ABOLITIONIST TWILIGHTS

D1598715

RECONSTRUCTING AMERICA
Andrew L. Slap, series editor

Abolitionist Twilights

*History, Meaning, and the
Fate of Racial Egalitarianism,
1865–1909*

Raymond James Krohn

Fordham University Press
New York   2023

Library of Congress Cataloging-in-Publication Data available online at https://catalog .loc.gov.

Printed in the United States of America

25 24 23 5 4 3 2 1

First edition

for Hannah

Contents

Introduction: What Is Abolitionism Now? From the Disposition of the AASS to the Determinants of Abolitionist History | 1

1   Antislavery Moderated: Samuel Joseph May and the Lessons of Respectable Reform | 19

2   Antislavery Elevated: William Wells Brown and the Purpose of Black Activism | 45

3   Antislavery Vindicated: Oliver Johnson and the Value of Abolitionism's Grand Old Party | 72

4   Antislavery Sanctified: Parker Pillsbury and the Spirit of Abolitionism in the Fields | 100

5   A Tale of Two Slaveries: Aaron Macy Powell and the Transfiguration of Abolitionism | 125

6   Songs of Innocence and Experience: Thomas Wentworth Higginson and the Abdication of Abolitionism | 154

7   What Was Antislavery For? From the Disbandment of the AASS to the Determination of Abolitionist Women | 191

Coda: Complicated Legacies | 219

Acknowledgments   221
Notes   225
Index   269

Abolitionist Twilights

Introduction: What Is Abolitionism Now?

From the Disposition of the AASS to the Determinants of Abolitionist History

As an intermediate state, twilight conjures ideas of beginnings as well as endings. Its anticipatory half-light and uncertain semidarkness symbolically underlie this study of antislavery thought in a United States where chattel bondage no longer existed. So, too, does the word's waxing and waning connotations, its forward-facing and backward-gazing evocations. Fascinated by the conceptual bipolarities surrounding twilight's in-betweenness, this book represents a rumination on veteran abolitionists' late-in-life ruminations, an exploration into abolitionism's history and meaning from the close of the Civil War to the coming of the Great War.

Amid a sectional military conflict that destabilized and permanently upended the southern system of slavery, the institution's most fervent northern adversaries contemplated not just the existence of organizations like the American Anti-Slavery Society (AASS) but also what abolitionism itself formally entailed. Their reflections on a decades-long campaign to immediately emancipate the enslaved hardly abated once an amendment forever outlawing enslavement entered the US Constitution in December 1865. Whether aligned or unaffiliated with the AASS, dozens of movement backers and fellow antislavery travelers recounted antebellum pasts throughout the postbellum period. The story that follows highlights the memorial and historical stories of some of those retrospective writers. By delving into the tales that they told, it seeks to ascertain the status of abolitionist-oriented racial egalitarianism during turning-point moments in American race relations.

Before and after the immediate emancipation campaign arose in the early 1830s, African Americans molded abolitionism's contours in profound ways. Because of, for example, their opposition to overseas expatriation schemes, as free Black community organizers and pamphleteers of protest in the 1810s and 1820s; their liberationist strategizing, as National Colored Convention planners and delegates beginning in 1830; their slavery exposés, as fugitive slave platform speakers and published authors during the 1840s and 1850s; and their resistance to captivity in the South and recapture in the North, as freedom seekers and Underground Railroad agents throughout the first half of the nineteenth century, African Americans were always abolitionist lifeblood. In an altered, postemancipation climate, they continuously quested for equity and inclusion—trying to advance themselves politically, economically, and socially as old barriers crumbled and new ones materialized in the Civil War's aftermath. At the same time, increasingly more whites lost interest in the fight for equal Black rights. Arguably no other veteran antislavery activist so strongly embodied an ongoing African American freedom struggle and conspicuously registered discontent with unreliable white allies as Frederick Douglass, the formerly enslaved Marylander who, after escaping to the nonslaveholding North in 1838, became famous on both sides of the Atlantic Ocean as a popular orator, social reformer, race leader, and public intellectual.[1]

In the final, 1892 installment of a life story that first appeared in print in 1845 and then in revised and updated 1855 and 1881 iterations, Douglass deplored intractable racism, derelict Republican officeholders, as well as the reemergence of the "slaveholding Democracy" in national political affairs and the reascendancy of the "spirit of slavery and rebellion" in the nation's highest councils. In the opening chapter of the autobiography's newly added third section, he made it clear that neither elderliness nor adversity had weakened his resolve. Despite the fifty years that had passed since his entry into organized abolitionism, Douglass admittedly still needed to mobilize youthful antislavery vigor well after slavery's death. "I find myself summoned again," he noted, "by . . . what is called the negro problem, to come . . . upon the witness stand and give evidence upon disputed points concerning myself and my emancipated brothers and sisters who, though free, are yet oppressed and are in much need of an advocate as before they were set free." Taking the attestation of that inveterate autobiographer as a cue, this book assays the post–Civil War humanitarian loyalties of others who had valued themselves as the slaves' steadfast friends, especially gauging how white abolitionists, as movement chroniclers and commemorators, interacted with an ongoing African American freedom struggle.[2]

Post-1830 abolitionism was never solely against slavery, as the founding documents of the AASS illuminate. Members, according to the group's 1833 constitution, pledged themselves to "elevat[ing]" African Americans and "removing public prejudice," so that they may "share an equality with whites of civil and religious privileges." The association's "Declaration of Sentiments" set forth a like promise on behalf of its adherents, proclaiming that they would seek to "secure to the colored population of the United States all the rights and privileges which belong to them as men and as Americans." The 1832 constitution of the New England Anti-Slavery Society (NEASS), which was a Massachusetts-based predecessor and subsequent branch of the larger AASS, sounded similar notes as well. A "mere difference of complexion," the preamble promulgated, "is no reason why any man should be deprived of any of his natural rights, or subjected to any political disability." In Article II of the NEASS charter, which lists its corporate raison d'être, three of the four stated aims pertain to free Blacks: One comprises uplifting their "character and condition"; another, extending "equal civil and political rights and privileges" to them. The 1833 constitution of the Philadelphia Female Anti-Slavery Society (PFASS), which was an early AASS auxiliary organized and led by women, also underscored that "dispel[ling] the prejudice against the people of color" and "improv[ing] their condition" were top priorities. As an against-racism initiative, post-1830 abolitionism represented a capacious quest for racial justice from the outset.[3]

Since the 1960s scholars have recognized, albeit not unanimously, the movement's pronounced equalitarian aspects. In a recent survey that reinforces the abolitionist centrality of Black people, enslaved and free, Manisha Sinha has attempted to recalibrate antislavery history over the eighteenth and nineteenth centuries on the grounds that abolitionism was a fundamentally radical, interracial syndicate, the constituents of which served as the democratic forerunners of the anticolonial and civil rights agitators of the twentieth century. In another recent account, Kate Masur has traced racially progressive policy milestones of the Civil War era to sustained civil rights endeavors that spanned the first half of the nineteenth century and encompassed countless African Americans and supportive whites, both working within and without formal abolitionist channels. Those and other scholarly findings thus corroborate Herbert Aptheker, who, years previously, reminded historians that, regardless of some white crusaders' limitations, "anti-racism [was] an indispensable component" of post-1830 abolitionism. Combating notions of inherent Black inferiority and backwardness remained part and parcel of the immediate emancipation campaign, because antislavery activists knew that the racist thinking undergirding the systemic exploitation of African Americans was not peculiar to the South but infiltrated all regions of the country.[4]

By similarly defining the immediate emancipation campaign as a wider push for racial justice, I do not suggest that white crusaders totally defied or entirely surmounted the racism—what they themselves designated as "colorphobia" or "caste prejudice"—that had structured American culture and society. Even though they could, and sometimes did, treat Black colleagues paternalistically or condescendingly, which complicated cross-racial partnerships and lasting friendships, historians should not dismiss their conscious efforts at, as well as conscientious striving for, antiracism. Nor did endorsing African American moral and intellectual uplift automatically render someone as racially narrow-minded. Partly impelled by a desire to topple white supremacism and expedite universal liberty, the abolitionist language of Black elevation emanated not from a race-based, or whiteness, standard of behavior. More than anything, it rotated around sociocultural ambitions and predispositions.[5]

Free Black community builders particularly embraced and spearheaded betterment proposals as bondage vanished across the northeastern United States in the late eighteenth and early nineteenth centuries. Instilling and attaining respectability thereafter ripened, as the historian Erica L. Ball has cogently demonstrated, into a deeply personal and subversive political program for rising and would-be middle-class African Americans across the nonslaveholding North. Besides an inherently goodly and godly thing, improving individually and collectively consequently enabled free people of color to habitually protest racial slavery in the South as well as the racism excluding themselves from bourgeois urban spaces and the broader body politic. White middle-class reformers, many of whom were evangelically motivated, also applied moral and intellectual uplift generously during the pre–Civil War decades. Whether as antislavery partisans or antiabolitionists, their improvement maxims and designs addressed free Black northerners, western white settlers, low-wage industrial laborers, and/or impoverished Irish immigrants. I therefore take seriously abolitionism's equalitarian values and aspirations, as neatly encapsulated in organizational constitutions and mission statements, and approach white abolitionists as the racial liberals that they were for their times. I also remain cognizant that Black activists had grown disappointed with white coworkers over the intertwined matters of antislavery and antiracism.[6]

Martin Robison Delany, for instance, trenchantly critiqued white coadjutors in an 1852 publication regarding the development of people of color in the United States and their special destiny elsewhere in the Americas. While praising them as the "truest friends" of African Americans among all whites, the author diagnosed a major allyship deficiency. Since abolitionism was not exclusively emancipatory in orientation but elevatory as well, he asserted that white "converts" to a Black-originated crusade had largely failed to deliver on their promises. Rather than facilitating opportunities for African Americans to acquire the necessary education, skills, and experience in order to rise in a racially hostile society, well-intentioned whites predominantly "propagated good and wholesome sentiments." Even though Delany expressly renounced faultfinding and bade Godspeed to such allies in their dissemination of holy principles, he nevertheless deduced that the Black condition was no better as a result of twenty years of white abolitionist leadership. "Instead of realizing what we had hoped for," African Americans occupied "the very same" rank in both the antislavery and proslavery segments of the North: a "secondary, underling position," in his assessment, and anything more "comes not by established . . . custom or right, but . . . by mere sufferance." Regardless of the scores of successful African Americans populating the narrative, the persistence of overall Black misery would have challenged the crusading authenticity of friendly white audiences. The allegation itself should induce the historian to regularly probe abolitionism's racial-egalitarian parameters.[7]

To map the place of a more transcendent, antislavery-and-antiracism conception of abolitionism in the minds of movement veterans, this examination concentrates on the book-length disquisitions that they issued shortly and long after the Civil War. Books afford worlds of possibilities to readers and interpreters. Since I am intrigued by the dynamics at play on and off the printed page, only a fraction of the sizeable body of antislavery memorial and historical literature can receive microscopic attention. Six retrospective writers and their authorial productions constitute my evidentiary foundation, namely, Samuel Joseph May (1797–1871), William Wells Brown (c. 1814–1884), Oliver Johnson (1809–1889), Parker Pillsbury (1809–1898), Aaron Macy Powell (1832–1899), and Thomas Wentworth Higginson (1823–1911). May's selective history of abolitionism, *Some Recollections of Our Antislavery Conflict*, appeared in 1869; Brown's intercontinental Black history, *The Rising Son; or, the Antecedents and Advancement of the Colored Race*, in 1873, and his personal and regional history, *My Southern Home: or, the South and Its Peoples*, in 1880; Johnson's homage to a pathbreaking crusader, *William Lloyd Garrison and His Times*, in 1880 (which he revised and expanded in 1881); Pillsbury's participant history of grassroots activism, *Acts of the Anti-Slavery Apostles*, in 1883; Powell's philanthropic autobiography, *Personal Reminiscences of the Anti-Slavery and Other Reforms and Reformers*, in 1899; and Higginson's autobiographical and biographical essays, *Cheerful Yesterdays* and *Contemporaries*, in 1898 and 1899, respectively.

The main research cohort evolved from the basic problems at the center of this controlled experiment: (1) to evaluate veteran abolitionists' fidelity to key antislavery articles of faith in the years and decades following enslavement's destruction and during new periods of adjustment in southern race relations, and (2) to determine the interconnections between the rise and fall of Reconstruction and the stable or shifting meanings of abolitionism throughout the late nineteenth and early twentieth centuries. A focus group principally consisting of *white* abolitionists came about from an impetus to interrogate the very historiographical tradition that generally profiles them as proponents of an exceptional and forward-looking enterprise. Yet a research cohort ostensibly containing only *male* abolitionists emerged not because their book-length accounts outnumber those created by female counterparts. This study showcases the memorial and historical literature of antislavery advocates who associated with the AASS before and/ or after the institutional schism of 1840, as well as movement chroniclers and commemorators who performed highly visible roles in the immediate emancipation campaign, acquiring prominence, if not celebrity, in the process.[8]

Samuel J. May assisted in the 1833 formation of AASS. Oliver Johnson cofounded the NEASS, in 1832, as well as the Vermont Anti-Slavery Society, in 1834. Both routinely filled leadership posts in the various state and national coalitions to which they respectively belonged. Parker Pillsbury dedicated much of his abolitionist profession to consciousness raising and community building throughout New England, the Mid-Atlantic, and the Old Northwest as a commissioned lecturing agent of the AASS and its subsidiaries. Aaron Macy Powell also toiled as an itinerant speaker for the parent organization, until he took on a settled post as editor of its official mouthpiece, the *National Anti-Slavery Standard*, starting in early 1866. Powell directly succeeded Pillsbury's brief tenure as the periodical's supervisor (which covered a few months), as well as Johnson's previously longer one (which ranged over multiple years). The latter's management of abolitionist weeklies across the North additionally involved extended stays at the *Anti-Slavery Bugle* (Salem, Ohio) and *Pennsylvania Freeman* (Philadelphia) and guest stops at Garrison's *Liberator* (Boston). As a newspaperman, Johnson thus made his greatest contributions to the immediate emancipation campaign. Besides preaching abolitionism on the lecture circuit and from the Unitarian pulpit, the Reverend May further distinguished himself as a benefactor of Prudence Crandall's short-lived boarding school for Black girls in the early 1830s and a plotter of the 1851 rescue of the detained fugitive slave William "Jerry" Henry.

Soon after fleeing from Missouri thralldom in 1834, William Wells Brown moonlighted as an Underground Railroad conductor from Lake Erie bases of operation. He obtained formal institutional affiliations in 1843, by participating in a Buffalo gathering of the National Convention of Colored Men as well as a meeting of the Rochester-headquartered Western New York Anti-Slavery Society (WNYASS). The self-liberated Brown, who legally gained his freedom in 1854, subsequently championed immediate emancipation and antiracism at home and abroad tirelessly, wielding the spoken and written word often on behalf of the AASS or Massachusetts Anti-Slavery Society (which was a modification of the NEASS original). Thomas Wentworth Higginson initially established an abolitionist reputation, locally, as a Free-Soil Party congressional candidate for Essex County, Massachusetts, in 1850, as well as an 1853 founder, and premier president, of the Worcester Anti-Slavery Society. Higginson's activist star soared, regionally and nationally, alongside his surging militancy: via forcible resistance to the 1850 Fugitive Slave Law during the 1854 Anthony Burns rescue attempt, clandestine ties to John Brown's 1859 plot to incite a southern slave insurrection, and taking command of freed-slave soldiers amid a slaveholders' rebellion of the early 1860s. Like the other focus group members, he, too, generated printed paraphernalia—pamphlets, articles, speeches, and so on—in abolitionism's defense.

Unfortunately, such influential AASS-affiliated reformers as Maria Weston Chapman, Lydia Maria Child, Betsy Mix Cowles, Sarah Mapps Douglass, Sarah Otis Ernst, Abigail Kelley Foster, Mary Grew, Sarah and Angelina Grimké, Frances Ellen Watkins Harper, Sallie Holley, Lucretia Mott, Amy Post, Sarah Parker Remond, and Lucy Stone did not publish their own memoirs. Elizabeth Cady Stanton represents a seeming exception. Her 1898 exposition *Eighty Years and More* only briefly recounts abolitionist experiences. Even though Stanton supported the immediate emancipation campaign throughout the Civil War era—launching, for example, a massive petition drive in 1863 as cofounder and president of the Women's Loyal National League—she was, foremostly, a pioneering feminist, both before and after slavery's wartime annihilation. Despite traveling within impressive antislavery networks—her cousin, Gerrit Smith; her spouse, Henry Brewster Stanton; and her collaborator and book dedicatee, Susan B. Anthony, all actively promoted abolitionism—her recollections prioritize the women's rights cause to which she devoted her adult life and forever made a name for herself. That she helped compile the multivolume *History of Woman Suffrage* during the 1880s additionally verifies which type of reform meant more to her, exactly why this analysis does not test her racial justice commitments as an abolitionist memorialist and historian.[9]

In contrast to Stanton's autobiographical tome of some 475 pages, three other white abolitionist women who had identified with the AASS or an offshoot authored abbreviated narratives of their humanitarian careers during the 1890s. To round out the focus group, I consider the remembrances of Elizabeth Buffum Chace (*Anti-Slavery Reminiscences*, 1891), Lucy N. Colman (*Reminiscences*, 1891), and Sarah H. Southwick (*Reminiscences of Early Anti-Slavery Days*, 1893) in the seventh chapter. During the immediate emancipation campaign's inaugural decade, Chace's father—Arnold Buffum—was a founding member and the first president of the NEASS; Chace herself (1806–1899) cofounded the Fall River (MA) Female Anti-Slavery Society and furthered its objectives in high-ranking capacities. Alongside the Buffum paterfamilias, Southwick's dad, Joseph, assisted in the AASS's creation; he also headed the new association in the mid-1830s. Southwick's mom, Thankful, worked for enslaved people's deliverance, too, as a lifelong member and four-time chief executive of the Boston Female Anti-Slavery Society (BFASS). Besides entering her mother's organizational ambit as a teenager, Sarah (1821–1896) twice served as the BFASS's recording secretary in the 1840s. After Chace's 1840 relocation to Rhode Island, her Valley Falls residence functioned as a magnet for wayfaring northeastern abolitionists as well as escapees from southern slavery. For her part, New Yorker Colman (1817–1906) backed abolitionism as a lecturing agent for the Western Anti-Slavery Society (WASS) during the 1850s; as secretary of the Women's Loyal National League in 1863; and as a relief worker and school administrator for Black refugees in and around the District of Columbia during the Civil War's last years.

I also scrutinize Laura Smith Haviland's monumental personal history, *A Woman's Life-Work*, in the same section in order to contest or confirm the primary outcomes of my controlled experiment. Despite a final book edition that surpasses six hundred pages, her 1897 publication does not receive a separate, chapter-long treatment, because the Michigan-anchored Haviland (1808–1898) had chiefly navigated organized abolitionism independently. Rather than frequent antislavery conventions, contribute to antislavery fairs and sewing circles, preach antislavery homilies, or prepare antislavery propaganda for the press, she labored on her own as an operative on the Underground Railroad, bravely roving about the Old Northwest, South, and Canada across the 1840s and 1850s. If nothing else, a research cohort comprising a white-male-abolitionist majority exposes the advantages stemming from legal and social categories rooted in race and sex. Regardless of how enlightened they were or unaware of their privileges, white antislavery men could more easily choose whose rights to encourage or evade.[10]

Without a doubt, the abolitionists—white and Black, male and female—hoped and believed that from the ashes of sectional conflagration a disenthralled and expiated Union would arise, wherein the inalienable-rights ethos of the Declaration of Independence unequivocally applied to all persons, regardless of racial background or skin color. The ratification of the Thirteenth, Fourteenth, and Fifteenth Amendments (in 1865, 1867, and 1870, respectively) seemingly made those expectations into a reality. Yet the regenerated American phoenix that they envisioned had a fleeting lifespan. Acts of violence, intimidation, and fraud repeatedly sabotaged the Republican Party's southern rebuilding project, sorely taxed the reconstruction energies of northern voters, and fully restored Democratic rule across the former Confederate States of America by 1877. With the downfall of Republican state governments throughout the South, the reactionary architects of which baptized as "Redemption," something resembling an antebellum arrangement ultimately, but not inevitably, returned to the area.[11]

To be sure, the postbellum reconquest of white supremacy did not reestablish a property-based regime of perpetual Black servitude. State-by-state developments nonetheless ushered in another epoch of white mastery and Black subordination beginning in the 1890s. To say that the writings of antislavery chroniclers and commemorators intersected with pivotal alterations in American race relations is truly an understatement. Of the study's six core subjects, two—May and 1873 Brown—thought and wrote about the past during the congressional, or "radical," phase of Reconstruction. Three—Johnson, Pillsbury, and 1880 Brown—did so in the years after unreconstructed ex-Confederates had scored counterrevolutionary triumphs that effectively terminated Republican reengineering of the Southland. Two—Powell and Higginson—produced personal histories amid an emerging Jim Crow world in which African American disenfranchisement and separation of the races defined everyday life and law in the former Confederacy. The four white abolitionist women under consideration also fall under that third authorship grouping, with the caveat that since the first edition of Haviland's memoir debuted in 1881, she overlaps with the second one as well.

The ensuing chapters are very much adventures in ideas. Each one spotlights a particular text or combination of texts, situating them within a variety of contexts. Each one provides an intensive meditation on the surface and subterranean significance of what retrospective writers wrote and why. Each one offers an in-depth exegesis of antislavery memorial and historical literature, unearthing and weighing the issues, incidents, and impulses behind a text and its author. The study's overall findings spring from an intimate dialogue with the past. Scarcely a one-sided affair, such a conversation proceeds from my attempts at executing the role of what the historian and theorist Dominick LaCapra has termed the "good reader," whose responsibilities include piercing interrogation as well as "attentive and patient listen[ing]." The good reader does not simply apply frames of reference and interpretative models onto texts but should also ask new and unexpected sets of questions prompted by the challenges and contradictions that the authorial and textual voices pose. This study simultaneously takes as a premise the elegant and cogent plea that John Patrick Diggins once tendered—"Why cannot a text constitute its own context?"—in order to better identify and explain the meaning of memorial and historical texts and the messages that they convey. This inquest, then, is the end product of close reading and rereading, viewing and reviewing.[12]

By deploying those strategies, I uncover a trajectory whereby the retrospective writers under examination mostly extricated themselves from an ongoing African American freedom struggle. I concomitantly show that even though focus group members remained robust reformers, the reformism of otherwise lapsing or lapsed veteran white abolitionists orbited a variety of new causes after 1876. The diminishing strength of antislavery-oriented equalitarianism hardly manifested itself uniformly over time. That declension nevertheless unfolds progressively throughout these pages. Chapters 1 and 2 exhibit unflagging racial justice advocacy and engagement; Chapters 3 and 4 disclose racial justice ambiguity and retrenchment; Chapters 5 and 6 reveal racial justice defeat and retreat. The quartet of white antislavery women featuring in the finale composed memorial and historical literature that further amplifies the overarching theme of atrophy and demise. A process gaining steam during the last years of William Wells Brown's remarkable life (1884) reached practically full force by the expiration of Frederick Douglass's (1895). The dramatic twists and turns in the standing of the freedpeople and their descendants thus affected the perceptions and cogitations of veteran white abolitionists in surprising ways. Such conclusions diverge sharply from those of other scholars.

Stating that by the 1880s Africans Americans could no longer rely on white northerners to enforce the letter or extend the spirit of the Reconstruction-era constitutional amendments strikes no novel chord among historians. Discordant historiographical noise certainly surrounds the argument that veteran white abolitionists, as representatives of the most outspoken antebellum advocates of racial justice, steadily ignored the topic as postbellum chroniclers and commemorators. By comparison, in *The Abolitionist Legacy: From Reconstruction to the NAACP*, which is the only full-scale treatment of the late-nineteenth-century activities of former antislavery agitators and their younger adjuncts, James McPherson described an unrelenting battle for equal Black rights. Regardless of reformist frustrations and setbacks, his portrayal of durable, dependable, and inspirational humanitarianism culminated in the founding of a "neoabolitionist" agency in 1909—the National Association for the Advancement of Colored People.[13]

The generally lesser attention that Julie Roy Jeffrey allocated to some of the same, as well as other, retrospective writers resulted in a research outcome contrary to mine. In *Abolitionists Remember: Antislavery Autobiographies and the Unfinished Work of Emancipation*, she argued that authors recorded their personal histories not merely to dispute popular accounts that had negatively delineated antebellum abolitionism or romanticized Old South servitude. Recollecting the movement also allowed her memoirists to keep "the reform spirit alive" and tenaciously press for a more racially just and inclusive society. In "Memory as History, Memory as Activism: The Forgotten Abolitionist Struggle after the Civil War," Manisha Sinha echoed Jeffrey's assertions. Referring to the written narratives of former antislavery agitators as "isolated voices crying in the wilderness," she reasoned that they recalled their stories of the past in order to "resuscitate the fight for black rights" in the present. By digging deeply into a carefully curated source base and inspecting all elements of a text, I differently appraise the authorial preoccupations of veteran white abolitionists and how they affected postbellum depictions of the campaign to immediately end slavery.[14]

Finally, in *An Old Creed for the New South: Proslavery Ideology and Historiography, 1865–1918*, John David Smith, while surveying the vitality of slavery in American racial thought well after the Thirteenth Amendment definitively prohibited it, displayed the neoabolitionist postures assumed by various amateur and professional historians as they pondered the cruelties of the slaveholding past. The antebellum zeal that several of those postbellum researchers mustered, which prompted them to question the emerging neoslavery circumstances of the 1870s, 1880s, and 1890s, lost out to the recycled proslavery arguments that came to dominate the historiographical landscape by the early twentieth century. Most of the antislavery chroniclers and commemorators herein investigated, however, did not marshal immediate emancipation reminiscences on behalf of racial egalitarianism. Rather than try to arrest or reverse disturbing trends in southern race relations, they accommodated to them. For that alone, I invite scholars to thoroughly (re)consider the late-nineteenth-century lives and careers of veteran white abolitionists. Whether that happens, the payoffs from this limited sample are quite huge.[15]

By complicating abolitionist history, my findings uniquely shed light on the disempowering repercussions of two powerful historical facts. Whether figuring in the foreground or hovering in the back, the collapse of Reconstruction and commencement of Jim Crow subtly and strikingly shaped a retrospective writer's understanding and representation of abolitionism. Whereas the Black activist Brown contested counterrevolutionary currents in American society and politics, the antislavery memorial and historical literature of white analogues, excepting May's, ultimately coincided with, capitulated to, and/or celebrated an advancing genius of reconciliation that enabled most northerners, in particular, to embrace former Confederates and overcome outstanding Civil War resentments by the dawning of the twentieth century. Indeed, the very event that originally divided a nation of people into warring sections evidently brought it together once more. My study therefore benefits from and builds upon the scholarship of David Blight, Edward J. Blum, K. Stephen Prince, Kirk Savage, Nina Silber, and others, which has shown how culture—in such forms as public monuments, commemorative gatherings and rituals, novels, plays, travel brochures, illustrations, popular songs, and evangelical religion—paved the way for an intersectional comity and a new national solidarity that came at the expense of interracial governance across the Southland as well as social justice for African Americans.[16]

Well before white Americans effectuated a reunification among themselves, the many deaths that enslavement underwent strained the cords that had unified exponents of the AASS. Since the critical abolitionist disagreements spawned by the 1860s revolved more and more about the future of organized abolitionism, plumbing their contents indicates whether past attitudes about the movement's nature and purpose remained widespread during a wartime present. Hardly insignificant, such quarreling further elucidates to what extent the immediate emancipation campaign supplied the necessary linguistic resources for long-term antislavery and antiracism advocacy.[17]

An existential discussion initially came up in early 1863, after President Abraham Lincoln had signed an executive order decreeing freedom for the enslaved throughout the rebellious regions of the South. At that year's annual AASS gathering, celebrants not only commented on the Emancipation Proclamation; they also mulled over three decades of fearless institutional activism. In an opening-day speech, the group's perennial president William Lloyd Garrison addressed both topics and broached a third: associational disbandment. Despite acknowledging that abolitionists could not slacken their efforts "until every slave in the land is set free," he espied a cessation rapidly approaching. Speaking on everyone's behalf, he exclaimed that if Congress "will only abolish slavery, I pledge the country that there shall be no more anti-slavery agitation." Frederick Douglass wholeheartedly disagreed. Toward the tail end of a two-day event, he proclaimed that organizational actions should not cease until the "black men of the South, and the black men of the North, shall have been admitted, fully and completely, into the body politic of America." A "mightier" labor therefore "loom[ed] up" before the abolitionists, according to his reckoning, one that transcended the disintegration of chattel bondage. Indeed, so long as anti-Black prejudices tightly held on, Douglass advised that the AASS must hold fast, "continually protesting, continually exposing" racism.[18]

The dissolution issue developed into a pressing situation by early 1865, once the US government did what Garrison, as well as all other antislavery congregants, had wanted and urged it to do. After Lincoln secured a second presidential term in 1864 under the National Union Party banner and on a platform calling for slavery's "utter and complete extirpation," both congressional chambers finally adopted a proposed constitutional amendment guaranteeing the emancipatory consequences of a disruptive civil war. At the thirty-second anniversary meeting of the AASS, an intensifying debate between the forces for and against the alliance's discontinuation reached a confrontational crescendo. Its settlement would determine antebellum abolitionism's potential relevance to a forthcoming post-bellum era.[19]

Stephen Symonds Foster essentially sparked a two-day showdown after submitting a motion that nominated a new slate of officers for the next year. In reply, the society's chief executive put forward an opposite docket for the conference participants. Reading aloud a set of resolves, a countermotioning Garrison announced that "after thirty years of faithful testimony and untiring labor," the moment had arrived for the abolitionists to formally retire their consortium. Expressing his "joy unspeakable that 'the year of jubilee has come,'" he declared any supplementary antislavery agitation as unwarranted. The age of humanitarian "exclusiveness," Garrison averred, would instantly expire with slavery's obliteration. Given a nonexistent need to constantly isolate the abolitionists "from the great mass of the people," the present AASS convocation, in his judgment, should serve as its last. A substantial number of the attendees starkly departed from Garrison's outlook. Once deliberation on his recommendations began, the detractors seized the limelight, rhetorically commanding the assemblage, as the published minutes demonstrate.[20]

Among the dissenting speakers, Charles Lenox Remond delivered an especially forceful admonition. The Black activist affirmed that based on his comprehension of founding documents, the AASS's "original objects" comprised "the emancipation of the slave and the elevation of the free people of color." Given that twofold program, he deemed an institutional breakup as horribly premature and woefully irresponsible. Remond thus remonstrated against any conflation of perpetual servitude's legal extermination with a glorious conclusion of abolitionism. He politely chided Garrison, in particular, because the abolitionist patriarch had taken that very stance, thereby misleading others in the AASS about their all-important business. Before doing so, he prefaced his displeasure with a potentially stunning admission: "While I defer to some and reverence others, I do assume here that it is utterly impossible for any . . . white friends . . . fully to understand the black man's case in this nation." "Our friend Mr. Garrison," he more pointedly observed, "told us to-day, that anti-slavery being the order of things, there is no further necessity for our anti-slavery work." Regardless of the societal progress signified by a constitutional amendment eradicating enslavement, Remond possessed no personal illusions about the prestige of his dark complexion among the bulk of Americans.[21]

To disabuse white compatriots of any misguided impressions, he pointed out that the essence of racism persisted in spite of racial slavery's impending death rattle. As corroboration, he alluded to the hostility that he frequently faced on public railcars by bigoted white conductors and the animosity that greeted him on city streets by prejudiced white passersby. With such antipathy still prevalent in the North, Remond boldly stated: "I deny, from beginning to end, that anti-slavery, according to this [society's] platform, characterizes any State in this country." "I deny," he iterated more emphatically, "without fear of successful contradiction, that the anti-slavery which takes its color from this platform has a majority in this nation at the present time." A contrarian Henry Clarke Wright, however, flatly dismissed the expansive notion of the AASS as an equal-rights or antiracism fellowship. Narrowly interpreting abolitionism, he pontificated that neither racially directed proscriptions at polling places nor "hatred of the negro because he has a black skin is . . . slavery." Despite his attempted refutation, far more abolitionists seconded Remond's views and enlarged his critique.[22]

Foster provocatively rejoined the proceedings, quoting the same sources that Remond had mentioned in order to explicate abolitionism's overriding ambitions as well as quash the closure push. He also inserted an uncomfortable fact into the conversation, as a corrective to the untimely hosannas of certain co-workers. Because of "a bitter prejudice . . . that puts its heel upon the negro, and treads him into the very dust," the abolitionists could currently claim no celestial victories. Unlike Garrison's exultant mood, Foster considered the get-together as a "most solemn" occurrence, for the "future of our country" hinged on the fortunes of the AASS. After others interjected, he poignantly recapitulated the associational agenda: "We organiz[ed] . . . simply and solely to write the law of justice on the American heart." Since colorphobia still polluted the national soul, an undeterred Foster propounded that he and his comrades had but one option: persevere in their collective venture. A concurring Anna Dickinson both consoled a seemingly despondent Foster and energized the assembled. She maintained that antislavery crusaders will disperse only when "there is no longer reason for me or any one else to stand up and demand the rights of any human being in this country," a prediction that garnered "loud applause," according to the newspaper coverage.[23]

Notwithstanding the vocal opposition, Garrison never relaxed his posture. Following Remond's observations, he brusquely informed the conclave that he required no one's permission to resign from the AASS and that he would freely do so "at the end of this anniversary." References to the "Declaration of Sentiments" apparently irked him, too, because he had penned that manifesto himself. He subsequently invoked the authoritativeness that authorship presumably granted. "Unless I have grown demented," according to President Garrison's blunt pronouncement, "I ought to know what I meant." The "thought never entered my mind then, nor has it at any time since," that the AASS would outlast servitude in the South. Mounting pressure in favor of upholding the coalition only hardened his convictions. "This is the fitting time," the *Liberator*'s editor broadcasted once Dickinson had stopped talking, "to dissolve our organization, and to mingle with the millions of our fellow-countrymen in one common effort to establish justice and liberty throughout the land." "My friends," he entreated after a series of verbal exchanges with Wendell Phillips, "let us not any longer affect superiority when we are not superior . . . let us not assume to be better than other people, when we are not any better." Given the achievement of abolitionism's paramount goal, Garrison believed that the AASS now represented a superfluous and outdated body. In a postemancipation United States, he saw it as the wrong vehicle to bolster the freedpeople's rights. His logic proved unpersuasive in 1865.[24]

Despite the reported clapping that accompanied Garrison's remarks, it did not match the exuberant reception for what Dickinson had articulated. Concerning the suggestion that the recently formed freedmen's aid squadrons should supplant the AASS, she professed that "if these new workers stood as earnest, as willing, as eager" as the tried-and-true abolitionists, "they would come up to your platform, not ask you to go down to theirs." Whereas that statement elicited "enthusiastic applause," even louder and longer-lasting approval hailed her heartfelt request to the "father of this Society." Turning toward Garrison, she predicted that his name "humanity will . . . call blessed" for all eternity and the emancipated bondman will intone in "his prayers forever." She then implored him to remain as the association's chief executive, to retain that charge "until God takes it out of your hands, and says, 'Come up higher!'" Such an appeal exerted little, if any, influence on the intended target. Having lost the motion to shutter the AASS for good, by a tally of 118 nays to 48 yeas, the *Liberator*'s editor nonetheless enacted his rejected resolution. In fulfillment of his earlier avowal, he, along with several like-minded associates, withdrew from club abolitionism after the annual exercises had concluded.[25]

Before the climactic floor vote on disbandment, Phillips, who would supersede Garrison as the AASS's president, proffered a compelling query to the audience: "What right have we to dissolve?" Since antislavery crusaders constituted "a banner, a principle, [and] a symbol," they could not, in his estimation, halt their operations. "We keep together," the soon-to-be new boss trumpeted, "because we want the country to understand that there is work to be done" and that the abolitionists themselves planned on doing it. Shortly following the verdict to sustain the AASS, Abigail Kelley Foster notified peers that even though "the whole community" evinced a readiness for almsgiving on behalf of the freedpeople, they themselves must engage in the more difficult task of African American enfranchisement. "I hope," she added, "that every Abolitionist will consecrate himself, or herself, anew to this special work." Joseph Evans Snodgrass also weighed in on the importance of concerted abolitionist exertions. Speaking as a southerner by birth, as well as a former slaveholder by inheritance, he avouched that "the fight is far from being over," escalating "more than some of you, perhaps, have ever dreamed." That multiple convention goers summoned the language of half-finished business not only accounts for the thwarted bid to disband the AASS in early 1865. It also denoted a general persuasion among organizational defenders that they must carry on in order to carry out racial justice.[26]

Arguably no AASS partisan made a more moving case for nonstop abolitionism than Remond. After remonstrating with Garrison, he mused on everybody's humanitarian constancy. "Standing as we do at this moment between the fires of rebellion in the South, and this hatred of the colored man in the North," he opined, "I hope nothing will be done within this Society that shall look like a betrayal of our movement." The immediate emancipation campaign undeniably equipped its proponents with a rich and multivalent vocabulary from which to wage prolonged philanthropic warfare, prior as well as subsequent to slavery's abolition. How, when, and why members of the focus group used and/or failed to use the movement's linguistic resources factors into each chapter. If the representatives of the most outspoken antebellum advocates of racial justice steadily ignored the topic as postbellum chroniclers and commemorators, as this study postulates, it should come as no surprise that their less principled or idealistic white contemporaries neither mourned nor sought to revive a fading biracial democracy that had momentarily taken hold in the Reconstruction-era South. If, moreover, creators of antislavery memorial and historical literature increasingly neglected unresolved or emergent problems in American race relations, then the contemporaneous prospects for indisputable and enduring racial equity and inclusion were always slim.[27]

This inquiry operates from the proposition that the retrospective writings of veteran abolitionists contained instrumental capabilities. Just as the backers of immediatism were extremely conscientious reformers, they were also highly conscious of the opinion-making qualities of authorship. Publishing from the Age of Emancipation to that of Jim Crow conceivably amounted to incessant propaganda. It could function, on the one hand, as a decidedly political act befitting politically driven, as well as popularly politicized, actors. It presented a unique opportunity, on the other, to bequeath a final and possibly undying testament on behalf of equal Black rights. Regardless of whether such calculations actually animated the focus group members, this reader interprets written narratives in ways that their originators likely never imagined or anticipated. If, in the process of excavating the intended and unintended meanings and messages of antislavery texts, it appears that veteran abolitionists are somehow on trial, fairness mandates that their authorial productions should obtain a full hearing. The legacy of abolitionism bore and still bears tremendous import, precisely why this study seeks to pinpoint what really mattered to the creators of antislavery memorial and historical literature throughout the late nineteenth and early twentieth centuries. Even though the chapters may be consulted in any order, sequential reading is recommended given the phenomenon that this controlled experiment charts—the eclipse of abolitionist-oriented racial egalitarianism.[28]

1 Antislavery Moderated

*Samuel Joseph May and the Lessons
of Respectable Reform*

In an 1869 memoir, Samuel Joseph May recounted an "earnest conversation" with the Unitarian preacher and theologian William Ellery Channing. Notwithstanding the passage of thirty-five years, the author recalled the exchange clearly. In reply to Channing's complaints about the excesses of antislavery crusaders like William Lloyd Garrison—their "severity" and "harshness," as well as "vehemence, heat, and excitement"—a frustrated May momentarily shed customary deference toward an esteemed Unitarian colleague. "'We Abolitionists are what we are,'" the personal historian quoted his 1834 scoff, "'babes, sucklings, obscure men, silly women, publicans, sinners, and we must manage this matter [the slave's cause] just as might be expected of such persons.'" That a seemingly ragtag combination of inconsequential reformers sympathized with "'suffering humanity'" called attention, in this instance, not to the actual composition of abolitionism but the appalling irresponsibility of society's pillars—that is, "'the scholars, the statesmen, the clergy.'" The historical question of who had listened to the loud supplications of "'oppressed, crushed colored countrymen'" factors heavily in *Some Recollections of Our Antislavery Conflict*. So, too, does the memorial issue of individual abolitionist character and abolitionism's group characteristics.[1]

In the years and decades following that remembered confab, many formerly negligent northern intellectuals, politicos, and divines arrived at some variant of abolitionism. The recollected Channing raised his own voice in remonstrance not long after May had chided him for not pleading on behalf of the enslaved. His 1835 treatise *Slavery*, the commemorator professed, created "a great sensation." Despite delivering "a fearful *exposé* of the sinfulness of holding slaves and the vices which infested [such] communities," May nonetheless criticized the publication's unevenness. To his disappointment, then and since, a revered Unitarian minister reinforced, albeit unintentionally, "several of the most serious misrepresentations" about the abolitionists. That an otherwise admired "Christian moralist" should inaccurately portray the motives and methods of antislavery activists elicited another acerbic rejoinder. "It is left for imprudent men, enthusiasts, fanatics," the chronicler declared, "to begin all difficult enterprises." The passing of time in no way healed all wounds. The constant charge of zealotry, which had beset the champions of immediate and unconditional emancipation from the campaign's early-1830s onset, galled both a younger and an older May.[2]

The retrospective writer did not repeatedly rely on sarcasm in order to rectify previous and persisting movement fallacies. He summoned a specific humanitarian type instead: the morally and socially responsible reformer, that is, the respectable agitator. In the postbellum quest to ensure a suitable reputation for the profoundly upright men and women populating his narrative, May noticeably moderated stories of antebellum antislavery persons and events. That his reminiscences often stress qualities that contemporaries rarely correlated with abolitionism render his annals as idiosyncratic, all the more so since he collaborated with highly controversial Garrisonian abolitionists. Given their real and imaginary ultraism, May took on a potentially tough assignment. However exacting, it ultimately redounded to the freedpeople's benefit, as the septuagenarian author also sought to advance an ongoing African American freedom struggle.[3]

In December 1837, the *Liberator* released a publishing prospectus for the forthcoming year that cogently displays both the editor's expanding radicalism and the challenges it posed for May's respectably inclined memorial and historical project. At one point the announcement apprised readers that subsequent copies would promote "the emancipation of our whole race from the dominion of man, from the thraldom of self, from the government of brute force, from the bondage of sin." With that statement alone Garrison shared a dramatically altered antislavery vision: from a campaign largely targeting a regional system of servitude to a larger crusade against exploitation nationwide. That mindset buttressed a host of Garrisonian positions thereafter, such as anticlericalism and antisectarianism, religious perfectionism and Christian anarchism, and feminism and disunionism. The nonresistance theory encapsulates the sundry isms surrounding the *Liberator*'s editor and his acolytes by the late 1830s and beyond.[4]

As an extreme form of pacifism, nonresistance entailed a categorical disavowal of warfare and anything war related. The 1838 "Declaration of Sentiments" of the New England Non-Resistance Society, which Garrison had drafted, dismissed armies and navies, armaments and fortifications, and governmental appropriations for martial things. It also scorned civic monuments and communal celebrations in honor of military exploits. The new pacifists, quite simply, rejected all manifestations of violence and coercion by individuals and nations alike. Not even earthly rulers and their organizational structures and controlling apparatuses—including legal proceedings, incarceration, and capital punishment—evaded their indictment. By pledging loyalty to the kingdom of God and rallying around the Prince of Peace, Jesus Christ, nonresistants proscribed themselves "from every legislative and judicial body," according to the Garrison-composed manifesto, as well as repudiated "human politics, worldly honors, and stations of authority." In a democratizing United States of mass political parties and widespread suffrage rights for white men, preaching no voting, no officeholding, and no government only magnified abolitionism's disreputable public image.[5]

As an ideological hothouse, nonresistance rapidly fostered other radical Garrisonian stances. Around 1842 the *Liberator*'s editor escalated his barrage against southern slavery, demanding its annihilation regardless of the disastrous ramifications for church and nation-state. His strident rhetoric birthed another assertive mantra, "No Union with Slaveholders," for the "uncompromising" abolitionist's consideration during the 1840s and 1850s. When Garrisonian advocates of disunionism insisted that nonslaveholding states must split from their slaveholding counterparts, they did so from the premise that a rotten document formed the country's core. Because of the sinful concessions that allegedly transpired at the 1787 Philadelphia Convention, the northern disunionists' irredeemably proslavery US Constitution substantiated an 1837 Garrison claim that "the governments of this world . . . are all Anti-Christ."[6]

In the same publishing prospectus in which the *Liberator*'s editor notified subscribers about the prominence of nonresistance in upcoming issues, he further indicated that feminist concerns would garner more awareness. "To redeem woman as well as man from a servile to an equal condition—we shall go," according to the pronouncement, "for the Rights of Woman to their utmost extent." Initially, the Garrisonian brand of feminism upheld the freedom of women to publicly defend the immediate emancipation campaign before gatherings of both sexes. It also backed the full participation of women in antislavery societies on the same basis with men. By the late 1840s, it encompassed the overthrow of traditions and statutes that had relegated women to a separate, subordinate, and unequal sphere. Such convictions only hardened the antiabolitionist biases of conventional Americans who deemed the outspoken and unorthodox Garrison as symbolic of a thoroughly dangerous undertaking. They also embroiled the abolitionists in an internal squabble that resulted in an irreversible breach.[7]

By 1838, the *Liberator*'s editor could boast that his paper had grown incredibly "liberal in its spirit." Rivals within the American Anti-Slavery Society saw his provocative progressivism as massive impediments to abolitionism's popularization. Some detractors wanted to bring about enslavement's demise through the establishment of a moral majority consisting of evangelical Protestant clergymen and congregations throughout the North. Others preferred to undermine southern slavery at the ballot box and possibly field an abolitionist political party to wage electoral warfare against it. After failing to reduce Garrisonian influence and reclaim the national association, Garrison's church-oriented and politically focused opponents removed themselves in 1840.[8]

Fifteen years later, the *Liberator*'s editor clarified his reputed extremism by citing, for example, the Hebrew prophets, Jesus and the Apostles, Martin Luther, John Calvin, and George Fox as precedents and peers. Whether initiated in the ancient Mediterranean, early modern Europe, or nineteenth-century North America, all "great reformatory movement[s]," for Garrison, were fundamentally alike. Since each and every one assailed "colossal" transgressions and disrupted entrenched hierarchies, root-and-branch reformers across space and time faced an identical arraignment: "fanatical, insane, destructive, treasonable, infidel." Such grand crusaders also similarly encountered "popular violence" and "religious opprobrium" and received early support from persons "destitute of resources, uninfluential in position, without reputation." Another fifteen years later, May proffered a more detailed explication of perennially mistreated and maligned antislavery agitators. Whereas the antebellum Garrison briefly ruminated on the character assassination endured by history's holiest warriors, the postbellum memoirist hoped to finally save the *Liberator*'s editor and other abolitionists from deadly mischaracterizations.[9]

Even though that endeavor culminated in a four-hundred-page volume, it originated as a simpler errand. Based on the "special request" of the *Christian Register*'s editor, May regularly contributed to that Unitarian periodical via his 1867–1868 "Reminiscences of the Antislavery Reformers" column. For the book, which allegedly came about at the behest of "so many persons," the author collected the already published articles as well as composed new remembrances. Regardless of who set his retrospective writing in motion, the end product amounted to May's last philanthropic actions, as he passed away in 1871. Premonitions of death did not necessarily preoccupy his late-in-life memorial and historical tasks. Both the insecure standing of the abolitionists and the freedpeople's unresolved situation certainly had done so.[10]

In a single-sentence paragraph concluding the narrative, May issued a moving appeal on behalf of racial justice. "May the sad experience of the past," he declaimed, "prompt and impel our nation . . . to do all for the colored population of our country, South and North, that righteousness demands at our hands." Despite the ratification of important constitutional amendments, eliminating chattel bondage and erecting a colorblind US citizenship, in his assessment, were egalitarian starting points only. The proponents of immediate emancipation always urged, the commemorator emphasized elsewhere in the text, that "our enslaved countrymen . . . should forthwith be admitted to all the rights and privileges of freemen upon the same conditions as others." A just resolution to "their long enslavement," however, involved not merely another constitutional amendment that would ensure Black manhood suffrage. It also mandated that public officials provide the formerly enslaved with access to confiscated lands and educational opportunities. The chronicler thus tendered his selective account as a serviceable guide for Reconstruction-era policy making. If readers abided by the abolitionist lessons that he wished to impart, they would, he firmly believed, avert more warlike calamities in the future.[11]

For May, then, reflecting on abolitionism comprised no easy exercise. While preparing recollections for the *Christian Register*, the divisive matter of which branch of the US government should determine the national reintegration of eleven secessionist states climaxed in a nearly successful congressional attempt to remove an obstreperous president from office. Before the impeachment and trial of Andrew Johnson occurred in early 1868, the Republican-controlled Congress had adopted, over the chief executive's veto, three Reconstruction Acts. Intended to complete the Union's restoration once and for all, the legislation placed governmental reorganization across the former Confederacy under temporary military oversight. It further reordered the Old South by extending voting rights and officeholding opportunities to African American males. Given that May's racial justice criteria necessitated additional reparations, his authorial context disallowed simple movement nostalgia or hallelujahs. As the first veteran abolitionist to publish a book-length memoir after the Civil War, he went about that venture as an ageless crusader.[12]

In the timely tale that he crafted, May particularly underscored responsible and respectable antislavery agitators. If Reconstruction-era Americans actually needed such models, then May was the perfect candidate to construct them. Genteel culture permeated his upbringing, maturation, and adulthood. As a descendant of the Sewalls and Quincys on his mother's side, he possessed an impressive Bay State ancestry. As a graduate of Harvard College and Harvard Divinity School, he obtained a prestigious education. As a Unitarian pastor, moreover, he belonged to a mostly urban-based denomination in which affluence, distinction, and learnedness typified many parishioners. However consciously, that pedigree, training, and vocation informed the memoirist's representation of abolitionism in subtle and complex ways.[13]

In one biographer's apt estimate, the Boston-born, Harvard-educated, and elite-connected May not only effectively renounced his "social class" upon entering the antislavery crusade. He "alienated many friends" as well by embracing a campaign that Boston Unitarians had generally deemed as "vulgar and a threat to their respectability." If traveling in immediate emancipation circles lowered May's status among New England blue bloods, he never relinquished it himself. As the memorial publication illustrates, the author viewed a stereotypically inflammatory campaign through a personalized gentility lens. Since the Thirteenth and Fourteenth Amendments had no sizable impact on May's humanitarianism, he utilized a uniquely themed history in order to redress generations of African American captivity.[14]

During the Civil War, May had succinctly articulated the program that awaited antislavery agitators once the sectional turmoil dissipated. About a year after President Lincoln affixed his signature to the Emancipation Proclamation on January 1, 1863, which raised abolitionist expectations of enslavement's imminent collapse if and when Union armies prevailed on the battlefield, May sensed no approaching day of jubilation. At the AASS's annual meeting, he asserted that members should not retire from their advocacy "until . . . all that can be done to repair the damages caused by slavery to the population of our country, black and white, shall have been done." The short period in between that pronouncement and the appearance of his printed reminiscences did not modify May's personal obligations or outlook. As the 1870s neared, some potential finalization of his altruistic agenda loomed nowhere in sight. "If the portents of the day be true," the memoirist proclaimed, "our conflict with the enemies of liberty, the oppressors of humanity, is not yet ended." A recently divided nation of people could truly learn much from his chronicle, especially the honorable and dutiful citizen-reformers whom he commemorated.[15]

Even though moderating the past did not result in gross distortions, encircling abolitionists with a respectable and responsible aura nevertheless obliged the retrospective writer to excuse specific antislavery crusaders. His overview of the *Liberator*'s editor offers a case in point. Early in the narrative May predicted that "the people of our reunited Republic will [someday] gratefully" salute Garrison as "among the greatest benefactors of our nation and our race." The latter warranted such recognition, in the author's analysis, because he selflessly dedicated himself to the arduous libertarian work that late-eighteenth-century revolutionaries had begun but left unfinished. Indeed, he billed the 1831 inauguration of patriotic Garrison's Boston-headquartered weekly as the opening salvo of the

Second American Revolution. Whereas May ranked as an original recruit and loyal Garrisonian soldier, he noted that many others reacted differently to abolitionism's commanding general. From the *Liberator's* get-go antiabolitionists had smeared its director as a "Fanatic! Incendiary! Madman!" The ferocious way that he verbally fought "to exterminate . . . the tremendous sin of slavery" evidently prevented a broader acknowledgment of his excellence. The memoirist therefore strove to legitimize Garrison's actions so as to secure a well-earned apotheosis. In so doing, he upheld the propriety and refinement that marked his own ancestry, schooling, and profession.[16]

That the *Liberator's* editor constituted a messianic minister the commemorator left no doubts. He vividly depicted how initial interactions with that abolitionist had instantly changed his world in 1830. Having been exposed to Boston-area advertisements for a slate of lectures in which Garrison proposed to expound on the rightfulness of immediate and unconditional emancipation and concomitantly disclose slaveholding's utter iniquity and the American Colonization Society's (ACS) sheer duplicity, an older May recalled that he eagerly wanted "to see and hear" the lecturer. That the latter was a cause célèbre at the time additionally piqued his interest. Only recently had Garrison surfaced from a two-month Baltimore jailing, his punishment for libeling a Massachusetts ship owner linked to the interstate slave trade. Returning to his native New England, the unfettered philanthropist in possession of "a sacred mission" captivated a younger May. "'This is a providential [and prophetic] man,'" the chronicler recited his reception; "'he will shake our nation to its centre, but he will shake slavery out of it.'" Virtually from that moment May orbited a Garrisonian sun. His divine words, the author avowed, left an "impression upon my soul [that] has never been effaced; indeed, they moulded it anew." Even though the born-again May wholly absorbed the spirit of Garrison's message, the spirited fashion by which Garrison delivered it made him feel uneasy at first.[17]

More than anything else, the blistering invectives dispensed by the *Liberator's* editor tested the memoirist's genteel sensibilities. Such comportment not only defied the proper modes of polite and civil conduct that period etiquette books had codified. As the apparent antithesis of self-restraint, Garrison's immoderate activism also undercut May's notions of respectability. In the posthumously published *Memoir of Samuel Joseph May*, the compilers affirmed that their subject had "greatly disliked the neglect of courtesy." "Manners," they accented, "were morals with him, and the disregard of the little amenities of behavior in domestic and private life always tried his feelings and offended his taste." An 1897 discourse in which Joseph May celebrated the one-hundredth anniversary of his father's birth sheds even more insight onto the topic.[18]

While praising a deceased parent's "personal graces," the son's filiopietistic address occasionally reads like a Victorian-era advice manual. The orator described the elder May's bearing as "easy, but always dignified"; "elegant, but unstudied." He remarked that dad's "tastes were correct and controlling over his own demeanor." He mentioned that "vulgarity, pretension, rudeness, and even [the] mere disregard of social conventionalities" distressed the bourgeois paterfamilias. Equally interesting, the speaker attested that the latter's high "moral ideals" never amounted to "fanatic[ism]." Despite such impeccable attributes, one of the elder May's earliest biographers indicated that abolitionism had alienated him from good society. "In almost all the refined and delightful [Boston] homes . . . in which he had been familiar," the son averred, "he lost the old welcome." That synopsis readily suggests how Garrison's linguistic intemperance could pose a quandary for someone with Samuel Joseph May's disposition. To certify the decency of a trailblazing abolitionist, the retrospective writer made allowances for his dear friend.[19]

To elucidate the *Liberator*'s editor, May meditated, in part, on his exceptional faculties. Only Garrison, to his wonderment, "had his eyes so anointed that he could see that outrages" inflicted on African Americans "were wrongs done to common humanity." Only Garrison, he worshipfully added, "had his ears so completely unstopped of 'prejudice against color'" that the entreaties of enslaved Black people "sounded to him as if they came from brothers and sisters." Yet uncommon senses alone did not enliven his antislavery assaults on wicked practices and heinous institutions; the author also italicized a higher calling. The narrator thus exculpated an infamous reformer by classifying him as a divinely commissioned agent. As such, he denounced "the inhumanity and hypocrisy" of popular religious sects and their priestly overseers in an appropriately Christlike way. Since nothing was more precious to him, the Reverend May avowed, than the "religion of Jesus Christ," assailing American Christianity as horribly corrupted and proslavery was anything but unseemly and irreverent. Those and other anti-Garrison canards, according to the memorial testimony, flowed from "the hollow-hearted pretenders of piety," precisely the latter-day scribes and Pharisees of Judea whom the historically misunderstood *Liberator*'s editor had excoriated.[20]

In another commemorative justification of the diatribes that Garrison unloaded on southern slaveholders and their northern abettors, the author returned to the problem of racism in the United States. "*Colorphobia*," he unceremoniously announced, "was a disease that infected all white Americans." To blast through the anti-Black biases vitiating every sector of society—the "most elevated," "humblest," and everyone else in between—the *Liberator's* editor needed "fiery indignation." An otherwise notorious facet, however, the chronicler himself did not immediately grasp. In a related conversation with Garrison shortly following the commencement of his antislavery weekly, May divulged that he had sought to restrain him. The activist's "undue severity," feared the fresh convert to abolitionism, "was damaging the cause." Regarding the friendly request to "'keep more cool,'" a quoted Garrison memorably retorted: "'Brother May, I have need to be *all on fire*, for I have mountains of ice about me to melt.'" For the memoirist, that self-defense permanently assuaged his reservations. Besides proving that he harbored no grievances about a heavenly crusader's temperament, the retrospective writer expressed contrition for the "mistaken" complaints that he and others had previously aired.[21]

If the *Liberator's* editor ever seriously taxed the author's code of respectability and responsibility, he did so only fleetingly. Garrison's traducers, he trenchantly observed, "knew nothing of his private life"; May's knowledge, by comparison, was exhaustive. Even though the memoirist never delved into that personal dimension, Joseph May's parental tribute once more shines informative light. Within the sanctuary of the family hearth, according to his recitation, Garrison and his father, the best of companions, could place their worldly cares aside. Thus reposed, "their sportiveness, their jests, their tales and songs," he affectionately reminisced, would fill the household with merriment well into the evening. The habitual truculence of the *Liberator's* editor, in other words, represented a daytime persona, which the antislavery agitator had publicly donned while fighting for the enslaved. By nightfall, the seldomly seen convivial Garrison took a starring role.[22]

Paradoxically, the very heatedness that had discomforted May emanated from his own Unitarian pulpit. Joseph May's homage, yet again, illuminates the Garrisonian tone of dad's ministry. "Offenses against the dignity of manhood or womanhood," the son acknowledged, engendered a "righteous anger" that sometimes took the form of "scathing censure." The orator also declared that in the elder May's sermons and speeches on reform, he deplored "the evil things of his day" in "unqualified," "unsparing," and "scorching" terms. But his rhetorical "fires," the offspring assured listeners, "blazed forth against the sin, not the sinner." That differentiation evidently mattered to two May generations; the *Liberator's* editor, conversely, rebuked both indiscriminately. Still, that the abolitionist disciple occasionally duplicated his leader's unrestrained intensity means that the memoirist basically moderated himself as well.[23]

Remembrances of Gerrit Smith, more so than recollections of Garrison, show how the retrospective writer recast abolitionism amid an unfolding congressional Reconstruction. May forged an "intimate" acquaintanceship with the upstate New York reformer beginning in 1845, after he had left ancestral New England to assume the pastoral responsibilities of a Syracuse church. Even though the political abolitionist Smith discontinued an AASS affiliation during the 1840s and 1850s, he and May nonetheless worked across organizational boundaries along the Erie Canal corridor. On the particulars of that history the author lavished only a little attention; he fixated on more marvelous stuff instead. To supplement his portrait of Garrison as a Christ-like figure, the commemorator pictured Smith as the incarnation of Christian charity. Whereas the chronicler primarily pondered the amazing earnestness of the former, he mostly mused on the astonishing stewardship of the latter. By spotlighting deeds that exhibited Smith's liberality, the narrator did not accidentally suppress those concerning his distinctive radicalism.[24]

As the holder of a real estate empire that traversed several states and approximated *"seven hundred and fifty thousand acres of land,"* May's Smith keenly comprehended his obligations while presiding over an immense tract of the Creator's dominion. That the New Yorker subsequently comported himself not as a feudal landlord but a noble servant of the Lord verified his preeminence and continued relevance. Several Smithian feats of munificence earned unstinting memorial accolades. May started by alluding to his allocation of nearly ten thousand dollars to the ACS. Once Smith had lost confidence in that association's antislavery bona fides and converted to the doctrine of immediate emancipation, as the author specified, he disbursed even more generous contributions to authentic abolitionist groups. To apprise readers of the significance of that humanitarian coup, May estimated that Smith earmarked at least *"fifty thousand* dollars" total for the AASS and a state-level auxiliary.[25]

The memoirist next stressed that Smith's magnanimity aided other progressive establishments. To assist Ohio's interracial, coeducational Oberlin College, he bestowed money as well as "twenty thousand acres of land in Virginia," from the sale of which the school earned "more than fifty thousand dollars." Smith similarly patronized New York's Oneida Institute, whose curriculum combined traditional coursework and manual labor training for Black and white enrollees. Besides aiding inclusive education, the narrator pointed out that he brilliantly managed vast assets by distributing forty-acre homesteads to some three thousand African American men and their families (a bequest that he extended to five hundred impoverished whites as well). Since May's Smith "profoundly pitied the landless" and sincerely cared about the hardships of a "proscribed race," he granted about 120,000 acres to Black settlers by the middle of 1847. Postbellum readers, then, could profit immensely from that antebellum role model. Such socially conscious largesse, though, the retrospective writer carefully curated. Unlike Garrison's extremism, which required simple rationalization, Smith's resulted in authorial evasiveness.[26]

In May's survey of a wealthy backer of racial justice, one spectacular benefaction turns up nowhere. As a New York associate of a clandestine alliance known as the "Secret Six"—which additionally comprised the New Englanders Thomas Wentworth Higginson, Samuel Gridley Howe, Theodore Parker, Franklin Sanborn, and George Luther Stearns—Smith helped finance John Brown's 1859 raid on the United States Armory and Arsenal at Harpers Ferry, Virginia. Brown personally conceived his expedition as a first strike in a broader insurgency throughout the Southland. Before embarking southward, he secured hundreds of pikes with which to arm African Americans escaping from bondage. That insurrectionary plot terminated not in the liberation of enslaved multitudes but the ringleader's execution. A seemingly innocuous closing statement demonstrates that the commemorator preferred to mask Smith's conspiratorial involvement. He "has entertained and freely expressed some opinions that have been peculiar to himself," the chronicler conceded, "and has done some things that have appeared eccentric." In that way, May sustained a respectable and responsible story of abolitionism.[27]

A curious report of a nervous breakdown amplifies the memoirist's attempted concealment of a politically and socially divisive incident. Smith's herculean philanthropy, according to this retelling, thoroughly exhausted him by late 1858, so much so that he suffered from "a serious [bout] of typhoid fever, which was followed by months of mental prostration." Since his philanthropic labors were laborious, as May underlined, they alone caused Smith's collapse. The psychological strain from his share of the Harpers Ferry business purportedly had nothing to do with it. Nor did the possible legal ramifications once a discovered cache of Brown's letters incriminated his silent partners. Such a memorial sleight of hand suggests that May viewed that chapter in Smith's past not merely as a personal irregularity but too scandalous for historical review. To offset the circumlocution, the author issued a testimonial on his behalf: "I believe that he has never consciously done or said anything unfriendly to an oppressed or despised fellow-being, white or black." Consummate selflessness and enlightened generosity thus defined Gerrit Smith's career and deserved emulation, not a momentary lapse in judgment.[28]

Even though the retrospective writer strategically withheld the Secret Six from his narrative of Smith, he did not altogether omit the Harpers Ferry imbroglio from the text. The smidgen that he recounted indicates the problematic place of violence in his delineation of the Second American Revolution. Information about Brown's squelched operation initially reached May during a homecoming voyage to the United States after a nine-month European sojourn. He recalled that he "felt at once that it was 'the beginning of the end' of our conflict with slavery." References to Lincoln's 1860 presidential election and an ensuing secession crisis corroborated his forecast about the foiled raid's galvanizing effects. The chronicler noted that while aboard a steamship, the news generated "deep excitement" among his fellow passengers, eliciting "words of bitter execration" from some southerners and their northern sympathizers. It occasioned "a state of high excitement" in Syracuse, too, preoccupying public and private debates for months. Other than those comments, May offered nothing substantive about Brown's abolitionist ambitions. The commemorator's apparent reticence significantly diverged from the unreserved sentiments that he had originally vocalized.[29]

In an 1860 American Peace Society address, May proclaimed that the defeated and detained Brown had risen to an "an almost unexampled sublimity as the *martyr of impartial liberty*." By juxtaposing the Harpers Ferry architect with Revolutionary-era patriots, the speaker seemingly carved out a more flattering space for the former. In contrast to late-eighteenth-century colonial rebels who had taken up arms to gain national independence from imperial Britain, their mid-nineteenth-century successor deployed forceful measures against American slavery in order to win the freedom of enslaved men and women. As a dedicated pacifist since 1819, as well as a supporter of the defunct Non-Resistance Society, May scarcely showered encomiums upon either. Neither Brown nor the "Fathers of 1776," he avowed, commanded a "wise and Christian" cause. Seizing the oratorical opportunity, May propagated a transcendent truth about warfare's elemental wrongfulness.[30]

While jailed for the Harpers Ferry incursion and awaiting trial in a Virginia court of law, May's Brown allegedly learned something priceless: "that the God of the oppressed is not the God of battle; that the doctrine and spirit of Moses and David are not sanctioned by Christ and his apostles; that there is another and a better way of overcoming any evil than by killing or harming evil doers." For May,

New Testament messages of peace and love superseded the vengeful Old Testament ethos that had apparently animated Brown. By drawing that moral, he presented the latter as an exemplary figure after all, but in a cautionary sense. Others should not replicate his earthbound abolitionist techniques, for they strayed from Jesus's spiritually superior path. That "Great Teacher," he sermonized, "has taught us . . . *that no cause, however righteous, that no life however valuable, may wisely, safely, effectually be maintained or defended by violence, by bloodshed, by doing any harm to the erring, injurious party.*" By May's standards, the avenging Brown constituted a flawed hero, at best; an "unchristian" one, at worst.[31]

Regardless of such qualified acclaim and adverse conclusions, the memoirist skirted the question of Brown's heroic status later in the decade. Since he mostly covered the immediate emancipation campaign's first two decades, the author could easily sidestep a subject that fell outside his chronological parameters. The same did not pertain to an 1837 skirmish that had produced abolitionism's first reputed martyr, which May considered in "The Alton Tragedy" memorial sketch. Even though Elijah Lovejoy never reached the legendary heights that the Harpers Ferry raider quickly attained, his case nonetheless complicated a history of respectable and responsible activists. On the one hand, the *Alton Observer's* editor ultimately enlisted firearms while protecting his printing press against a southern Illinois mob that had sought to demolish it. On the other hand, that musket-toting newspaperman died from the shotgun wounds that he had incurred in the process. Remembering on behalf of "Mr. Garrison and most of the oldest Abolitionists," May stated that they had "regretted" Lovejoy's reliance on "deadly weapons," preferring, instead, an "unresisting martyr[dom]." As that more righteous scenario never transpired, the retrospective writer endeavored to explain away that fatal encounter.[32]

By solely blaming the antiabolitionist rabble, May exonerated Lovejoy for his part in the Alton affair. He mentioned that local ruffians had twice wrecked the *Observer's* business office and equipment before another pack of "madmen" gathered outside a warehouse containing the determined journalist's recently arrived machinery. Destruction, the chronicler avowed, represented the mob's "declared purpose." The offensive against the structure, as well as the persons and objects within, opened with the launching of "stones and other heavy missiles"; it soon proceeded to the firing of more lethal projectiles. Even though members of the "besieged party" responded to the gunshots with their own—thereby causing an enemy fatality—Lovejoy himself did not vacate the premises and charge the armed assailants until someone had torched the roof. Such a menacing situation, the commemorator conveyed, compelled the *Observer's* editor to use force; he discharged his musket as a last resort only. Despite the uneasiness of May's anti-slavery colleagues over how Lovejoy had met his demise, they apparently believed that "our devoted brother had been governed by his highest sense of right [and] had acted in accordance with the accepted morality of the Christian world, and in the spirit of our Revolutionary fathers." May applied that same logic to account for the bellicose Brown in his American Peace Society speech. By reapplying it to Lovejoy exclusively in his postbellum reminiscences, he revised the past.[33]

Whereas the memoirist finessed historical facts while reflecting on Smith's altruism, he silenced them in his representation of the Alton tragedy. The very reasoning behind Lovejoy's posthumous pardon May absolutely abjured decades beforehand. In an 1837 communication to *The Emancipator*, he both deplored a violent *Observer*'s editor and reproached AASS leadership. How other abolitionists mourned the deceased newspaperman particularly incited his epistolary reprimand. Even though May condemned the Alton rioters as "murderers," he refused to recognize the slain Lovejoy as a sacrificial victim or saintly sufferer. By relying on force, he had violated Christ's teachings, which, according to the correspondent, made him an unworthy candidate for veneration. Since the AASS's executive committee eulogized Lovejoy as a valiant defender of civil liberties, May worried that such memorializing endangered "the *evangelical* character of that great enterprise which aims to effect the *peaceful* emancipation of millions in our land." By transforming the killing of the *Observer*'s editor into an undeserved martyrdom, the antebellum May thought that his comrades had terribly strayed from their chosen direction. He therefore emitted a "strong disapprobation of the course pursued by my brethren" because they had virtually betrayed abolitionism's Christ-derived precepts.[34]

Unlike that unmistakable discontent, the retrospective writer nondescriptly remarked that the Alton excitement had led some AASS members to repudiate crucial organizational tenets. Besides the absence of any analysis regarding which abolitionist segment did so and why, May inserted that passing observation into a different book section—one concerning the founding of the AASS. At the 1833 Philadelphia Convention from which that national association materialized, the narrator confirmed that a peace-loving mood had suffused the proceedings. As a participant himself, he recalled that the delegates "emphatically and solemnly" disowned physical violence, or an "arm of flesh." Such paladins of the slave's cause placed their faith wholly "in the power of truth and the influence of the Holy Spirit" in order to convert white Americans to the doctrine of immediate and unconditional emancipation. Their consciousness-raising activities, then, would center on printed and spoken appeals to the hearts and minds of readers and listeners, a tactic known as "moral suasion."[35]

In the *Emancipator* dispatch, May reminded coworkers that inaugural campaign documents had committed them to a nonbelligerent credo. A few years later, he revisited the ethical retreat of leading abolitionists in the aftermath of the Alton tragedy via a series of remembrances for the *National Anti-Slavery Standard*. While musing on the drafting and ratification of the AASS "Declaration of Sentiments," he once more identified commitment to nonviolence as a movement fundamental. From the inception of crusading abolitionism, the memoirist professed many years later, exponents "had determined not to harm our foes." But if the behavior of the *Observer's* editor constituted an irregularity, only the postbellum May acknowledged it as an outlier. His antebellum self flatly disallowed that concession. Even though the commemorator buried his dissension toward Lovejoy's manufactured martyrdom, he fully vented the ire accompanying the 1850 Fugitive Slave Law. In so doing, the chronicler nearly jeopardized his meticulously tailored narrative.[36]

With the adoption of that "Bill of Abominations," the United States had descended into abject dreadfulness, according to the memoirist. In verification of its "execrable" nature, the author quoted some provisions and paraphrased others. He fulminated against the inability of accused runaways to testify on their own behalf because the law forbade the admission of such evidence at adjudicatory hearings. He seethed at the heavy fines and potential imprisonment that the law mandated for anyone assisting freedom seekers or interfering with their rendition. He castigated the law's apparent inducement to remand all accused runaways to southern servitude because, under its terms, judicial commissioners would collect a ten-dollar fee when they ruled in the slaveholding claimant's favor but only five dollars if they decided against the latter. Since northern congressmen and senators had voted for the measure, a still-livid May thundered at how their "concurrence" had turned the North into the "hunting grounds" of enslavers. Despite a nearly two-decade vantage point, he admittedly lacked the words to adequately express his revulsion for such legislative wickedness. Notwithstanding that communicative inability, the retrospective writer shared how he had redoubled antislavery exertions in retaliation.[37]

Through the incorporation of a nearly seven-page sermon, May divulged that a "'diabolical'" statute had triggered a metamorphosis to his abolitionism. In an impassioned homily upbraiding the enactment and its enactors, the Unitarian pastor also implored his parishioners to contest an egregious wrong by practically any mechanism. Everybody, he counseled, "'is bound, as I am, to do for the protection or rescue of a fugitive from slavery what, in your hearts before God, you believe it would be right for you to do in behalf of your life or liberty, or that of a member of your family.'" Exactly how his churchgoers disobeyed the congressional dictate did not necessarily concern the Reverend May; that they do something to thwart its enforcement mattered to him more than anything else. If their consciences permitted "'maim[ing] or kill[ing]'" in security of themselves and loved ones, the normally genteel May had no qualms with his listeners' using the "'the same degree of violence'" to shield freedom seekers from southern oppressors and northern tormentors. That 1850 May thus tolerated, if not encouraged outright, what he had categorically eschewed.[38]

Besides disclosing that a loathsome piece of legislation upset a pacifistic vow, that clerical call potentially altered the memoir's tone. "'There never was, there cannot be,'" according to an incensed preacher, "'a more righteous cause for revolution than the demands made upon us by this law.'" Hardly showcasing some responsible or respectable undertaking, a defiant discourse condoning "'force and arms'" more likely buttressed ingrained stereotypes about the fanaticism of antislavery crusaders. Some of the persons whom that supplication targeted, the author himself conceded, had found it objectionable on those grounds. However problematic, the excerpted tirade did not nullify the author's moderating proclivities. Under his handling, actual resistance to the Fugitive Slave Law unfolded not recklessly but downright orderly. In his historical audit of the 1851 William "Jerry" Henry rescue, May rendered an 1850 philippic as nothing more than a memorable exception to the memorial rule. Recollections of how a collection of upstate New Yorkers liberated an arrested runaway from a Syracuse police station, which made flight to Canadian freedom possible, authenticated the direct-action commandments of his ministerial broadside. They also indicated that his conversion to civil disobedience did not entail a concurrent disavowal of Christian nonviolence.[39]

As he and others devised plans for Jerry's deliverance, the chronicler notified readers that given "strict injunctions," everyone "agreed not to intentionally injure the policemen" guarding the apprehended fugitive from slavery. They consequently pledged themselves to overwhelming the foe not by "blows" but "numbers." By rushing into the room and crowding around the constables, the more plentiful rescuers could leave the officers "powerless by the pressure of the bodies about them." That, in turn, would allow the intruders to seize the prisoner and lead him to an outside buggy. Even though the remembered conspirators realized the likelihood of casualties, the commemorator qualified that ostensible compromise with a telling interjection. After the schemers had finalized their preparations, May said, should anyone get hurt, "'I hope it may be one of our own party.'" As it happened, the liberators inflicted no wounds while abducting Jerry from his confinement. The authorial description of a basically peaceable rescue defuses the narrative tension surrounding his seeming advocacy of forcefulness against a reviled statute. Without a doubt, the Fugitive Slave Law had infuriated antislavery agitators. Documenting it did not derail May's story of abolitionist respectability. To his infinite satisfaction, the protestors channeled their rage responsibly—at least they had done so in Syracuse in 1851.[40]

In contrast to the philosophical dilemmas and interpretative conundrums that antislavery violence provoked, contemplating abolitionist character presented no such memorial or historical predicaments. While detailing the superlative traits of fellow philanthropists, however, the narrator inadvertently unveiled their aberrant features, too. The nonconformity of May's antislavery crusaders stemmed not from their brazenly flouting cultural norms and social mores. Their deviance revolved, instead, about their efforts at upholding and universalizing core values, such as the natural rights enshrined in the Declaration of Independence and the individualism at the heart of a developing middle class. Only the advocates of immediate emancipation, the retrospective writer posited, embodied the equalitarian promise of the Founding Generation. A triumphant abolitionism, he averred, "was indispensably necessary to complete the American Revolution, and verify the truths which it declared to the world." However unconsciously, his abolitionists operated as a liberal-bourgeois vanguard.[41]

If May's associates truly possessed a liberal-bourgeois mentality, progressive inclusivity distanced it from competing middle-class outlooks. A recapitulated 1833 conversation between Garrison and an anonymous "gentleman" encapsulates abolitionism's ecumenical liberalism as the memoirist understood it. After that nameless interlocutor invoked "commonplace objections" to discredit the formation of the AASS, the recollected Garrison countered not with the burning rhetoric that emblazoned the *Liberator*'s pages but plainspoken commonsense. Enslaved people of color, according to May's mentor, "were men, entitled as much as the whitest and most exalted in the land to their liberty, to a residence here, if they choose, and to acquire as much wisdom, as much property, and as high a position as they may." Such points, which May raised in an 1834 discussion that appears elsewhere in the text, coincided with and diverged from the individualistic attitudes of many other contemporaries. The very American mission on which antislavery crusaders generally embarked entailed augmenting the rights of self-ownership, personal improvement, and equality of opportunity.

Since their broader appreciation of national ideals contradicted widespread anti-Black prejudices, they always attracted limited support. What the abolitionists alone had ideated, however, evolved into a political and legal reality because of a cataclysmic civil war. With good reasons, the author strove to standardize the example of eminently bourgeois reformers.[42]

Beyond the retrospective writer, scholars have explored abolitionism's liberal-bourgeois proportions. Yet, attributing the justification of an emerging industrial capitalist economy to a reputedly middle-class-directed campaign overestimates the promoters' weightiness. The abolitionist few did not validate a widening capitalist marketplace, which ultimately placed a premium on the free, wage-earning worker. Nor did that same capitalist marketplace, which easily accommodated the commodity-constituting and -cultivating enslaved laborer, help legitimize the abolitionists' appeal among most white Americans. To be sure, the presumptions and arguments of antislavery agitators often reflected the changes occurring within and without the antebellum United States. Since capitalism was bigger than abolitionism, it simply did not require a small cadre of humanitarian outsiders for reinforcement. In an 1837 sermon, May took a critical stance toward the era's economic transformations. Delivered amid a financial panic, the preacher expressed his abhorrence at the entrepreneurial extravagances and individual greediness attending increasing commercialization. Thirty years later, he elaborated not on that critique but on the moral magnificence of incomparable middle-class activists.[43]

Despite noting that abolitionism had attracted "persons of every class in society . . . each of the three learned professions . . . and of all the various trades and occupations in which men and women engage," the memoirist concentrated on its middling-sort makeup. Simple materialism, however, did not unite May's crusaders and define them as paragons of the bourgeoisie. Nor did religious devotedness on its own confer a singular social status upon those immaculate philanthropists. Espousing the doctrine of immediate emancipation, in conjunction with already heartfelt religiosity, solidified their avant-garde footing. The morality that catapulted such antislavery agitators to the forefront of middle-class altruism simultaneously consigned them to pariah standing among antiabolitionist counterparts. For May, the abolitionist vocation of bourgeois reformers was fraught with difficulties. He repeatedly stressed the occupational hazards that they endured.[44]

To demonstrate that the champions of immediate emancipation braved manifold privations, the commemorator pinpointed the earthly abundance and prestige that they had to forgo. The remembered Charles C. Burleigh surrendered all manner of emoluments when he accepted an 1835 offer to serve as a lecturing agent for a Massachusetts antislavery society. Rather than pursue remunerative employment—specifically the legal profession for which he had prepared himself—May's Burleigh opted for highly trying grassroots activism. He subsequently knew that "he would have to renounce all hope of wealth or political preferment, and lead a life of continual conflict with ungenerous opponents; be poorly requited for his labors, and suffer contumely, hatred, persecution." Such a person amounted to an unusual bourgeois, and not just because of an eccentric physical appearance that consisted of long hair and a full beard. Yet, as a "purehearted, conscientious, self-sacrificing" individual, he epitomized the delayed gratification typifying the middle-class activists of May's chronicle.[45]

Whereas Burleigh's embracing immediate emancipation required that he relinquish prosperity in the foreseeable future, the recollected Lydia Maria Child risked an already lucrative livelihood as soon as she decided on an abolitionist calling. Her 1833 publication *An Appeal in Favor of That Class of Americans Called Africans* not only powerfully exposed, in May's appraisal, slavery's "essential barbarity" and "dehumanizing influences." It also reversed the commercial viability of a formerly popular writer of novels, advice books, and juvenile literature. The southern market for her literary products, the narrator elucidated, virtually disappeared, and the northern demand seriously declined as well, so much so that her income had "lessened six or eight hundred dollars a year." Regardless of the negative shocks to the household economy, such a consumer rebuke never prompted May's Child to soften her antislavery protest. On the contrary, it "roused" her to toil even more energetically on behalf of the slave's cause. By putting people before profits and conscience calculations ahead of the capitalist marketplace, Child represented yet another antebellum anomaly that the memoirist wanted postbellum readers to normalize.[46]

A conspicuous professional slump also befell the recalled German émigré Dr. Charles Follen. That veteran of the Napoleonic Wars, who had fled from Central Europe lest his advocacy of "liberal institutions" resulted in official Austrian or Prussian repression, experienced harassment of another kind in the supposedly more tolerant United States. By rallying around the immediate emancipation banner that Garrison had unfurled, Follen lost his German language and literature professorship at Harvard College. "If he had been like too many other men," according to May's moralizing, "worldly wisdom, prudential considerations" would have prevented his joining something so unpopular. "But liberty, the rights of man, and his sense of duty," he certified, "were more precious . . . than physical comforts or even life." Since the "illustrious German" had unhesitatingly forfeited academic contentment for the sake of a "great moral enterprise," the author painted him as a commendable bourgeois reformer.[47]

The middle-class exceptionalism of May's Burleigh, Child, and Follen thus hinged, in part, on the economic betterment that their personal probity and industriousness seldom produced. The extraordinary virtues of such humanitarians had nothing to do with social mobility per se, precisely why they symbolized the bourgeoisie's cutting edge. By preaching a high standard of morality and practicing a comprehensive code of ethics, the immediate emancipation faithful evinced, in the memorialist's evaluation, that a huge gulf existed between themselves and other middling-sort Americans. Apart from highlighting that historical divide, the retrospective writer tried to narrow it, too. The effectiveness of his gambit depended on whether postbellum audiences internalized and externalized the antebellum lessons of irreproachable abolitionists.

Since antislavery agitators were no respecters of persons, May emphasized that their movement encompassed "both sexes and all complexions." In memorial sketches respectively reserved for Child, Sarah and Angelina Grimké, and Lucretia Mott, he recognized the "valuable services" of female colleagues. He also mentioned the abolitionist contributions of Susan B. Anthony, Maria Weston Chapman, Abigail Kelly Foster, and Sallie Holley. In a book section revealingly entitled "Distinguished Colored Men," the memoirist applauded William Wells Brown, Frederick Douglass, James Forten, Lewis Hayden, Jermain Loguen, William Cooper Nell, Robert Purvis, Charles Lenox Remond, and David Ruggles. That May assimilated white women and Black men into his narrative further substantiated the unmatched catholicity of the immediate emancipation campaign. Abolitionism, the author proudly professed, "has shown that there is neither orthodox nor heterodox, neither white nor black, neither male nor female, but all *are one in the work of the Lord.*" To properly edify Reconstruction-era audiences, he traced the ways in which respectable and responsible reformers had struggled against structural inequities.[48]

Across six memorial sketches, for instance, the retrospective writer surveyed the 1833–1834 plight of Prudence Crandall, addressing in the process the succor that he and other abolitionists had extended. For the "*crime* of keeping a boarding-school for colored girls in the State of Connecticut," the memoirist declaimed, the indomitable Quaker educator encountered public animosity and legal persecution. The concerned citizens of Canterbury, mustered by the bigotry that viewed a "'nigger school'" as incalculably evil, first reacted by organizing a meeting and issuing resolutions. Since an undeterred Crandall persisted, townspeople sought to intimidate the headmistress and drive out her equally "resolute"

African American pupils by hurling insults at them, vandalizing schoolhouse property, and enforcing an "obsolete vagrant law." When such local pressure had failed, the narrator explained that the state legislature then intervened, adopting a "Black Law" that partly targeted educational initiatives like Crandall's. May's story did not end there, though. It reached a denouement with the disgraceful jailing and trial of a "generous," "disinterested," and determined woman, as well as the harrowing destruction of the home from which she had launched her "Christian enterprise."[49]

The antipathies that had quashed the Canterbury school and other abolitionist efforts on behalf of Black education during the early 1830s comprised but one portion of a larger memorial and historical problem. In the section "Prejudice against Color," May took on the malevolent mentality behind systemic racial oppression. Because of generations of African American captivity, according to his explication, white Americans regarded subjugation as the condition naturally suiting an "*inferior race* of beings [located] somewhere between monkey and man." That free people of color were generally "poor, uneducated, and . . . engaged in menial employments" only cemented such racist thinking. To continuously counter ideas about immutable Black ignorance and degradation, the chronicler deployed an inconvenient truth: Antebellum African Americans could not rise en masse from a "low estate" as a result of the "laws, customs, and contemptuous treatment" inhibiting their advancement. After several paragraphs describing free-state discrimination and segregation, the commemorator alluded to an old antislavery procedure whereby activist-authors gathered and disseminated "numerous evidences" of Black capabilities. May effectively updated it in the "Distinguished Colored Men" sketches, depicting notable people of color as exceptionally bourgeois. In so doing, he not only furthered his distinctive agenda but also cooperated in an antiracism uplift project that free Black northerners had themselves commenced well before the immediate emancipation campaign had begun.[50]

Besides lauding James Forten's opposition to the ACS, the narrator touted the business acumen that had made him a well-to-do Philadelphian and an important person of color. As the proprietor of the "largest private sail-making establishment" in the City of Brotherly Love, the remembered Forten garnered the respect of his forty employees, most of whom were white, as well as "prominent merchants." Such successfulness in a competitive marketplace superbly carried over to the domestic sphere as well. Forten "lived in as handsome a style as anyone should wish," May attested, and "entertained with as much ease and elegance as I could desire to see." The cultivation of the household patriarch additionally characterized his "lovely, accomplished daughters." Their education, though, cost the father dearly, as the area's "best schools" denied Black pupils. Even though riches did not shelter Forten or his family from "accursed" caste prejudices— racial slavery's "offspring"—that possessor of a "commanding mind" constituted no antebellum abnormality. However compactly drawn, May created other cases of African American aptitude and gentility.[51]

The recollected Jermain Loguen emerges from the text as the quintessence of American individualism, a veritable Black Benjamin Franklin. The author recited how, through undaunted perseverance, he had broken away from Tennessee servitude in 1834 and continually improved his economic and educational stations in life thereafter. Within three years of his self-liberation, Loguen earned the "confidence" of a Canadian employer, who entrusted to him the management of a two-hundred-acre farmstead. After saving "several hundred dollars" from his Hamilton labors, he then relocated to Rochester, New York, where he obtained employment at a top hotel. Since May's Loguen totally abstained from "intoxicating liquors and tobacco," he amassed, in short order, several hundred more dollars in savings, thereby allowing him to pursue formal schooling. Training at Oneida Institute enabled him to assume, beginning in 1841, the pastoral care of Syracuse's African Methodist Church as well as teach local Black children. "By industry, frugality, and the skillful investment of his property," the memorialist pontificated, "he has gained a good estate." That the Reverend Loguen should also ascend to the rank of bishop of his denomination befitted such a stalwart history.[52]

The recalled Frederick Douglass similarly personifies the middle-class sociocultural values that had shaped May's interpretation of abolitionism. The memoirist pointed out that within a decade of his 1838 escape from Maryland enslavement, an assiduous Douglass arose as a first-rate antislavery agitator, a "favorite" public speaker on both sides of the Atlantic, and an owner and operator of a weekly newspaper. While summarizing that stellar trajectory, which Douglass himself famously told and retold, May interspersed references to an unparalleled autodidacticism. As an unfree laborer in Baltimore, Douglass had "contrived . . . various ingenious ways" by which to procure literacy. As a newly arrived resident of New Bedford, Massachusetts, he expertly "improved his enlarged opportunities to acquire knowledge." As a freshly appointed abolitionist lecturing agent, he "applied himself diligently to reading and study" so that he could carry out his responsibilities effectually. Should the hardworking Douglass ever enter Congress as a representative or senator, the retrospective writer predicted that he would quickly achieve prominence. That simple declaration mirrored both May's admiration for Douglass and the sincerity of his racial egalitarianism.[53]

As a subgroup within a middle-class subgroup, the talented people of color whom May extolled therefore executed loftier authorial tasks as socially and politically useful race representatives. Even though the narrator designated white and Black comrades as phenomenally bourgeois, he nevertheless suggested that they had led divergent middling-sort existences. White reformers, in his analysis, often forsook conventional aspirations as they set out on immediate emancipation journeys. Moral richness, not material accumulation, separated their bourgeois lifestyles from others. May conversely accentuated the personal attainments of Black activists, reconfiguring several of their life stories as middle-class epics. Whereas the commemorator essentially isolated white antislavery crusaders from the mainstream bourgeoisie, he integrated African Americans within a broader middling-sort milieu. Regardless of those differences in treatment, the chronicler beckoned all postbellum whites to do what only the antebellum abolitionists allegedly had done: rise above racism.

The refinement of America according to abolitionism's specifications thus comprises a memorial key to solving historical ills. The author, however, held no illusions about colorphobia in the past or present. The pervasiveness of anti-Black biases, he announced, blocked an earlier eradication of chattel bondage and still formed "the greatest obstacle in our country to the progress of liberty and the establishment of peace." Yet the postwar prospects for the latter necessitated not the rehabilitation of ex-Confederates exclusively, from May's standpoint, but the redemption of racist Americans more widely. Since the Old South's master class had enjoyed countrywide backing, the memoirist accordingly censured antiabolitionist northerners while reviewing the careers of paradigmatic bourgeois reformers.[54]

Among the legions of northern whites culpable for the crime of slavery, the "'gentlemen of property and standing'" headed the retrospective writer's list. Ditto for the countless editors of sacred and secular newspapers and virtually all the foremost orators, ministers of religion, and members of major political parties. Whether the willing agents or submissive lackeys of "the slaveholding oligarchy," those dishonorable and delinquent citizens had solidly arrayed themselves against the slaves' friends. In the short term, the malicious attacks that they fired occasioned fierce antiabolitionist hostility. The "counsels of the Abolitionists were spurned," May concisely tabulated, "their sentiments and purposes were shamelessly misrepresented, their [reputations] traduced, their property destroyed, their persons maltreated." Rather than suppress abolitionism, such sinister assaults ultimately caused what May provocatively labeled a "fratricidal, parricidal, and [nearly] suicidal war."[55]

To prove the misconduct of affluent antiabolitionists, the chronicler allocated dozens of pages to the crowd violence that had broken out in cities, towns, and villages across the North during the 1830s. Memories of that physically abusive and emotionally traumatic "Reign of Terror" prompted an authorial chastisement not of the brutal and disorderly rabble but of the irresponsible and disrespectable rabble-rousers. May publicized, for example, that more than a thousand of Boston's finest inhabitants gathered at Faneuil Hall, in August 1835, to supply their collective seal of disapproval against the immediate emancipation campaign. Their "harangues," according to his pithy indictment, exacerbated the unrest among the lower sort. The commemorator subsequently wondered if those and other better-sort instigators ever felt "heartily ashamed" at how their ignoble actions had released the "demon spirits" of the mob.[56]

Besides singling out the abysmal record of the gentlemen of property and standing, the narrator impugned Protestant clergymen. Indeed, nothing had menaced abolitionism's growth like a woeful American Christianity, which purportedly provided decades of reprehensible guidance. As corroboration, May stressed that churchmen neither accepted nor denounced slaveholding as an absolute sin. He underscored that the ecclesiastical bodies in which ministers met to discuss doctrinal matters and formulate denominational regulations had never severed ties with churches that had admitted slave-owning congregants. He also called attention to the priestly antagonism to the gospel of immediate emancipation within and without meetinghouse walls. Such wrongdoing, according to May's tally, infiltrated "ninety-nine hundredths" of the nation's religious leadership. It also brought about direful repercussions. Self-proclaimed Christians, the memoirist avowed, effectuated "the most violent conflicts [and] most outrageous mobs" against the abolitionists. If Christian clerics, he contended, had simply enjoined "the impartial love of the Heavenly Father" for all persons, as well as insisted on the "equal, inalienable rights" for all men that "Divine justice" mandated, then "our late civil war would have been averted!"[57]

Such an accounting of antiabolitionist offenses only heightened the exceptionalism of antislavery crusaders. Since they alone had taken the lead on a pressing human rights issue, the retrospective writer strengthened their timeliness, too. In the postemancipation America that he desired and demanded, US policy makers must additionally outfit African Americans with basic economic and educational tools. That just compensation for generations of captivity, May deduced, would permit the freedpeople "to maintain . . . their new condition, and work themselves out of the evils that were enforced upon them." Nor did his recommendation of unprecedented governmental assistance amount to a sectional punishment. Given the connivance of white northerners in "the enslavement of our fellow-men," their sinfulness, the author reminded readers, required nationwide atonement. From the outbreak of sectional military strife, he transmitted that message so as to deflate any notion that the Almighty had sided with the Union blue on the battlefield.[58]

In an early 1861 sermon, the Reverend May promulgated potentially startling truths. Even though southern slaveholders constituted "the principals in our national transgressions," their northern accomplices "can hardly claim to be less guilty." He particularly tongue-lashed "our selfish merchants," "our godless politicians," and "the timid, time serving ministers and churches in our free States" as the most flagrant abettors of wickedness. Since nearly all whites possessed a share in slavery's iniquity, he declared that Unionists and Confederates alike deserved the "heavy pecuniary losses, ruined hearths, [and] untimely deaths" that warfare always wrought. Americans could have avoided a resort to armaments, May preached, if millions of supposed "believers in the Prince of Peace . . . had followed his precepts, and manifested his spirit." "A terrible punishment," he pronounced, "is now upon us." The conclusion of combat brought about no revisions to those judgments.[59]

Regardless of the memoirist's fair-minded assertion that the general government "should be forbearing" toward rebellious southerners, he scolded Congress for leaving the freedpeople "at the mercy of their former masters." Despite the absence of contextualizing commentary, May probably had in mind the discriminatory Black Codes of 1865–1866, which state legislatures throughout the recently defeated Confederacy had enacted, under President Johnson's lenient restoration guidelines, in order to render the newly emancipated as slave-like as possible. The savagery unleashed by the Ku Klux Klan and other terrorist organizations, in order to dispute the expansion of African American rights and stem the reconstructionist tide in the South, likely impacted his textual ruminations as well.[60]

That persisting recalcitrance only magnified the sense of urgency infusing May's narrative. "Our country is not surely saved," the chronicler opined. "Discord still reigns in the land," he added, which meant that the abolitionists' commission had not expired. By noticeably moderating antislavery history, the commemorator unequivocally hoped to fulfill its racial justice promise. Rather than completely conceal the radicalism of the immediate emancipation campaign, he deftly revealed that honorable and dutiful citizen-reformers had waged a grand moral and spiritual fight for common humanity and universal liberty. Ensuring a proper recognition and emulation of abolitionism's sterling middle-class men and women allowed an elderly Samuel Joseph May to wage a final fight against problems anchored in a proslavery and antiabolitionist past.[61]

2   Antislavery Elevated

William Wells Brown and the Purpose of Black Activism

"A little more than forty years ago," William Wells Brown observed in a massive 1873 opus, "William Lloyd Garrison hoisted the banner of immediate and unconditional emancipation, as the right of the slave, and the duty of the master." Across a 550-page historical survey, the white champions of universal liberty appropriately take center stage at several narrative moments. Besides venerating the *Liberator*'s editor as abolitionism's pathfinder, as well as professing gratefulness for everything that the Boston crusader had done for African Americans, the author revered all abolitionists more generally. He admired them for battling a monstrous system of subjugation with "bold[ness] and seeming audacity," cherishing the "persistency" and "courage" that a numerically insignificant band of humanitarians had evinced. Despite ultimately singling out the Garrisonian agitators with whom he identified as the antislavery campaign's most "zeal[ous]" and "radical" exponents, Brown did not write about the past in order to fortify or enhance their reputation in the present. Far greater purposefulness guided the pen of a former bondman turned man of letters. In the intercontinental Black history *The Rising Son; or, The Antecedents and Advancement of the Colored Race*, as well as the 1880 personal and regional chronicle *My Southern Home: or, The South and Its People*, the historian and memoirist sought to finalize an ongoing African American freedom struggle that he himself uniquely emblematized.[1]

For Brown, like many other prominent African Americans of the Civil War era, abolitionism revolved about two paramount *E*'s—the emancipation of the enslaved and the elevation of people of color. Of the twin goals, the second interacted with and transcended the first in distinctive ways. Arising in the North as human bondage disintegrated during the late eighteenth and early nineteenth centuries, uplift strategies addressed both practical and principled affairs. On a simple level, an ethic of individual and collective improvement originally responded to the developmental needs of free Black communities gradually taking shape after generations of captivity. More subversively, it increasingly targeted the anti-Black prejudices that riddled American culture and society, in the slaveholding and nonslaveholding states alike. Improving oneself, in the eyes of community builders, would help advance the race; racial progress, in turn, would erode the racism that reduced African Americans to pieces of property in the South and second-class citizenship in the North. Because of such outlooks, southern servitude's demise, whenever it happened, could never end the abolitionist fight. The wartime death of enslavement and consequent birth of millions of freedpeople thus enabled leading Black northerners to enlarge and nationalize their longstanding betterment philosophy. Nor did postwar congressional enactments and constitutional amendments favoring equal African American rights lessen a program that went beyond pure politics.[2]

Both *The Rising Son* and *My Southern Home* powerfully illustrate Brown's engrossment in a postbellum respectability project that had deep antebellum roots. In each, the prolific public intellectual invested in and attempted to realize unfinished abolitionism as a Black middle-class moralist and conduct writer. The code bourgeois and uplift evangel defining the historian and memoirist notably stemmed from decades of assiduous personal application and the expertise that eventually ensued. Indeed, with the 1847 printing of the *Narrative of William W. Brown, a Fugitive Slave*, the autodidactic author formally embarked on an activist literary career in which he spectacularly surmounted the lack of cultivation embedding the southern school of slavery. An industrious Brown generated an impressive and unprecedented array of works thereafter, always as an exemplary elevator and antiracism messenger.[3]

For example, in 1848, he compiled an abolitionist songbook, *The Anti-Slavery Harp*; four years later, he issued a travelogue, *Three Years in Europe: or, Places I Have Seen and People I Have Met* (which he revised and rechristened in 1855). With the 1853 appearance of *Clotel; or, The President's Daughter* (the alterations to which reappeared under different book titles during the 1860s), Brown emerged as a novelist; with that of *The Escape; or, A Leap for Freedom* five years later, he further distinguished himself as a playwright. In the last three authorial roles, in particular, the Black man of letters achieved African American firsts. Even though Brown did not similarly prepare the first book-length African American history, his biographically driven examination of 1863, *The Black Man, His Antecedents, His Genius, and His Achievements*, and especially his martial-oriented investigation of 1867, *The Negro in the American Rebellion: His Heroism and His Fidelity*, nonetheless denote pioneering historical productions.[4]

"No man ever succeeded," the uplifting memoirist declared, "who lacked confidence in himself." "No race," he added, "ever did or ever will prosper or make a respectable history which has no confidence in its own nationality." Precisely because Brown wanted to instill such self- and group esteem and ensure that Black people were not "ashamed" to own their "colors," he studiously pursued the past for the benefit of African Americans in the present and future. Starting seriously in the mid-1850s, with the publication of the thirty-six-page lecture *St. Domingo: Its Revolutions and Its Patriots*, the grand result of that quest came twenty years later. As an epic account, *The Rising Son* repeatedly conveyed to Reconstruction-era Black readers that they possessed a rich heritage, one stretching back to antiquity. Ripped from Old World Africa by slave traders and rendered as the instruments of New World slave masters, historian Brown effectively restored what had rightfully belonged to African Americans—a living, breathing cultural patrimony.[5]

Regardless of how much Brown benefited from predecessors and contemporaries, *The Rising Son* amounted to a major authorial undertaking by any measure. Arguably no other abolitionist author before or after the Civil War approximated his encyclopedic scope. William Goodell's comprehensive history of 1852, *Slavery and Anti-Slavery*, constitutes an ostensibly comparable text. Totaling nearly six hundred pages, the white reformer's tome spans centuries and even crosses the Atlantic but largely concentrates on the enslavement problem in the United States from the country's colonial beginnings to the 1850s. Brown, by contrast, composed a panoramic portrait of the Black past that commences in Mediterranean-facing classical times and culminates in a modern-day United States. The African American and American Indian writer Robert Benjamin Lewis penned a more analogous work in 1843. *Light and Truth*, the original version of which debuted in 1836, chronicles people of color over an exceptionally long term—from the world that God made to the one that revolutionary Haitians remade. That ambitious four-hundred-page compendium, however, principally deals with sacred and secular ethnological matters of the very distant past.[6]

Of *The Rising Son*'s fifty chapters, eleven pertain to continental Africa, seventeen to the Caribbean, one to South America, and twenty to British North America and the United States. Interestingly, whereas Lewis concluded his volume with a fifteen-page discussion of Saint Domingue, Brown committed fourteen chapters and about one hundred pages to Haiti's inspirational and complicated history. The latter also allotted substantially more space to cataloging outstanding Black lives of the eighteenth and nineteenth centuries. Lewis's ancient-focused endeavor covers "Modern Eminent Colored Men," "Modern Historians," and "Female Writers" in less than fifteen pages; Brown's fiftieth chapter itself represents a compact book. Numbering 135 pages, it scans the careers of scores of people of color—all of which, regardless of how local the prestige, contributed to the "Freedom of the Race" and accordingly made each figure a "hero." In that final section, moreover, the Black man of letters gleams at his bourgeoisie finest. Before unpacking the middle-class messages saturating it, the other race-pride contents require consideration.[7]

The story that Brown reclaimed for African Americans was not only diasporic; it rivaled, at times, the glorious histories of European states and empires. In chapters respectively on the Ethiopians and Carthaginians, the author interlaced his narrative with references to sophistication. Regarding the former, Brown located the general origins of the "African race," the source of multiple Egyptian pharaohs, and the cradle of European civilization. Well before the Common Era, Brown's Ethiopia boasted of pyramids of unsurpassed "architectural beauty," which, however smaller than Egyptian ones, predated their world-renowned neighbors. Ethiopian excellence in the "art of building" carried over to pottery making; the "taste[ful]" and "elegan[t]" vases adorning its monuments, according to the argument, had no parallel elsewhere, then or since. The "greatness" of Brown's Ethiopia also encompassed commerce—its strategically positioned mother city was a caravan trading center—as well as the military sphere. As a trailblazing nation, it "organized a regular army" earlier than almost anyone else, thereby establishing "the foundation . . . of ancient warfare." It also made the chariot a fundamental fighting unit and the bow a national weapon. Even though no other people "paid more attention to archery," the historian maintained that regardless of a well-trained warrior class, Ethiopians were not particularly aggressive or warlike. With good reasons, then, the Black man of letters traced Western social and cultural evolution from an Ethiopian birthplace. In his estimation, Ethiopia's civilizing influence spread to Egypt, from Egypt to Greece, from Greece to Rome, and from Rome to around the globe.[8]

Brown's Carthage, a precious jewel of the Classical-era Mediterranean, also performs an important textual task. As the architects of a prosperous commercial society, the "enterprising" Carthaginians engaged in trade with area peoples and conquered some of their lands, too (the historian specified parts of Spain, sizable portions of Sicily, as well as Sardinia). Whereas the fleets of Carthage blanketed the sea, nearby Rome, the author remarked, could claim not "a single vessel." In stark contrast to the former's maritime dominance, Roman citizens were mired in nautical crudeness. The Carthaginians of this narrative therefore function not as the equals of the latter but their envy, so much so that Brown dedicated the bulk of the chapter to outlining the strife that persisted between the two for more than a century. In so doing, he detailed the exploits of the military "genius" Hannibal, the "heroic" resistance of besieged Carthaginians, and the savage cruelty of invading Romans. Yet the destruction of ancient Carthage and the dispersion of its surviving inhabitants did not merely signify the collapse of a city that was, for Brown, "the model of beauty and magnificence" as well as a "repository of immense wealth." The Black man of letters additionally noted that cold-blooded Romans strove to "obliterate every vestige" of Carthaginian existence from the face of the earth. A historical pattern thus began whereby a European imperialist attempted to extinguish a "proud" African people's history.[9]

In the Ethiopian and Carthaginian chapters, furthermore, the historian first broached a topic that permeates that entire study: skin pigmentation. Brown enlisted sundry ancient voices, from Homer and Strabo to Josephus and Eusebius, as well as sound logic, to confirm that color had nothing to do with curses. He specifically meditated on the Greek meaning of the word "Ethiop." That it meant "sunburn" comprised an important piece of authorial evidence that something much less supernatural accounted for the blackness of Ethiopians. "Although the descendants of [the biblical] Cush were black," the author explained, "it does not follow that all the offspring of Ham were dark-skinned; but only those who settled in a climate" that had altered their appearance. The same environmentalism applied to the Egyptians, "for Herodotus tells us," Brown indicated, "that the latter were colored and had curled hair." Ditto for the similarly complexioned and headed Carthaginians, who, "though not as black as the present African population, w[ere] nevertheless, colored." Quite significantly, then, the light of classical antiquity in this historical tale emanated not from pale-skinned Europeans but nonwhite Africans.[10]

The author unquestionably called attention to the physical traits of ancient Ethiopians, Egyptians, and Carthaginians as part and parcel of a larger effort to undercut racist ideas about the natural inferiority of Black people. Brown's spiritual, intellectual, and philanthropic credo, of course, surrounded the unity of humanity. When the Protestant Christian and activist-historian addressed variety within races and among nations, he did so from the knowledge that God, as set forth in Acts 17:26, which he quoted, had made all persons of one blood. Even before the Black man of letters proceeded to discuss the condition of contemporary Africans, he more fully explored the workings of the climatic principle in back-to-back chapters—one concerning "Causes of Color," the other, "Causes of Difference in Features."[11]

Brown ascribed gradations of color on the continent of Africa to environmentalist factors. The northernmost populaces, he elucidated, "are whitest," but as one journeyed southward toward the equator and beyond, especially to "those countries in which the sun's rays fall more perpendicularly, the complexion gradually assumes a darker shade." Besides the "deep black" of the southern-hemisphere "Negro" and the "copper or olive" tones of northern-hemisphere "Moors," Brown discerned degrees of darkness and lightness among Europeans themselves, depending on locality: from the comparatively "swarthy" Spanish and Italians to the "fair and florid" English and Germans all the way to the "bleached" Scandinavians. "Climate and climate alone," he opined, "is the sole cause" of such diversity.[12]

Environmentalism shaped other racial characteristics, too. By alluding to "heat" as "the great crisper," Brown universalized his previous statements about ancient African hair. He also invoked Africa's hot temperatures in order to shed insight onto questions about reputedly common continental attributes: "the large, wide mouth and flat nose" of many peoples. The author simultaneously extended the climatic principle to include the impression of human-made habitats on populations over time. To further contest popular notions of Black backwardness, he expatiated on how barbarity was no discriminator of races. "From the grim worshippers of Odin in the woods of Germany, down to the present day," Brown axiomatically asserted that "all uncivilized nations or tribes have more or less been addicted to the barbarous custom of disfiguring their persons." In making that observation, the historian displayed his own sociocultural biases, which he fully revealed while attesting that "the farther the human mind strays from the ever-living God as a spirit, the nearer it approximates to the beasts; and as the mental controls the physical, so ignorance and brutality are depicted upon the countenance." Yet by decreeing that physiognomy and morality or visage and civility went hand in hand, he continued to dispute anti-Black stereotypes.[13]

Even though a monotheistic Brown contended that heathenism modified African features wherever and whenever its evidently degenerating influence had prevailed, he quickly shifted such derogatory analysis from nonwhite to white peoples on behalf of a transcendent, antiracism interpretation. "We all acknowledge the Anglo-Saxon to be the highest type of civilization," the Black man of letters decreed. After rhetorically asking about the wellsprings of that allegedly virtuosic race, the historian mulled over the latter's utterly wretched genealogy. "Go back a few centuries," he invited audiences to imaginatively time travel, additionally requesting that they look closely at the Anglo-Saxons' frightening ancestors who had occupied Teutonic forests. "See them," according to this verbal recreation, "sacrificing to their grim and gory idols; drinking the warm blood of their prisoners, quaffing libations from human skulls; infesting the shores of the Baltic for plunder and robbery; bringing home the reeking scalps of enemies as an offering to their king." Brown followed that gruesome picture by citing the British historians David Hume and Thomas Babington Macaulay, both of whom referred to the savagery of other sires of the Anglo-Saxons: the ancient Britons.[14]

Brown stressed identical points in the 1863 publication *The Black Man*, wherein he cogitated on the abject incivility of Anglo-Saxon forebears in slightly more detail. Amid an escalating sectional military conflict at home in the present, the Black abolitionist reflected, in this scenario, on human bondage abroad in the past. Britain's native inhabitants, he noted, once suffered "a state of vassalage as degrading as that of slavery in the Southern States." After their enslavement under Roman occupiers, the author added that later Norman invaders had dispatched "thousands" of captured Britons to foreign slave markets hundreds of miles away. Given such a servile pedigree, Brown chastised the prejudicial "white American," who should not speak of ancestry, "unless with his lips to the dust." That antiquity's master-class members, such as Julius Caesar and Cicero, had deemed British bondservants as uniformly stupid and ugly prompted more authorial provocativeness. "I am sorry," he acerbically proclaimed, "that Mr. [Abraham] Lincoln came from such a low origin; but he is not to blame. I only find fault with him for making mouths at me." Knowledge, Brown implied, was truly empowering; nor was it, he explicitly declared, "innate." 'Nothing in . . . blood," he avowed, "imparts susceptibility of improvement to one race over another." "Development makes the man," the Black abolitionist pithily pronounced, a judgment that he more deeply probed after the Civil War.[15]

In a postbellum setting, however, the historian did not broadcast the wretched background of a currently "refined, proud," and "haughty" racial group with the intentions of angering any white American readers. After all, he prefaced his recitation of such aboriginal degradation by observing that Anglo-Saxons, thanks to centuries of ascending "the scale of humanity," had gotten smarter and more physically attractive. Whatever the sarcasm, the author delivered those words sincerely, too. Even though Brown, as suggested by his review of ancient Ethiopia and Carthage, generally adhered to conventional Western historical wisdom about naturally rising and falling states and empires, his organic conception of societal growth and decay was never one way. Races and nations undoubtedly progressed and atrophied, but they could (and did) flourish again according to his thinking. That zig-zag doctrine the Black man of letters based on changeable circumstances (and on God's eternal one-blood dictum). Immutable biological differences originating from separate racial creations had nothing to do with his worldview, save that he relentlessly challenged polygenist theories proffered by mid-nineteenth-century scientists and their anti-Black popularizers.[16]

Page by page, Brown therefore bettered the race and battered the racists. Through historical instruction, he demonstrated that Black people had elevated themselves, kept on elevating themselves, and still needed to elevate themselves. To be sure, the author did not issue a vast paean to all things Africa and of African descent. For example, in two chapters collectively totaling thirty pages, he resumed an examination of continental skin-color dynamics by surveying Africa during the eighteenth and nineteenth centuries. The historian also launched a new investigation into social complexity across the landmass. What he found, unsurprisingly, varied from region to region, as well as within regions, and was perpetually contingent on "moral [state] and physical surroundings." If a hypothetical white supremacist ever seized on certain findings as confirmation that in a hierarchy of global races, nonwhites always occupied the bottom rungs, Brown effectively anticipated such bigoted cherry-picking.[17]

Among African peoples, the author espied "the lowest type of Negro character" along the western coast and presumably "the lowest condition of man" near the southern tip. For Brown, however, such extreme lowliness derived from corrosive encounters with Europeans. Concerning the natives of West Africa in and around Guinea, he pinpointed the "progenitors" of the American South's Black populations: an ancestral people thoroughly "degraded and unhumanized" by an area that had long served as a Middle Passage epicenter. Slave trading's "demonizing" impact, the historian announced, "defies all description." Whereas a Protestant Brown earlier articulated his views about monotheism's civilizing effects and did so elsewhere in the text, at this narrative juncture he highlighted Christianity's corruptive consequences. "Christian gold" and "contact with Christian nations," in his evaluation, engendered diabolical human trafficking and subsequently degenerated the locals.[18]

The natives of South Africa the Black man of letters initially portrayed even more pejoratively. According to Brown's humanity index, the "Hottentots" ranked beneath the inhabitants of man-stealing Guinea because they roamed deserts, resided in caves, ate "roots or raw flesh," and lacked "religious ideas." Despite that negative inventory, the author assembled it so as to assay a perceived problem that white specialists in "'anatomy and ethnology'" had never conscientiously considered—how did the Khoikhoi become so "degraded?" Reenter the Christian European answer. "Before the evil hour" when light-skinned outsiders upended their realities, the numerous locals of this accounting lived under a governmental system headed by chiefs and elders; held rudimentary notions of religion; subsisted, if not thrived, as nomadic pastoralists; and were "courageous in warfare, yet mild in their tempers and dispositions." The arrival of suppos-

edly civilized colonists from Europe unleashed waves of unmitigated viciousness. Treating the indigenous peoples like prey, the newcomers "exterminated"
most and plundered their possessions; the survivors fled to barren hinterlands,
"where their miserable descendants exist as wandering Bushmen." For a race
elevator who was always an environmentalist, context explained everything; it
represented an analytical sine qua non.[19]

That the "Timanis" of Sierra Leone, to give another example, were allegedly
"depraved, licentious, indolent, and avaricious" indicated nothing essential about
the Temne in particular or people of color more generally. Such perceived qualities said a lot, once more, about a monotheistic Brown, who simply deduced
that a "heathen tribe" in Africa was akin to all others "on the globe." The historian, however, did not deploy similar adjectives in his censorious assessment of
an African location wherein the "worship of snakes" made it the most superstitious and paganistic spot on the continent. He, instead, deplored the Kingdom
of Dahomey, partly because its tyrannical ruler claimed absolute ownership over
lands and their occupants. Since Dahomean seaports functioned as transatlantic
slave-trade capitals and soldiers operated as "slave hunters," the Black abolitionist especially denounced a large, powerful dominion and its despotic king. "The
atrocious cruelties that are constantly perpetrated at the command and bidding of this monarch, has gained for him the hatred of the civilized world," the
activist-historian added.[20]

In contrast to those critical traversals, the Black man of letters praised such
western coastal peoples as the "very dark" complexioned Vai, whose "ingenuity" had recently resulted in the invention of an alphabetic writing system. That
alone, Brown maintained, "should silence forever the cavils and sneers [about]
the intellectual endowments of the African race." He also set aside a four-page
chapter to positively representing the modern successors of the ancient Ethiopians. The Abyssinians, whom Brown described as mostly of "a ginger-bread, or
coffee color," constituted an "intelligent" and prosperous nation. Besides possessing "fine schools and colleges," as well as a "flourishing military academy," the
author reported that they expertly practiced "agriculture, that great civilizer of
man." (He mentioned in a different section, however, that a "complex civil war"
had broken out there after Emperor Theodore II's death.) Finally, in a six-page
chapter, he exuberantly advertised Liberia not as an appendage of the white-
controlled American Colonization Society but as a sovereign and independent
Black republic. Owing to already established "schools, seminaries, a college, and
some fifty churches," Brown virtually guaranteed that thirty thousand "civilized"
Liberians would steadily uplift the hundreds of thousands of natives falling

under their governmental purview. Based on their rich natural resources and commercial potential, he prognosticated that they would also transform jungles into vibrant cities and bustling ports, and turn a moral and cultural wilderness into a fertile field for religion and literature. Liberia, the historian gushed, "is destined to hold an influential place in the history of nations."[21]

Whereas the downfall of slavery in the United States and the emergence of biracial governments across the Southland constituted the dawning of a new day for African Americans, *The Rising Son*'s author additionally made it clear that the sun had never set on the peoples of Africa. "It is a pleasing fact," the Black man of letters remarked, "that the last fifty years have witnessed much advance towards civilization" throughout the continent. The historian's agents of African progress encompassed, for instance, manufacturing development, from the growth of "iron-smelting villages" to skilled workers of various wares; gifted political orators and talented musicians; as well as self-sacrificing missionaries from overseas, those who, "forgetting native land and home-comforts, have given themselves" to the hard work of education. Brown was brimming with optimism in the early 1870s, because centuries-long sources of debasement had ended or were ending in the New and Old Worlds. Enslavement, the Black abolitionist stated in the section on physical differences, "is the great demoralizer of the human race," imbruting the oppressed and oppressor alike. In another section, he identified slave trading as the "great obstacle" to civilizing Africa as a whole, for it incited ceaseless marauding and kidnapping and flooded communities with "gunpowder and rum." Expressly thanking the English and Liberians for their instrumental services, Brown happily pronounced the suppression of an "inhuman and unchristian traffic" in West Africa, one that had wreaked immense damage on both sides of the Atlantic Ocean.[22]

But telling traumatic tales did not particularly interest the historian. It does not follow that he simply narrated success stories across the book's thirty-nine other chapters. Revolving about freedom-struggle Black histories from the transatlantic Age of Revolution to the Era of Emancipation in the United States, the Afro-Caribbean and African American themes that the author perused over four hundred pages build up to an unequivocally triumphal closing. *The Rising Son*'s lengthy fiftieth chapter, wherein Brown set forth seventy-nine race representatives, readily attests that regardless of the dismal days surrounding generations of captivity, the sun had never set on African-descended peoples either. Indeed, the Black man of letters transmitted a motivational feeling that at no point in human history did it shine so brightly with promise. Before reaching an empowering finale, the middle-class activist sought to navigate, for instance, Haiti's tricky past.

Substantive authorial engagement with the subject preceded *The Rising Son* by twenty years. After the 1855 printing of *St. Domingo*, Brown further immersed himself in that historical initiative by devoting at least seven of fifty-three biographical sketches to eminent Haitians in *The Black Man* of 1863—from founding-figure Toussaint Louverture (1743–1803) to President Fabre Geffrard (1806–1878). The diasporic 1873 history thus represents the summit of his thinking on Haiti. In the fourteen chapters and some one hundred pages on the topic, the author unsurprisingly drew upon his earlier research, extracting entire paragraphs and pages for the new text. He also enlarged on the preexisting work, excluding some inflammatory observations and excusatory remarks in the process.[23]

Even though much of *St. Domingo*'s information reappears in *The Rising Son*, only in the former did the Black abolitionist share his vision of a redemptive, Haiti-styled conflagration in North America. The lecture itself signaled Brown's return to the United States after seeking refuge thousands of miles overseas following the enactment of the 1850 Fugitive Slave Law. A three-year European sanctuary not only guaranteed, thanks to English funds, a freedom seeker's personal liberty in 1854. It also significantly emboldened him, as the published speech illuminates. After reviewing the course of a fierce antislavery and anti-colonial conflict in Saint Domingue, under the leadership of Louverture, Henri Christophe, and Jean-Jacques Dessalines, the lecturer proclaimed that American slaveholders should shudder at its memory. He rhetorically pondered whether a similar uprising could surface in the South as well, quickly predicting that it certainly would someday soon.[24]

"The spirit that [had] caused the blacks" to risk their lives during the American War of Independence, the propagandist opined, "is still amongst the slaves" of the Southland. His avenging calculations revealed that as would-be Haitians, the latter "are only waiting [for] the opportunity of wiping out their wrongs in the blood" of white enslavers. If and when that clash burst forth, he expected cataclysmic outcomes in the United States: Africa's "exasperated genius" will arise "from the depths of the ocean, and show its threatening form." In the mid-1850s, then, a formally free Brown shied away from retributive violence neither in retrospect nor prospect. Nor did he mince words about a revolutionary event that produced "greater heroes" than any other before or since. Even "if the blacks were guilty of shedding blood profusely" in the French Caribbean, according to the speaker's subversive justification, "they only followed the example set . . . by the more refined and educated whites." True, the Toussaint whom he celebrated was not especially sanguinary, but the recollected rallying cry of "'To arms! to arms!'" rendered insurgent Haitians as eternally thrilling freedom fighters.[25]

The historian steadfastly championed Haiti's father in *The Rising Son* but generally omitted proclamations of righteous retaliation from its narrative. Quite simply, given the Civil War's eruption and termination, he no longer needed to demand a Haitian Revolution for the United States. Besides the fact that Black soldiers in blue uniforms had helped annihilate southern slavery, which he chronicled briefly in this text and more fully in another, antebellum bloodletting prophesies resonated very differently with the postbellum Brown. The Black abolitionist of the mid-1850s, as an incensed antislavery agitator, expressed apocalyptic wishes for a slaveholding republic that both enforced the enslavement of millions of African Americans in the South and endangered the tenuous autonomy of thousands of slavery's escapees in the North. The Black abolitionist of the early 1870s, as an indefatigable racial elevator, articulated a pacifistic antiracism vision of individual and communal improvement to the formerly enslaved. Bourgeois inflected or not, that unending mission affected his discourse on Haiti's post-revolution problems.[26]

The interpretative difficulties posed by that country's history, however, had nothing to do with Louverture or his legacy. Throughout four chapters, the author repeatedly lionized the "negro chief," extolling his kingly African heritage; admiring his physical attributes, personal demeanor, and "private virtues"; and lauding his "genius" on the battlefield and for nation building. One praiseworthy passage encapsulates Brown's treatment of Toussaint, who "passed the greater number of his days in slavery, and rose to be a soldier, a general, a governor, and to-day lives in the hearts of the people of his native isle." "Endowed by nature with high qualities of mind," the middle-class activist added, Louverture "owed his elevation to his own energies and his devotion to the welfare and freedom of his race." Such plaudits the historian did not regularly bestow on the "heroic" chieftain's immediate successors—Dessalines, then Christophe.[27]

Whereas Haiti's saintly father "was entirely master of his own appetites and passions," a moralistic Brown painted the other leading Haitians as slaves to their worst inclinations and apprehensions. Even though the Black man of letters assessed the revolutionary accomplishments of both in generally sympathetic terms, as peacetime magistrates, he scarcely complimented either. On the contrary, he stressed the ferocity and vindictiveness surrounding the autocratic regimes of "Jean Jacques the First" and "Henry the First." Of the two monarchs, one was a vampiric "monster," the other, a latter-day "Caligula." In a single chapter on

Dessalines (1758–1806), the author elucidated how the ruler committed countless atrocities against white French populations. Fearful of their sovereign's unslakable "vengeance," the "mulatt[o]" followers of Dessalines, Brown informed readers, carried out the murderous orders; so, too, did "dread surveillance" pressure subordinate "black chiefs" to act similarly. As for the despot himself, he allegedly "gloated with secret complacency over the scene of carnage, like some malignant fiend glorying in the pangs of misery suffered by those who had fallen a sacrifice to his wickedness." After the spilling of white blood, as the historian indicated, Dessalines turned his perversely hemophilic attention toward Black and mixed-race bodies.[28]

The rise and fall of Christophe (1767–1820), which the narrator dissected over five chapters, elicited more references to unquenchable bloodthirstiness. With a "despotic temper" that duplicated his predecessor's, Brown's monarchical Henri loathed the rival republican government headquartered in Port-au-Prince, as well as the mixed-race Haitians administering and inhabiting it. The next tyrant, according to the authorial explanation, early "resolved to rest the foundation of his power upon the support of the pure blacks, and he [eventually] determined to make his administration one of ceaseless hatred and persecution to the mulattoes," whether they lived within his northern domain or that of the southern competitor. The historian, of course, emphasized that a racial civil war between light- and dark-skinned people of color had initially exploded during the Haitian Revolution itself. For the Black man of letters, though, Louverture contained it, Dessalines revived it, and Christophe intensified it, driven as he reputedly was by genocidal fury. Since the latter's tyranny purportedly lacked boundaries, Henry I also outdid Jean-Jacques I in "excessive cruelty" against his own subjects, which encompassed heavy taxation, corporal punishment, indiscriminate imprisonment, military execution, and political assassination. "So unlimited and habitual was his severity," adjudged Brown, "that he would put a man to death with as little hesitation as a sportsman would bring down an article of game."[29]

Such gruesome abuses of power the author either muted or bypassed in *The Black Man*. Concerning Christophe, a diplomatic Brown succinctly decided that his "aims were great, and many of them good." Regarding Dessalines, a forgiving historian postulated that despite "the blood that marked his course, the circumstances attending it will, no doubt, be made to extenuate some of his many faults, and magnify his virtues as a general, a ruler, and a man." No collateral consideration or approbation occurs on the pages of *The Rising Son*. The narrative restraint and apologetic tone that the Black man of letters manifested during an uncertain Civil War, when defeating the slaveholders' rebellion and razing the house of bondage preoccupied him, he effectively discarded ten years later. At the same time, exposing the abominable reigns of previous Haitian rulers in the early 1870s disclosed nothing about the inherent capabilities of African-descended peoples either in the Caribbean or anywhere else in the Americas.[30]

Since the abysmal statesmanship of Dessalines and Christophe deviated from the sterling standard that the remembered Louverture had established, the middle-class activist could only lament that postcolonial dictators had impeded Haiti's nineteenth-century progress. Even though Brown commended other heads of state, especially such presidential figures as Alexandre Pétion (1770–1818), Jean-Pierre Boyer (1776–1850), and Geffrard, he ultimately concluded his discussion with a startling forecast. Given the "poverty and want of development" among Haitians and neighboring Dominicans alike, he presumed that the island of Hispaniola would "fall into the hands of some more civilized nation or nations." If Brown insinuated annexation by the United States, he offered no explicit allusions to the 1869 Santo Domingo treaty that the Ulysses S. Grant administration had negotiated but the Senate never adopted. Whatever the inferences behind that imperialistic assertion, it signifies a meaningful textual transition from Afro-Caribbean to African American content.[31]

In the twenty chapters and 150 pages pertaining to Black experiences in British North America and the United States (not including the biographically focused finale), the author largely addressed enslavement's introduction and expansion, persistent resistance to perpetual servitude by the enslaved, the emergence of radical abolitionism and corresponding antiabolitionist public reaction, and African American military contributions from the American Revolution to the Civil War. In one chapter, the historian listed sundry slave upheavals throughout the eighteenth century, stopping with the thwarted Gabriel conspiracy of 1800. In a subsequent chapter, he covered the daring 1822 plot of Denmark Vesey and the deadly war that Nat Turner had waged in 1831. In another, he touched on Joseph Cinqué and the 1839 *Amistad* revolt as well as Madison Washington and the 1840 *Creole* mutiny. In yet another, he contemplated the African American members of John Brown's 1859 band of insurrectionists. Based on firsthand knowledge and historical inquiry, Brown accordingly avouched that "discontent always pervaded the black population of the South, bond and free." Besides reflecting on that open and "undeveloped" defiance, the narrator cited the damages sustained by northern African American communities caused by the racist rioting that had taken place during the 1830s and early 1860s. He also referred to Black migrations to safer Canada as a result of the disruptive 1850 Fugitive Slave Law.[32]

As in the Africa-themed sections, the Black man of letters once again accented enslavement's awful repercussions for everyone involved. In the slaveholding South, human bondage had made the enslaved an animalistic possession, thereby denying "every characteristic of manhood." It "degraded the mind of the master," too, imbruting emotions and benighting the conscience. In the nonslaveholding North, that "curse of curses" had rendered African-descended peoples as a separate, unequal, and despised caste. "Wherever the blacks are ill-treated on account of their color," the author explicated, "it is because of their identity with a race that has long worn the chain of slavery." In that way alone, a racial system of servitude begat white racism, for an environmentalist Brown underlined how racists were never born but always made. Even though the postbellum historian pictured the antebellum United States as a perilous place for African Americans, he did not simply point out that a proslavery, "negro-hating" atmosphere had corrupted the country's statutes and corroded many of its Christian churches. Rather, the narrator prominently showcased Black resiliency and toughness. Nowhere did he so compellingly, and no less upliftingly, detail those attributes than in the last chapter.[33]

Thanks to the Civil War's splendid denouement and Reconstruction's progressive unfurling, Brown viewed his disenthralled homeland as a redemptive racial site. He also recognized that additional renovations must occur before the historical fulfillment of all people of African descent transpired in the United States. In the book's penultimate chapter, "The New Era," he called attention to present-day problems tethered to a still-living past. Efforts to politically enfranchise African American men, the author noted, had brought about a resurgence of the "virus of negro hate" in both the Union-saving North and ex-Confederate South. He further commented that generations of captivity had "bequeathed . . . nothing but poverty, ignorance, and dependence" to the freedpeople. Despite previously relying on slaveholders for "employment" and the "means" of sustenance, Brown also announced that the latter were "honest," "sincere," and "industriou[s]." To unlock their potentialities and constantly challenge anti-Black prejudices, the greatest obstacle to African American improvement, the historian sought to inspire people of color to improve themselves.[34]

Before President Lincoln's emancipation edict officially went into effect, Brown memorably wrote: "All I demand for the black man is, that the white people shall take their heels off his neck, and let him have a chance to rise by his own efforts." As a graduate of the southern school of slavery himself, the autodidactic author therefore underscored, in 1873, the necessity of formal education for the formerly enslaved. The middle-class activist next proselytized on behalf of temperance, "that John the Baptist of reforms," in order to buttress the equal Black rights recently inscribed into the Constitution by the Thirteenth, Fourteenth, and Fifteenth Amendments. After prescribing to African Americans the same methods "resorted to by the whites for their elevation," a moralistic Brown concluded his counsel with a Benjamin Franklin flourish. "An ignorant man will trust to luck for success; an educated man will make success. God helps those who help themselves." Hardly empty rhetoric, such self-help advice served as a prelude to the august assemblage of race representatives that followed.[35]

By crafting an archive of superlative Black men and women, Brown endowed the freedom struggle with new sets of meaning, new models of emulation. After commencing with an American Revolution martyr, Crispus Attucks, a distinctive group portrait comes into sharper focus with each accomplished person of color whom the biographer delineated. Overall, the historian's catalogue of eighteenth- and nineteenth-century heroes comprises lay preachers, ordained ministers, and high-ranking ecclesiastics; college graduates, educators, and scholars; school teachers, administrators, and organizers; newspaper editors and publishers; orators and reformers; entrepreneurs and artisans; lawyers, physicians, and scientists; governmental officers and veteran soldiers; essayists and historians; and literary, visual, and dramatic artists. The well-educated African Americans that the narrative features had earned undergraduate or advanced degrees from such colleges and universities as Cambridge, Glasgow, Harvard, Knox, and Oberlin, as well as from various institutes, normal schools, and seminaries. Regardless of education level, the Black man of letters routinely appraised his hall of famers as eloquent speakers, keen observers, skillful writers, and fine thinkers.[36]

Of the seventy-nine individuals composing Brown's personal pantheon, eight are women—from the poet Phyllis Wheatley and the sculptor Edmonia Lewis to the Underground Railroad operative Harriet Tubman and the activist and journalist Mary Ann Shadd Cary. Of the seventy-one men, thirteen stand out as embodiments of Radical Reconstruction in the Deep South. The trailblazing African American officeholders consist of five who were based in South Carolina (Richard Cain, Francis L. Cardozo, Robert Brown Elliott, Joseph H. Rainey, and Alonzo J. Ransier), four in Mississippi (Thomas W. Cardozo, James Lynch, John Roy Lynch, and Hiram Revels), two in Louisiana (Oscar James Dunn and P. B. S. Pinchback), and one in Florida (Josiah T. Walls) and Alabama (Benjamin S. Turner), respectively. As evidence of Reconstruction's wider impact, the biographer also mentioned two Black state legislators in Massachusetts (Lewis Hayden and George Lewis Ruffin) and the first African American diplomatic agents (Ebenezer Bassett, ambassador to Haiti; and J. Milton Turner, consul general to Liberia).[37]

Among the fifty-four remaining men whom Brown commemorated, he reviewed such leading members of the antebellum Black community as Frederick Douglass, Martin R. Delany, Henry Highland Garnet, Leonard Grimes, Jermain Loguen, James W. C. Pennington, Robert Purvis, David Ruggles, William Still, and William Whipper. Even though the author occasionally acknowledged Black excellence across the Atlantic World—for example, the Jamaican editor and assemblyman Edward Jordon; another Jamaican, the newspaperman and lecturer Henry Garland Murray; and the New York-born but London-centered Shakespearean Ira Aldridge—his exhibition concentrates on renaissance people of color who actively uplifted themselves and others in the United States. *The Rising Son*'s lengthy fiftieth chapter thus foregrounds a very specific racial rebirth, one that would evidently have large-scale race ramifications. The wonderful range of past and present African American achievements, for Brown, constituted vital nourishment for the current generation of aspiring African Americans. Given what people of color had attained when slavery ruled America and what they would attain now that its reign was over, the Black man of letters saw an exalted epoch looming in the near future.[38]

That the biographer issued a stirring middle-class manifesto he amply demonstrated via the preferred nomenclature that he marshaled across 135 pages. On the one hand, Brown often invoked such descriptors as "industry," "upright," and "refined" while applauding race representatives. Altogether, he utilized those words on at least twenty-one textual occasions in the last chapter. On the other, Brown more habitually enlisted "genteel" and "gentlemanly" in order to solidify the bourgeois credentials of his cohort. Of the seventy-one Black men whose careers the author traced, a minimum of forty-one explicitly bear such respectability hallmarks. (Edward Jordon qualifies as a possible forty-second; the uniqueness of his case surrounds an 1860 knighthood, which made his status as a "gentleman" more literal.) By compiling a record of African American civility and cultivation—which also encompasses such ladies as Louise De Mortie, Charlotte Forten, Frances Ellen Watkins Harper, and Fanny M. Jackson—the chronicler repeatedly scored antiracism victories.[39]

Since the exceptional men and women whom he saluted were anything but exceptions to a racist rule about African American backwardness and inferiority, the biographer torpedoed any notion that Black gentility was fundamentally contradictory or naturally impossible. Brilliance and ingenuity, he attested, knew no skin color. Still, Brown's collection of race representatives was especially marvelous, because members obtained social, cultural, political, and professional distinction in spite of entrenched racial bigotry. They arrived at prominence in a white-dominated society wherein far more barriers had existed to block Black advancement than did bridges facilitating African American mobility. The author made similar points throughout the fifty-three biographies making up *The Black Man*, twenty-eight of which he incorporated, either wholly or in part, into the 1873 "Representative Men and Women" book section. Since the 1863 vignettes are genuinely transatlantic in scope (highlighting persons of color in England, France, Cuba, Haiti, Jamaica, and Liberia), the overwhelmingly African American orientation of the latter endows *The Rising Son*'s uplifting agenda with greater potency. Indeed, after the 1873 historian had evoked the self-making spirit of a famous white American at the end of chapter 49, in the fiftieth he enumerated dozens of Black people who seemingly lived a Benjamin Franklin life. Brown, however, needed no recourse to the illustrious Philadelphian in order to draw his subjects appropriately. A different Ben was much more instructive.[40]

Immediately following a discussion of Wheatley's poetic talents, the biographer reviewed Benjamin Banneker's impressiveness (which Brown similarly canvassed in the 1863 text). What that Revolutionary-era polymath had "rendered to science, to liberty, to the intellectual character" of African Americans, the author annunciated, "are too great for us to allow his name to sleep, and his genius and merits" to go unnoticed. Equipped with a rudimentary training from "an obscure country school," Brown's Banneker was an extraordinary lifelong learner. Under his own tutelage, he mastered classical and modern languages. He additionally devoured all literature that crossed his path, so much so that the heroic mathematician of this account amassed herculean amounts of knowledge: in "every branch of history, both natural and civil," as well as "criticism, metaphysics, morals, politics, voyages, and travels." Brown particularly acclaimed the almanacs that Banneker had published during the mid-1790s, the astronomical calculations and charts of which, the author assured readers, he devised "without the least assistance from any person." The Black man of letters unquestionably saw himself in Benjamin Banneker. Writing on the latter's behalf, Brown professed that he "never lost sight of the condition of his race." He frequently promoted racial equality with "whites whom he could influence" and "ever urged the emancipation and elevation of the slave." Just like Brown, moreover, Banneker "felt that to deprive the black man of the inspiration of ambition, of hope, of wealth, of standing, among his brethren of the earth, was to take from him all incentives to mental improvement." As a precious race representative, then, the 1873 historian wanted African American readers to ruminate on and reproduce not Poor Richard but the "'Negro Philosopher.'"[41]

In the early 1870s, the Black man of letters proclaimed that "revolutions seldom go backward." Even though he applied that personal truism to the Civil War's aftermath, in order to account for how equal civil and political rights for the freedmen ultimately, but not initially, accompanied universal liberty, it captures the book's overarching tenor. In *The Rising Son*, Brown clearly emitted radiant optimism, as a postemancipation sun brightens the historical pathway of African Americans in the concluding chapters. Such ebullience considerably dimmed by the end of the decade, as *My Southern Home* of 1880 reveals. To be sure, Brown's confidence in the capacity of the formerly enslaved for improvement underwent no seismic changes. In *The Black Man*, after all, the one-blood apostle professed that he never succumbed to "despair," regardless of how bleak things looked for people of color, because "the negro has that intellectual genius which God has planted in the mind of man . . . and which needs only cultivation to make it bring forth fruit." With that unshakeable faith Brown doubled down on purposeful Black abolitionism in his next book-length project, which represented his last. The authorial mood nevertheless shifted, for reactionary white southerners had halted Radical Reconstruction by 1877 and began dismantling its forward movement after the restoration of Democratic rule throughout the ex-Confederacy.[42]

My Southern Home's 250 pages thus materialized from a retrogressing backdrop. Of the book's twenty-nine chapters, the first seventeen revolve about an omniscient, third-person storyteller; the other twelve, a more conventional first-person chronicler. Chapters 1 through 13 pertain to life and labor in the Old South, to what the author had seen, heard, and faced while in thralldom during the 1820s and 1830s. The next four constitute a transition, wherein the author touched on such topics as the "hard lot" of free Black southerners, the national political domination of the southern slaveholding oligarchy, and the "War of Races" that took place once the slaveholders' rebellion had failed. The following eight relate to the purportedly New South, to what the author had witnessed and experienced while touring the region during the late 1870s. The last four comprise a general racial assessment, wherein the author expounded on what the formerly enslaved must do in order to overcome adverse circumstances. *My Southern Home*, then, is a genre-bending work that defies simple categorization: an autobiography refashioned from earlier autobiographical sources; a dramatized memoir that obfuscates, at times, the narrator's identity; a historical evaluation of the Southland before and after the Civil War; a post-Reconstruction travelogue of a race leader and middle-class activist.[43]

From 1877 to 1880, the former fugitive completed a series of southern so-journs—particularly in Alabama, Tennessee, Virginia, and West Virginia. Re-gardless of how imaginatively the memoirist revisited the antebellum past during a worsening postbellum present, his musings on recent visits italicized a do-it-yourself respectability project as the only viable option for African Americans. Amid a regionwide collapse of interracial governance, the Black man of letters provocatively suggested that people of color possessed few trustworthy white al-lies in or outside the halls of Congress. Brown, however, still enjoyed some inti-mate philanthropic connections. Indeed, he traveled southward from his Boston base of operations as an officer and commissioned agent of the Right Worthy Grand Lodge of the World, a transatlantic antialcohol association centered in Great Britain and Ireland that had split from the International Order of Good Templars in 1876 because of the racially segregationist practices of the organiza-tion's leading American affiliates. A special mission therefore underwrote Brown's peregrinations: spreading the good news of total abstinence among the freedpeo-ple. In reporting back on what he had encountered, the uplifting autobiographer delivered not an ordinary rebuke of what the slaveholders had originated. Rather, he indicted current counterrevolutionary efforts aimed at rehabilitating an older social order.[44]

Even though the author communicated to readers that ignorance, supersti-tion, and barbarity saturated the antebellum South, he reserved his sharpest criticisms for domestic slave trading. Such a profit-driven enterprise, for Brown, amounted to the evilest component of the whole plantation-slavery business. Nothing else so plainly exposed the inhumanity of enslavement as the buying and selling of bodies. The brutalization that human trafficking had intensified entailed, in this depiction, the sundering of slave marriages and families, inuring white southerners to African American suffering, and even making the enslaved callous toward other Black people. Despite decreeing that the house of bondage owed its eventual "overthrow" to the nefarious interstate slave trade, elsewhere in the text the narrator interjected mystifying announcements. That Brown stated in a nondescript, three-sentence preface, "No attempt has been made to create heroes or heroines," scarcely foreshadowed the bombshells that he would peri-odically drop.[45]

At one point, the autobiographer seemingly substantiated proslavery rhetoric about the benevolence of the ruling race and the slave-like tendencies of African-descended peoples. He conceded, for instance, that some truth surrounded the often-repeated phrase about enslaved happiness. Such contentment, according to his ostensible qualification, added up to a very "low kind . . . existing only where masters were disposed to treat their servants kindly, and where the proverbial light-heartedness of the latter prevailed." More surprisingly, he augmented that observation with essentialist assertions that potentially undermined his abolitionist stature and contradicted his antiracist writings. "Sympathetic in his nature, thoughtless in his feelings, both alimentativeness and amativeness large, the negro is better adapted to follow than lead," Brown averred. "His wants easily supplied, generous to a fault, large fund of humor, brimful of music, he," the racialist explanation continued, "has ever been found the best and most accommodating of servants." If the memoirist intentionally donned a deceptive guise or experimented with divergent voices, he certainly succeeded when referring to people of African descent as better suited for enslavement than any other race, as "History shows." Such confounding remarks have consequently prompted literary critics to interrogate, in one scholar's characterization, the "racially indeterminate" narrator who presides over the book's slavery-oriented contents.[46]

Whatever the authorial motivations behind that racial stereotyping, the Black man of letters dedicated greater textual space to disclosing the subversive survival tactics of the enslaved, to how they had wielded wit and guile in order to lessen daily burdens, avoid harsh punishments, and resist slaveholding authority. He also unmistakably described a Southland that had degraded all parties and prepared no one for alternative arrangements. Unlike the difficult-to-define storyteller of the previous chapters, the recognizable chronicler of the postemancipation sections additionally portrayed the New South as more savage than the highly uncivilized original. By candidly demarcating areas for African American improvement, as he perceived them, the discernible middle-class activist of the later chapters persistently challenged late-nineteenth-century audiences. Despite posing some fresh puzzles, he proffered no Sphinx-like riddles as the indecipherable narrator did (and still does) earlier in the text.[47]

Nothing fictionalized or literary distinguishes the New South autobiographer, as demonstrated by his terse commentary on Reconstruction's inception and expiration. Brown opened a four-page chapter 17 with a discussion of the "Negro equality" question—the urgency that had surrounded it as a result of racial slavery's wartime doom and the senseless responses of bigoted interlocutors before and after the Emancipation Proclamation. He closed that analysis with a nearly two-page diatribe against a race problem that always represented a white one. Because of "the policy adopted by the Democrats in the late insurrectionary States," a terroristic onslaught subsequently rendered the "colored citizen . . . a nonentity in politics." "Through fear, intimidation, assassination, and all the horrors that barbarism can invent," Brown further inveighed, "every right of the negro in the

Southern States is to-day at an end." Whereas an adroit sense of humor and deft cunningness had sustained African Americans under chattel bondage, another oppressive system necessitated revised strategies. "Complete submission to the whites," according to the memoirist, "is the only way for the colored man to live in peace."[48]

The author returned to the subject of anti-Black bloodletting in chapter 25. Rather than retell numerous massacres that unreconstructed ex-Confederates committed in order to regain power, Brown referred to an incident that had occurred in Gibson County, Tennessee. By quoting a pages-long newspaper report about the killing of sixteen African Americans, he sought to prove white ruthlessness and "inhumanity," as well as the "hideous race prejudice" plaguing an entire region. Since a racist "reign of terror" had reversed Reconstruction-era gains, Brown specifically chastised the US government for not upholding constitutionally guaranteed liberties. And since equipping adult African American males with the same rights as whites neither compensated the formerly enslaved nor strengthened their communities in the long term, the Black abolitionist issued another, more proactive recommendation in chapter 28—evacuate and emigrate. With southern lands in the hands of unchristian, "rebellious, and "negro-hating" populations, as many freedmen and women as possible should relocate to safer territory. The autobiographer thus endorsed a nascent Exoduster Movement to Kansas, Oklahoma, and other western locales, which, he believed, would not only secure betterment opportunities for Black people fleeing from neoslavery. The actual and perceived threat of migration would also compel Deep South "planters to pursue a different policy," thereby bettering the situation of the area's integral African American workforce.[49]

While recounting postbellum injustices and atrocities, the memoirist manufactured occasional narrative tension. A decade of white-supremacist vigilantism evidently prompted him to reevaluate the utility and allure of violence altogether. He especially reflected on physical resistance in racially paradoxical ways. On the one hand, Brown defended the courageousness and masculinity of African American males. "In all the Southern States," he maintained in chapter 27, "we have some of the noblest specimens of mankind,—[Black] men . . . ready to do and die for the race." Earlier, he indicated that "brute force," as opposed to simple fear or harassment, had caused the freedmen to capitulate during the Second Civil War.[50]

On the other hand, Brown reenlisted racial essentialism when thinking aloud about the supposed quiescence of African Americans. In a contradictory chapter 27 paragraph, concerning an assault against a Black West Point cadet who had made no preparations to resist a forewarned attack, the author extrapolated from that "want of courage and energy" a universal race trait. In the next chapter, he claimed that African Americans never seriously did what other "oppressed nations or communities" had done: "throw off their chains." "The fact is," the autobiographer pontificated, "the world likes to see the exhibition of pluck" among subjugated groups. Yet if libertarian outbursts historically "gai[n] respect and sympathy for the enslaved," Black people had largely failed, in his eyes, a crucial racial test of vindicating their natural rights. Twenty-five years after releasing the *St. Domingo* lecture, the 1880 narrator argued that the present-day successors of heroic Haitian revolutionaries shed "little or no honor on the race." Seven years removed from *The Rising Son*, he curtly dismissed Nat Turner as an "insane man," whereas the nuanced historian of 1873 repeated his 1863 self by eulogizing that insurgent Virginian as "a martyr to the freedom of his race" as well as "a victim to his own fanaticism." Even though Brown recognized the "good service" of Black soldiers in blue uniforms, such passing praise hardly replicated past summaries of their "undaunted heroism" or "unsurpassed bravery" on the battlefield.[51]

Despite such dichotomous positions, the memoirist never betrayed his abolitionist stature or his antiracism writings. Brown definitely vented frustration and dissatisfaction, which he sometimes directed against the freedpeople. The latter, however, were not exceedingly problematic; a racially disintegrating state of affairs assuredly was. Just as the adoption of the 1850 Fugitive Slave Law had impelled the Black man of letters to look closely at Haiti's revolutionary history for inspiration, Radical Reconstruction's recent death instigated a revised authorial stance toward bloodshed. Resorting to arms represented no real solution for the formerly enslaved, according to the autobiographer's new calculations, because (1) recalcitrant white southerners would eagerly restart a war of races that was only temporarily "suspended" and (2) indifferent white northerners, by implication, would do nothing if and when that racial warfare burst forth again. By 1880, then, Brown apparently pulled back from fighting in the typical combat sense. Despite strongly backing emigration, he did not exclusively or predominantly embrace flight as a substitute. However desirable, voting with one's feet comprised no perfect panacea, for the South's Black populations generally lacked the resources to capitalize on Great Plains homesteading. The most feasible freedom-struggle method in the present and foreseeable future therefore centered on a gospel of elevation, which the middle-class activist preached throughout *My Southern Home*'s final ninety pages.[52]

The reportedly widespread degradation that the traveling temperance crusader had detected among the freedpeople motivated him to dispense some tough love in the 1880 text. The prefatory remark about making no conscious "appeal[s] to the imagination or the heart" effectively prefigures the author's unsentimental approach after chapter 16. By frankly treating the condition issue and assigning partial blame to African Americans themselves, the self-help guru anticipated a critical backlash from "numerous" Black readers. Chronic ignorance and superstitiousness, of course, long predated slavery's abolition, precisely why the memoirist denounced a southern system of servitude that had ill-equipped everyone for postemancipation realities. Since generations of captivity shackled Black faculties and abilities, "crippl[ing] their energies, darken[ing] their minds, debas[ing] their moral sense, and obliterat[ing] all traces of their relationship to the rest of mankind," Brown made the acquisition of knowledge a perennial uplift priority. Since "nations are not educated in twenty years," formal Black schooling "is the most important matter that we have to deal with at present," according to his uncontroversial charge, "one that will claim precedence of all other questions for many years to come." More contentiously, the bourgeois moralist seemingly scolded the formerly enslaved for their insufficient refinement.[53]

After Brown identified Black impoverishment as another legacy of chattel bondage, just as he had done in *The Rising Son*, the author listed in a following chapter the ways in which the freedpeople required a vigorous outreach program. Regarding living standards, the African Americans of *My Southern Home* generally inhabited "small unventilated houses" in dilapidated urban spaces or "poorly-built log huts" unfit for horses across the countryside. Besides the absence of "bathing conveniences" from their inadequate abodes, the formerly enslaved, whom the autobiographer classified as "inveterate eaters," survived on limited nutritional regimens. For those reasons, the middle-class activist insisted that "lecturers of their own race, male and female, upon the laws of health, is the first move needed." Of the two causes of African American debasement that the memoirist isolated, unhygienic modes of life warranted much less consideration than religious enthusiasm.[54]

For the Black man of letters, the surfeit of spirituality from which the freedpeople allegedly suffered involved their absorption in season-long revivals and late-night meetings, excessive displays of emotion, membership in multiple dues-paying benevolent societies, as well as welcoming hucksters of faith masquerading as missionaries. His proposed correction for the latter "evil," in particular, was theoretically straightforward: the proliferation of a well-trained ministry. He forecasted, however, a difficult implementation of that proposal because "the uneducated, superstitious masses" will not readily "receive and support an intelligent Christian clergyman." The autobiographer further projected that the formerly enslaved would unwillingly relinquish such worship practices as "[ring] shouting, the loud 'amen,' and the most boisterous noise in prayer." Whereas the Black southerners with whom Brown had interacted held those "outward demonstrations [as] necessary adjuncts to piety," the respectable memoirist adjudged them as paralyzing race vices. In a later section, the narrator also voiced his disapproval of extravagant sartorial choices—all the "silk," "satin," and "costly feathers" worn by poorly compensated laboring folk—in order to reinforce the aspects of religion that churchgoing freedmen and women needed to moderate.[55]

Brown, however, counterbalanced his admonitions by consistently referencing a disadvantageous upbringing. "Long years of training of any people to a particular calling," the redoubtable environmentalist opined, "seems to fit them for that vocation more than for any other." Since perpetual enslavement had accustomed African Americans to execute someone else's thoughts, wants, and orders, the "black man's position as a servant," the author instructed readers, "has not only made the other races believe that is his legitimate sphere, but he himself feels" the same. "In the olden time," the autobiographer declared elsewhere in the text, slaveholders had done the planning, whereas the enslaved performed all the work. Even though the Civil War dispossessed slaveholders of chattels personal, the former master nonetheless owned an "education, backed up by the lands" that he still controlled. The "negro," by comparison, merely had "his hands." Whether toiling in the fields or Big House structured their antebellum existences, the memoirist regularly called for systematic retraining of postbellum Black southerners, for otherwise the push for racial amelioration and advancement would amount to very little. "The race," he announced, "must be educated out of the ignorance in which it at present dwells, and lifted to a level with other races." To upgrade themselves individually and collectively, the self-help guru accordingly arranged a lengthy middle-class checklist.[56]

In chapter 26, for example, the uplifting autobiographer intoned: "We must cultivate self-denial," "repress our appetites for luxuries," and "inculcat[e] . . . the principles of total abstinence from all intoxicants." African Americans needed, the chant continued, "more self-reliance, more confidence in the ability of our own people; more manly independence" from whites, as well as increased interdependence among themselves. In subsequent sections, the author resumed the elevator's song, sounding old themes and introducing new ones. Since "all civilized races have risen by means of combination and co-operation," he deduced in chapter 27, the freedpeople must create and sustain their own alliances. The "time for colored men and women to organize for self-improvement has arrived," he uttered more broadly in the next one. While constantly vocalizing moral, social, and intellectual maturation, the memoirist especially privileged "inward culture" in the twenty-eighth chapter.[57]

For the Black man of letters, literature was indispensable to enlightenment and evolution. Great writers, in his estimation, served as the noblest measurement of attainment by any group or nation. To quickly demonstrate the point, the narrator cited the influence of Homer on the ancient Greeks, Virgil and Horace on the Romans, Dante and Ludovico Ariosto on the Italians, Johann Wolfgang von Goethe and Friedrich Schiller on the Germans, Jean-Baptiste Racine and Voltaire on the French, and Shakespeare and John Milton on the English. In so doing, he deemed transformative authors as additional African American must-haves. Literary artists, Brown elaborated, "possess the most gifted and fertile minds," joining together "all the graces of style with rare, fascinating powers of language, eloquence, wit, humor, pathos, genius and learning." To cultivate such cultivators and gather invaluable insight and stimulation from them "should be," the autobiographer asserted, "one of the highest aims of man." In that way, the race leader conjoined art and uplift on behalf of the freedom struggle.[58]

"No nation has ever been found," Brown professed in *The Black Man*, "which, by its own unaided efforts, by some powerful inward impulse, has arisen from barbarism and degradation to civilization and respectability." In 1863, the Black man of letters envisaged a dynamic historical process, one that flowed from a divine fountainhead, epically unwinding in a postemancipation United States, whereby "nation learns from nation" and "civilization is handed from one people to another." Despite similarly promulgating that "amalgamation is the great civilizer" in *My Southern Home*, he felt very differently about its prospects by 1880. Given the retreat from Congressional Reconstruction in the North and the concomitant decline of equal Black rights in the South, Brown recalibrated the postwar promise of racial intermixing, cultural diffusion, and African American fulfillment. "In America, the negro stands alone as a race," the autobiographer observed at the outset of chapter 29. "Whatever progress he makes," a dismayed Brown declared, "it must be mainly by his own efforts. This is an unfortunate fact, and for which there seems to be no remedy." Pages previously, he more constructively expressed that outlook: "We possess the elements of successful development; but we need live men and women to make this development. The last great struggle for our rights; the battle of our own civilization, is entirely within ourselves, and the problem is to be solved by us." Interestingly, in that do-it-yourself program in the present, for the future, the self-help guru as memorialist momentarily divorced from the past.[59]

However racially empowering were the memories of historically renowned people of color, the narrator further amplified the call for "our men and women of the day" in order to carry out the task of African American improvement. In other words, he insisted on iterations of, rather than reliance on, prior prominence—the historic importance of the next crop of first-rate Black professionals, scientists, entrepreneurs, poets, and so on. Whether as a historian or memoirist, the author manifested, time and again, an understanding of abolitionism that was always bigger than immediate emancipation. For Black activists like Brown, the transcendent uplift mission would surely prosper from white involvement. In the event that such allies ever lost interest, he ultimately recognized that African Americans must rely on themselves solely. That realization, when it finally came, was nonetheless distressing and aggravating. As a chronicler of the race as well as himself, the middle-class activist never withdrew from racial-egalitarian environmentalism or relaxed an antiracist elevation campaign. To do otherwise would have totally denied the Benjamin Banneker life that William Wells Brown so carefully imitated and reframed for the benefit of others.[60]

3

Antislavery Vindicated

*Oliver Johnson and the Value of
Abolitionism's Grand Old Party*

Toward the end of a revised and expanded 1881 biography, Oliver Johnson declared that any open-minded student of abolitionism could not fail to see that William Lloyd Garrison's "relation to it was like that of the North star to the slave in his flight from the Southern prison-house, and that the band he led was always at the battle's front." For the veteran abolitionist ruminating on a dear friend and fellow activist, whose death had occurred in 1879, the *Liberator*'s editor undoubtedly constituted a revelatory source of inspiration. In *William Lloyd Garrison and His Times; or, Sketches of the Anti-Slavery Movement in America, and of the Man Who Was Its Founder and Moral Leader*, Johnson paid tribute and personally testified to an epochal career. As the title suggests, the author also operated as a partisan historian. The book's nearly five hundred pages demonstrate that despite dedicating the volume to antislavery advocates of every stripe, he had no intentions of celebrating all things abolitionism indiscriminately. Vindicating a departed comrade therefore structured the retrospective writer's thoughts and formed a blueprint for the remainder of his public life.[1]

Before embarking on a lengthy memorial, Johnson honored the living Garrison at an 1874 antislavery reunion in Chicago, where an attendee read his biographical portrait aloud. He also eulogized the deceased Garrison in the *New-York Tribune* and an 1879 pamphlet. The newspaper panegyric specifically resulted in more widespread reminiscing. At Whitelaw Reid's editorial request, he produced a *Tribune* column that appeared on a weekly-to-biweekly basis over a seven-month span. Totaling twenty-one installments, "The Fall of Slavery. Recollections of an Abolitionist" established a groundwork for the larger undertaking, one that went beyond an extended obituary. Since the remembered Garrison represented the first American philanthropist "to unfurl the banner of IMMEDIATE AND UNCONDITIONAL EMANCIPATION, and to organize upon that principle a movement which, under God, proved mighty enough to accomplish its object," he appropriately lay at the center of Johnson's commemorative universe. To craft a fuller story of abolitionism, the memorialist featured a constellation of Garrisonian reformers, too.[2]

Even though the narrator never overtly disparaged the altruists who bolted from the American Anti-Slavery Society in 1840 and whose philosophies deviated from polestar Garrison's, his reverencing a single abolitionist school effectively downgraded, without completely disregarding, the achievements of others. If Johnson bore any lingering resentment toward AASS defectors, such an authorial choice seemingly confirmed it. Notwithstanding a disavowal of narrow partisanship, the self-styled "conscientious if not . . . quite impartial observer" depicted the Garrisonians as an illustrious grand old party. They alone, in his estimation, remained faithful to core immediatist values, tactics, and institutions from crusading start to finish. By delineating Garrison and Company as abolitionism's essence and epitome, Johnson endeavored to preserve not a mere version of the humanitarian past but an important account that would shape future historical perceptions.[3]

The author plainly announced his aspirations from the outset. If the text, he commented in the first edition's preface, provided current and subsequent generations "a clearer apprehension of the instrumentalities and influences by which American slavery" met its demise, then his "highest ambition will be fulfilled." Claiming the ability to "speak with something like authority," the lifelong Garrisonian and longtime associate of Garrison's envisioned his personal chronicle and intimate biography as a critical resource for researchers and writers. In the enlarged edition's preface, Johnson acknowledged the limitations surrounding his enterprise. The moment to prepare a detached and unbiased report of the antislavery crusade, he avouched, had yet to arrive, and would not "until long after those who took part in it are in their graves." As a prominent actor in the immediate emancipation campaign from its organizational inception, he nevertheless "sought to make a contribution of some value" to the bedrock materials of later scholarship. Fortifying the posthumous reputation of the *Liberator*'s editor went hand in hand with supplying the documentary needs of posterity.[4]

As an individually designated guardian, Johnson's activism underwent a substantial makeover in the late 1870s. Keeping a particular past approximated an all-consuming reformatory initiative, one that originally coincided with the restoration of Democratic regimes across the Southland. After racially conservative white southerners supposedly rescued the region from Reconstruction-era corruption and misrule, the retrospective writer engaged in a distinctively redemptive quest of his own: salvaging the Garrisonian history and legacy from denigration and disrepute. Even though the unsure standing of the Republican Party's southern rebuilding efforts did not directly impel his venture, it certainly affected his record of abolitionism. From 1879 to 1889, Johnson's busy pen disclosed how an obsession with abolitionist historical matters marginalized his awareness of other issues, especially those pertaining to the formerly enslaved. As the antebellum antislavery crusade developed into a quasi-scholarly pursuit under his postbellum care, it arguably ceased to function as a living and breathing phenomenon.

Congressional Reconstruction's disintegration, though, did not categorically bring about a Johnsonian abandonment of racial egalitarianism. In the concluding paragraph of a chapter about the creation of Garrison's Boston-based newspaper and the popular outrage greeting it, the narrator bombarded weak-kneed officials. "On every side," his rhetorical salvo opened, alleged "statesmen . . . brand as enmity to the South every earnest plea for the equal rights of the negro." They "ask us," the author bristled at the audacity, "to stop our ears to the cry of men driven from the ballot-box and defrauded of their wages by violence, and to close our eyes to the frauds by which the South has . . . gain[ed] by political power the substance of what she failed to achieve by the sword." On at least one textual occasion, he notably summoned an undying abolitionist spirit on behalf of an ongoing African American freedom struggle.[5]

Postbellum northern officeholders, according to Johnson's calculations, perpetrated the same dereliction of duty that their antebellum counterparts had committed. Both evinced extraordinary sensitivity toward southern white sensibilities, manifested little concern for the South's Black populations, and discountenanced anyone criticizing the area's race relations. With good reasons, he likened present-day functionaries to the toadying and timeserving northern men with southern principles of the past whom antislavery agitators had endlessly excoriated. Just as the pre–Civil War political originals were "always ready with some new compromise in the interest of the slaveholding class," their post–Civil War progeny evidently bent over backward to appease the South's white elites. The commemorator did not explicitly refer to anyone or anything, but the reigning mood of sectional reconciliation since the election of 1876 plausibly factored into his blistering assessment.[6]

In a face-off in which neither contender obtained an electoral-vote majority, the Republican candidate Rutherford B. Hayes emerged as the victor after a congressionally appointed commission resolved the impasse. The fifteen arbitrators—consisting of five representatives, five senators, and five Supreme Court justices—narrowly determined that all the disputed returns from South Carolina, Florida, and Louisiana, as well as a solitary Oregon vote—justly belonged to Hayes. Whatever the role that political affiliation played in the election's resolution, and without delving into the behind-the-scenes negotiations that purportedly transpired amid the standstill, the final outcome had significant repercussions. The decision of the newly inaugurated president to withdraw US troops from the statehouses of South Carolina and Louisiana, wherein embattled Republican governors fought to maintain the party's weakening grip over the governments of each, helped complete a regional process that had begun, in Georgia, in 1870. The let-alone approach of the incoming Hayes administration, which its devisors hoped would pacify white southerners and simultaneously broaden support for the Republican Party among them, symbolized Reconstruction's termination. With the return of Democratic rule throughout the former Confederacy, national protection for equal Black rights steadily diminished and eventually disappeared across the South.[7]

Regardless of exactly what prompted Johnson to equate obsequious postbellum politicos with submissive antebellum analogues, he detected a disturbing continuity in countrywide affairs—a conciliatory connection between the past and present. While experiencing such moments of déjà vu, the retrospective writer expressed his discontent accordingly. He specifically updated an argument that the abolitionists had routinely deployed in order to advance the slave's cause and stamp out anti-Black prejudices. "If the enfranchised [African American] men of the South were white," he opined, folks in "the North would be all on fire with indignation over their wrongs, and ready to exert the last iota of constitutional power for their protection." To shake fatigued northern voters of their sluggishness toward southern race relations, Johnson challenged them to "do for the negro what we should not hesitate to do for the white man." As the culmination of a sentences-long diatribe, that dare illustrates sympathy for the freedpeople's plight.[8]

The commemorator waved the "bloody shirt," too, but not in the same way as Republican campaigners and strategists. Often exploited during presidential election years, the latter often reminded white northerners that the Party of Lincoln saved the Union against treacherous Democrats who had sought to subvert and destroy it. Johnson, in contrast, appropriated and redefined Republican rhetoric not solely to energize the electorate but ostensibly reactivate philanthropic audiences as well. "The voice of Garrison cries to us out of his freshly-made grave," he rhapsodized, "bidding us not to waste the heritage won for us by his indomitable courage, and by the blood and bravery of our soldiers." The memorialist thus urged readers to cherish and sustain the drive for universal liberty that valiant men in blue uniform *and* fearless antislavery freedom fighters had waged. Such declarations, however, sharply diverge from the primary purpose of Johnson's personal chronical and intimate biography. His remarkable castigation of cowardly and deferential northern officeholders, when viewed within the wider narrative context, registers as a digression only. In an otherwise vast desert of preservative Garrisonian partisanship, it approximates not an oasis of unflinching abolitionism but a mirage.[9]

Whereas defending William Lloyd Garrison and Company preoccupied the author, the status and condition of liberated African Americans entered his consciousness fleetingly by comparison. Given his own approval of the Hayes administration's southern plan, Johnson himself had resembled, albeit temporarily, the very placatory statesmen whom he so memorably chastised. His initially sanctioning a policy that attempted to mollify sectional tensions and cultivate regional white favor, by removing the threat of US governmental involvement in the Southland's racial business, suggested one of two things. At worst, it represented an abolitionist defection; at best, it revealed disillusionment with Radical Reconstruction. Yet Johnson's dissatisfaction with the Republican Party's handling of the postwar peace settlement actually antedated Hayes's ascendancy by several years.

In 1872, for example, he sponsored the potential presidency of Horace Greeley, who was the nominee of both the newly formed Liberal Republican Party and customarily pro-southern Democratic Party. In his acceptance letter, Greeley proclaimed that if elected, he would serve "as President, not of a party, but of the whole People." He additionally articulated, as his firm belief, that the "New Departure" in politics set in motion by Liberal Republicanism would receive the hearty embrace of Americans North and South, most of whom were "eager to clasp hands over the bloody chasm which has too long divided them." That statement encapsulated the tone of appeasement permeating Greeley's candidacy, concomitantly indicating the growing northern disaffection with certain Civil War topics. The very platform of the Liberal Republicans reflected such a mood shift. It stressed, as an established fact, the "equality of all men before the law" and opposed "any reopening" of the debates that the Thirteenth, Fourteenth, and Fifteenth Amendments had settled. It further insisted on "the immediate and absolute removal of all disabilities imposed on the account of the Rebellion"—that is, unlimited amnesty for politically proscribed ex-Confederates—and championed local self-government and "the supremacy of the civil over the military authority."[10]

To assist team Greeley in its push against the incumbent chief executive and Union war hero Ulysses S. Grant, Johnson penned a praiseworthy piece that circulated in the public press and as a separate tract. Writing as an "abolitionist . . . who took an earnest though humble part" in the campaign to immediately emancipate the enslaved, he assured voters that Greeley's election "would promote the best interests of the country and the welfare of the whole people." Readers could presumably rely on his words because Johnson spoke from a place of familiarity: He was the managing editor of Greeley's *New-York Weekly Tribune* from 1870 to 1872 and had held a position on his *Daily Tribune* editorial staff during the early 1840s. Johnson advertised that relationship by alluding to his decades-long friendship with the famous newspaperman. He then endorsed the nominee's character and integrity against Republican imputations, which had maligned him not only as a "wavering, unstable man" but also as someone who "made a corrupt and disgraceful bargain" with the Democrats.[11]

Even though Greeley's bid for the Executive Mansion had failed miserably— he carried the electoral votes of only three states—the contest's one-sidedness apparently hastened Johnson's deteriorating stance on Reconstruction. In March 1877, for instance, he promulgated his preferred solution to a southern racial conundrum. In the New Jersey *Orange Journal*, which he managed from 1876 to 1879, an evidently exhausted radical broadcasted a Hayes administration bromide: "It will be best, in the long run, to leave [white and Black southerners] face to face, with the slightest possible interference, and trust to moral influences chiefly to secure peace and good-will." Not until the year before the inaugural, 1880 publication of *William Lloyd Garrison and His Times* did Johnson transmit a decisive break from laissez-faire rationalizations.[12]

In an 1879 epistle to the *Tribune*, a seemingly regenerated reformer deplored both the "persecution of the negro" and "'the shot-gun policy' of 'the Solid South.'" Despite his pronouncement that elevating ex-slaveholders and former slaves from the "debasement" of chattel bondage would require "the slow operation of moral forces," Johnson did not publicly notify AASS colleagues to resume their associational exertions. He, instead, beseeched the Republican Party to resuscitate its moribund project in the Southland, demanding that the general government "go to the very verge of its rightful powers" on behalf of every American citizen, but especially those who must still "drink [servitude's] bitter dregs." Since such a positive application of US authority was contingent on the retention of Republicans in office, the missive writer advised northern voters that in order to check southern "barbarism" at the ballot box, they must prevent a Democratic victory in the upcoming presidential showdown. If the South could make itself "solid in the cause of oppression," Johnson posited, the North should undergo consolidation on behalf of "civilization and justice." However much his communication sounded a resurgent radicalism—"human rights" violations, he averred, "are not [and] can never be sectional"—it did not infuse the book-length memorial with an electrifying humanitarian aura.[13]

To be sure, as enslavement's eradication transitioned into "an event of the past," Johnson admittedly worried about historical ignorance. He wanted to rescue from possible oblivion not the generations of captivity that African Americans had endured but the epic deeds of antislavery agitators. The mostly white abolitionists whom the author brought into "full view" consecrated some three decades to the onerous, and sometimes dangerous, responsibility of telling the truth about slavery. It took prodigious valor to expose "the wrongs and woes of the slaves, the duty and safety of immediate emancipation, and the terrible guilt of those who, whether in church or state, lent themselves to the support of so atrocious a system." As the commander of a cadre of steadfast and intrepid activists, Johnson's Garrison unleashed the revolutionary currents that dramatically changed the philanthropic landscape of the United States. The massive opposition over which the *Liberator*'s editor ultimately prevailed, the memorialist postulated, would have quashed a momentous crusade if someone else had occupied its helm. Had Garrison "faltered and retreated," he exclaimed, "what calamities might not have befallen the Nation!" The "fate of the Republic," he provocatively added, "depended on the fidelity of a single man."[14]

In justification of those assertions, the commemorator recalled Garrison's Baltimore jailing, as other antislavery chroniclers had done and would do. He remembered that during Garrison's postconfinement speaking tour, the orator encountered a generally "hostile" and "apathetic" reaction to his ardent abolitionist message. He reminisced about how an undeterred Garrison, "without so much as a single dollar of capital, or even one subscriber," started the *Liberator* in order to publicize the sinfulness of slavery and the American Colonization Society's deceptive benevolence. He recollected Garrison's feats of self-denial while maintaining his periodical during its hard-knocks upbringing, for he resided in a dark and "dingy" printer's shop and subsisted on a paltry diet of bread and water. He related that Garrison, as a delegate to an 1833 convention from which the AASS arose, prepared a rousing manifesto that amounted to abolitionism's "Magna Charta." As cruel compensation for such pioneering labors, Johnson reminded readers that an 1835 mob nearly lynched Garrison, beating and dragging his body through Boston's streets. If that recitation did not persuade postbellum audiences to seriously consider how the country's existence hinged on the determination and faithfulness of a lone crusader, they strengthened the author's prediction that posterity would hold Garrison in the utmost esteem for his glorious ministrations.[15]

To explicate the ways in which Garrison refocused the lives of individual abolitionists and reconfigured the meaning of abolitionism, the partisan-cum-participant historian emphasized the doctrine of immediatism. It invested his "arm with strength," Johnson observed, and "made all the difference between success and failure in the movement" that he conducted. Predicated on "God's outraged law of justice and love" as well as "the inalienable rights of man," the transformational activist preached the good news of immediate emancipation on the antislavery lecturing circuit, at antislavery assemblies, and via antislavery media outlets. Despite the seemingly severe language that the remembered Garrison had marshaled on behalf of the new humanitarian creed, the memorialist explained that he "wounded only to heal." He always "weighed his words," according to the commemorative assurance, "exactly and scrupulously" and never allowed intense emotions to arrest and displace "calm judgment." A red-hot zeal unquestionably actuated Johnson's Garrison. Yet his prophetic voice, "crying in the wilderness and calling the people to repentance," received a special ordination from on high. "Divine Providence," the author avowed, had "raised [him] up" so as to carry out a magnificent work.[16]

Even though Johnson harbored no doubts that "God and Christ" sustained the immediate emancipation campaign, the negative stereotypes bedeviling its visionary messenger troubled him deeply. Before the Civil War, most Americans did not merely rebuff his abolitionist exhortations, as the author indicated. Rather, the evangelical Protestants whom Garrison especially targeted had branded him as a heretic or infidel. Of the fallacies that still threatened the stature of the *Liberator*'s editor, nothing so rankled the retrospective writer as the slanderous charge of irreligiousness. Exonerating Garrisonian abolitionism as rightful and righteous imbued his personal chronicle and intimate biography with an obvious purposefulness. So, too, did uncovering how Garrison's purportedly Christian opponents scorned a Christ-centered cause.[17]

In the chapter "Mr. Garrison's Early Orthodoxy," Johnson decreed that the biographical subject emitted not the slightest "odor of heresy of any kind." To remove a foul stain from the Garrisonian mantle, the memorialist underscored that "by inheritance and through the influence of his noble . . . mother," the *Liberator*'s editor possessed a strong Baptist background. Organizing an antislavery crusade did not jeopardize that churchly upbringing at all. When the recollected Garrison unfurled the immediatist banner, he traveled fully within the parameters of

evangelicalism. As a "friend and champion of the revivals of religion," he originally believed that the outpouring of faith, thanks to the preachers of the Second
Great Awakening, would only "hasten the day of emancipation." Johnson's Garrison was similarly confident, at first, that the widespread diffusion of the Bible
would serve as the "chief instrumentality" of abolitionism's advancement. The
commemorator further noted that the reputedly sacrilegious Garrison had once
"held and inculcated" a strict observance of the Sabbath's total sacredness. Such
a religiously normative reformer even counseled free Black northerners to "set
apart a day for fasting . . . and prayer on account of the wickedness of slavery, and
the oppressions arising therefrom." Because of that "sort of infidelity," the author
acidly remarked, churchmen across the nation decidedly turned "their backs" on
the immediate emancipation campaign.[18]

The narrator also showcased the tragic irony of clerical aversion to abolitionism through yet another evangelical wellspring of Garrison's crusading philanthropy. The *Liberator's* editor, he announced, had acquired the doctrine of immediatism from an enforcer of religious orthodoxy—the famous New England
divine and uncompromising antialcohol evangelist Lyman Beecher. That Presbyterian pastor emboldened antislavery agitators by preaching that sinners were
duty bound "to repent instantly and give . . . [their] heart[s] to Christ." The remembered Beecher, however, never did what the abolitionists whom he helped
galvanize had done. Even though he and like-minded ministers adjudged "sin in
general" as reprehensible and unjustifiable, the author asserted that they betrayed
their own teachings. As a comeback to the abolitionists' demand that slaveholders must immediately recognize and renounce slavery's sinfulness, Beecher and
his ilk hypocritically reasoned that "the particular sin of treating men as chattels
and compelling them to work without wages could only be put away, if at all, by
a process requiring whole generations for its consummation!" Since Johnson's
Garrison never bartered over such serious personal, social, and spiritual considerations, an ostensibly reckless activist was a far better representative of prevailing religion than the very ecclesiastical purveyors of evangelicalism.[19]

Besides a significant hermeneutical point, that deduction allowed the retrospective writer to settle a vital historical score. Since the "fanaticism of the
Abolitionists" merely entailed the application of mainstream religious tenets to
the problem of enslavement, their low popularity had nothing to do with Garrison's alleged extremism. Duplicitous clergymen, the commemorator argued,
comprised the real reason, for they deliberately fanned the flames of antiabolitionism. One recollected incident cogently captures how the postbellum Johnson
illuminated the ignominy of antebellum hierarchs. It involves the same "consci-

entiously and strictly Orthodox" Garrison, on the one hand, and Beecher the "Orthodox pulpit" headman, on the other.[20]

After his Baltimore imprisonment, the remembered Garrison counted on men like Beecher to aid the nascent immediate emancipation campaign, wholeheartedly and without hesitation. Instead, the eminent revivalist sought to dissuade him from pushing that specific agenda. In what approximates a latter-day temptation scenario, the memorialist counterpoised a nearly Mephistophelian Beecher with a Christ-like Garrison. "'Your zeal is commendable,'" a quoted Beecher uttered to Garrison, "'but you are misguided.'" "'If you will give up your fanatical notions and be guided by us (the clergy),'" the former reportedly propositioned, "'we will make you the [William] Wilberforce of America.'" By refusing the offer, Johnson's Garrison overcame the enticement to worldly prestige; he also "left Dr. Beecher with a . . . saddened heart." Even worse, he soon discovered that other leading clergymen throughout New England shared Beecher's disapproval of anything that condemned southern slavery as a sinful institution and combated the ACS scheme to relocate manumitted Black people overseas. In short, the Beecher-Garrison episode foreshadows the more flagrant and pervasive church-based antagonism to abolitionism that the author spotlighted elsewhere in the text.[21]

That the *Liberator*'s editor needed to wage an altruistic war without the stewardship of venerable ministers paled in comparison to the clerical intransigence that he confronted from the antislavery crusade's onset. Hard-line resistance, among the very persons from whom Garrison had anticipated encouragement, consequently induced a reassessment not of his abolitionist ideas but conventional religion. The partisan-cum-participant historian briefly surveyed a spiritual evolution in which Garrison questioned the Bible's divine inspiration, the Sabbath's sanctity, and the Christian clergy's heavenly authority; incorporated elements of Quakerism and Unitarianism into a nonsectarian Protestantism; and developed the biblically derived theory of nonresistance. For the commemorator, however, it did not matter how he eventually understood Christianity or applied newfound devotional insights to his humanitarianism. The American religious establishment, Johnson propounded, repudiated immediatism well before the *Liberator*'s editor espoused supposedly ungodly views. Had evangelical leading lights acted differently, as the memorialist proposed, Garrison might have remained a part of, rather than parting from, their fold. Whatever the soundness of such conjecture, he nonetheless attempted to construct an unassailable argument: Those who arraigned Garrison with heterodoxy primarily did so to excuse their own hostility to abolitionism.[22]

Rather than gloss over a divorce from evangelicalism, the author clarified and legitimated it. Contrary to the malicious allegations, the recollected Garrison never surrendered or violated fundamental Christian precepts or ethics. His pure and simple faith, Johnson attested, was intensely conservative in orientation. In "theory and practice," according to the commemorative explication, the Christianity of the trailblazing abolitionist repeatedly revolved about the ministry of Jesus, which concentrated on the commandments that "require us to love God with all our hearts, and our neighbor as ourselves." The remembered Garrison displayed his reverential bona fides not by belonging to a certain denomination or accepting a particular theology. He did so by submitting to "Christ as a leader and guide," obediently walking "in his footsteps, at whatever cost or hazard." Given that lifelong *imitatio Christi*, the narrator conceived that few individuals qualified for the Christian name better than Garrison. Johnsonian verities about the *Liberator*'s editor equally pertained to his disciples as well.[23]

In validation of the Garrisonians' religiosity, the author relied on a basic binary formulation. "The Abolitionists," he annunciated, distinguished "between *Christ*ianity and *church*ianity, between piety and 'piosity,' between sincerity and cant." Whereas Johnson's antislavery agitators occupied the one side and abided by the "Church of Christ," their antiabolitionist adversaries inhabited the other and adhered to the "pro-slavery churches of the United States." The implacable enmity of clergymen subsequently compelled Garrison's proselytes to spurn sectarian attachments and disconnect from disingenuous "representatives of Christ and religion." The beliefs of Johnson's Garrisonians "in Christianity and its Divine Founder" only deepened thereafter. Such devoutness, under the memorialist's handling, comprised a prerequisite for those who went down the same road as the *Liberator*'s editor. It rendered them, in his evaluation, as the "best fitted to carry on a moral warfare" against slaveholding wickedness that had vitiated not just the Southland but the entire country.[24]

Given their saintliness, the partisan-cum-participant historian also claimed that if Jesus himself had suddenly descended from Heaven and returned to the realm of mortals, he would have "bless[ed]" the immediate emancipation campaign and directed it to "victory." No other observation more provocatively conveyed the commemorator's confidence in the sacredness of Garrisonian abolitionism. The retrospective writer thus overturned historical misinterpretations with apparent vengeance. While comparing and contrasting the spirituality of the Garrisonians and their churchly foes, to the advantage of the former and detriment of the latter, Johnson dismissed any vindictive intentions. Presenting "the truth of history for the instruction and warning of other generations," he promised readers, constituted a peak priority. They should not, then, impute any ulterior motivations behind his ledger of American Christianity's appalling track record on the slavery issue. Johnson suggested that evangelical Protestants, as befitting moral free agents, were wholly culpable for their own misdeeds; he simply recounted them. Regardless of those memorial disclaimers, avenging previous injuries and documenting the past were hardly mutually exclusive endeavors. His appraisal of the havoc wreaked by a national network of proslavery Christian ministers and sects illustrates how implied and explicit authorial aims worked in tandem.[25]

Since northern faith leaders had entered into an unholy alliance with the Old South's ruling race, they alone, according to the commemorative indictment, accounted "for all the blood spilled and treasure lost in the war of the Rebellion!" Whatever the denomination, all "were essentially alike" in Johnson's analysis. Mainline churches, he reported, firmly resisted immediatism and "refus[ed] or neglect[ed] to adopt any efficient measures for the overthrow of slavery." So that audiences fully grasped "the courage, foresight and self-sacrificing spirit of Mr. Garrison and his associates," they needed to comprehend the ways by which antiabolitionist churchmen, to a greater extent than recalcitrant slaveholders, had impeded abolitionism's momentum. The retrospective writer therefore listed, in vivid detail and with palpable disgust, the sordid crimes of pre–Civil War clerics. By remaining "insensible of the humanity of the negro" and "indifferent to the sin and shame" of enslavement, their willful connivance with iniquity invited, and finally warranted, divine retribution. With that post–Civil War judgment, Johnson joined a swelling chorus of veteran abolitionists who recited similarly as antislavery memorialists and historians.[26]

As evidence that pulpiteers deliberately prejudiced their parishioners and led them horribly astray, the commemorator catalogued how they had distorted both the nature of southern slavery and the reformers who attempted to uproot it. To their eternal dishonor, the North's priestly classes professed that the drive for immediate and unconditional emancipation was (1) "dangerous," because freed slaves would "cut their masters' throats"; (2) unnecessary, because enslaved people were "contented and happy"; (3) "cruel," because unfree African Americans constituted the "property" of their owners; (4) objectionable, because enslaved people "ought not to be set free in this country, but . . . taken back to Africa, where they belong"; (5) obnoxious, because antislavery agitators were "too indiscriminate in their denunciations"; (6) disruptive, because abolitionist organizers "divide[d] the churches and divert[ed] their attention from religious work"; (7) seditious, because antislavery talking points threatened sectional "peace" and national harmony; and (8) mistaken, because "the Bible sanction[ed]" servitude. Given such a rap sheet, the responsible author could not "blot from the page of history the sad and disgraceful truth." As the postbellum guardian of the House of Garrison, he dutifully unmasked antebellum wrongdoers, no matter whom or what his exposé offended.[27]

Johnson additionally vented his indignation against a US government and constitution that master-class interests had thoroughly manipulated and controlled. He also voiced his ire against elected officials and political parties that had functioned as tools of the Slave Power. Nothing in the narrative, however, rivals the disdain that the author reserved for Protestant clergymen and the ecclesiastical bodies, voluntary associations, and faith-based periodicals over which they presided. For the retrospective writer, a religious establishment that repulsed an overwhelmingly Christian movement was itself antithetical to genuine Christianity. By shunning oppressed people of color and sustaining the slaveholding oppressors, it deserved precisely what it had earned: nothing but commemorative reproach and historical infamy.[28]

In stark contrast to a blind Protestant ministry, the recollected Garrison clearly discerned the path to humanity's redemption. Only he, the memorialist sermonized, recognized that "the millennium could never be realized until slavery should be put out of the way." For that visionary figure, revival meetings, as well as bible, tract, and missionary societies, were insufficient devices for bringing about Christ's one-thousand-year reign on earth if they did not liberate masters and bondservants alike from a sinful arrangement. Such perceptiveness alienated Johnson's Garrison from evangelical orthodoxy. It heightened his sense of mission, too. Buttressed by a belief in the invincibility of a righteous cause and forever revering the "heavenly voice" that had summoned him into action, the remembered Garrison accordingly did what he had to do. While setting down those ideas as biographical facts, the commemorator largely served the dictates of personal conscience and the perceived needs of history.[29]

Despite an impressive rhetorical supplication that conjured the heritage of a deceased Garrison, Johnson volunteered few answers to any unresolved or emergent racial justice questions. Reminiscences of how white abolitionists had defied ensconced anti-Black biases in the antebellum North often occasioned paeans to the exceptionalism of the *Liberator*'s editor. They did not elicit any reflections on postbellum race relations. As an epoch-changing reformer, Johnson's Garrison premised the doctrine of immediatism on a startling truth: "the absolute humanity of the negro." Endowed with an "unqualified and complete" knowledge of humankind's underlying oneness, that holy crusader expected others to accept it without reservations, both "in principle and practice." As proof that Garrison obeyed his own directives, the memorialist mentioned that he had successfully challenged a Massachusetts antimiscegenation law. He addressed Garrison's assistance for a planned manual labor school and college for African Americans in New Haven, Connecticut. He also discussed how Garrison discredited the ACS, which had "the hateful spirit of caste as its chief corner-stone." Such actions previously "won" for the *Liberator's* editor "the grateful confidence of the free colored people," according to the author, but he never broached their present-day applicability.[30]

At another narrative point, the retrospective writer referred to the same "hateful racial prejudices" that had ruined Prudence Crandall's short-lived boarding school for African American girls. In comparison to his recurring coverage of the authentic piety of the Garrisonians and the false religiosity of their ecclesiastical nemeses, Johnson treated the abolitionists' enlightened egalitarianism sparsely. Even though the commemorator cited Garrison's long-held affirmation that the immediate emancipation campaign was "rooted alike in Christianity and Humanity," he prioritized the mantra's former quality in order to rectify incessant antiabolitionist complaints. His handling of the "meanness and cruelty" of early-nineteenth-century colorphobia shows that he lacked any intentions of instilling new life into an old fight. Regardless of the racial terrorism that defined the Reconstruction era, as well as the post-1876 ambiguity encircling equal Black rights, racism in the recent past and present apparently did not match the kind that had once predominated.[31]

"Anglo-Saxon prejudice against the negro is strong even yet," the partisan-cum-participant historian declaimed, "but it is weak to what it was." That statement preceded remembrances of the bigoted customs and attitudes that had suffused the prewar North—racial segregation in churches and on public conveyances, as well as the anti-Black biases of Christian clerics and ACS benefactors. It also followed recollections about the absence of African Americans among the founders of the New England Anti-Slavery Society, which Johnson ascribed to the fear that their participation would incite a racist backlash, thereby imperiling the fledgling immediate emancipation campaign. By underscoring the rigidity and intolerance of white New Englanders, in particular, he alerted readers to a highly inhospitable environment. "I am simply trying to make clear," the author averred, "the darkness, ignorance and moral degeneracy against which the . . . Abolitionists had to contend." Unlike the ostensible omnipresence and omnipotence of antebellum colorphobia, the postbellum variety evidently exercised no such ubiquitous or overbearing effect.[32]

Despite marveling that long-suffering African Americans had weathered white hatred, thanks to God's making them especially "gentle, patient and forgiving," Johnson never elucidated how or why the racial climate markedly improved. Authorial comments elsewhere in the text suggest that he had in mind constitutional milestones that outlawed enslavement and implemented colorblind criteria for US citizenship and suffrage rights. The modified national compact, he stated, "is not that which" the *Liberator*'s editor once "burned on a certain Fourth of July in Framingham [in 1854]; nor is the [slaveholding] Union which he sought to dissolve any longer in existence." Yet if a bloody civil war revolutionized an allegedly proslavery document that the antebellum Garrison, armed with the biblical language of the Prophet Isaiah, had reviled as a "covenant with death, and an agreement with hell," it never extinguished an ex-Confederate ambition to restore an Old South order. When the retrospective writer upbraided postbellum northern politicos for their spineless stances toward the solidification of a Democratic Southland, he acknowledged the sheer brutality surrounding a reactionary regional quest to reassert traditional white dominance. Whereas the veteran abolitionist formerly urged voters to retaliate to southern outrages by filling elective posts with Republicans, he issued no such public plea in the years after the release of *William Lloyd Garrison and His Times*.[33]

In an 1884 *North American Review* essay, which appeared as part of a roundtable discussion on "The Future of the Negro," Johnson pondered the theme with outright optimism. From the start, the contributor shared an unshakeable conviction, grounded in abolitionism, regarding the fundamental sameness of white and Black Americans. Besides an "identical" humanity, he stressed that they possessed indistinguishable "attributes and capacities." He consequently pictured a not-too-distant day of interracial concord. Slowly "but surely," the author forecasted, "the vulgar 'prejudice of color' will fade out of the minds and hearts of people of culture, and a black skin, no more than red hair or blue eyes, will be regarded as a badge of social inferiority." As African Americans steadily attained "education and refinement" and increasingly overcame "the scars which slavery inflicted," all impediments to racial intermixing, according to his reasoning, would eventually crumble.[34]

Johnson further painted an impending tomorrow in which the ideal of colorblindness itself would become irrelevant. The "tendencies of the times," he pronounced, "are towards the obliteration of race distinctions and a union of all branches of the human family in a common struggle for mutual protection and development." Unlike his previous electoral solution for neutralizing unreconstructed ex-Confederates as well as aiding the freedpeople, the veteran abolitionist now counseled patience. African American progress, he noted in closing, "will not be the fruit either of concession or self-assertion, exclusively, but of a wise resort to the one or the other method, as circumstances may require." Regardless of that vision's admirable features, the essayist's stated panacea basically relied on Black improvement over generations. Less than two decades after the Civil War, the antebellum champion of immediatism now advocated what he had hitherto despised—gradualism. Remarkably, but a short spell separated this Johnson from the seemingly rejuvenated version who, in the lead-up to the election of 1880, maintained that the "powerful healer" of "Time" needed active intercession in order to enable its beneficence. The absence of US governmental intervention, according to that 1879 reckoning, would only "hinder" racial amelioration in the South.[35]

Imagining gradually occurring African American *social* equality did not automatically signify a regression from prior reformism. Most, if not all, white abolitionists had subscribed or still subscribed to it, consciously or not. Johnson's supposition that racial elevation, in and of itself, would resolve America's troublesome race relations constituted a far more cautious, and possibly retrograde, perspective in 1884. The politics of respectability, of course, predated the rise of the immediate emancipation campaign in the 1830s and persisted well after the AASS shut down in 1870. Whereas Black leaders continually invoked uplift as a freedom-struggle maneuver, it had received much less emphasis among many white Garrisonians by the 1840s and 1850s, if only because bigoted northerners had squelched their initial attempts at facilitating African American educational opportunities. By boosting betterment without white involvement, Johnson placed the onus of antiracism solely on Black shoulders.[36]

Revealingly, the 1884 essayist did not rebuke the holders of anti-Black prejudices as he had censured the owners of Black bodies since the 1830s. As an antislavery crusader, he demanded an immediate and unconditional extirpation of a personally and nationally sinful system of slavery. The former abolitionist, in contrast, conceded that the total and complete extermination of socially evil colorphobia must conform to some indefinite timetable. The rediscovery of uplift, even though it never devolved into a flat-out surrender to white supremacists, denoted a capitulation nonetheless. A gradualist mechanism of change was anything but scientific, regardless of the certainty with which Johnson expressed his progressive outlook. Yet given the egalitarian design that he unequivocally entertained, his chosen means could assuage the consciences of retired, as well as tired, white humanitarians. "As the negro qualifies himself . . . [for] the privileges and amenities of cultivated society," Johnson anticipated that "he will find the color of his skin no bar to these advantages." Antiracism in the Age of Redemption simply did not exact the sense of urgency as abolitionism had before the Civil War. Otherwise, the author might have insisted on instantaneous adjustments to southern race relations during the last decade of his life.[37]

Years before the *North American Review* piece, he urged the nation's youth to emulate the abolitionists. At the 1863 annual meeting of the AASS—wherein some of the attendees celebrated the Emancipation Proclamation, and others even speculated about their associational future—Johnson vocalized his gratitude for all the "blessings" and "benefit[s]" that a "noble cause" had bestowed. Memories of trials endured and sacrifices made, while laboring on behalf of the enslaved, hardly pierced his address. The approaching day of liberation overpowered them. As the orator rejoiced at the striking alterations to popular antislavery sentiments, as well as saluted the integral role of his partners in shaping them, he seized on the speaking moment to offer vocational advice to younger audience members. To "enrich and ennoble their lives," he recommended that they give themselves "unreservedly to reform." They should back "the oppressed and the wronged," he pontificated, "cast their influence on the side of truth, however unpopular, and . . . allow no temptation of wealth and fame to swerve them . . . from the principles of justice and righteousness." Such altruistic rules later figured into the narrative of *William Lloyd Garrison and His Times*, but neither an 1863 nor 1880s Johnson visualized ensuing waves of white reformers mainly toiling for the freedpeople.[38]

Concomitant with his joyful expectation that the ultimate "triumph" of the immediate emancipation campaign was nigh, Johnson readily accepted that "much remains to be done" before anyone could set aside philanthropic "armor." He also affirmed that the abolitionists themselves, and not their heirs, must finish the crusade that they had commenced. After slavery's disappearance, "other moral issues will be presented, other reforms [will] arise, to test the courage and devotion of the new generation." The speaker never diagnosed the next concerns or whom or what they might affect. So confident was Johnson that antislavery values exceeded the boundaries of abolitionism, he presumed that the old crusaders would steer successors until "the end of time." On the pages of his personal chronicle and intimate biography, Garrisonian godliness stands out as a transcendent facet. Exactly where that holiness could or should lead aspiring humanitarians did not factor into any authorial equations.[39]

Not long after that 1863 gathering, the congressional adoption of the Thirteenth Amendment prodded Johnson to problematize the abolitionists' corporate identity. In his final issue as the *National Anti-Slavery Standard*'s editor, which he had conducted with someone else or by himself since 1853, he advertised his re-tirement and encouraged peers to do the same. As enslavement's irrevocable col-lapse neared, the exponents of immediatism "have now no distinctive function," in his opinion. The AASS and its auxiliaries, he added, "are an anachronism." Rather than retain their "isolated position[s]," Johnson advised colleagues to do as Garrison himself enjoined: "mingle with others in the great work" of assisting the emancipated in their transition to freedom and securing an equal African American citizenship. Despite recognizing that responsibilities still beckoned soon-to-be former abolitionists, he nevertheless communicated a limited con-ception of organized abolitionism in 1865—and the 1880s.[40]

As a movement memorialist, Johnson surveyed the rightfulness of Garrison's innovative pathway and the righteousness by which he and other avant-garde ac-tivists had followed it. If, indeed, the author wanted would-be reformers to draw upon his account for stimulation or sustenance, he imparted a two-part phil-anthropic code for their edification: (1) absolute acceptance of Christ-derived precepts and (2) strict adherence to moral-action strategies. Since all propo-nents of abolitionism fulfilled those criteria at first, the narrator initially made no distinctions among them. In a succinct description of the Methodist min-ister Orange Scott, for instance, Johnson itemized the very credentials that had rendered one as an antislavery crusader: "He opposed the Colonization scheme, denounced slavery as a sin," and espoused "the doctrine and duty of immediate emancipation." Besides establishing his abolitionist footing, such faithful indica-tors ordained him an "avowe[d] Garrisonian." That observation supplies another clue to ascertaining the patrimony that the commemorator aimed to preserve. Given what the remembered Scott represented, he was not merely intellectually indebted to the *Liberator's* editor but, ipso facto, an apostle of Garrison's as well. The same pertained to everyone else, so long as he or she absorbed and per-formed those fundamentals.[41]

Despite a Johnsonian terminology that classified all abolitionists as techni-cally Garrisonian, in actuality, many had disassociated themselves from the cam-paign's ostensible prime mover by the early 1840s. The author honored virtually the entire antislavery vanguard throughout the first half of the book, including such future AASS bolters as James Birney, Beriah Green, William Jay, Amos A. Phelps, Gerrit Smith, Alvan Stewart, Arthur and Lewis Tappan, and Elizur Wright. After recounting the 1840 organizational rupture, he ceased to extoll im-mediate emancipation personnel universally. Of the three movement schools—the Garrisonian, church-oriented, and political abolitionists, respectively—only the upholders of founding practices, standards, and alliances, in his evaluation, comprised the cause's best and truest embodiments. Vindicating abolitionism evolved into an even more restrictive undertaking in the book's second half.[42]

Regardless of Johnson's denial that he had any "enmities to gratify," his commemoration of a specific antislavery way came at the expense of non-Garrisonian reformers. Once Liberty Party promoters immersed themselves in the hustle and bustle of electoral politics, they reportedly forfeited the ethical high ground afforded by the abolitionist tactic of moral suasion. Rather than seek out the votes of individuals, Johnson's Garrisonians perpetually strove to "enlighte[n] the people" about slavery's real character. By winning the hearts and minds of white Americans through printed and spoken appeals, they sought to fashion "a public sentiment that would impel the National and State Governments to exercise all their constitutional powers" against chattel bondage. The *Liberator's* editor and his coadjutors therefore appreciated the value of "political action"; they just rejected the Liberty Party's necessity.[43]

The recollected Garrisonians resisted that abolitionist entry into party politics on the premise that a preexisting partisan coalition would draft an emancipatory platform as the electorate became morally and religiously renovated. They also believed that such activism would contaminate abolitionism's "purity" because the quest for ballot-box success inevitably required compromises of principle. That the Libertyites merged with antislavery-leaning Democrats and Whigs in 1848 was undeniable evidence of backsliding in the retrospective writer's analysis. Thus, by joining the Free-Soil Party they not only endorsed the presidential candidacy of the "political trickster" Martin Van Buren but also embraced a diluted humanitarian agenda that merely protested slavery's expansion westward.[44]

The church-oriented abolitionists, whom the author dubbed as "New Organizationists," reputedly abandoned the ecumenical scope of the immediate emancipation campaign once they left the AASS and set up the rival American and Foreign Anti-Slavery Society (AFASS). Their bid to purge founder Garrison from the national association needled Johnson decades after the fact. So too did their attempts at concurrently blocking the admission of women to full AASS membership status, which, in the end, permitted them to vote on institutional matters, serve on committees, and hold executive positions on an equal basis with men. Despite asserting that he had no desire to "revive the controversies of that day" or to "impeac[h] the motives of others," the partisan-cum-participant historian cast the architects of the AFASS in an unflattering light.[45]

While reflecting on how the church-oriented abolitionists processed the perceived religious extremism of the *Liberator's* editor, Johnson mustered some restraint. The narrator accordingly relayed their uneasiness toward Garrison's growing unorthodoxy, which supposedly frightened away conventional Christians and deterred the movement's overall success. Such evenhandedness vanished when he attributed the AASS schism itself to a sectarian conspiracy. The plot to oust Garrison constituted an "insidious effort to narrow" abolitionism, claimed Johnson, so that it "conform[ed] to the wishes of men, who, however sincerely they loved the cause, yet loved their sects far more." The defender of everything Garrisonian scarcely let bygones be bygones. He settled outstanding historical scores against all his chieftain's critics and adversaries, both within and without the antislavery crusade.[46]

Unlike the narrow-minded schemers, Johnson's Garrisonians clasped onto one of abolitionism's "noblest [and] most conspicuous" qualities—its openness. Only they, the author avouched, heartily received "every friend of immediate emancipation, without distinction of sect, party, caste, or sex." Such inclusiveness evidently triggered an internecine abolitionist confrontation at the AASS's 1840 annual meeting. Affairs reached a boiling point amid the nomination of Abigail Kelley to sit on an otherwise all-male business committee. After Kelley's Garrisonian supporters ensured her appointment, by an ample hundred-vote margin, the church-oriented sort exited the assemblage. The separatists, Johnson wryly commented, quickly forged a new affiliation under a "constitution [that] carefully guarded against the intrusion of women." By thwarting the machinations of a disgruntled faction, the remembered Garrison and Company fended off "a most mistaken and dangerous assault upon the [movement's] integrity." Whatever the sources of discord, an undisputedly Garrisonian AASS amounted to a crucial event for the retrospective writer. On a simple level, the group's organizational victory meant that only the doctrine of immediatism acted as a membership determinant. More substantively, it guaranteed the "pristine and vibrant" institutional "catholicity" that its leader Garrison had formulated.[47]

As custodians of cardinal abolitionist virtues against Libertyite innovators and New Organizationist usurpers, the Garrisonians surface from Johnson's personal chronicle and intimate biography as uniquely conservative. Nor did the author resort to any rhetorical sleight of hand by depicting radical agitators as stellar fundamentalists. The "Old Organizationists," he declared, stayed loyal to the AASS's "original foundation," as set down in the Garrison-composed "Declaration of Sentiments." Equipped with "the old plan," they battled "the enemy with constantly increasing energy and power" until the jubilation day of liberation had arrived. Such tenacity generated memorial wonderment, all the more so since abolitionism's splintering had "fearfully crippled" the post-1840 AASS in resource terms. Despite lacking "numbers," "wealth," and "social position,"

Johnson's Garrisonians took solace from the knowledge that "theirs was a war-fare . . . in which one, with God, is a majority." In so doing, they verified the potency of "purely moral instrumentalities" in remolding populations, further proving that they had divine providence on their side.[48]

Whereas fealty to abolitionist originalism allowed Garrisonian conserva-tors, whatever the logical paradox, to persist as "the advance guard of the whole anti-slavery host," the New Organizationists did not fare so well. The breakaway activists, the memorialist revealed, executed some good works, via the publica-tion of antislavery tracts and periodicals especially. Despite "a formidable show in the beginning," the AFASS, in his judgment, "expired for want of moral vi-tality after a feeble [thirteen-year] existence." Regardless of the "high standing and great popularity" of some, the church-oriented abolitionists never gained the backing of the spiritual communities whom a heretical Garrison had alleg-edly repelled. Since the New Organizationists "still denounced slavery as a sin and urged immediate emancipation as a duty," the supposed stigma that they so diligently wanted to avoid nonetheless accompanied them and their alterna-tive consortium. The evangelical divines of the North, as Johnson pointedly ob-served, "would no more follow" Lewis Tappan's lead than that of the *Liberator*'s editor, whose antislavery witness they always resented. Notwithstanding autho-rial statements to the contrary, vindicating Garrisonian abolitionism occasion-ally resulted in vindictiveness.[49]

For the partisan-cum-participant historian, Americans needed his testimony. "Ill-informed and prejudiced men" continuously belittled the consciousness-raising efforts of Garrison and his allies, he proclaimed, insisting that they had no impact on the Free-Soil or Republican Parties. The narrator knew better. His hardworking abolitionists plowed the very terrain of future vote-getting har-vests. Without the grassroots agitation of dedicated men and women, "who trod the field with bleeding feet" and withstood the "fiery trials as beset only the paths that martyrs . . . tread," the rich popular opinion that nourished both the Free-Soilers and Republicans would not have arisen. Time and again, Johnson con-tended that party operatives merely reaped what he and his collaborators had sown. Accurate or not, the argument pinpoints how the commemorator situated Garrisonian crusaders at the fore of an antislavery *Iliad*.[50]

Just as all abolitionists constituted a disciple of Garrison's, Johnson addition-ally posited that "every earnest anti-slavery worker in the field of politics was, however unconsciously, a follower" as well. Sympathetic politicians, he affirmed, immensely appreciated the Garrisonians, relying on them as "an independent influence" pushing "their parties up to a high [antislavery] level." Unimpaired by legislative stratagems and the expediency of party politics, they functioned, according to the authorial lesson, as an invaluable ethical compass. That principled minority also fortified the Union during a perilous secession crisis and civil war. Northerners, the retrospective writer vociferated, "needed all the strength which a whole generation of MORAL AGITATION had developed." Hardly a negligible factor in southern slavery's extinction, the crusade initiated by Garrison reached its destination, "more or less directly," thanks to his heroic service. Without a doubt, past and present misconceptions goaded the partisan-cum-participant historian.[51]

During and after the personal chronicle and intimate biography's preparation, the author engaged in multiple public rows that further document what fixated his post-Reconstruction thoughts. An epistolary spat framed the writing of the first edition of *William Lloyd Garrison and His Times*. While running the "Recollections of an Abolitionist" column, wherein Johnson impugned the mainline religious sects of the North, the *New-York Tribune* featured a lengthy 1879 letter in which the Reverend D. D. Whedon came to his denomination's rescue. As confirmation that Methodist-erected congregations always acted as northern "anti-slavery societies," the correspondent referenced, for example, church founder John Wesley. He also chided Johnson's "Garrisonian spectacles." Nobody so myopic, the epistler charged, "can write a true history" of abolitionism. Whedon, by comparison, suggested that he could assay things more veraciously, in spite of his never identifying with the abolitionists as a result of Garrison's notorious excesses. The Garrisonian "moral enterprise," in his brusque estimate, "was an ignominious failure," causing nothing but sectional turmoil and warfare. A Johnsonian communiqué materialized shortly thereafter.[52]

Johnson's reply began by ostensibly welcoming Whedon's admonitions. "I shall not wince," he professed, should the Methodist divine completely "tear my history to pieces." Rather than admit that such a dismantling had occurred, the single-minded Garrisonian countered another churchly onslaught. Methodism in the Old South, he pointed out, disciplined no one for trafficking in human flesh or extracting involuntary labor from Black people. In contrast to the denominational founding father, who memorably castigated slave trading as the "'sum of all villainies,'" northern Methodists, according to a censorious Johnson, reliably fellowshipped with slaveholding sinners. Such complicity only "emboldened" the master class to devise "an unqualified" justification of a "diabolical system." The Civil War's coming thus rested not on unrelenting Garrisonian reprobation of unchristian behavior but on those who "apologized" for enslavement, "compromised" with it, or silently watched its "deadly work."[53]

Since a second Whedon dispatch alluded to the good Christian slave owner so as to demolish Garrisonian moral reasoning, Johnson summoned straightforward abolitionist logic in his next reply. The notion of "'pious slaveholding,'" he opined, "is as much a solecism as 'pious gambling.'" A sin was a sin was a sin, according to that immutable antislavery worldview, and any past or present prevarication on the subject was itself sinful. Besides shredding the apparently slipshod thinking of his Methodist disputant, the partisan-cum-participant historian ripped the unfavorable reviews that had greeted his volume in the book's revised and expanded version. The section's descriptive title trumpets the combative tone and contents, for in it "the Criticisms of two Religious Journals are Weighed and Considered, the Subterfuges resorted to in Defense of a Recreant Ministry and Church exposed and swept away, and the Truth of History vindicated." Whatever his supposed receptiveness to outside critiques, Johnson consistently reacted to detractors by discrediting their commentaries.[54]

In 1882, the battle-tested Garrisonian crossed swords with George W. Julian of Indiana. With the *International Review* as the forum, the erstwhile radical abolitionist and the one-time Radical Republican disputed the issue of "modern" abolitionism's originator. Whereas a revisionist Julian claimed that Charles Osborn, an early-nineteenth-century Quaker active in Tennessee, Ohio, and Indiana, represented the movement's "real germ," a protective Johnson adamantly upheld Garrison as its paramount prophet and preacher. Osborn personally discovered the idea of immediate and unconditional emancipation in 1814, according to the Hoosier historian, when "Garrison was nine years old, and nearly a dozen years before . . . [England's] Elizabeth Heyrick" coined a similar phrase herself. As proof, he cited statements of contemporaneous Friends and reformers and passages from a short-lived newspaper that the Quaker in question had edited in 1817–1818, which Julian adjudged as the country's first antislavery periodical. Oliver Johnson was unimpressed.[55]

Despite nixing "any prejudice or personal feeling" in his rejoinder, Johnson wasted little space while picking apart Julian's findings. Osborn's advocate, he counterclaimed, entirely misunderstood the matter and mishandled primary sources, so much so that he fell "victim of a credulity more amiable than discriminating or judicious." For Garrison's guardian, Osborn could not have subscribed to the doctrine of immediatism beginning in the 1810s because of a key historical fact: The Garrisonian nomenclature had yet to exist. If the concept actually entered his head, the respondent argued, "the words would have dropped from his pen." Even though Johnson recognized the "tender-hearted" man as a "sincere opponent" of slavery, conferring an exalted status on him was preposterous. Unlike the pathbreaking *Liberator*'s editor, whose activism fundamentally altered American abolitionism, Osborn's reformism, Johnson observed, generally took place in out-of-the-way locales and "within the walls of his sleepy and almost apostate [Orthodox Quaker] sect." Nor did he approximate a Benjamin Lundy, whose *Genius of Universal Emancipation*, Johnson added, circulated as an unmistakable abolitionist publication, whereas Osborn's *Philanthropist* merely touched upon enslavement.[56]

Some months preceding the Johnson-Julian tussle, Theodore Bourne politely corrected Garrisonian dogma about who or what revolutionized antislavery. In the Whedon-managed *Methodist Quarterly Review*, he alerted readers that his father, the Reverend George Bourne, had laid the foundation upon which the *Liberator*'s editor and his associates rebuilt abolitionism. Starting in the 1810s, the elder Bourne championed "'immediate abolition without compensation,'" the very credo, the son explained, that demarcated new-school "*Abolitionists*" from old-school "*Emancipationists*." The "keen" and "pungent" language by which the Presbyterian pastor, lecturer, and writer had lambasted chattel bondage also established an arsenal of invectives that empowered subsequent crusaders. To enhance his case, the essayist incorporated an 1858 endorsement from no less an authority than Garrison himself. With such a reference letter, maybe Johnson felt constrained to promptly respond. Since the younger Bourne's modernist trinity included the *Liberator*'s editor, he had no compelling reason to do so. When Johnson formally assessed those acclamations, in 1885, he unhesitatingly commended a Garrisonian forerunner of the 1810s. Yet while noting that Bourne also authored "immensely serviceable" writings as an 1830s follower of Garrison's, the assessor less charitably indicated that he had suspended his strife with southern slaveholders in order to "fight against Roman Catholicism" during the 1820s.[57]

Shortly after the release of the updated *William Lloyd Garrison and His Times*, Elizur Wright, a founding member of the AASS and an important movement journalist, indirectly complicated Johnson's contention that the Garrisonians had made antislavery at the ballot box possible and successful. As a proponent of political abolitionism himself, he advanced that the upstate New Yorker Myron Holley did the groundwork that resulted in the Liberty Party's creation during his lifetime, as well as the formation of the Free-Soil and Republican parties that followed his passing. Even though Wright noted that the *Liberator*'s editor suffered from some limitations—namely, his proslavery interpretation of the Constitution and nonresistance ideology—his criticism sparked no Johnsonian retort. Perhaps, the privately printed study simply escaped the staunch Garrisonian's notice. If it had not, he would have encountered plaudits echoing his own.

Wright's Garrison occupied both the "heart and head" of the great "moral" campaign against slavery, and was a vaunted humanitarian deserving of "more glory than he has received." Johnson could not have asked for anything more.[58]

The keeper of all things Garrisonian, however, did not allow a blatant 1883 broadside by Leonard Woolsey Bacon to go unreturned. In a *Century Magazine* piece praising the accomplishments of a deceased parent—the Yale-educated divine and Congregationalist minister Leonard Bacon—the filial eulogist berated Johnson's companions. For Woolsey Bacon, the sensible and moderate antislavery advocacy of reformers like the Bacon patriarch eventually carried the day for emancipation, not the AASS's perennially unsuccessful "long-haired men and short-haired women." The younger Bacon specifically disdained abolitionism's putative leader, whose "false positions, bad logic, and in some cases malignant passions" annoyed the son as much as they had bothered the father. Barely anyone beyond Garrison's "little ring" of sycophants, he asserted, believed in slaveholding sinfulness. To further undercut the cachet of the *Liberator*'s editor, Woolsey Bacon stressed that enslavement's demise came about from "principles which he abhorred" and "by measures . . . he denounced." Since Garrison and his crew needlessly antagonized many "good men at the South," the remembered Bacon appropriately focused his energies on those purportedly dangerous fanatics and the damages that they had inflicted.[59]

In retaliation, Johnson discharged an open letter wherein he strategically resurrected a topic studiously avoided by Woolsey Bacon. Regardless of the elder Bacon's later opposition to slavery's territorial extension, Johnson accented the colonizationist bigotry that blighted much of his philanthropy. For more than two decades, the inveterate Garrisonian harangued, he lent his "voice and pen" to African American removal. Equally heinous, Bacon never "publicly renounced" the ACS, even after moving away from it. The sins of the father only got darker, though. The esteemed divine, whom Johnson quoted in this takedown as well as the book, once wickedly stated that Black liberation could not transpire on domestic soil, because "'you cannot raise him [the slave] from the abyss of his degradation [or] bleach him into the enjoyment of freedom.'" The missive writer reminded the younger Bacon, himself a Congregationalist clergyman, of a "simple truth"—his daddy ranked as "one of the blind leaders of the blind multitude." Swathed in a dense "metaphysical cloud" of his own choosing, this recollected Bacon always sought to obstruct the clear-sighted Garrisonians. A vigilant Johnson never shrank while facing antiabolitionist sectarian plots.[60]

Nor did he let slide a venomous attack on the Garrisonian legacy by Eli Thayer. In a pair of 1886 lectures, which appeared as a pamphlet during the next year,

Thayer voiced magnificent hosannas on behalf of the New England Emigrant Aid Company (NEEAC) that he had founded. By supposedly spoiling the Slave Power's expansionistic designs on the Kansas Territory, his agency forever changed the course of US history. It allegedly set the Republican Party in motion; stiffened the antislavery will of northerners; spurred desperate slaveholders toward secessionism; saved "the white race of the South, as well as the negroes, from the evils of Slavery"; and spawned an everlasting Union that still produced "regenerating" effects throughout the former Confederacy. While acclaiming "ORGANIZED AND ASSISTED EMIGRATION," Thayer repeatedly ridiculed Garrison and his acolytes, so much so, that denigrating a "noisy and pugnacious . . . cabal" often made lauding the NEEAC a secondary consideration.[61]

As a result of the "persistent clack and endless scribbling" of Garrisonian hero-worshippers, Thayer spotted a terrible historical trend whereby Americans increasingly assumed that the *Liberator*'s editor was an antislavery "Alpha and Omega." Except for the waves of "crying women and children" at their sentimental get-togethers, the paltry and minuscule Garrisonians whom he recalled wielded no influence whatsoever. The coterie's "revolutionary methods," according to this appraisal, only rendered devotees as a collection of out-of-touch activists and attention-getting charlatans. Thayer therefore charted sundry Garrisonian defects and defeats, the most provocative of which accused an otherwise inconsequential group with worsening the "burdens" of unfree African Americans. Nothing but his own quietus would have inhibited a nearly eighty-year-old Oliver Johnson from counterattacking.[62]

He initially aired his grievances before the patrons of the Worcester Society of Antiquity, the same Massachusetts site where Thayer had delivered his talks. At the outset, Johnson granted that "no individual, society, party, or clique" could take sole credit for slavery's annihilation. Aspiring annalists of the antislavery crusade, especially if they had contributed to it, should not abuse others "who labored . . . by means different from his [or her] own, or in ways that he [or she] did not wholly approve." Despite that precautionary advice, Johnson mainly shielded the Garrisonians from yet another defamatory barrage. In so doing, he introduced nothing new while returning Thayer's fire. His riposte, about twenty pages in its printed form, parsed the combatant's "boastful," "exaggerated," and "vituperative" handiwork, ultimately deeming it as "worthless" history. Given the "gratuitous and flippant abuse," however, Thayer's assayer pondered aloud his late-in-life mission. Since the passing of the *Liberator*'s editor, he modestly remarked, "it has been my duty to write on several occasions in defense of him and the movement" that he animated.[63]

In February 1889, Johnson proffered a seemingly final Garrisonian justification. Unlike the aggressive posture typifying his regular clashes with Garrison's
posthumous calumniators, the Brooklyn Congregational Club's special guest
evinced greater ease as he discussed favorite themes. Despite softening the edges
of arguments regarding a spiritually dilapidated Christianity before the Civil
War, the partisan-cum-participant historian still noted that the North's evangelical ministry and churches wrongfully stonewalled a deeply religious cause.
Regardless of a comparatively balanced treatment of the AASS "seceders"—the
movement, he stated, had grown "too vast in its ramifications to be represented
exclusively by any single organization or method of work"—the stalwart Garrisonian predictably hailed the *Liberator*'s editor as abolitionism's indispensable
man. At one point, he divulged a Lincolnian acknowledgment about how the
crusading Garrisonians had nurtured "the public sentiment" that enabled the
Emancipation Proclamation. The speaker also shared a less-heralded presidential pronouncement, whereby Honest Abe, in conversation with a South Carolina
officeholder, accredited his antislavery policy "to the fidelity of the soldiers and
'the logic of Garrison.'" Even though Johnson did not explicitly scuffle with anyone, his skirmish with real and imaginary enemies at the gates of history scarcely
subsided.[64]

The story of abolitionism undeniably consumed Johnson's twilight years. He
told and retold how a small but irrepressible band of agitators spearheaded the
immediate emancipation campaign against immense obstacles and considerable
setbacks. In a synopsis of the book's first edition, a *New-York Tribune* reviewer
commented that the "volume abounds in passages of true descriptive power,
sometimes rising to impassioned eloquence, showing that the inspirations of
youth and the convictions of manhood have not been impaired by the lapse of
[time] and the vicissitudes of life." That combination of boyish enthusiasm and
elderly insight did not translate into any involvement in an ongoing African
American freedom struggle. It motivated, however, a decade-long project concentrating on present and future interpretations of antislavery's actual GOP—the
Garrisonians.[65]

Amazingly, not even death stopped Johnson from speaking afresh, for he
buoyed his mentor's exceptional and exemplary spirituality once more in a post-
mortem pamphlet. As a compilation of quotations on organized religion and
personal faith, the author gifted readers with Garrison's aphorisms for their contemplation. Even though Johnson never exhibited outright indifference toward
the fate of the formerly enslaved, as a retrospective writer he heavily invested
in safeguarding the historical significance of Garrisonian abolitionism. In the

personal chronicle and intimate biography, he proclaimed that the *Liberator*'s editor had educated and improved him more than "any college or theological seminary could have done." That schooling arguably comprised his most precious possession, precisely why he frequently wrote and spoke in vindication of a transformative teacher. While taking shelter behind Garrison the glorious emancipator, the partisan-cum-participant historian sidestepped emancipation's problematic aftermath.[66]

4 Antislavery Sanctified

*Parker Pillsbury and the Spirit
of Abolitionism in the Fields*

"Everybody now is anti-slavery," an exasperated Parker Pillsbury announced in an 1883 memoir. Safely removed from a fiery and contentious antebellum past, startling amounts of postbellum Americans falsely claimed, according to the allegation, an abolitionist appellation or bloodline. Even worse, such after-the-fact activists reportedly assumed an unmerited accolade, too. To Pillsbury's infinite annoyance, philanthropic poseurs and latecomers rejoiced at how they themselves had effaced "the sublimest scourge and curse that ever afflicted the human race." As a veteran foot soldier of the decades-long fight to immediately free the enslaved, he knew that limited numbers of adherents had actually populated and propelled the campaign. The retrospective writer consequently intended *Acts of the Anti-Slavery Apostles* to enlighten the public on the interrelated questions of who the bona-fide abolitionists were and what their "genuine, uncompromising" activism entailed. Ironically, disabusing or reproving anyone who had misappropriated the movement prompted the author to reappropriate it himself. The mission to sanctify the immediate emancipation faithful, in many respects, had nothing to do with abolitionism itself.[1]

Constructing an honest and accurate account certainly motivated the memoirist. His stated desire to serve "the cause of truth and the demands of history" contained deeper mainsprings as well. On a basic level, Pillsbury sought to bridge a perceived knowledge gap. The current generation, he observed, possessed a meager understanding of "the outrages and horrors" surrounding southern slavery. Nor did it appreciate the abolitionists' "desperate and deadly encounters with th[at] monster." Other factors added a sense of urgency to his undertaking. While preparing his volume, abolitionism's "old opponents or their children," he apprised readers, issued articles "declaring that they or their fathers" had brought about enslavement's elimination in the United States. They further asserted that that difficult endeavor could have happened earlier and more easily "'had [William Lloyd] Garrison and his small, but motley following' been out of their way!" Pillsbury thus confronted not only the misdirected pretensions and self-congratulations of bogus reformers in the present but also longstanding accusations that had distorted and still tarnished the immediate emancipation campaign. Each problem, as it turned out, emanated from a common source.[2]

That Protestant ministers propagated flagrant misinformation in the 1880s an unsurprised commemorator adjudged as wholly consistent with vigorous ecclesiastical antagonism to the abolitionists since the 1830s. The perennial misdeeds of abolitionism's reverend nemeses therefore provided the chronicler with a highly meaningful mandate to reflect on and record historical rights and wrongs. In a narrative spanning five hundred pages, he seemingly did what similarly inclined memorialists had already done. An ostensibly unoriginal Pillsbury honored the morally courageous and religiously outstanding Garrisonians with whom he intimately associated. He also exposed, as irredeemably corrupted and spiritually moribund, the nation's Christian clergy and denominations. As the book's principal villains, however, dreadful antiabolitionist churchmen function as a dramatic foil to the saintly antislavery agitators whom only Pillsbury eulogized at length—itinerant field workers.[3]

Meditating on the brave and selfless exploits of those crusaders comprised a very special authorial assignment. During the 1840s and 1850s, Pillsbury had traveled across New England, the Mid-Atlantic, and the Old Northwest in order to disseminate the gospel of immediatism and accumulate converts for the American Anti-Slavery Society. As a battle-scarred lecturing agent, he witnessed and withstood the personal suffering, physical hardships, and financial sacrifices that had defined such a career. The memoirist, then, did not indulge in sheer hyperbole by equating the apostolic abolitionists of his epoch to ancient biblical predecessors. Both, he averred, "literally 'went everywhere preaching the word,' often with their lives in their hands." In the process of highlighting the ordeals by fire that he and other grassroots organizers habitually endured, the retrospective writer underscored how community builders and consciousness-raisers epitomized both authentic abolitionism and unalloyed religiosity. Since many field-service collaborators had passed away, the septuagenarian Pillsbury subsequently deemed himself as duty bound to "cherish their memory . . . with tenderest affection" and "shield it from any unjust reproach to the full extent of my power." Not all antislavery circuit riders, however, were suitable candidates for canonization.[4]

The abolitionist holy warriors whom the author revered also championed some variety of "comeouterism," that is, acts of secession from supposedly proslavery-infested churches. By contesting American Christianity's collusion with chattel bondage, Parker's pilgrims did not just cleanse themselves of all attachments to spiritually contaminated institutions. They also manifested "true" credentials as modern-day prophets, in his evaluation, given their obeying the Book of Revelation decree: "'Come out of them, my people, that ye be not partakers of their sins, and receive not of their plagues.'" A devout Pillsbury enacted that scriptural commandment himself within a couple years of embracing abolitionism. As a Garrisonian defender of the "unimpeachable doctrine of human equality before the law," he broke away from a conventional pastoral calling as well as a corresponding Congregationalist identity by the early 1840s. With good reasons, the comeouter ethos in which he had steeped his own brand of reformism fittingly informed and revealingly suffuses his narrative. Yet the memorial and historical errand on which he set out ultimately came at the expense of racial egalitarianism. The martyr spirit of antislavery in the fields was unquestionably mighty; for Pillsbury, however, it no longer affected American race relations.[5]

During the same year that the memoirist placed "a thirty years moral [and spiritual] conflict" in a seemingly inapplicable past, the Supreme Court struck down the 1875 Civil Rights Act. That measure, a version of which Senator Charles Sumner of Massachusetts had introduced in 1870 but died nearly twelve months before its passage, prohibited racial discrimination in public accommodations (hotels, restaurants, and theaters) and on public conveyances (steamboats, streetcars, and railroads). It also forbade the exclusion of citizens from jury service based on considerations of race, color, or previous condition of servitude. In its original form, the wider-ranging bill that Sumner had crafted, and for which the African American congressmen James T. Rapier of Mississippi and Robert Brown Elliot of South Carolina prominently campaigned, disallowed racial segregation in public schools, too. Since the Fourteenth Amendment, according to the high court's ruling majority, pertained to state actions only, Congress lacked the constitutional authority to adopt legislation regulating the private behavior of individuals. Whatever the logic behind that decision, it signaled a jeopardized status for equal Black rights under US governmental protection. If those postbellum events emboldened or aggravated Pillsbury, he expressed no such emotions in his rendition of antebellum abolitionism.[6]

While thinking about deceased antislavery saints, a defunctive southern reconstruction never directly entered the retrospective writer's ruminations. Regardless of returning white Democratic rule and the uncertainty that it created for the formerly enslaved, Pillsbury's stories testify, in subtle and perceptible ways, to his absence from an ongoing African American freedom struggle. Elucidating how the abolitionists had grappled with northern Protestantism's endemic moral degradation represented a more potent and pressing theme for reminiscing. By recounting their headway against spiritual tyranny in the past, the chronicler concurrently suggested the need for eternal watchfulness on behalf of soul liberty in the present and future. The commemorator produced a useable antebellum history, after all, and it overlapped with his postbellum liberal religious allegiances and perpetual mistrust of Christian orthodoxy. As will be seen, matters of faith—namely, his Spiritualist sympathies and involvement with the Free Religious Association (FRA)—surpassed and displaced those of race.[7]

Even before the collapse of Republican state governments across the Southland by 1877, Pillsbury evinced a personal modification of, but not an outright retreat from, the abolitionist quest for racial justice. By the late 1860s, he had distanced himself from colleagues seeking to uphold abolitionism's institutional existence amid a rapidly changing postemancipation world. More than anything else, his alliance with Elizabeth Cady Stanton and Susan B. Anthony, whose shared goal comprised equal rights for *all* people, resulted in alienation from peers pushing for the freedmen's civil and political rights first. Whereas most antislavery crusaders celebrated Reconstruction-era constitutional amendments as movement capstones, Stanton, Anthony, and Pillsbury reacted less cheerfully. They criticized the Fourteenth Amendment, because its framers thrice inserted the word "male" into the language of Section 2, thereby implying sex-based criteria for US citizenship and voting privileges. They also opposed the ratification of the Fifteenth Amendment because its enfranchisement provision benefited African American men only. Such criticism and opposition generated friction among AASS backers. Despite directing the *National Anti-Slavery Standard* from June 1865 to May 1866, Pillsbury essentially withdrew from the network not long after relinquishing his editorial duties.[8]

Unlike their former AASS allies, Stanton, Anthony, and other feminist abolitionists believed that the times warranted across-the-board advancements, especially a fully impartial suffrage. With such aims in mind, they commenced the radical women's rights journal *The Revolution* in 1868; founded the National Woman Suffrage Association in 1869; and, after the 1870 ratification of the colorblind Fifteenth Amendment, called for another constitutional addendum that would grant a gender-neutral franchise. The "emancipation of woman," according to Stanton's pithy explanation in her 1898 autobiography, constituted "the most momentous reform yet launched upon the world." As an avid supporter, Pillsbury coedited the New York–based *Revolution* during a two-year tenure. After his close affiliation with Stanton and Anthony had ended, he continued seconding their views in lectures and pamphlets.[9]

Even though the postbellum Pillsbury steadily shifted his reformist resources, he did not entirely abandon African Americans once the US Constitution forever

outlawed enslavement. In numerous *Revolution* pieces, he censured northern political conservatism on the issue of Black rights and called attention to the freedpeople's impoverishment. In two 1867 tracts, furthermore, he chided the Republican Party for its purportedly sham liberality and progressiveness. By the early
1870s, however, the church of humanity dominated his philanthropic energies.
In the pursuit of freedom of conscience and universal spirituality, the FRA, as
its 1867 charter affirmed, prioritized a rational, scientifically oriented study of
religion and ethics. Fundamentally against religious sectarianism and customary
modes of authority, the group formed a "spiritual anti-slavery Society," in the
words of its founder, William J. Potter. That veteran abolitionists participated in
the inaugural meeting, such as Charles C. Burleigh, Octavius Brooks Frothingham, Thomas Wentworth Higginson, Oliver Johnson, and Lucretia Mott, only
strengthened Potter's reference. Besides supplanting feminism, Pillsbury's espousal of Free Religion superseded his diminishing racial justice activism.[10]

The FRA's quarrel with mainstream clergymen and churches, according to
Pillsbury's reckoning, replicated and augmented comeouterism. He formally
joined the coalition in 1870 and frequently contributed to its official periodical,
The Index. He also peddled Free Religion throughout the North via a tried-and-
true technique: interacting with potentially receptive audiences as a traveling field
agent. In so doing, the seasoned evangelist revived the community building and
consciousness-raising that had characterized his abolitionist experiences. Past
and present seamlessly dovetailed as the Free Religionist program approximated,
for Pillsbury himself, another antislavery venture. Whereas he had originally
sought the release of enslaved men and women from the unchristian thralldom
of despotic slave masters, the resolute crusader now targeted the superstitious
servitude that oppressive ecclesiastics inflicted on many more souls. The new
campaign did not simply fill a humanitarian void in his life; it simultaneously
rendered the older one's loftier racial equity objectives as personally irrelevant.
Abolitionism remained instructive, but mainly as a guide in the unending battle
against spiritual slaveholders.[11]

In a series of early 1870s communiqués that the *Index* circulated, the FRA
missionary reminded readers of a "hateful, horrible system of religious faith,
practice, and worship" that had prevailed in the United States. Spiteful or not,
Pillsbury dispatched muckraking epistles about antebellum Christianity in order
to instigate an up-to-date exodus. "I sometimes think," he relayed to the editor,
"that could you . . . only disclose the history of that religion and its ministry as
connected with American slavery, your work and warfare would be done." The
inextricable ties between Christian congregations and a nefarious institution,

the correspondent opined, irreparably disfigured the former with "an audacity of wickedness *in practice* unparalleled in the annals of human depravity." The evidence that Pillsbury marshaled in this and other missives made his point abundantly clear: Responsible individuals should have separated from such a religious establishment, and that religion's proslavery past still required them to do so in the present. *Acts of the Anti-Slavery Apostles* allowed him to make both cases more exhaustively.[12]

The confluence of pre- and postwar spiritual concerns recurs in Pillsbury's narrative. It uniquely surfaces in the opening chapter on Garrison. Like other commemorators before him, the chronicler deified the *Liberator*'s editor. Besides figuring as abolitionism's "divinely constituted leader," Pillsbury designated him as the first to annunciate "the prophetic word" that sealed what the American Revolutionary generation had started. Since that heavenly activist had initiated an abolitionist renaissance in the United States, he and his disciples personified the immediate emancipation campaign to an extent unlike any of their contemporaries or rivals, at least for the memoirist. The "Garrisonian movement" and the antislavery crusade, in his eyes, were consequently identical and indivisible. Despite the internecine divisions that had flared up during the 1860s, he never reassessed that axiomatic fact.[13]

At the beginning of the Civil War, the Garrisonians disagreed on the proper relationship between the AASS and the Lincoln administration. Once the sectional hostilities had reached a terminus, they quickly diverged over the society's responsibilities toward the freedpeople. Such infighting did not reappear in Pillsbury's memorial portrait of the abolitionist patriarch—not in an obvious manner, anyway. In the book's closing chapter, however, he alluded to the 1865 annual assemblage wherein AASS members debated their association's fate. Even though the author quoted a resolution that he had submitted, in which he urged partners to carry on with their corporate activities until African American men possessed the same civil and political rights as whites, he never brought up Garrison's contrary wartime stances. Had Pillsbury done so, he might have revealed how the respective positions that he and the *Liberator*'s editor held mirrored a broader organizational rift.[14]

Whereas Garrison eventually defended Lincoln's handling of emancipation and endorsed his presidential reelection, Pillsbury was one of Honest Abe's sharpest abolitionist detractors, so much so that he engaged in a short-lived effort to elect a different Republican—John C. Fremont—in 1864. Unlike Garrison, Pillsbury rejected the notion that southern slavery's destabilization, in conjunction with congressional approval of a constitutional amendment that would demolish it, had finalized the business of abolitionism. The discrepancies that upset Garrisonian solidarity, as well as culminated in Garrison's vacating his AASS membership, did not hang around indefinitely. By referring to an 1879 letter wherein he saluted the antislavery chieftain on the "successful completion of his life-mission," the retrospective writer implied that a mending of their friendship, in particular, had taken place. That Pillsbury largely omitted the Garrisonians' Civil War–era bickering from his historical storytelling should come as no surprise. How he utilized the humanitarianism of the *Liberator's* editor on behalf of past and present comeouterism spotlights something far more significant.[15]

In a nineteen-page synopsis of Garrison's legendary career, the memoirist mostly concentrated on key incidents of the 1830s. Whatever the narrated episode—from his stint as coeditor of *The Genius of Universal Emancipation*, in 1829–1830, to his cofounding the New England Non-Resistance Society, in 1838—Pillsbury emphasized that the spirit of Jesus always animated the visionary abolitionist. When the *Liberator's* editor trumpeted a "new and more excellent [antislavery] evangel," as the chronicler attested, he unequivocally represented a "New Testament Christian." Certifying that a radical activist subscribed, at first, to viewpoints of "the whole Evangelical church" comprised a strategically important authorial move, just as it had for commemorative precursors. Once again, the reality of a religiously orthodox Garrison undercut the infidelity charge— passed on "from the university and theological seminary down to the humblest village pastors, churches, and Sunday-schools"—that continuously harried him. That Garrison believed wholeheartedly in "the inspiration and authority of the Bible," as well as "the Trinity and Atonement," also displayed the hypocritical religiosity of his critics. Only after clergymen widely condemned the good news of immediate and unconditional emancipation, according to a common Garrisonian refrain, did the *Liberator's* editor reorient his sacred compass and march in other directions. However derivative or clichéd, that recited progression nicely melded with Pillsbury's singular preoccupations, as his pious wayfarer discarded a decayed evangelicalism in search of greater authenticity.[16]

As a Sermon on the Mount Christian, Pillsbury's Garrison strictly abided by the injunctions to "Resist not Evil" and "love your enemies." Virtually unceasing "opposition and persecution" prodded him to reconsider those precepts not at all. Antagonistic evangelical ecclesiastics nonetheless liberated the *Liberator's* editor, prompting him to scrutinize their "faiths and formulas." The recollected Garrison thus arose from his reexamination convinced that the predominant Protestant sects were empty moral and spiritual vessels. He also questioned the verbal, plenary inspiration of Holy Scripture. Yet, the comeouter of this specific tale never succumbed to doubtfulness. Despite abjuring the nation's religious establishment, his "venerat[ion]" of the Bible continued unabated. Besides unfailing devotion to "the christian doctrines of peace, purity, and liberty," the remembered Garrison became infinitely open-minded to "whatever new truth might appear." Unique among Garrisonian hagiographers, Pillsbury crowned his discussion of the abolitionist seer by delineating him as a Spiritualist seeker.[17]

Materializing in the late 1840s, Spiritualism offered Pillsbury's Garrison with a much-needed sanctuary from, as well as surrogate for, evangelical Protestantism. Since no downtrodden or maltreated being "appealed in vain" to the *Liberator's* editor, that enlightened and exalted reformer, in turn, constituted a safe haven for the Spiritualists. Their conviction that departed souls could communicate with the living consummated, for the retrospective writer, a lifetime of altruistic striving in which Garrison, envisaging humanity's universal reformation, had battled against the sins of "intemperance, slavery, war, capital punishment, and woman's enslavement." Whereas many antislavery peers evidently regarded the Spiritualists "with contempt and scorn," the exceptional *Liberator's* editor "found, and to the end of his life believed, that he had literally entertained angels, and angels not unawares." Interestingly, in an 1871 letter to the *Index*, the FRA missionary seemingly isolated himself from Spiritualism, maintaining that he "in no way" affiliated with the phenomenon. That assertion, however, does not problematize the 1883 portrayal of Garrison's evolving credo.[18]

Lacking alignment never approximated sympathetic absence, for Pillsbury trusted that interactions with spirits of the dead, through mediums and at séances, empirically proved the soul's immortality. Indeed, in the same 1871 dispatch, the grassroots organizer proposed that the Free Religionists should themselves take the Spiritualists as an activist model. "Wherever I go," he proclaimed, "no other single association is doing more, if so much, for human emancipation and elevation." The field agent specifically extolled the Spiritualists' forward-thinking exertions on behalf "of Temperance, Rights of Woman, of Labor, and of religious . . . toleration." The memoirist, then, could accentuate Garrison's Spiritualism without the slightest reservation. The prophetic abolitionist whom he praised was a vital link between the liberal religious past and present.[19]

To illuminate the subject, the chronicler incorporated an 1854 *Liberator* piece on "'spiritual manifestations'" witnessed by the editor at a New York gathering, as well as an 1870 funerary address in which Garrison vindicated the Spiritualist persuasion of a recently departed Henry Clarke Wright. Equipped with such evidence, Pillsbury confirmed that Garrison "yoked" Spiritualism "to his chariot of salvation," regardless of the "deep regret" that some unnamed friends had felt about his transformation. For the commemorator, though, Garrison's Spiritualist advocacy approximated his earlier promulgation of the abolitionist gospel of immediatism, as the revelations of the new cause composed another "sublime Evangel." That the author closed a nineteen-page survey with a multipage appraisal of that antislavery saint's alternative faith indicated that his usefulness, in the 1880s, had nothing to do with racial justice. Nor did Pillsbury seize the memorial moment ten years later to make any historical amends.[20]

A public unveiling of a Garrison statue on July 4, 1893, presented a seemingly perfect occasion to expound on the patriotic services of the *Liberator*'s editor and expand the revolutionary boundaries of a nationally celebrated day. Despite railing against the "cruelties and horrors of the whole slave system," speaker Pillsbury offered nothing substantive about the enduring meaning of the Second American Revolution that a towering figure supposedly fomented. Apart from rejoicing that the progenitor of the immediate emancipation campaign in the United States had "lived to see the triumph of his warfare" and recommending a multivolume biography of Garrison by his children, much of Pillsbury's oration consists of references to George Washington, the Marquis de Lafayette, and Boston's Bunker Hill Monument. Even though he treated Garrison's abolitionism as a thing of the past, the latter's legacy was palpable nevertheless. For anyone unsatisfied with traditional religion, Garrison's broad-mindedness, as recorded in *Acts of the Anti-Slavery Apostles*, provided an uplifting example.[21]

Next to the *Liberator*'s editor, Nathaniel Peabody Rogers and Stephen Symonds Foster also play starring roles in Pillsbury's production. The retrospective writer idolized those agitators in part because of their contributions to the Garrisonian crusade against slavery's ecclesiastical accomplices in the North. Pillsbury devoted ample space to cherishing them for more intimate reasons as well: He shared their trials, as they did his. Stationed in New Hampshire, all three struggled to sow abolitionist seeds across the Granite State's hostile terrain. The Rogers and Foster of this tale therefore completed an antislavery trinity and anticlerical triumvirate that had commenced with prime mover Garrison. Their antebellum lives afforded instructive lessons to postbellum readers, too, none of which was relevant to racial egalitarianism.[22]

Since Americans knew "far too little" about the *Herald of Freedom*'s editor, Pillsbury sought to restore a reputedly forgotten comrade to a rightful historical place. He initially attempted to do so in an 1869 *Revolution* essay, which he enlarged upon nearly fifteen years later. The memoirist articulated Rogers's deserved preeminence by designating him as "a high priest in the great fellowship of humanity" and declaring that the newspaperman had carried out his duties "wondrously" and "divinely" until an early death prevented further achievements. From the moment that he donned an abolitionist mantle, Pillsbury's Rogers was an "unshaken" and "uncompromising" friend of the slave as well as a loyal associate of the "Garrisonian school." Besides depending solely on moral-action strategies and tactics in order to "rescue" the enslaved and "redeem" the world, he demonstrated both a catholic humanitarianism and well-rounded humanism.[23]

As a universal reformer, the Rogers of this narrative espoused "temperance, peace, rights of woman, abolition of the gallows and halter, and other" movements. As a renaissance man, he possessed an impressive knowledge of poetry, history, and jurisprudence. Overflowing "with music . . . and culture of every kind," the memory of Rogers's fireside recitations of Shakespeare, Robert Burns, Walter Scott, and Lord Byron left an indelible imprint on Pillsbury. Such an individual apparently posed a compositional problem. Any suitable commemoration, the author propounded, "would require a genius and inspiration like his own." To better communicate the "character and work" of a mentor and friend, he simply sampled Rogers's oeuvre. Enlisting two *Herald of Freedom* writings, for instance, allowed the chronicler to capsulize his subject's fine intellect and expert craftmanship.[24]

In one, entitled "The Presence of God," an evangelically directed Rogers trenchantly reviewed an article that a Unitarian periodical had printed. In the other, a sightseeing Rogers evocatively described an Irish Sea topographical attraction— the jutting rock formation known as the Ailsa Craig—which he had encountered during an 1840–1841 expedition to the British Isles. Of the eighteen-plus pages that make up the biographical sketch, those journalistic excerpts jointly consume about half the chapter's length. Neither concerns abolitionism. It does not follow that Pillsbury overlooked Rogers's antislavery dissent. Elsewhere in the book, he copiously cited the latter's newspaper reports on abolitionist comings and goings in New Hampshire, specifically those regarding the labors of local field agents. In so doing, the retrospective writer documented both his personal experiences and Rogers's philanthropic significance. Whereas the memoirist himself represents the historian of antislavery comeouterism, the frequently quoted Rogers operates as a historic comeouter columnist. In addition to furnishing vital press coverage, his very own pilgrim's progress bolstered Pillsbury's confrontations with conventional Christianity.[25]

Evincing the utmost integrity, the recollected Rogers "was a christian in the divinest, sublimest sense of that still mysterious and much abused word." Similar to Garrison, Rogers entered the abolitionist fold thoroughly committed to evangelical Protestantism. Unlike Garrison's Baptist upbringing, Rogers grew

up in the denominational home of the New England Puritans. After noting a
nine-generation Congregationalist pedigree, the author stressed that passivity
or thoughtlessness in no way characterized his fealty to the ancestral church.
Having diligently "studied and considered" its doctrines, Pillsbury's Rogers promulgated them "eloquently" and no less "tenderly." That conscientious disciple
ultimately rejected not merely the faith of his fathers but the American religious
establishment more generally. Pillsbury related how the fierce antiabolitionism
of pastors and parishioners induced the *Herald of Freedom*'s editor—just as it had
the *Liberator*'s—to reevaluate evangelicalism's holy foundations.[26]

As Rogers remembered those in bonds as bound with them in chains, another
biblically derived imperative enacted by every genuine Christian of Pillsbury's
memoir, he soon detected that coreligionists did not share the same compassionate outlook. To his astonishment, evangelical ecclesiastics, rather than serve
as "the divinely appointed instrumentality" for immediately emancipating the
slaves, emerged as inimical foes of a Christ-imbued mission. Indeed, because of
his antislavery agitation, Rogers's reputation drastically deteriorated among fellow members of the Plymouth Congregational Church. Previously commended
for charitable deeds, seemingly everyone, Pillsbury pointed out, suddenly reproached him as a "disorderly, contumacious disturbe[r] of the peace." Uncou-
pling from time-honored ties did not transpire until Rogers realized that false
Christians could do what true ones could not.[27]

Since his place of worship "welcome[d] to the pulpit and sacramental table"
visiting slaveholders and denied that courtesy to devout abolitionists, a purifying Rogers separated himself from such wickedness. He thenceforward strove,
the comeouter historian elucidated, to liberate others. To no one else, Pillsbury
broadcasted, "does the . . . [American public] owe more . . . for exposing and
rebuking the arrogance and insolence, not to say down-right fraud and dishon-
esty," of an entire class of people. He particularly lauded the *Herald of Freedom*'s
editorials as "fresh and new" but dispersed them throughout the text not because
they forcefully transmitted the iniquity of southern enslavers or inhumanity of
perpetual servitude. Their freshness and newness rotated, instead, about the editor's powerful revelations of slavery-abetting northern clergymen.[28]

Whereas Pillsbury esteemed Rogers's "descriptive articles" as "unsurpassed in
life and vigor, brilliancy and beauty," he upheld his newspaper denunciations of
antiabolitionist churchmen as "scathing, withering, but always eminently just."
With good reasons, he hoped that readers would personally revisit or discover
a supremely "gifted writer." That a single-volume collection of Rogers's handiwork vanished from the marketplace "long ago" prompted an impassioned

appeal from Pillsbury. He urged some publishing firm or enterprising individual to "scatte[r] everywhere" up-to-date editions, which would stand out, according to his prognostication, as a "shining constellation among the dimmer stars." For the memoirist, postbellum reformers could prosper immensely from that antebellum light source. Specially "anointed to perceive all spiritual and moral truth," the rich and thrilling words of the *Herald of Freedom*'s editor had exposed an ungodly religious ministry and subsequently formed an invaluable patrimony for Free Religionists. Pillsbury, however, invoked a very different Rogerian tradition as the *Revolution*'s coeditor. He beseeched Reconstruction-era Americans to replicate Nathaniel's root-and-branch essence because ending enslavement via "'military necessity' is not justice, nor repentance, nor righteousness." A "dense forest" of racial inequity blanketing the 1869 United States evidently disappeared by 1883.[29]

Besides sparking a revival of interest in Rogers's literary activism, the retrospective writer tried to repair a broken partnership. In his rendering of Garrison, Pillsbury ignored the discord that marred his collaboration with the illustrious abolitionist during the 1860s. He similarly suppressed an 1840s falling out with Rogers. By publicizing that an exchange of letters occurred before Garrison's passing, fully reproducing the missive from the *Liberator*'s editor, Pillsbury signified to insiders that their estrangement had expired. By glorifying the virtues of Rogers and summoning his journalistic voice for clarity and insight, the commemorator likewise suggested that he wanted to heal another breach. Unlike his rapprochement with Garrison, Pillsbury did not reestablish camaraderie with the *Herald of Freedom*'s editor. Nor could he ever do so, as Rogers had died in 1846. Reverencing him consequently amounted to a therapeutic exercise, one enabling the septuagenarian chronicler to atone for prior mistakes.[30]

The increasing radicalization of Rogers led to his split from the Garrisonian community by 1845. His distinctive variety of antiauthoritarianism precipitated dissension among tightly knit New England crusaders, many of whom, as nonresistance advocates, theoretically opposed all institutions and procedures predicated on force. Even though Pillsbury alluded to Rogers's support of the Non-Resistance Society, noting that "none ever more highly adorned [its] doctrine" than he, the memorialist never explicated his anarchistic philosophy at length. The historical Rogers believed that unlimited freedom of speech should hold sway at antislavery convocations, which did not constitute an intrinsically troublesome proposition. He additionally insisted on purely open and spontaneous participation at abolitionist get-togethers, which should themselves unfold extemporaneously and without ceremony. An emerging no-organizational approach toward organized abolitionism undermined the legitimacy of elected officers and business committees. It also cast aside, as arbitrary and coercive, the formal meeting agendas and resolutions, as well as the time restraints on speaking, that had typified antislavery assemblies.[31]

For the Garrisonian leadership in Boston, such views corroded movement cohesion, especially when pronounced by a journalist whose vituperation and outspokenness matched that of the *Liberator*'s editor. Internal strife had already ruptured abolitionist unity, climaxing with the 1840 decampment of politically focused and church-oriented activists from the AASS. High-ranking Garrisonians worried about the ramifications of another out-in-the-open schism. In this family feud, matters came to head not over dissimilar mindsets on no-organizationism per se. Rather, an intragroup tempest ensued from the localized issue of who properly owned the *Herald of Freedom*: either editor Rogers and printer John R. French or the managerial board of the New Hampshire Anti-Slavery Society. When Garrison, Wendell Phillips, Edmund Quincy, and other Bostonians favored the latter's control of the press, Rogers interpreted their intervention as a barely concealed repudiation of his antiauthoritarian principles. In response, he started a rival publication—the nearly identically named *The Herald of Freedom*—and severed his Garrisonian relations.[32]

Amid those developments, Pillsbury perpetrated actual or perceived betrayal. He not only sided with the state antislavery society during a sometimes-heated affair but also agreed to temporarily replace Rogers as the editor of the original *Herald*. The goodwill and comity between the two faded away thereafter. Decades later, the remorseful memoirist resurrected a meaningful connection. By saluting the newspaperman's intellectual brilliance and moral excellence, he conceivably searched for absolution. He had a compelling motivation to do so. "After Rogers's death," according to a Pillsbury biographer, "some New Hampshire abolitionists accused him of contributing to his mentor's demise," charges that greatly stung, then and since. Nagging guilt did not determine how the retrospective writer enshrined Rogers in an altruistic hall of fame. However latent, that emotion nonetheless affected his monumentalizing.[33]

In the book's concluding pages, the author briefly reflected on the in-house arguments among AASS proponents. "Abolitionists did think, and deeply too," he mused. Since "they felt as intensely as they thought," opinionated clashes, according to Pillsbury's reasoning, inevitably erupted. Despite admitting that those altercations "were not all reconciled before death sundered the parties to meet on earth no more," he, of course, never mentioned his rift with Rogers. Eulogizing a former friend as "one of the brightest, noblest, truest and every way most gifted sons, not only of the Granite state, but of any state" in the Union, must have comforted him. Intimating that he had piloted many a sojourner to the "hallowed spot" of Rogers's final resting place must have assuaged his conscience as well. Public expiation, in this context, was a personalized process only.[34]

Pillsbury lacked any compulsory need to restore amity or display its reinstatement while surveying the third facet of his antislavery trinity and anticlerical triumvirate. Among abolitionist companions, he enjoyed no closer affinity than with Foster; years of arduous fieldwork together had cemented their lifelong rapport. The chronicler conveyed as much in his thirty-three-page examination, which expands on an 1882 panegyric about a recently deceased Foster. Even though Pillsbury waited until the seventh chapter to formally delineate his confidant's career, reminiscences of Foster permeate the overall storytelling. Yet in contrast to the textual omnipresence of the often-quoted Rogers, the memoir's surrogate narrator, the repeatedly recollected Foster arises from the narrative as an omnipotent figure, one whose spiritual precedent and philanthropic feats had and continued to have empowering qualities. "To him," the commemorator avowed in an autobiographical chapter 5, "was largely due my first and best lessons in anti-slavery work." The wisdom acquired under Foster's tutelage Pillsbury sought to dispense to successive generations of Americans. Undoubtedly pertaining to the Christ-like way by which that crusader had protested enslavement, its post-Reconstruction significance nevertheless pivoted on the face-off between a transcendental comeouter saint and a domineering religious establishment.[35]

Like the other visages of Pillsbury's godhead, Foster was a many-sided reformer, backing temperance, peace, women's and workers' rights, as well as the moral and social "improvement of the city and neighborhood where he lived." He was profoundly pious, too. As the embodiment of the "christian minister and teacher, in all that those words . . . could ever be rightly made to mean," he possessed a commanding awareness of church history and consecrated himself to the precepts that Jesus had set forth in the Sermon on the Mount. Pillsbury's Foster thus based his abolitionist advocacy of nonresistance on the pronouncements of the Prince of Peace, the seminal nonresistant, and modeled his antislavery comeouterism after the Good Shepherd's comportment, the archetypal comeouter. The immediate emancipation campaign, the memoirist moralized, in no way impaired Foster's religiosity. The decision to enroll, though, dramatically altered the fate of his Congregationalism.[36]

The retrospective writer explained that before taking up the antislavery crusade, Foster had belonged to his parents' Congregational church and initially hoped to multiply the denominational following as a clergyman himself.

Individual awakenings at institutions of higher learning halted that allegiance and aspiration. As an undergraduate at Dartmouth College, the remembered Foster began questioning the "christian name and character" of evangelical Protestantism, principally because of its "persistent countenance of slaveholding." As a divinity student at New York City's Union Theological Seminary, he espied a dubious spiritualty among theology instructors, partly because of their lacking pacifism. Accumulated misgivings therefore led to his 1839 admission to a new school—abolitionism. Thenceforth, the author affirmed, "the cause of freedom and humanity, justice and truth, had no more faithful, few if any more able champions." To support that contention, Pillsbury elaborated on how Foster's escalating contest against entrenched religious tyranny revolutionized the movement.[37]

While attempting to spread the good news of immediatism across New England, Foster quickly "made the popular, prevailing religions his main point of attack" for two reasons. First, countless clerics regularly banned antislavery missionaries from their pulpits. Second, those disgraceful churchmen actively discouraged parishioners from attending the public meetings of itinerant abolitionists. Even though such things appalled other crusaders, Pillsbury's Foster uniquely challenged both. To reach the hearts and minds of self-professed Christians, he deployed the confrontational stratagem of showing up at places of worship, "as frequently as possible, at whatever cost." More provocatively, he intentionally disrupted Sunday services by suddenly addressing congregations during the appointed sermon hour. That proselytizing did not cease until someone physically removed the unexpected evangelist.[38]

Irrefutably controversial, Pillsbury justified Foster's behavior on the grounds that he acutely understood that delinquent divines had rivaled "depraved politicians in their determination to prevent the people, both in and outside the churches, from learning the truth" about an issue involving "the national preservation or destruction." The antislavery apostle accordingly braved meetinghouse lion's dens so that he could preach on behalf of the enslaved millions whose shackles American Christianity had helped fasten. Since he defied ecclesiastical adversaries on their own territory and in front of their flocks, contemporaries denounced Foster as "insane." The comeouter historian lamented that more persons did not suffer from a like madness. If just a small fraction of white northerners had, then the crime of slavery "would never have attained such proportions" that only the blood of millions of young men, in his estimation, could cleanse a reprobate United States.[39]

Rather than warding off a deadly civil war, Foster's prophesying resulted in personal abuse and punishment. No other grassroots agitator, Pillsbury observed, met with "more mob opposition and violence." By implementing his preferred method of consciousness-raising, he wound up in jail "as many as ten or twelve times, in New Hampshire and Massachusetts." If nothing else, the incarceration that heroic antislavery witnessing had brought about allowed Pillsbury's Foster to more directly identify with enslaved people. He "comforted himself that he not only 'remembered them that were in bonds as bound with them,' but that he actually *was bound with them*, and for their sake." Besides referencing that imagined community, the retrospective writer returned to a previous biographical fact in order to clarify what sustained a persecuted Foster. Based on a masterful comprehension of church history, the latter contended that Christian gatherings should permit the same freedom of speech that "Christ and the early apostles . . . [had] preached and practiced." The churchmen whose Sabbatarian ceremonies he interrupted thought otherwise. They demanded silence when he spoke, Pillsbury recounted, gesturing for his expulsion when he did not comply. Even though the recollected Foster always acquitted himself in a "decent and respectful" manner, his unwelcomed sermonizing prompted the parish lackeys of infuriated ministers to seize the unresisting prophet, upon which they dragged his body along aisles and hurled him through opened doorways and downstairs.[40]

By bringing his forbidden meetings to religious audiences themselves and relying on the apostolic directive that authorized everyone, with "psalm, doctrine, interpretation or revelation," to have a voice during worship, Pillsbury's Foster unmasked an antebellum priestly class as irresponsible and unregenerate. The memoirist chastised evangelical ecclesiastics for never contemplating the rightfulness or wrongfulness of Foster's conduct, as they had automatically assumed "that he was wrong, and . . . that they were right." The brutal repressiveness that the Sadducees of the North afterward unleashed, he alleged, replicated a "Spanish inquisition with all its terrors and tortures." The filled-with-faith Foster, by comparison, reminded the author of a New Testament Stephen whom an enraged throng had "stoned *to death*." That modern analogue would have "cheerfully" sacrificed himself in honor of an "equally holy cause"—presumably, the annihilation of a sinful system of servitude. Yet, even a cursory reading indicates that the chronicler had comeouterism on his mind. A saintly Foster thus accepted a prospective martyrdom on behalf of *all* slaves, for the benefit of abolitionism as well as anticlericalism. To be sure, the two sides of his activism formed a single coin: The Christ-inspired abolitionist implored conscientious individuals to renounce horribly polluted Christian churches. The commemorator, however, ultimately privileged one aspect of that humanitarianism.[41]

Beyond the widespread enmity of foes, even some friends, concerned about Foster's mental balance, "doubted" the appropriateness of his course of action. His methodology, Pillsbury acknowledged, "did not meet the approval of Mr. Garrison nor many of the most prominent abolitionists." Whatever the tension, the retrospective writer defused it, assuring readers that anyone on affectionate terms with Foster never suspected "his entire honesty, indeed deep, solemn conviction of religious duty, in what he did, and in all that he did." The seemingly iconoclastic Foster of this analysis only disturbed the ordinary peace of Protestant meetinghouses thanks to extraordinary circumstances. As a good American and genuine Christian, he keenly felt that he belonged to a nation that "in the name of republicanism and christianity, enslaved down to the lowest brute-beast level, one-sixth part of the people." That his country contained so many "immortal beings" whose marriages no law or religion had sanctioned absolutely disgusted him. Necessity therefore drove Pillsbury's Foster to disorder places of worship and urge repentance and reformation among slavery's unknowing abettors and abolitionism's willful antagonists. So, too, did anger. With the same earnestness and intensity as his spiritual paragon, he stormed New England's "synagogues" on the Sabbath, brandishing "terrible words of warning, expostulation, and rebuke."[42]

In that showdown with pervasive inhumanity and immorality, the remembered Foster launched the opening salvo in a dispute that equaled and exceeded the Second American Revolution inaugurated by the *Liberator*'s editor. Breaking away from all proslavery associations, as "far as it was possible," had tremendous repercussions according to Pillsbury. In the short run, Foster's tactic of religious disobedience alerted the citizenry to the dangers surrounding enslavement. Even though few contemporaries heeded his admonitions, the chronicler maintained that no other antislavery agitator "so stirred the whole people" until John Brown and his Harpers Ferry raiders dared slavery's defenders to "mortal combat." In the long run, Foster's pietistic army of one grew in strength and size. Setting that "sublime example" elicited imitators, so much so that his personal contest developed into a magnificent quest. The comeouter gatherings that had sprouted in New Hampshire and Massachusetts, the commemorator stated, prepared the culture for a future crop, specifically the "present Free religious societies, now so widely known." Truly, the series of events that Foster purportedly set in motion perfectly corresponded with and promoted the memoirist's preoccupations.[43]

Even though the dynamic comeouterism that the narrated Garrison, Rogers, and Foster collectively bequeathed provided relatively paltry sustenance for an ongoing African American freedom struggle, it does not follow that Pillsbury disregarded racial injustice completely. In the twenty-five-page chapter "Slavery— As It Was," he demonstrated that regardless of the passage of time and adoption of other endeavors, his hatred of Old South servitude had softened none whatsoever. He excoriated the world that slavery had made partly because slave masters, as man-stealers, committed heinous acts against their enslaved victims, whose persons they claimed as property and lives they subsequently imbruted. Since slaveholding southerners had perpetuated a regime of "wholesale, legalized, sanctified concubinage, or adultery, from first to last," that "unquestionable fact" triggered Pillsbury's memorial and historical fury. He inveighed against an arrangement that had negated the divine institutions of marriage and parenthood as if it still existed. To verify the Southland's barbarity and murderousness, he incorporated articles and advertisements from period newspapers. His condemnation, however relentless and striking, never segued into a rant about racist wrongdoing in the New South. By recalling "the torture-chambers of the imprisoned slave," for which all white Americans were culpable, he erected yet another foundation upon which to carry out grander FRA designs.[44]

Despite marketing abolitionism as a majestic "movement in behalf of liberty and humanity," the author seldom tackled racism. On one of the rare occurrences in which Pillsbury did, he relied heavily on someone else to illustrate how anti-Black prejudices had tainted the nonslaveholding North. In a nearly four-page discussion of the discriminatory policies on public conveyances, he excerpted information from an 1872 disquisition, *History of the Rise and Fall of the Slave Power in America*, by the former US senator and vice president Henry Wilson of Massachusetts. The antebellum practice by which the Bay State's Eastern Railroad barred African American passengers from first-class cars, requiring that they sit in separate and inferior ones of their own, provoked the retrospective writer's scorn. So, too, did the violence directed against Black and white antislavery agitators who had protested such bigotry and unfairness. Exactly why Pillsbury did not wholly anchor that disdain on what he witnessed himself or read in the abolitionist press remains an uncertainty. Whatever the reason, his fleeting contempt for racial segregation in the past stimulated no examination of race in the present.[45]

Elsewhere in the text, the memoirist depicted Salem, Massachusetts, as "almost fatally infected with prejudice against the African color." He remarked that white townspeople felt aggrieved when "respectable, intelligent, well-dressed, [and] well-behaved" free Black people had "presumed to exercise the plainest . . . of the inalienable rights of humanity." Precisely what prompted him to single out that northern locale constitutes a mystery, for he neglected to investigate whether its antebellum race relations were abnormal or representative. Despite classifying colorphobia as the most "frothing, foaming madness . . . [ever] visited on the human family," he never expatiated on how white abolitionists had successfully avoided or overcome that malady. Inoculating other Americans against it did not mobilize his post-Reconstruction pen.[46]

Given that the comeouter historian possessed so many scarring memories of Christian churches and clergymen, he barely chided the racially prejudicial rituals of the mainline Protestant sects. He stated that the "'negro pew,'" which had set Black parishioners apart from whites, provided the model for the "'negro car'" of railway companies. He also noted the persistence of such apartheid in religious meetinghouses across the United States. Neither assertion, however, garnered any scrutiny. The anti-Black biases of white Americans simply did not rile Pillsbury to the same degree as the misdeeds of antiabolitionist ecclesiastics. Even though racism undergirded the latter, the retrospective writer never ruminated on that matter. Original positions toward the immediate emancipation campaign functioned as his historical litmus test for determining someone's true or false Christianity. The equal or unequal treatment of free African Americans, within and without houses of prayer, factored nowhere significantly into the memorial equation.[47]

To be fair, reminiscences of well-known Black activists occasioned allusions to antislavery-oriented racial egalitarianism. Pillsbury particularly applauded the abolitionist oratory of Charles Lenox Remond, the brilliance of which led to his mulling over whether young white men, equipped with all the advantages of formal education, might address audiences remotely as well. That few could, as he confidently surmised, did not fully validate Remond's rhetorical skills. Stating that colossal obstacles had beleaguered Black northerners allowed him to satisfactorily encapsulate his subject's proficiency. With "our codes, customs, constitutions, schools and churches" arrayed against them, the author averred, "the colored people, a half-century ago," enjoyed but scanty resources "to set up the business of 'self-made men' making!" Unfortunately, Pillsbury used the past tense while proving a point about racist roadblocks and Remond's attainments. That he referred solely to a bygone era's racially exclusionary features further suggests what cause and whose rights no longer galvanized him.[48]

The memoirist also touted Frederick Douglass as a personally manufac-tured American par excellence; ditto for a mentioned-in-passing William Wells Brown. Even though Pillsbury scarcely touched on Douglass's accomplishments, he nonetheless underlined the overarching greatness of his story. As a recently appointed US marshal for the District of Columbia, that former fugitive slave, the narrator exclaimed, directly "spurn[ed] the lingering evolutionary processes of Darwin, and mount[ed], as in an instant, from the deep dead level of mules, horses and old wagons, to the very proudest manhood yet achieved in the nine-teenth century!" Despite such complimentary, but slight, coverage, Pillsbury evi-dently trusted in his readers to decide how African American superstars quashed notions of inherent Black inferiority and backwardness. The comeouter historian did not permit them to infer anything about who was a genuine abolitionist and authentic Christian.[49]

Regardless of enslavement's eradication, the abominable record of antiaboli-tionist churchmen permanently incensed Pillsbury. Echoing his memorialized trio and other Garrisonian memorialists, he announced that virtually all north-ern pulpiteers warmly received slave owners, breeders, traders, and hunters but "universally cast out" God-fearing emissaries of immediate emancipation. The region's religious leadership, he added, "traduce[d] and vilif[ied]" the Christ-centered abolitionists yet offered excuses for slaveholders and "defend[ed] their right . . . to the christian name." Comeouterism thus comprised the only reason-able option for anyone desiring a valid and pure faith. Notwithstanding the his-toric evacuations that did happen, Pillsbury thought that many more Americans should have seceded from morally and spiritually bankrupted bodies. That failure certainly reflected poorly on self-professed Christians, but the author pinpointed the machinations of a treacherous evangelical ministry as the core problem, so much so that antislavery crusaders "had almost to abolish the church before we could reach the [Southland's] dreadful institution." Or, in Rogers's ever-quotable words, they needed to be the "'mortal enemies of slavery, and of its patrons, the priesthood.'" Such "everlasting truth" fueled the retrospective writer's unended work—against clerical despotism.[50]

Time and again, Pillsbury pilloried Protestant ministers and their denomina-tions. Throughout the narrative, he exhumed the vicious antiabolitionism of the New England Congregationalism with which he originally fellowshipped. In a two-chapter diatribe, "Some Acts of the Pro-Slavery Apostles," he charted the cursed histories of the Presbyterians, Baptists, Methodists, and Episcopalians; criticized such smaller sects as the Free Will Baptists and Disciples of Christ; and

castigated the intersectional bible, tract, and missionary groups that northern ecclesiastics had helped organize and administer. Exposing the impious multitudes
that had buttressed the master-slave relationship and succored man-stealers
verged on a retaliatory inquisition. Grand inquisitor Pillsbury therefore found
that "the leading clergy never held slavery to be a sin, in any such sense as even
mere *heretical* offenses." In the accompanying efforts to silence supplications on
behalf of suffering bondservants, clergymen, bishops, and doctors of divinity exerted a baleful influence on churchgoers and emerged as the bane of antislavery
apostles. "True christian abolitionists," according to a recurring textual theme,
had no choice but to loosen "the bands of wickedness in the church."[51]

At the commencement of the "anti-slavery apocalypse by Garrison," the Slave
Power, Pillsbury harangued, totally controlled the country. By zealously detailing how evangelical Protestantism had fallen under its dominion, he put forward
an account whereby the religious establishment impeded an earlier and peaceful
emancipation. Antiabolitionist clerics, however, did not simply spawn anticlerical abolitionists. Sounding judgments similar to other Garrisonian chroniclers
and commemorators, Pillsbury contended that American Christianity's connivance with slaveholders resulted in "*Retribution*" for sectional and national transgressions against God and humanity. Despite, or perhaps because of, the cold,
hard facts, abolitionism's priestly archenemies reputedly engaged in a malignant
side hustle after the Civil War. In addition to renewing "their old calumnies,"
the memoirist declaimed, they "would have the world believe that they always
opposed . . . slavery and sought its overthrow." More repugnantly, they or their
offspring "boldly declare[ed] through pulpit and press . . . that the abolitionists,
even Garrison, did more harm than good." Pillsbury cited an unidentified orator,
a reverend essayist, and the son of a highly regarded Congregationalist pastor as
the culprits of such fallacious information. Infinitely aggravating, such misrepresentations amplified his project's perceived necessity.[52]

If Christian ministers honestly preached and prayed abolitionism, Pillsbury
rhetorically asked, then "why did they not put it [chattel bondage] out of existence?" Had the communities under their pastoral direction amounted to "an
anti-slavery . . . society," another such organization, he avowed, would never
have arisen in the United States. Not until the *Liberator*'s editor rang the alarm
bell, according to his version of events, did enslavement's baseness and crimi-
nality actually upset churchmen. Their uneasiness allegedly emanated not from
the sudden knowledge of slavery's real nature. Rather, when Garrison and other
apostolic abolitionists "began to resolve and re-resolve that . . . a slave-holding
religion was essentially anti-Christ; a slave-holding church a synagogue of Satan;

and a slave-holding ministry and all the fellow communicants a brotherhood of thieves," pulpiteers finally took notice. From then on, in the comeouter historian's testimony, the fight between the antislavery saints and antiabolitionist sinners broke out "in deadly earnest." For the FRA field agent, it represented but a microcosm of the larger collision between the forces of spiritual liberation and ecclesiastical oppression.[53]

Since the Free Religionist Pillsbury squared off against a clerical adversary that apparently posed a threat more grievous than its slaveholding counterpart, he retrieved from the past exactly what he needed in the present. Beyond the antislavery trinity and anticlerical triumvirate, the retrospective writer recognized several more fearless and faithful Garrisonian reformers. He lionized some over pages, such as Nathaniel Allen, Thomas Parnell Beach, Erastus Brown, and Jesse B. Harriman. Pillsbury recalled that each had emulated Foster's comeouter mode of operation and likewise endured bodily harm and imprisonment at the hands of proslavery clergymen and parishioners. He also attributed their self-sacrificing activism with precipitating a new "Martyr Period." The author appreciated other saintly figures over a couple paragraphs, a few lines, or merely in passing, such as Susan B. Anthony, James Buffum, Charles C. Burleigh, Abigail Kelley Foster, Sarah and Angelina Grimké, Sallie Holley, Oliver Johnson, Samuel Joseph May, Loring Moody, Aaron Macy Powell, Sarah Remond, Lucy Stone, and Henry Clarke Wright. Regardless of how much or little Pillsbury discussed them, all partook in an "enterprise solely moral and religious." His latter-day apostles spoke "divinely inspired" words, "crying aloud and sparing not," until a deadly civil war "magnified and made honorable their ministrations, and showed to the whole world that there was yet a God in Israel!" Furthermore, in the shared revolt against southern slavery and its churchly fortresses, those genuine abolitionists and authentic Christians laid the groundwork for an even wider, though incomplete, emancipation.[54]

Besides the book, shorter publications prove that equal Black rights did not actuate the late-in-life Pillsbury. A dictatorial priestly class and the perils of traditional Christianity form the leitmotif of an 1891 tract that went through at least three subsequent printings. In *Ecclesiastical vs. Civil Authority: God in the Federal Constitution; Man and Woman Out*, he wanted to awaken the public to a frightening theocratic conspiracy. Calling attention to the National Reform Association's (NRA) push to amend the US Constitution, the indefatigable Free Religionist warned that its lobbying initiatives would revolutionize America for the worse if they succeeded. To convey the dangerousness of the situation, he quoted the constitutional preamble as modified by scheming clergymen: "'We, the people of the

United States, *recognizing Almighty God as the source of all power and authority in civil government, our Lord Jesus Christ as the ruler of nations, and the Bible as the standard to decide all moral issues in political life, in order to form a Christian government, and in order to form a more perfect union. . . .*'" Even though Pillsbury enlisted italics to offset the proposed alterations, that typeface accented the grim character of the NRA plot as he comprehended it—to make Trinitarian Christianity as the country's official faith and sacred scripture the arbiter in secular affairs. The staunch comeouter could stomach neither; he toiled diligently, even as an octogenarian, to counteract both.[55]

In an 1893 pamphlet, *Things New and Old*, Pillsbury disparaged the regnant Christian order as irrational and reactionary. Despite championing reason, science, and antiauthoritarianism in religion, the former Congregationalist entreated current and prospective Free Religionists to effectuate an activist-attuned spirituality, one formatted on the living example of Jesus, what he labeled as the "Christ idea, truly interpreted." "The world must be *led* by pure and holy men and women," he proclaimed, "not *driven* by pretenders, hypocrites, liars, and libertines into the heavenly highway of salvation." Whereas biblical literalism and ministerial misrule, according to his inexhaustible comeouterism, obstructed that road to deliverance, a humanistic and progressive creed embracing peace, women's rights, temperance, tolerance, and the "Labor and Capital Problems" would assuredly irradiate the path to the promised land. Tellingly, the status and condition of the freedpeople warranted no authorial allusions.[56]

By reissuing 1840s antislavery literature that had unveiled conventional Christianity's depravity and underpinned a nascent comeouter crusade, the former abolitionist further exhibited that freedom of conscience and universal spirituality outstripped every other consideration. While republishing polemical classics by Foster and James G. Birney, whose stinging indictments the memoirist often referenced, Pillsbury released a revised 1885 edition of his own 1847 broadside, *The Church as It Is: or, The Forlorn Hope of Slavery*. In the updated preface, he explained that reproductions of past anticlerical writings would fulfill the informational requirements of present and future generations. Because of "the strange mendacity or ignorance of an unscrupulous clergy, who insist that they or their predecessors were the main instruments" behind southern slavery's destruction, he felt obligated to reprint vintage treatises from the same motives that he prepared a memoir of abolitionism. Should inquisitive or incredulous postbellum readers wish to confirm the veracity and dependability of those antebellum materials, Pillsbury recommended that they consult *Acts of the Anti-Slavery Apostles* itself. The retrospective writer asserted that "strict truth and justice to everybody concerned" comprised his "one constant study and care." Under his handling, historical truthfulness and justness hardly aided Black southerners by the 1880s.[57]

Even before Reconstruction's downfall, Pillsbury already located a replacement for an evidently obsolescent strain of abolitionism. In a published lecture, he indicated that an autocratic clerical regime had begun to monopolize his philanthropic priorities. Included in the 1873 book *The Sunday Question, and Self-Contradictions, of the Bible,* Pillsbury's contribution provocatively reinforced the volume's underlying aims. In the editorial preface, S. S. Jones emphasized that the collection of essays would "show the utter inconsistencies of singling out one day of the week for special devotion, rest, or worship," thereby stamping out "the effects of false teachings" from people's minds. Pillsbury's piece also captures his smooth transition from one antislavery movement to the next.[58]

Mustering the moral might of comeouterism, the inveterate crusader absolutely refuted the divine origins of the Sabbath. The latter, in his critical assessment, "was made *by* the priesthood, *for* the priesthood . . . and fearfully have they used it to perpetuate, as well as exercise," their mastery over humankind for centuries. Censuring Christianity's habitual day of rest and worship as a tool of "usurped authority, arbitrary power, and . . . outrageous cruelty," the FRA field agent possessed but one assignment: setting free the enslaved. Quite fittingly, he summoned the spirit of antebellum abolitionism, as well as its linguistic devices, to enhance the presumptive postbellum analogue. "Break this one yoke [the Sabbath]," he bellowed, "and priestly domination is no more." If and when that occurred, he revealingly concluded, the slaves of the American clergy's "40,000 spiritual plantations . . . would rise up redeemed, regenerated, and disenthralled by the spirit of God [and] the genius of universal emancipation." The shifting commitments of such a reformer did not signify a positive omen for any continuing interest in southern race relations. During his final twenty-five years, Pillsbury remained a vigilant and uncompromising agitator, but primarily against religious intolerance and perceived subjugation.[59]

As a fascinating window into Pillsbury's changing humanitarianism, *Acts of the Anti-Slavery Apostles* serves as an inspirational resource for anyone involved in an enduring confrontation with a purportedly repressive Christian orthodoxy. Audiences, specifically religiously liberal ones, viewed the author's magnum opus in that light. An 1898 review in *Free Thought Magazine* swiftly noted the tome's instructive potential. The periodical's editor, Horace L. Green, hailed it as the finest one currently available on abolitionism, "especially to the young people of this country, who have come to the age of understanding since the late war." Americans of all ages, however, should ponder the exploits of Pillsbury's amazing altruists, for they "will learn very much about the apostles of Freedom." Such knowledge, in the reviewer's appraisal, was useful, crucial, and hopefully vitalizing. "The Free Thought Cause needs to-day," he pontificated, advocates like those recorded in *Acts*: individuals "of the purest characters, of the highest aspirations, willing to sacrifice everything that is held dear by the [masses] . . . for the sake of benefiting Humanity." Parker Pillsbury, the antebellum comeouter-turned-postbellum Free Religionist, expected nothing less and arguably envisioned nothing more.[60]

Amid a slaveholders' rebellion, however, he occupied dramatically different altruistic turf, as evidenced by a communication appearing in the *National Anti-Slavery Standard*. About a year before President Lincoln signed an executive decree freeing millions of enslaved men and women throughout mutinous regions of the South, an Argus-eye abolitionist anticipated no such turn of events in the Union war effort. Even if Pillsbury had done so, it would not have mitigated his antipathy toward racism, which, as he observed, both bolstered southern slavery and blinded white northerners to the misery of chattelized humans. In a powerful sequence of sentences, the ardent activist dissected the immemorial loathing that mostly all whites felt for African Americans. They abhorred the Black bondman, Pillsbury bemoaned, because of the "skin in which his Creator clothed him," the "crisped hair" that crowned him, the "form of his features," the "fancied ill odour of his body," et cetera. So long as white countrymen denied the "humanity of the African race" and refused adult Black males the same civil and political rights, the epistler apprised fellow antislavery agitators that they must forever preach "*repentance*." Even though a sinful system of servitude did not survive a sectional conflagration, the "devil" of color prejudice still thrived decades later. Other demons, however, tormented Pillsbury's twilight years.[61]

5 A Tale of Two Slaveries

Aaron Macy Powell and the
Transfiguration of Abolitionism

In a posthumously printed memoir, *Personal Reminiscences of the Anti-Slavery and Other Reforms and Reformers*, Aaron Macy Powell depicted his first abolitionist convention as a life-altering experience. Held under the auspices of the American Anti-Slavery Society, it featured such leading lights as the visiting English activist and orator George Thompson, the formerly enslaved New Yorker and religious visionary Sojourner Truth, and the roving husband-and-wife organizers Stephen S. and Abigail Kelley Foster. That 1851 event figures as "momentous and influential" in the 1899 narrative because of what someone had said to and about a nineteen-year-old Powell as he engaged with the wider world of abolitionism. During a session intermission, Truth, bound from her 1797 birth until she seized her freedom in 1826, singled out the would-be crusader among a cluster of his relatives and acquaintances. Powell vividly recalled, as if the encounter had recently transpired, that a Michelangelesque sibyl slowly marched down the aisle from the pulpit, perched "her big black hand on my head," and, "with prophetic tone," uttered: "'I'se been a lookin' into your face, and I sees you, in the futur', pleadin' our cause!'" With such a baptism into the immediate emancipation campaign, the retrospective writer appropriately showcased the incident early in his account.[1]

Initially championing abolitionism as a grassroots lecturing agent, Powell would assume an even more conspicuous position in order to advance the AASS's larger racial justice objectives. As the editor of the *National Anti-Slavery Standard* from 1866 to 1870, he steered the organization's flagship periodical at a time when members pressed for the freedmen's civil and political rights. In so doing, Powell seemingly fulfilled the expectations of the quoted Truth, making her an astute judge of character and a skillful soothsayer in process. What she had predicted in 1851, Isaac H. Clothier confirmed nearly a half-century later. In the memoir's introduction, he remarked that among the "radical anti-slavery workers" of the 1850s and 1860s, Powell represented one of the "very youngest." Among the movement's fresh recruits, Clothier's Powell also ranked as "one of the most faithful and energetic." Even though death prevented the project's completion, the two hundred pages that Powell himself authored give credence to such encomiums. The book, however, does not merely broadcast the story of a devout abolitionist of the Civil War era. On the contrary, it exhibits a postbellum transfiguration that rendered a memorable antebellum prophecy as antiquated.[2]

By the 1890s, Powell had responded to the sounds of another philanthropic bugle and had done so for quite a while. More than anything else, he reflected on the past from the perspective afforded by a present-day social purity crusade. That emergent endeavor inflected the chronicler's celebration of fellow Garrisonian agitators appreciably, so much so that their relevance largely hinged on how they laid a foundation for, and even lent their own assistance to, a different abolitionism. The commemorator therefore delineated the connections between reformers who respectively challenged modes of slavery before and after the Civil War. Intentional or not, he constructed a teleological narrative whereby the transatlantic fight against the enslavement of African-descended peoples reached a denouement with an Occidental offensive against "white slavery" (that is, sex trafficking in women and girls). The intertwined antiprostitution and antivice undertaking undeniably refocused Powell's reformism throughout the late nineteenth century, concurrently distancing him from an ongoing African American freedom struggle.[3]

The retrospective writer placed the old abolitionism at the service of what he and like-minded others deemed a new one during a resurgent period of racial violence and oppression. To be sure, masked and unmasked vigilantes—from the Ku Klux Klan and Knights of the White Camelia of the 1860s to the Louisiana White League, Mississippi Rifle Clubs, and South Carolina Red Shirts of the 1870s—no longer roamed the southern countryside terrorizing Black communities and their white Republican allies. During the 1890s, however, lawless mobs lynched scores of African Americans annually across the Southland, allegedly in defense of white womanhood against sexually aggressive Black men (as the area's white apologists contended) but unequivocally to reassert white supremacy and Black subordination (as the African American journalist Ida B. Wells powerfully exposed). Even though southern state legislatures did not adopt rigid Black Codes in the 1890s as their ex-Confederate counterparts had done in the 1860s, previously customary segregation in local schools, restaurants, theaters, hotels, and public conveyances increasingly entered municipal and state law as the twentieth century neared. If those historical parallels disturbed Powell, his memorial publication hardly registers that impression.[4]

Regardless of whether the American South still resembled a region in revolt, that the country's highest tribunal gave its imprimatur to unfolding Jim Crow developments accentuates Powell's lacking dissent. Despite the 1866 Civil Rights Act and 1868 Fourteenth Amendment, which ensured the national citizenship status of African Americans and prohibited any state from abridging the privileges and immunities of US citizens or denying them with equal protection of the laws, a formalized structure of apartheid gathered momentum in the 1890s. In the 1896 case *Plessy v. Ferguson*, the Supreme Court ruled on behalf of the constitutionality of an 1890 Louisiana statute requiring separate railway carriages for white and Black passengers, provided that they equally accommodated patrons of both races. Judicial review further narrowed Reconstruction-era achievements two years later.[5]

Notwithstanding the enfranchisement of the freedmen under the 1867–1868 Reconstruction Acts, as well as the 1870 Fifteenth Amendment, which expressly forbade any state from refusing US citizens the right to vote based on racial criteria, state after state throughout the former Confederacy instituted procedures to drastically curtail and virtually eliminate the Black suffrage beginning in the late 1880s. The resulting poll taxes, literacy tests, and grandfather clauses, which determined who could formally participate in elections, the Supreme Court upheld in the 1898 case *Williams v. Mississippi*. Those provisions, in the written opinion of Justice Joseph McKenna, "do not on their face discriminate between the races, and it has not been shown that their actual administration was evil; only that evil was possible under them." If Powell squandered an authorial chance to disrupt the evolving Jim Crow times, he disallowed a divergent activist opportunity to slip away. Assessing the changeover from antislavery movements in the past and present amounted to an apparently more meaningful errand.[6]

While attending an 1872 international prison congress in London, the future memoirist gained exposure to a campaign that would alter his life once again. The drive to abolish state-regulated prostitution opened in the late 1860s, as British reformers mobilized against the parliamentary Contagious Diseases Acts of 1864, 1866, and 1869. Conceived as a sanitary measure to reduce bouts of syphilis and gonorrhea among military personnel in the United Kingdom, a third of whom had contracted sexually transmitted infections, the CD Acts implemented a limited system of legalized prostitution. Proponents of the enactment's hygienic benefits sought to extend them to Britain's civilian populations, too. The legislation mandated medical examinations for suspected sex workers in and around garrison towns and seaports, as well as ordered the detention of infected persons in specialized "lock hospitals" for up to an entire year. Anyone resisting inspection risked incarceration, with hard labor, for at least a month. The enlisted soldiers and sailors patronizing prostitutes, by comparison, faced no compulsory testing or enforced isolation. Enter Josephine Butler and the back-ers of the Ladies' National Association for Repeal of the Contagious Diseases Acts (LNA).[7]

On January 1, 1870, the *Daily News* (London) issued an eight-point manifesto in which 124 women denounced the CD Acts as unfair, misguided, and iniqui-tous. Point 4, for example, stated that "it is unjust to punish the sex who are the victims of a vice, and leave unpunished the sex who are the main cause, both of the vice and its dreaded consequences." Point 5 asserted that any method of legal-ized prostitution, however minimal, cleared a pathway to perdition for "our sons" and all England's youths because a righteous constraint "is withdrawn the mo-ment the State recognises, and provides convenience for," a vile practice "which it thereby declares to be necessary and venial." Finally, point 8 announced that since the "conditions of this disease . . . are moral, not physical," the protestors believed that "wiser teaching and more capable legislation" would successfully check "the *causes* of the evil" in question. Partly because of "astonished editors and eager newsmongers," that document, Butler later observed, materialized in other media outlets across the realm. The war of words that LNA advocates waged against illicit sex and governmental sanctioning of it quickly spread be-yond the United Kingdom as well. As a globalizing contest, antiregulationists universally heralded a single standard of morality whereby everyone obeyed the dictates of constancy within marriage and chastity without. For an expanding network of campaigners, internal restraints—self-control—comprised the best means of purifying individuals and society. By the mid-1870s, the new abolition-ism found an enthusiastic ally in Aaron Macy Powell.[8]

On behalf of Butler's far-reaching operation to dismantle state-supported prostitution, Powell helped arrange the local itinerary of British antiregulation-ist missionaries while they toured the United States in 1876. As a go-between, he coordinated New York City conferences and speaking venues for Reverend J. P. Gledstone and Henry J. Wilson and introduced them to benevolent circles elsewhere in the Northeast. The humanitarian dignitaries, in turn, motivated Powell and other receptive New Yorkers to establish an auxiliary branch of the recently created British, Continental, and General Federation for the Abolition of State Regulation of Prostitution (rechristened the International Federation for the Abolition of State Regulation of Vice by 1888, then the International Aboli-tionist Federation in 1902). Their warnings, Powell propounded in an 1877 paper that he published during the next year, aroused listeners to a "sense of Christian obligation and duty to join in the holy crusade against legalized . . . immorality."

They induced audiences, the metamorphizing old abolitionist added, to actively aid "heroic . . . women and men who are laboring in the 'new abolitionist' movement abroad."[9]

Equipped with an arsenal of British-forged arguments and similarly donning "'the whole armour of God'" that a crusading Butler had required for herself, American reformers alerted compatriots to the impending danger of governmentally tolerated or protected vice, specifically at the municipal and state levels. Powell, in particular, dedicated twenty-five years to the antivice (counter) revolution. In so doing, he not only arose as a premier proselytizer at home and a well-known devotee overseas. The reconsecrated activist also uniquely persevered as an antislavery agitator. Whereas the old abolitionist had preached the immediate and unconditional emancipation of the slaves, the up-to-date version proceeded as a paladin of the new abolitionism's "one standard of morality." Whereas he formerly espoused equal Black voting rights as the culmination of the old abolitionism, the new abolitionist endorsed, "in the interest of purity," a fully impartial suffrage. Since women must "everywhere make their voices heard and their influence felt against . . . the most arbitrary and unjust type of oppressive legislation," they absolutely needed the ballot, according to Powell's logic. He thus grounded his feminism on the presupposition that women, as voters and officeholders, would ensure the passage of antiprostitution policies that so "vitally" affected their welfare and the commonweal.[10]

Since death halted Powell's project, his incomplete narrative retraces the dramatic impact of just one antislavery campaign. Remembrances of the wayfaring Fosters nicely highlight the ways in which pre–Civil War crusaders had transformed his life trajectory. The retrospective writer related how, during an 1850 series of consciousness-raising events that the dynamic duo had arranged for his hometown of Ghent, New York, the visiting abolitionists' "stirring appeals" deeply awakened him to the wrongs endured by enslaved people. The Fosters' private statements on southern slavery, as household guests of Powell's parents, "more profoundly impressed" him than their public speeches. That domestic stopover subsequently produced the regular presence of other abolitionist callers, namely, the *Liberator* and *National Anti-Slavery Standard*, which supplied, according to the personal historian, "the basis of my anti-slavery education." The Fosters further primed Powell four years later. The narrator shared how, while vacationing with the immediate emancipation community builders, Abigail had unexpectedly invited him to address a Stoneham, Massachusetts, rally. Shortly thereafter, he befriended the AASS's Boston-based leadership and decided to pursue abolitionism full-time. The work of reform thus prompted Powell to suspend his teacher training at the Albany Normal School and, as it happened, permanently abandon aspirations for a higher education at Ohio's Antioch College. Besides that "boyhood ideal," he eventually set aside original abolitionist commitments, too.[11]

Regardless of the memoir's fragmentary nature, the chronicler still conveyed how post–Civil War crusaders reshaped his calling. The appended "Memoranda of the Unwritten Chapters" illustrates that the volume's second half would have encompassed copious recollections of antiprostitution and antivice, not surprisingly, because those dual concerns had formed Powell's philanthropic bedrock since the mid-1870s. Of the sixteen proposed sections, at least eleven would have focused on new-wave abolitionism, the spirit of which pervades the book's pages in more revealing ways as well. Numerous references to social purity amid reflections on old-wave abolitionism designate for whom the author wrote. By charting a line of succession from one antislavery enterprise to another, the commemorator authenticated the appropriation and purported enlargement of the American abolitionist tradition by European purity activists. His serviceable stories predominantly benefited the latter's global initiative despite, or perhaps because of, chattel slavery's troublesome legacy in the United States.[12]

Yet the memoirist did not categorically forget or ignore the equalitarian impulses that had animated the immediate emancipation campaign. At one narrative point, he recognized the current usefulness of an entity modeled after the AASS, the business of which had ceased following the Fifteenth Amendment's 1870 ratification. Expressing disappointment "that it had not been possible to . . . indefinitely" continue the syndicate in some capacity, Powell professed that a lasting alliance of nonpartisan agitators could have applied "effective moral censorship of public men and measures, especially as involving the rights of the colored people." On the surface, such an autobiographical lament conceivably summoned renewed racial justice demonstrations. While proffering it, however, Powell never mentioned his prior attempts at retaining an institutional presence for steadfast abolitionists. Had he fully executed the writing assignment, the topic would have gotten covered (as the third section of the memoranda of the unwritten chapters indicates). In contrast to his generously sprinkling social purity among reminiscences of the old abolitionism, cogitating on a still-necessary AASS spinoff notably triggered no allusions to the short-lived Reform League or its publishing clearinghouse, the National Standard. What Powell did not appraise, even in passing, sheds further insight onto why he deployed the memorial and historical pen.[13]

MEMORANDA OF THE UNWRITTEN CHAPTERS.

[IN the memoranda left, the unwritten chapters are not even sketched. But it seems due to the writer's generous purpose, that this barely hinted outline should be given, of work and workers for Temperance; for the Indians; for Prison Reform; for the Equal Rights of Women; for Peace and Arbitration; and in behalf of Purity.]

Emerson, John Brown, George L. Stearns, George W. Julian, Rev. Samuel May, Lucy Stone, Rev. Antoinette Brown Blackwell, Gerrit Smith, Frederick Douglass, Rev. Beriah Green, Parker Pillsbury, Charles C. Burleigh, Oliver Johnson, Giles B. Stebbins.

Julia Ward Howe, Mary A. Livermore, Abby Hopper Gibbons, Elizabeth Gay, Dr. Elizabeth Blackwell, Dr. Emily Blackwell, Louisa M. Alcott.

The appended "Memoranda of the Unwritten Chapters," which demonstrates both the amount of memorial attention that the purity crusade would have received by Aaron Macy Powell and special mission animating his history of old and new abolitionism. (*Personal Reminiscences of the Anti-Slavery and Other Reforms and Reformers*, pp. 200–3.)

National Standard 1872. Indian Civilization—Journey to San Francisco—Chicago Fire—Barclay White—Chinese.

First Trip to Europe 1873—International Prison Congress. Drink Episode—Cardinal Manning—Mr. Raper and Mr. Barker, Sir Wilfred Lawson and Exeter Hall. Continental Trip—Mrs. Butler—Liverpool.

Standard and *National Temperance Advocate*, Editorship and Secretary. Wm. E. Dodge, J. N. Stearns, Gen. Neal Dow, Dr. Cuyler, Miss Willard, Dr. Richardson, Dr. Lees, Mr. Rae, Mrs. Lucas. Congress, Commission of Inquiry, Senator Frye, Mr. Dingley, Joseph D. Taylor. National Prohibitory Amendment. Canon Wilberforce, Archbishop Farrar, Gen. Fisk, Ramabai.

New York Committee State Regulation of Vice. H. J. Wilson, M. P., and Rev. J. P. Gledstone. Second European Trip 1877—First International Congress and Federation. Canon and Mrs. Butler, Mr. Stansfeld, Sir Harcourt Johnstone, Prof. Stuart, Prof. Humbert, M. Henri Pierson, Madame De Morsier, Mme. De Gingins, George Gillet, Henry Richard, Maria Richardson. Reformation Hall—Mrs. Butler, Eliza Wigham and Mrs. Howe, Dr. Blackwell.

PERSONAL REMINISCENCES.

Third European Trip 1883.—The Hague. Mrs. Butler, Count and Countess Hogendorp, Madame Klerck. Socialism—the King—Motley Palace.

Fourth European Trip—Fourth International Congress—London 1886. Mr. Stead, M. De Laveleye. Toynbee Hall—Dr. Nevins, Mr. Minod.

Fifth European Trip—Fifth Congress, Geneva 1889. Paris Exposition—Absence of Mrs. Butler. Canon Butler died March 14, 1890, in his 71st year. Mrs. Ballington Booth and the Servia.

Sixth European Trip—Sixth Triennial Congress —1891 at Brussels, Belgium. Mrs. Butler and others.

World's Congress on Social Purity. Chicago— Archbishop Ireland, Mr. Gerry, Father Cleary, Judge Bonney, Mr. De Watteville, Mrs. Livermore, Rev. Anna Garlin Spencer.

Seventh European Trip—London, July 1894— Rosebery, Salisbury, Devonshire, etc.

National Purity Congress, Baltimore, Md., October, 1895 — First National — Characterize.

PERSONAL REMINISCENCES.

Rev. Dr. McVickar, Rev. Dr. Lewis, Dr. Emily and Dr. Elizabeth Blackwell—Woman's Medical College, Rev. Dr. Sabine, Dr. J. H. Kellogg and others.

Eighth European Trip—Congress at Berne, 1896. Birmingham Conference. Visit at the Clarks' at Street—John Bright.

Ninth European Trip—London 1898—International Congress. Social Purity Alliance. Archdeacon of London. National Vigilance Association. Mr. Stead. Canon Rawnsley, English Lakes.

In May 1870, the abolitionist lecturing agent and *National Anti-Slavery Standard* editor launched a liberally conceived experiment after the AASS's dissolution. Headquartered in New York City, the Reform League targeted an array of societal issues. The group's first annual report, prepared by Powell, identified the "great wrongs" that made up its program, explaining each under the following headings: "The South-Caste," "Woman's Rights," "The Labor Question," "Temperance," "Indian Civilization," "The Chinese Question," "Peace," and "Slavery Abroad" (that is, in the Caribbean and South America). That an unresolved regional "race problem" constituted item number one on the organizational docket readily suggests the vitality of founding AASS precepts and values among Reform League sponsors.[14]

Since a "true pacification" of the defeated Confederacy had yet to arrive, the Powell-composed document insisted on vigilant antiracism. "Though legally free and enfranchised," it declaimed, the freedpeople "are objects of a bitter hatred, persecution, and murderous violence." As a modernized AASS, the Reform League accordingly approached the postemancipation Southland as the setting for an "old conflict in a new form." Its promoters, the 1871 digest communicated, not only excoriated the atrocities that hooded Klansmen had perpetrated against Black southerners but reviled all manifestations of white supremacy across the country. To exterminate the "caste prejudice" stemming from systemic racial servitude, publicist Powell claimed the very heritage that he strove to maintain and augment.[15]

For the originator of another abolitionist outfit, the AASS and its adherents eternally proved "the power of simple fundamental principles, embodied in faithful, persistent appeals to the hearts and consciences of the people." Whoever sided with the Reform League and sought to achieve its "broader and more comprehensive demands" must consequently emulate such paragons. Fealty to antebellum moral-action strategies and freedom from "political and sectarian limitations" would therefore allow postbellum humanitarians to mold popular views and sway policy makers. Unfortunately, Powell folded his neoabolitionist venture within two years. Nor did its official gazette, which he also managed, fare much better. Despite an originally wide-ranging mission, the *National Standard* underwent substantial revisions. On December 23, 1871, for instance, Powell pronounced that "earnest, radical Temperance reform" thereafter represented the newspaper's paramount consideration. By forecasting its 1872 merger with an antialcohol journal, that editorial signified the demise of virtually everything for which the *National Standard* had briefly stood.[16]

With the Reform League's descent into obscurity, Powell took on the editorship of the *National Temperance Advocate*, a task that he performed until 1893. In 1873, he accepted the position of assistant secretary of the National Temperance Society, a role that he filled until 1894. More significantly, amid a collapsing Congressional Reconstruction the transfiguring abolitionist fervently enlisted in the battle against prostitution and vice. In 1876, he cofounded the New York Committee for the Prevention of Licensed Prostitution, which would slightly rebrand itself as the New York Committee for the Prevention of State Regulation of Vice. That same coalition undergirded the nationwide American Purity Alliance, which materialized in 1895 and subsumed the older groundbreaker.[17]

From 1876 until his 1899 death, Powell carried out executive functions on behalf of social purity, serving as the vice president of the New York Committee for many years, the consortium's president between 1893 and 1895, and the inaugural presiding officer of the American Purity Alliance. He spread its crusading message via the *American Bulletin*, a monthly newsletter that commenced, under his care, in 1878, and recirculated as the *Philanthropist* starting in 1886. From 1886 to 1899, Powell directed that periodical alongside his wife, Anna Rice Powell. For years, it appeared once a month, then reappeared as an enlarged quarterly beginning in January 1897 (and resumed as a monthly in January 1910, under the banner of *Vigilance*). Besides those jobs, Powell promulgated post-Reconstruction antiprostitution and antivice commandments through public presentations and addresses, as well as printed speeches and pamphlets. As a new abolitionist, he also frequented movement convocations overseas: in Geneva, in 1877 and 1889; in The Hague, in 1883; in London, in 1886, 1894, and 1898; in Brussels, in 1891; and in Berne, in 1896. Stateside, he helped orchestrate a weekend World's Congress on Social Purity, which convened in Chicago, in June 1893, among the festivities and exhibits of the Columbian Exposition. He additionally organized and chaired a days-long National Purity Congress that occurred in Baltimore, in October 1895. Immersion in the new abolitionism, then, symbolized the rebirth of the old abolitionist, a fact to which the memoir's contents and design abundantly testify.[18]

At first, Powell simply added antiprostitution and antivice to the assortment of causes that he had accumulated by the 1870s. Just before embarking on a new abolitionist vocation, and irrespective of the Reform League's rapid rise and fall, his commitment to racial egalitarianism wavered not at all. For an 1875 event honoring the centenary of a still-existing Revolutionary-era organization, Powell sent a dispatch in which he advised members of the Pennsylvania Abolition Society (PAS) to persist in their "important and much needed efforts." The Quaker-led PAS, which had overseen slavery's gradual eradication in the Keystone State, should not terminate its activities, according to the veteran immediatist, "until colored people are also emancipated from the yet prevalent, oppressive, cruel, and unchristian spirit of caste." As the *Philanthropist*'s editor, however, he seldomly tackled that matter. Even though his press occasionally ruminated on the moral condition of the formerly enslaved—and that of ex-slaveholders to a lesser extent—the freedpeople's political status and socioeconomic situation never seriously factored into any journalistic examinations. Unlike the Reform League Powell, the new abolitionist iteration saw generations of African American captivity resulting not in embedded anti-Blackness but endemic sexual immorality.[19]

At an 1883 meeting commemorating the fiftieth anniversary of a defunct AASS, the celebrant's temperament seemingly harmonized with the tone of his PAS communiqué. Before an audience that included retired antislavery advocates and the adult children of deceased crusaders, Powell praised the association's hallmark "moral method." While describing it as a majestic "moving power" whose mightiness exceeded that of any "military spirit," he beckoned other reformers to continually abide by that technique. He simultaneously reminded the attendees, whatever their ages, to remain loyal to the codes and ethics that the AASS and its framers epitomized. "The one lesson of the hour," Powell opined, "is that there must be no retrograde step; that no party shall be permitted to give license to the spirit of oppression and race-prejudice," both of which, he noted, afflicted Chinese immigrants in the West and imperiled African Americans in the South. Everyone, according to his solicitation, must exert themselves in order to "keep the public opinion . . . sensitive to the principles of justice and right upon which [the AASS] was founded." Despite apparently invoking Reform League tenets, Powell nevertheless exalted the antebellum past with fresher postbellum priorities on his mind.[20]

After cautioning against altruistic backsliding, the speaker's social purity swiftly took center stage. While upholding a paradigmatic AASS, he cited the helpful "precedent" that it set "for workers in other directions." Whom the club instructed Powell did not leave open to inference or interpretation. He outlined how, as a delegate to a conference at The Hague pertaining to "a wider slavery, wherein woman is victim," he had heard participants eloquently "quoting the example of Garrison and the American abolitionists, as an assurance of the justice and humanity of their cause." Besides thanking God for that experience, Powell articulated what he, and presumably many others, already knew: The record of the AASS amounted to a rich repository. "All who think and labor in our own country, and particularly those who are contending for great interests," he concluded, will find guidance from its institutional history "for all time to come." Antiprostitution and antivice undoubtedly figured uppermost in Powell's thoughts. Nothing else so absorbed his reformist thinking during and after the 1880s.[21]

Besides the direct correlation of the two antislavery movements in his own career, the retrospective writer memorably interconnected them while recalling philanthropic lives that social purity had only lightly touched. His handling of William Lloyd Garrison offers a case in point. In a thirty-page depiction, Powell summarized the early phases of Garrison's abolitionism as well as the crowning moments of that decades-long humanitarianism. He allotted some space to the "gentle, genial, and lovable" side of a popularly controversial and publicly combative agitator. Finally, the author polished the portrayal by showing the ways in which the old abolitionist patriarch emboldened new abolitionist descendants in the years before his death.[22]

While enumerating basic facts about the *Liberator*'s editor, Powell relied on the historical expertise of others, particularly the multivolume biography that two Garrison siblings had written as a tribute to their illustrious father. Equipped with that resource, the narrator traversed well-trodden memorial ground, such as his subject's apprenticeship as a printer in Newburyport, Massachusetts; subsequent experiences with reform-oriented journals in sundry New England locales; truncated partnership with Benjamin Lundy as coeditor of the *Genius of Universal Emancipation*; imprisonment in Baltimore for libeling, on the pages of that aforementioned publication, a Massachusetts ship owner attached to domestic slave trading; postincarceration lectures on abolitionism in Philadelphia, New York, New Haven, Hartford, and Boston; and launching an epochal antislavery weekly in 1831, the message of which was so "emphatic morally" that Americans, North and South, quickly "heard and felt" it.[23]

Powell's recapitulation of iconic episodes comprises a lengthy preamble to a self-evident truth, at least for Garrisonians. Echoing previous chroniclers, the commemorator decreed, "It was Garrison who made [President] Lincoln . . . a possibility." Pointing out that Secretary of War Edwin M. Stanton had invited the *Liberator*'s editor to attend an April 1865 flag-raising ceremony at Fort Sumter, where Powell too was a spectator, neatly attested to Garrison's cachet among Lincoln administration officials. It also symbolized the invaluable role that he purportedly played in the Civil War's greatest emancipatory accomplishment: the ratification of a constitutional amendment forever outlawing human bondage in the United States. The memoirist consequently submitted a bold prediction about the venerable old abolitionist, for "in the sight of the impartial historian of the future," his manner of working "will put to shame the much lauded statesmanship of the [John] Calhouns, [Henry] Clays, [Daniel] Websters, and other eminent Americans of the pro-slavery era." Yet Powell never gauged, in any depth, Garrison's diagnosis of "the slavery question" or why it was so "vital to the well-being of the nation." Nor did he presume that audiences already knew something about those matters, because his intended readership—the "young"—likely had no intimate knowledge of generations past. That the author discussed his subject's new abolitionist sympathies indicates what he really wanted neophytes to take away from the tale.[24]

Even though Powell likened the antebellum Garrison to "a prophet of the olden time [who] had returned to exhort and admonish a guilty slave-holding people," he prized the "all-round" reformism of the *Liberator*'s editor. Earlier Garrisonian hagiographers also highly valued such universalism, but Powell alone situated postbellum social purity on a list that additionally encompassed pacifism, temperance, women's rights, and liberal religion. In the latter-day movement against white slavery, as well as for an "equal standard of morals alike for both men and women," the pioneering old abolitionist of this narrative seamlessly merges into a pronounced and unbending new antislavery crusader. Despite identifying "equal rights for women, in all the relations of life," as the issue nearest to Garrison's heart after the immediate emancipation campaign, Powell pondered that feminism via a solitary paragraph. Ties to antiprostitution and antivice, in contrast, warranted a five-page exploration. The retrospective writer thus magnified but a tiny segment of his subject's half-century of activism.[25]

Extracted personal correspondence uniquely reinforced the memoirist's passion for purity. Of the six letters from Garrison that he partly or fully quoted, one deals with the old abolitionism indirectly, as it addresses the Civil War's outbreak and anticipated results. Two—one of which Powell interwove into the storytelling; the second, he replicated on a separate page—concentrate on the new abolitionism. The remaining three refer to more private affairs: Garrison's musings on nature before visiting Powell's rural residence, Garrison's condolences to Powell upon the loss of a family member, and Garrison's congratulations to Powell on his forthcoming matrimony. As authorial beacons onto the book's ultimate purpose, the antiprostitution epistles require some scrutiny.[26]

In the short missive that appears in facsimile, Garrison expressed his appreciation for the complimentary copy of Powell's 1877 paper "State Regulation of Vice." The very theme, he remarked, commanded widespread awareness, "as it relates to habits, usages, and legal sanctions of immorality, which are sapping the foundations of society on both sides of the Atlantic, especially in Great Britain and on the Continent." That evaluation supplied not merely a virtual advertisement for Powell's pamphlet but also a key endorsement of the new abolitionist proposition. The chronicler, in turn, apprised readers that the emeritus editor of the *Liberator* had promptly espoused the crusade against white slavery. Indeed, Powell and Garrison each did so at about the same time—during the sojourn through the United States of the traveling Gledstone and Wilson. In 1876, as the New Yorker Powell scheduled lecturing engagements for the British antiprostitution apostles, Bay Stater Garrison contested "the threatened encroachment of American regulation propagandists" by assisting in the formation of a Boston vigilance committee. To be sure, the younger Powell more energetically applied himself to the purity agenda; his elderly associate, who died in May 1879, nonetheless labored on its behalf. The ephemeralness of Garrison's antivice efforts, however, did not inconvenience the commemorator, for he equated them with the vigorous struggle against southern slavery.[27]

Toward the bottom of the same missive, Garrison informed his recipient about an approaching voyage to Liverpool, where he hoped "to meet the devoted

Mrs. Butler and other noble co-workers in the cause of purity." An expounding memoirist confirmed that the august old abolitionist had personally met with the new crew's leader. He indicated as well that the holidaying Garrison had spoken at antiregulationist gatherings across England. Furthermore, the autobiographer reported that at a homecoming reception that the New York Committee had held in Garrison's honor, seeing and hearing the revered reformer speak elicited feelings of déjà vu. His words on that occasion, according to Powell, "strongly reminded many . . . of his most eloquent, uncompromising anti-slavery [sermons] of an earlier period." Antebellum *and* postbellum actions therefore rendered the recollected Garrison as an unlimited fount of "inspiration and strength" for antiprostitution forces at home and abroad. Even though Powell's pre- and postwar pursuits illumined the historical congruence between the old and new abolitionism, the purity advocacy of an immediate emancipation founding father denoted another source of continuity. If Butler and her transatlantic allies truly represented the rightful successors of preceding antislavery crusaders, then Powell's Garrison provided indispensable memorial legitimization. The other incorporated communication about tolerated or protected vice fulfilled that very task.[28]

Unable to partake in the New York Committee's 1879 annual get-together, a feeble Garrison mailed a memo to Powell wherein he applauded the group's firm resistance. Its "timely warnings," "solemn appeals," and "faithful testimonies," he asserted, had helped stymie domestic bids at procuring "profligate legislation." The sagacious reformer accordingly recommended "constant vigilance," so that a falsely sanitary European system never gained a foothold in the United States. He acknowledged as well the new abolitionists across the pond and their courageous fight against the CD Acts. The "world has never before seen," in the old abolitionist's eyes, "such a morally sublime uprising against statutory licentiousness, and for the preservation of personal chastity and public virtue." The veteran immediatist even blessed the postbellum activists who attired themselves in the regalia of antebellum antislavery. In certain regards, the excerpted Garrison declared, the purity campaign "resembles the conflict that was hotly waged in this country for the abolition of chattel slavery." "We know," he added, that the latter necessitated "ardent consecration, noble self sacrifice and unfaltering trust in God." So, too, by implication, did the former. With good reasons, the author strategically inserted that note into his account. Received but a few months before Garrison would pass away, it apparently validated that a passing of the philanthropic torch had occurred, thereby solidifying the heir-apparent pretensions of the new abolitionism that the autobiographer delineated.[29]

To bring these remembrances to a close, Powell enlisted a resolution that the New York Committee had approved upon Garrison's decease. It not surprisingly catalogued him as a "prophetic, fearless, and uncompromising" defender and deliverer of enslaved African Americans. It also tellingly characterized him as a "foremost" and "outspoken antagonist" of licensed prostitution in the United States and "the enslavement of women and degradation of men" that would accompany such sinister lawmaking. With the departure of an extraordinary crusader, the New York Committee "commend[ed] to all" the lessons that he had bequeathed: "unswerving fidelity to convictions of duty and the right." By quoting that organizational declaration, Powell further amplified the significance of Garrison's twilight-years purity partnerships. Even though he alluded to the recent construction of a bronze statue of the *Liberator*'s editor as a suitable posthumous accolade, readers of his reminiscences might have contemplated to which William Lloyd Garrison had Bostonians paid homage. The sculpture assuredly monumentalized the old abolitionist, but the retrospective writer compounded and complicated its meaning by arguing for the new abolitionist as well.[30]

As the columns of the *Philanthropist* demonstrate, Powell's transfigured abolitionism entailed not only hostility to white slavery and advancement of a single moral standard. It also involved several ancillary matters by the 1890s, such as rescue work among female "victims of social vice," educational work among college-aged males on behalf of chastity before marriage, and pressure-group work in order to secure state and national policies in "protection of girlhood" (namely, raising the legal age of consent). Loyalty to that bigger campaign manifested itself from the memoir's opening pages. Once more, the introduction proves instructive. For Clothier—Powell's friend, Quaker coreligionist, and fellow new abolitionist—the late reformer had led an exceptionally "consecrated life." From the commencement of adulthood, Clothier's Powell completely gave himself to any good humanitarian enterprise, particularly the "least popular" ones. "The cause of the colored race," according to the eulogist's insightful inventory, "of the Indian, of peace, of temperance, of [Quaker higher] education . . . and above all the personal purity movement . . . received his earnest support, and the last named his unquestioned leadership." Whether in the preface, the body of the text or the memoranda of the unwritten chapters, every charitable endeavor of Powell's eventually reached a new abolitionist terminus.[31]

Not all representations of old abolitionists bear an unmistakable purity patina. Consider the chronicler's thirty-page traversal of Wendell Phillips. Similar to the remembered Garrison, Powell intimated his subject's tender qualities.

He culled passages from two letters in which Phillips had sent condolences to him following the loss of a four-year-old daughter in 1867 and an elderly mother in 1877. The commemorator also referred to the "loving devotion" that Phillips had bestowed on an infirmed spouse, Ann Greene Phillips, whom he "fondly cherished" throughout their marriage and attentively nursed at the end of her days. Like the recollected Garrison, moreover, Powell rated Phillips as an altruist of "the widest scope." His eclectic antebellum activism included abolitionism, women's rights, temperance, penal reform, and opposition to the death penalty and inhumane treatment of the mentally ill. Based on that rock-solid "sympathy for the wronged and the oppressed," his liberalism broadened throughout the postbellum period, extending to native peoples, Asian and Irish immigrants, and industrial laborers. As a labor advocate, he specifically called for a shorter working day and better educational opportunities for workers. He concomitantly condemned "the modern growth of corporations and the gigantic combinations of capital, especially as a controlling force in legislation." Fifteen years after his 1884 quietus, Powell's Phillips was a remarkably up-to-date agitator; in many respects a personification of the bygone Reform League's comprehensive ethos.[32]

The memoirist extolled Phillips's "oratorical gifts," too, spotlighting an 1837 Boston speech that he had given shortly after the killing of the antislavery newspaperman Elijah Lovejoy by an antiabolitionist mob in southern Illinois. Even though Powell did not witness the Faneuil Hall exploit himself, its legendary status pre- and postdated his old abolitionist attachments. Because of one attendee's "bitter" judgments, which denounced the fallen Lovejoy as "'presumptuous and imprudent'" and belittled his fate as one who "'died as the fool dieth,'" the Phillips of this tale (and others) scored a verbal coup, winning everlasting acclaim via a cutting retort. "'When I heard the gentleman lay down principles which place the murderers of Alton side by side with [James] Otis and [John] Hancock, with [Josiah] Quincy and [John] Adams,'" the quoted Phillips announced, "'I thought those pictured lips [pointing to the portraits in the historic hall], would have broken into voice to rebuke the recreant American—the slanderer of the dead!'" Such a commanding address, additional sections of which the narrator recited, inaugurated a stellar career from which Powell's Phillips emerged as "a master among masters, a leader of leaders." That preeminence, however, came at a price. His espousal of immediate and unconditional emancipation, the author averred, resulted in the "sacrifice of brilliant professional prospects, social position, [and] family and other . . . friendships." That Phillips's humanitarian prestige should outlast a lifetime constituted partial compensation for those costs.[33]

Despite painting him mostly as a universal reformer and incisive platform speaker, Powell nevertheless enhanced the likeness with new abolitionist highlights. In a different chapter, he observed that Phillips backed the same Boston vigilance committee as Garrison had in 1876, so as to thwart any potential schemes to license prostitution locally. About two-thirds into the memorial sketch, he stated that during various visits with antiregulationists overseas, "I have been much impressed with the marked influence of his [Phillips's] life and teaching [on] their great conflict" against a monstrous iniquity. The retrospective writer more substantively recalled how Phillips took a deep interest in his 1877 journey to Geneva, Switzerland, where antivice activists from Europe and North America convened in order to found an international federation. Powell underscored that Phillips had furnished him with two things: "a message of love," which he must transfer to "Mrs. Butler and others"; and "a general 'credential,'" which set forth his reformist bona fides. That the personal historian reproduced the reference letter, as a three-page facsimile, readily suggests the preciousness that he assigned to it then and since. As an opener of European doors, Phillips's certification esteemed Aaron Macy Powell as "so devoted, efficient & widely known a worker on all our Reform questions" that he needed no such voucher in the United States. At the time, that "especially helpful" document conferred a seal of approval on an unfamiliar American abroad. Yet the benefactor's famous name and hearty recommendation continued to "aid him anywhere" many years afterward, as it provided a visible purity figure, on both sides of the Atlantic, with another old abolitionist justification for the crusade against white slavery.[34]

Powell also celebrated Lucretia Mott as a multifaceted philanthropist whose pre–Civil War altruism spanned the immediate emancipation campaign, peace, temperance, women's rights, and liberal religion. As an antebellum antislavery agitator, in particular, the chronicler presented Mott as the movement's first lady. He mentioned her attendance at the 1833 conclave that gave rise to the AASS. Even though Mott did not personally sign the association's "Declaration of Sentiments"—the male delegates had neither expected nor invited her to do so—Powell emphasized that she nonetheless participated in the proceedings by proposing stylistic revisions and amendments to the founding texts under consideration. The commemorator referenced as well the managerial posts that she held "for many years" on behalf of the Philadelphia Female Anti-Slavery Society, which had functioned as an invaluable AASS affiliate.[35]

Besides her signal services as an old abolitionist organizer and officer, Powell lauded Mott's feminism. Early experiences as an undercompensated

schoolteacher, according to the authorial explication, awakened her to the economic "inequality between the sexes." The later objections that Mott encountered
at the 1840 World's Anti-Slavery Convention in London, wherein a majority of
the male conference-goers had decided that she and the other accredited female
delegates from the United States could not officially take their seats, convinced
her that concerted action was crucial for obtaining "equality of rights . . . and full
enfranchisement of women." Quite properly, the remembered Mott played an integral part at the 1848 Women's Rights Convention in Seneca Falls, New York.[36]

Mott's progressivism, unlike that of male counterparts, evidently required
extra defense. The memoirist maintained, for instance, that her domestic situation patently disproved the charge, "which used often to be made, and which
still survives in certain quarters," that women endangered their femininity if and
when they transgressed traditional gender boundaries. Powell warmly recounted
a dinner party at the Philadelphia residence of James and Lucretia Mott, following an antislavery meeting that had taken place earlier in the day. The in-
vitees included, besides himself, Garrison, Phillips, William H. Furness, Mary
Grew, Robert Purvis, and unnamed others. As a "delightful" hostess, Powell's
Mott possessed "the gift of leading and keeping the conversation general" for
everyone's gratification. More significantly, the adept entertainer remained an attentive homemaker. Powell reconstructed a "memorable" scene in which Lucretia, during dessert, executed two tasks simultaneously: She sustained her duties
as an engaging conversationalist, "bearing her full share with her guests," while
hand drying washed dishes from her table seat, so as to relieve "the heavily taxed
kitchen maids." Entering the public sphere in no way jeopardized Mott's womanhood, which a protective Powell treasured as "true and beautiful."[37]

The retrospective writer rounded things out by sketching an outstanding
woman as a model Friend. Whereas the recollected Phillips had distinguished
himself as an orator "without a peer" across the Atlantic World, Powell hallowed
Mott as a "religious teacher . . . without a peer in modern times." The latter's
activism, in his assessment, amounted to an outward reflection of inner spirituality. First and foremost, Powell's Mott was "liberal in thought, catholic in spirit."
He defined her utterances as "persuasive and truly eloquent." He admired the
patience that she had mustered toward "prejudiced opposition, and sometimes
marked discourtesy." He hailed, furthermore, the "mighty transforming influence" that her ministry had exerted, so much so that later in Mott's life, Quakers
"everywhere welcomed [her] with tokens of respect and affection." Even though
Powell never hinted at the new abolitionism in his reminiscences of Mott, he did

not restrict himself to the old one either. The same applies to other stories that the author told about the immediate emancipation campaign.[38]

While interlinking past and present crusades, Powell occasionally indulged in anecdotal asides that had nothing to do with chattel or white slavery. Likely designed for audience amusement, his digressions arguably disclose the widening humanitarian distances between the autobiographer of the 1890s and the racial justice agitator of the Civil War era. One colorful tangent pertained to a western Pennsylvania woman whom Powell had met while riding the AASS lecturing circuit throughout the Old Northwest states of Ohio, Indiana, and Michigan during the mid-1850s. A striking zeal for the slave's cause did not render the unidentified subject as singular or unforgettable. Instead, an out-of-body incident that the "chronic invalid" had relayed to him left an indelible stamp.[39]

Powell postulated that members of the Society for Psychical Research (SPR), the 1882 English original or 1885 American offshoot he did not specify, would have found the near-death account that he once heard absolutely fascinating, but their organization did not yet exist. Despite the absence of "exact notes," he salvaged as much as he could about the happening, apparently for the benefit of SPR investigations that initially centered on the parapsychological phenomena generated by Spiritualist mediums. A report of two-plus pages ensued, in which the narrator discussed how the person in question ultimately bypassed and delayed the "new life" that awaited her, which she characterized as so "delightful and grateful" that it surpassed explanatory capabilities. Rather than "sever altogether the cord" that tethered her to the body, she chose, according to Powell's retelling, to return to her earthly receptacle. The awareness of loved ones mourning her ostensibly lifeless form, and the sympathy that she felt toward grieving family and friends, "turned the scale" and prompted her bodily repossession.[40]

Elsewhere in his narrative of grassroots abolitionism in the developing Midwest, the memoirist fixated on the poor conditions that he had endured. Regarding northern Indiana, Powell recalled that "some of the old 'corduroy' roads" made for quite adventuresome antislavery outings. To avoid plummeting into the seemingly "bottomless" depths of muddy thoroughfares, he clung "vigilantly to the [wagon] seat." Presumably, he had reached his expected Hoosier destinations unscathed, for the retrospective writer provided no additional details. Concerning Michigan, he also reminisced about "primitive" transportation facilities, which had made his east-to-west trek, from Pontiac to Grand Rapids, into an "'exploring expedition.'" That, in tandem with the "intensely cold weather," exponentially multiplied the difficulties of coalition building on the frontier. The forbidding climate particularly reminded the itinerant speaker of the 1845 misfortunes of Sir John Franklin, whose venture into the Canadian Arctic resulted in his and his entire team's disappearance. Unlike the lost English explorer, Powell had found his way to "pioneer anti-slavery appointments" in the Wolverine State. To be sure, he did not think that those antebellum tours actually rivaled a major odyssey through unnavigated waters or across uncharted terrain. Even so, the lightheartedness with which the postbellum author relived those abolitionist jaunts stands out as noteworthy.[41]

Overall, Powell's "vivid" memories of philanthropic grunt work in the Old Northwest frequently revolved about the incidental and trivial, thereby problematizing their purported importance. Organizing meetings and disseminating propaganda on behalf of the AASS, he contended, had so thoroughly "educated and revolutionized" public sentiment that they "ma[d]e the abolition of slavery a possibility." Yet mulling over the paranormal in Pennsylvania and the primeval in Indiana and Michigan, which comprises nearly half the textual space that he earmarked for Midwestern activities, added very little to a chronicle of old abolitionism's headway. To whatever extent such anecdotes deflected readers' attention from the substance of his proselytizing forays, they certainly did not detract from the larger authorial objective. The commemorator regularly created opportunities to import the new abolitionism into his analysis of the immediate emancipation campaign.[42]

Thanks to eye-catching allusions, postbellum purity cuts a distinctive silhouette in Powell's publication. Its recurrence in recollections of antebellum antislavery corroborates exactly what consumed the memoirist at the dawning of the twentieth century. The remembered Garrison and Phillips constitute but the most prominent old abolitionists who directly and indirectly promoted antiprostitution successors after Reconstruction. Powell wrote about others who also had done so. For example, Edward M. Davis—whom he classified as a "forceful speaker," efficient executive officer of the Pennsylvania Anti-Slavery Society, and son-in-law of James and Lucretia Mott—proffered "helpful co-operation" to the antiregulationists. Personal modesty, however, constricted any public embrace of Powell's New York Committee. In excerpted correspondence, the quoted Davis politely declined an invitation to a group gathering because the prospect of conversing about the "terrible question" of illicit sex before a "mixed assembly" of men and women greatly discomforted him. In the absence of formal involvement, Powell revealed that his charitable confrere assisted the drive against tolerated or protected vice though gifts of money. "I send a mite . . . just to satisfy my conscience," according to the missive writer's self-deprecating remark, "for I know it is my duty to do something in some direction, so like all cowards or drones I accept the easiest way." Interestingly, in a three-paragraph reflection on Davis, the first concentrates on the old abolitionism; the second, the new abolitionism; and the last, friendship.[43]

Nor did antebellum antislavery delimit the activism of Joseph and Mary Post of Long Island, New York. Ever ready to "extend sympathy and aid to all humane, benevolent efforts," the couple, whom Powell adored as surrogate parents, especially sponsored his purity projects. In verification, the author, as was his habit, enlisted a written communication. "I keep hoping for better times," the quoted Mary declared in a five-paragraph dispatch, "but really it seems as though there never was a time when it was more needful to be on the alert to prevent evil legislation than the present." She subsequently entreated Powell and his antiregulationist collaborators to "keep up courage," so that, as in the past, they could inhibit the legalization of social vice in the future. After praising the "good work" that the *Philanthropist* carried out, she articulated a desire to do more for the new abolitionist fight, but advanced age admittedly impeded her from doing anything else. Nevertheless, Powell's Post, "not long before her transition to the larger life," supplemented epistolary encouragement with a "generous" cash donation.[44]

Besides recording monetary bequests, the autobiographer referred to the postbellum antiprostitution amity of still other veterans of antebellum abolitionism. Sarah H. Peirce of Pennsylvania, he avowed, furthered the crusade against white slavery as a "member of the General Council of the American Purity Alliance" and through her "judicious use of literature." Esther Carpenter Pierce of New York, he attested, was one of the "most valued and sympathetic helpers in our mission for the promotion of purity." He similarly affirmed that Mary Grew, after a wonderful old abolitionist career in which she operated as the longtime secretary of the PFASS, prepared imitable annual reports on that organization's behalf, and coedited the *Pennsylvania Freeman*, provided "most helpful sympathy and co-operation" to the new cause. Not coincidentally did the retrospective writer's list consist of women. As a Gilded Age activist on the front lines of the antivice conflict, though, he would have liked for more male coadjutors.[45]

The "purity reformation," Powell opined in an 1886 issue of the *Philanthropist*, "is not alone or chiefly the responsibility of women." He consequently predicted that an "era of more strict social accountability on the part of men is at hand." Three years later, however, he conceded that among the periodical's nationwide readership, "the majority are women." Men, the editor lamented, "appear to have

[much] less interest in the movement." Yet since the "degradation of one sex involves the degradation of both," he called upon adult males, as would-be advocates or acting legislators, to effectuate the one standard of morality for everyone.
That dichotomy in the makeup of the new abolitionism may additionally explain
why Powell heightened the antiregulationist contributions of both Garrison and
Phillips. Not only were they remarkable reformers, but they amounted to exemplary men, too.[46]

Whereas several old abolitionists of Powell's remembrances, regardless of gender, noticeably fostered his purity priorities, a few pushed for Black liberty and
equality solely. In a thumbnail sketch of Thomas Garrett of Delaware—reputedly
"one of the strongest pillars" of the AASS—the memorialist accented the historic
feats of an Underground Railroad conductor. Thanks to clandestine transactions
that had facilitated the escape of more than 2,500 freedom seekers, Powell styled
Garrett as "a Moses to a multitude of fugitives from slavery, and a terror to their
masters." The tremendous public interest in Garrett's 1871 funeral constituted,
for the storyteller, a fitting tribute to such a thoroughgoing foe of Old South
servitude. After a "continuous stream of humanity" passed by the casket and
dispersed from the home of the departed, Powell noted that "stalwart colored
men, who had asked the privilege," then carried the coffin through Wilmington's
streets, which were thronged with onlookers, to the local Quaker meetinghouse
for the closing services. Besides a recitation of some facts, the narrator never elucidated how Garrett had shepherded runaways to safety or whether his heroism
remained pertinent.[47]

In contrast to that superficial tabulation of a modern-day biblical rescuer,
Powell more specifically saluted the special humanitarian witness of a less famous
antislavery partisan and Underground Railroad operative. During the memoirist's seasons as an AASS lecturing agent, the New Yorker Joseph Carpenter
had set up his speaking opportunities in Westchester and accompanied him on
circuit-riding trips to nearby Mamaroneck, New Rochelle, and Port Chester. Not
only did African Americans always outnumber whites at those meet and greets,
as Powell related, but "there was [also] much prejudice against colored people"
in that Empire State region. As evidence of the latter, the retrospective writer
invoked a former prohibition against Black bodies in New Rochelle's cemeteries.
Reenter the recollected Carpenter. He memorably countered such discrimination by reserving a portion of his Mamaroneck farmland for African Americans'
burials, further stipulating that the same plot should compose his final resting
place. Powell deemed both deeds as "testimony against the then prevailing—and,
alas, still prevalent—unchristian color prejudice." The addition of a photographic

illustration, in which a seated Carpenter places his arm around a standing Black child, visually complemented the verbal rendition of the subject's antiracism. Copies of that image, Powell apprised readers, Carpenter had distributed to acquaintances upon request, "feeling at the same time that he was conveying silently the lesson he so much desired to teach." As part of a book, it presumably performed the same racial-egalitarian function in the late 1890s.[48]

The five-page homage to Carpenter shows that substantive reminiscences of an antebellum African American freedom struggle sometimes surface from the narrative. The author also interjected the topic of race while considering Black colleagues in the immediate emancipation campaign. Regarding the "educated, refined and sensitive" sibling reformers Charles Lenox and Sarah Parker Remond, Powell stressed that they constantly confronted "heartless and vulgar color prejudices." Hotels and lodges across New York, he averred, "rudely denied admission to them," whereas white patrons like himself and Susan B. Anthony had faced no such rejection. To fully impart the offensiveness of pre–Civil War colorphobia, the personal historian recounted a conversation at the home of old abolitionist comrades in Washington County, in which a guest described the hardships of an area family infected with the red plague and the unwillingness of neighbors to interact with the sufferers. The "distressing account" moved the remembered Charles Remond to express empathy for the diseased, because "'to colored people it is the same as having the small-pox all the time.'" If Remond's powerful words approximated an enduring parable, they elicited no such commentary. Powell simply repeated them and proceeded on to something else.[49]

The retrospective writer also grappled with racial matters in a compact portrayal of the Pennsylvanian Robert Purvis. Besides indicating his old abolitionist usefulness—he had worked with Benjamin Lundy before assisting in the formation of the AASS—Powell drew attention to the subject's mixed ancestry. Despite an English father and a mother of "Moorish descent," the freeborn Purvis, originally of South Carolina, firmly identified with "the victim and enslaved race." Such an affinity evidently shocked white contemporaries, who, at antislavery rallies, "would look at him with incredulity." They did so, according to Powell's clarification, not because he possessed an Amherst College degree or a "pecuniary competence." The disbelief stemmed, instead, from the "slight . . . connecting link" between Black bondservants and the light-skinned Purvis. That the latter did not conceal an African heritage verified the goodness of his character. Powell's remarks suggest that Purvis could have easily passed as white, thereby avoiding the social proscriptions and popular prejudices that had beset free Black northerners.[50]

Whereas the blackness of the darker-skinned Remonds, regardless of their education, refinement, and sensitivity, resulted in exclusionary incidents, the recollected Purvis apparently experienced no similar difficulties. In actuality, according to Powell, many fellow citizens "of the better class," with no affiliations to the immediate emancipation campaign, highly regarded that "public spirited" individual. Since the chronicler never offered any information about how Purvis, "marked [with] dignity and grace of manner," obtained such acceptance among certain white Americans, the meaning of that statement lacks transparency. The commemorator, then, did not capitalize on the Purvis case in order to expose the speciousness of racist customs and practices in the antebellum past and post-bellum present alike.[51]

Powell's ruminations on Garrett and Carpenter therefore represent unstable, old abolitionist harbors. The collective impact of Garrett's fifth-column accomplishments and Carpenter's equalitarian actions fails to offset the cumulative weight of repeated purity references. Racial justice, of course, never vanished from the memoirist's field of vision. Surveying antebellum antislavery for the sake of antiracism, however, did not galvanize him, as the recollections of Remond and Purvis disclose. Within the larger context of the autobiographical text, the new abolitionism not only subsumes the older one but finally submerges it as well. Despite the volume's unfinished state, the author nonetheless realized his overarching purity intentions. Furthermore, in the fifty-page panegyric that follows the central narrative, Elizabeth Powell Bond helped complete both her deceased brother's composition and his unique agenda.

"It is deeply to be regretted," Bond professed, "that we cannot have from his own hand the history of the three decades that he has barely" traced. The dutiful sister thus committed much of her paean to doing what the autobiographer had left undone. Since he had already recorded the antebellum antislavery past, the eulogist complimented old abolitionist Aaron briefly (via a page of prose). In an attempt to fill in the empty postbellum spaces of his personal story, she acclaimed antialcohol Aaron in greater detail (over approximately six pages of prose) and antiprostitution Aaron even more extensively (through some seventeen pages of prose). However unintentionally, Bond essentially adhered to and expanded upon a firmly established authorial pattern.[52]

Even though the eulogized Powell gave himself "wholly to public service" in the immediate emancipation campaign for more than ten years and dedicated twenty-one more to editing the *National Temperance Advocate* after southern slavery's annihilation, social purity formed the pinnacle of his humanitarianism. "For nearly a quarter of a century," Bond trumpeted, "my brother has used his voice and pen in behalf of the cause which touches the very fountains of individual character and of national life." When the new abolitionists overseas appealed to him, the encomiast asserted, he eagerly and entirely made their movement his own. What the memoirist divulged, the sibling memorialist confirmed: Crusading against white slavery allowed Powell to reexperience and reinvent the old abolitionism.[53]

In the process of reviewing her relative's purity vocation, Bond integrated private and published correspondence into the presentation. One communiqué encapsulates the historical intersections and conjunctions between pre- and postwar abolitionism that the retrospective writer sought to forever enshrine. In an 1883 letter that the *Women's Journal* originally printed, Powell heralded the antiregulationist contest abroad as the re-embodiment of an earlier showdown at home, proclaiming that it instantly reminded him of the "American Abolitionists in their warfare against slavery." Whereas the public had once abhorred the leader of the immediate emancipation campaign—the *Liberator*'s editor—but eventually appreciated him, Powell believed that popular opinion would similarly unite around Josephine Butler, whom he denominated as "the pioneer of this great crusade for the emancipation of the white slave of State sanctioned vice." He further prognosticated that when the reincarnated Garrison freed prostitutes from an "odious" enslavement, she and her allies would procure "a truer liberty for all women, an ennobling influence for all men." By sharing the sense of familiarity that antiprostitution activists had personally inspired, the newspaper correspondent likely wanted to gain broader support for them. That Bond quoted the epistle only reinforced the nexuses that the autobiographer had discerned and devised between the two antislavery causes. Whether in 1883 or 1899, however, Powell's thinking principally comprehended how the old abolitionists set the stage for their new abolitionist analogues. He compiled his reminiscences so as to irradiate the dramatic role of the latter.[54]

The memoir's marketing also reiterated Powell's motivations. An advertisement appeared in the April 1900 edition of the *Philanthropist* and reappeared in subsequent installments for several years thereafter—as late as July 1905. Publicizing that the volume contains vignettes of old abolitionists like Garrison, Phillips, Mott, Lydia Maria Child, and John Greenleaf Whittier, it particularly touted the production's new abolitionist features. Indeed, as a five-sentence summary of the book, only one line of the posting pertains to antebellum antislavery, but three others give prominence to its postbellum replacement. The announcement also plugged the inclusion of a photographic image of Butler and a facsimile letter from the *Liberator*'s editor, both displaying Powell's "profound interest" in the fight against white slavery. That his final testament should resonate with "all friends" of antiprostitution and antivice was not merely a pointed sales pitch, for the memoirist wrote about his philanthropic life and times as a purity advocate, for a purity audience, and with a purity objective.[55]

Hardly an arbitrary decision, the insertion of Butler's picture within the section about the remembered Garrison not only fastened the respective founders of the old and new abolitionism tightly together. It transmitted as well a message in which the social purity cause benefited from and built upon the campaign to immediately emancipate the enslaved. In the years following Powell's death, moral agitators persisted in a commission that he had commenced in the United States. Newspaper articles, published tracts, and other printed miscellanea, for instance, provoked a veritable white slave panic between 1908 and 1914, so much so that the Congress, under the constitutional authority of Article I, Section 8, adopted legislation criminalizing the foreign and interstate transport of women and girls for "immoral purposes." The 1910 White Slave Traffic Act—also known as the Mann Act, after the statute's Republican sponsor, Representative James R. Mann of Illinois—denoted an official recognition of and confrontation with the perceived problems of prostitution and licentiousness that Powell had formerly uncovered. Besides perpetuating such new abolitionist endeavors, Powell's Progressive-era descendants substantially minimized an issue that no longer strongly registered on his own humanitarian radar. Despite the acceleration of Jim Crow discrimination and segregation across the Southland, white reformers of the early twentieth century, with the exception of those backing the National Association for the Advancement of Colored People, largely ignored African Americans.[56]

Before Powell essayed on his memorial and historical assignment, yet another assemblage of surviving old abolitionists enabled him to promote first concerns. Unable to attend a Danvers, Massachusetts, commemorative event, he forwarded a dispatch that the participants could read aloud and deliberate. Similar in theme to his 1883 thoughts at a like gathering, Powell's 1893 memo still assessed the immediate emancipation campaign as "the grandest moral movement of modern times." After counting himself as fortunate to have served alongside "noble, self-sacrificing leaders," he pronounced their legacy as alive and well. "More and more," he observed, "do the early Abolitionists become, as an object lesson, helpers and teachers to younger workers of this generation in dealing with the prevalent evils of our time." Even though he did not specify the new abolitionism or refer to any purity crusaders by name, anyone slightly aware of his reformist whereabouts since the 1870s would have understood what he meant. Interestingly, Powell concluded the missive by sharing his relief and joy that "just now Boston comes again to the front . . . to protest against our oppressive treatment and scandalous injustice" toward Chinese immigrants. If nothing else, such a declaration reveals that the fortunes of the freedpeople and their descendants had ceased to preoccupy him.[57]

A younger Powell sang a contrary philanthropic tune thirty years previously. In May 1865, he cautioned AASS exponents against any missteps in the Civil War's aftermath. Despite the "peculiar pleasure" produced by southern servitude's wartime wreckage, he instructed abolitionist companions on their outstanding obligations. As they wrangled over institutional disbandment, Powell delivered a full-throated commitment to the association's constitutional clause relating "to the elevation of the colored people." Emphasizing its "binding force," the soon-to-be director of the *National Anti-Slavery Standard* called for the prolongation of AASS-inspired agitation. He thus proposed a perfectly principled and practical solution to an otherwise contentious dissolution debate. For those who had "in their hearts and consciences a sense of duty to labor," Powell urged them onward in a "greatly useful" activity, one that would "cove[r] the ground of the still not wholly abolished slavery, and the still broader ground of human rights."[58]

Without a doubt, antiprostitution and antivice brought about significant—albeit unexpected—repercussions. The year in which Powell aligned with British antiregulationists, potentially momentous changes unfolded domestically. First, the disputed presidential election of 1876 eventually resulted in the ascendancy of the Republican candidate, Rutherford B. Hayes, whose administrative strategies symbolically ended the Reconstruction era. Second, racial conservatives effectively exploited northern fatigue over seemingly endless US governmental intervention in southern race relations by finalizing Democratic home rule via legal and extralegal means. At the birth of a new political order, after the demise of Republican state governments across the former Confederacy, the old abolitionist Powell discovered an alternative antislavery crusade. Ever watchful and resolute, he remained faithful to reconstructing individual Americans as well as American society, but only according to the purity standard. Aaron Macy Powell's annals reflect that altruistic transfiguration. They document it, too.

6

Songs of Innocence and Experience

*Thomas Wentworth Higginson
and the Abdication of Abolitionism*

During the 1890s a retrospective Thomas Wentworth Higginson combined and reissued previously printed autobiographical and biographical writings. *Cheerful Yesterdays* (1898) narrates the author's life and times; *Contemporaries* (1899) recounts influential altruists and artists whose careers intersected with his own. Since Higginson's story represented a chapter in a broader account that encompassed Emersonian Transcendentalism and Garrisonian abolitionism, he confided that "whether I will or no, something worth chronicling" would crop up in his personal survey. Whatever the sincerity of that self-effacing remark, the memoirist's familiarity with the movers and shakers who respectively "created American literature" and "freed millions of slaves" rendered his stocktaking as potentially insightful. Yet his work commemorating a revolutionary past ultimately sheds light onto a reactionary man of letters in the present. Songs of antebellum innocence did not conceal the retrogression that postbellum experience had produced. A septuagenarian Higginson neither attempted to rekindle the spirit of radical antislavery agitation nor repurpose its values for another phase of militant activism.[1]

Cheerful Yesterdays and *Contemporaries*, in tandem with assorted magazine pieces, newspaper articles, and civic addresses, itemize how a one-time exponent of violent means to end enslavement entered the less aggressive trade of learned culture. Even before the disintegration of the Republican Party's southern reconstruction project, Higginson began to construct himself as a public intellectual and cultural authority. Such refashioning expanded amid the return of white Democratic rule across the former Confederacy and advent of a new regional regime of racial discrimination and subordination thereafter. That he similarly handled the lives and deeds of antislavery evangelists and Transcendentalist literati, despite their divergent ambits, elucidates the nature of his authorial enterprise. His depictions of abolitionism subsequently offered late-nineteenth-century readers not a useable past per se but the judgments of an erudite commentator and urbane belletrist.[2]

The author additionally portrayed his earlier humanitarianism in a storybook manner. By treating the subject of himself as an aesthetic creation, conceived and interpreted according to his artistic sensibilities, the autobiographer prepared no one for neoabolitionism. Higginson's antislavery activities, rather than augmenting a moral and religious crusade against individual and communal sinfulness, often form a colorful backdrop for romantic tales of derring-do. His memorial and historical publications thus constitute an abdication, mapping a long retreat from an abolitionist militancy that had materialized in the late 1840s, intensified after the enactment of the 1850 Fugitive Slave Law, and reached a crescendo in his 1859 backing of John Brown's insurrectionary plot as well as his Civil War colonelcy of the Union's first authorized Black regiment. Even though he witnessed a reinstituted racial justice campaign, an about-face Higginson openly questioned the appropriateness of the National Association for the Advancement of Colored People. As the oeuvre of that inexhaustible public intellectual and presumptive cultural authority attests, he was a reliable sectional reconciliationist decades before the NAACP's 1909 founding.[3]

That the postbellum Higginson prioritized the man of letters over the man of reform should not instantly sound alarm bells. His literary ambitions, after all, antedated—and outlasted—his abolitionism. Poems were his first publications, not antislavery orations or protest pamphlets. The memoirist remained particularly proud of the 1843 opus "La Madonna di San Sisto," which takes an Italian Renaissance painting as its source of inspiration (specifically, a copy after a Raphael masterpiece). Originally appearing in the *Present*, he mentioned that the distinguished New England poet and Harvard educator Henry Wadsworth Longfellow later anthologized it in *The Estray*. Other published works followed that initial foray, surfacing in such journals as the Brook Farm–based *The Harbinger* (before the Civil War), as well as *Scribner's Monthly* and the *Atlantic Monthly* (during and/or after the Civil War). The release of two volumes of collected verse, in 1889 and 1893, further illustrates his lifelong dedication to the poetic craft and concurrent quest for lasting fame. Finally, Higginson helped introduce the creative genius of Emily Dickinson to poetry lovers in the early 1890s, when he coedited two compilations of the deceased writer's hitherto unpublished and unknown compositions.[4]

A conspicuous literariness defines his autobiographical and biographical texts for other reasons, too. After the *Atlantic Monthly*'s 1857 establishment, Higginson regularly wrote for that Boston-headquartered periodical. He pointed out that nobody else, with the exception of James Russell Lowell and Oliver Wendall Holmes Sr., had contributed more to its "first twenty volumes" than himself.

Altogether, some one hundred of his essays graced the magazine's pages, which also serialized the author's 1869 novel *Malbone: An Oldport Romance*. Such a sophisticated venue not only constituted Higginson's publishing outlet of choice. It cemented his credentials as a public intellectual as well. Whereas prior writings had "attracted little notice," he proclaimed that thanks to the publicity and acclaim that the *Atlantic* bestowed on its contributors, his "literary life" commenced in earnest. Quite understandably, the autobiographer highlighted the cultivated concerns that he so personally cherished. *Cheerful Yesterdays*, however, does not fully reflect his other vocation as a social activist.[5]

Even though the sketches generally underscore a history of engagement, their tone and contents also reveal a process of deradicalization. Higginson reported on how he had heard, seen, and experienced much over the years: as an undergraduate and divinity student at Harvard; a Unitarian pastor of congregations in Newburyport and Worcester, Massachusetts; a prominent antislavery agitator; a Union Army officer; a civil service reformer and Independent Republican member of the Massachusetts state assembly; as well as a cultural insider at home and abroad. By sharing his memories, the storyteller certainly hoped to edify audiences. His conversational style suggests that he wanted to regale them, too. That the *Atlantic* initially circulated most of the memoir's chapters, from 1896 to 1898, indicates that the undertaking always comprised a belletristic one. The very way that Higginson related his past transforms the narrator on the printed page into a charming supper guest or witty parlor visitor. He could not have envisioned anything better himself.[6]

The *Atlantic's* discerning subscribers conceivably enjoyed, for example, the raconteur's image of romantic youth. They might have additionally appreciated how well-read he was. By routinely dropping the names of cultural luminaries without much commentary, the chronicler enhanced his learned bona fides and simultaneously indexed his readership's polish. Regarding a younger self, the littérateur did not delineate him as an outright Bohemian. Nor did he commemorate the Harvard divinity student of the early 1840s as an unduly staid theologian. While completing his formal religious studies, the memoirist amusingly observed that he had retained a "perilous habit" of "miscellaneous reading." The remembered Higginson enriched himself by repeatedly revisiting classic works by Homer and Dante. He derived even greater nourishment from a bevy of modern thinkers and writers, such as the German poet Heinrich Heine, the German novelist Johann Paul Friedrich Richter (better known as "Jean Paul"), the German idealist philosopher Johann Gottlieb Fichte, the French novelist Amantine-Lucile-Aurore Dudevant (better known as "Georges Sand"), the French socialist philosopher

Charles Fourier, the English poet Samuel Taylor Coleridge, the English political philosopher John Stuart Mill, and the New England Transcendentalist Ralph
Waldo Emerson. One author's tome, however, posed some difficulties.[7]

Thomas De Quincey's *Confessions of an English Opium Eater* (1821), a now-
serious autobiographer opined, amounted to a most "perilous" handbook. That
laudanum-soaked tale of personal addiction and trancelike euphoria "doubtless
created more of such slaves than it liberated." Hardly a hearsay assessment, Higginson admitted that "I myself . . . tr[ied] some guarded experiments in that direction, which had happily no effect." Whether a transgression or not, an artistic
impulse—the desire "of stimulating my imagination"—reportedly spurred that
short-lived descent into a narcotic counterculture. Whatever the rationale, the
narrator announced that as a theology student, he represented two of three per-
sonality types demarcating Harvard Divinity School at the time: a Transcendentalist seeker among the "mystics," an inquisitive doubter among the "skeptics,"
but never an irritable novice among the "dyspeptics."[8]

Higginson's romanticism, however, neither started nor stopped with an opi-
oid. Its roots purportedly sank deeply into the soil of his birthplace and upbringing, as well as undergraduate and postbaccalaureate matriculation. Despite describing antebellum Cambridge as a "distinctly graded society," the retrospective
writer declared an immunity to local hierarchical mindsets. Somehow, he myste-
riously personified a bygone egalitarian ethos. The traces of the "popular feeling"
that so stirred the American Revolution still lingered, the memoirist mused, "for
without aid or guidance" he was instinctively democratic. Possessing no professional proclivities following his 1841 Harvard graduation, the eighteen-year-old
Higginson nonetheless approached the age of majority with unimpaired excitement, partly because of the "seething epoch" that he inhabited, the one in which
Sage of Concord Emerson had inaugurated. The storyteller recalled that as a
young buck, he wanted to toil as "a mechanic of some kind . . . in order to place
myself in sympathy with all." Based on his habitual reading, newfound essays
and books had convinced him that he should place himself "on more equal terms
with that vast army of hand-workers who were ignorant of much that I knew, yet
could do so much that I could not." The intuitive democrat of *Cheerful Yesterdays*
consequently performed "honest labor" on a railroad, from which he pocketed a
single dollar each day.[9]

If the 1840s truly approximated an idealistic new era, the personal historian
promulgated that he eagerly imbibed the intoxicating brew. Nor did he ingest an
entirely American brand of romanticism. After Emerson, a German Romantic
"took possession" of him. A freshly minted biography of Jean Paul, as well as

a recently translated Richter story, "set before" the recollected Higginson "the attractions of a purely literary life, carried on in a perfectly unworldly spirit." Fortified by that Teutonic model, which the autobiographer pointed out but never explicated, he shared an epiphany in which "poverty, or at least extreme economy, had no terrors for me." If anticipated artistic hardships once comprised an imposing obstacle for a rudderless Harvard alumnus, its removal did not clear a pathway forthwith. A brief tenure tutoring a cousin's children, the memoir-ist divulged, only accentuated the loneliness that he then felt, causing him to spend countless hours "in the woods, nominally botanizing but in reality trying to adjust . . . to the problems of life." Sustained contemplation of Mother Nature (as a proper Transcendentalist should), combined with reveries about "German romances," deepened his longing for "a free life of study, and perhaps of dreams." With such stimuli, the remembered Higginson finally resolved to resume his education at Harvard.[10]

As if to assure readers that his Cambridge homecoming signified a *cause ro-mantique*, the man of letters cited Henry David Thoreau to make his case. The author presented himself not merely in a Thoreauvian guise but also as a precur-sor of Concord's other famous philosopher. Before beginning a graduate resi-dency, he had pondered a one-person husbandry initiative that would have pre-dated, by some two years, the Walden Pond excursion and bean-farming scheme that Thoreau later conducted. "I carefully made out," the raconteur disclosed, "a project of going into the cultivation of peaches . . . thus securing [temporary] freedom from study and thought by moderate labor of the hands." Overtaken by a yearning to break away from "prescribed bondage" and to presumably live more deliberately as Thoreau would do, the recollected Higginson emblema-tized "that desire for a freer and more ideal life[style]" then passing "through the whole community." Returning to Harvard evidently did not derail his search for a simpler existence.[11]

To commune more meaningfully with interior and exterior worlds, the story-teller explained that he had arranged for the "cheapest room" possible, where "at last I could live in my own way, making both ends meet by an occasional pupil, and enjoying the same freedom which Thoreau, then unknown to me, was after-wards to possess in his hut." To be sure, Higginson's living frugally in a college town, with the intention of sowing "intellectual wild oats," did not equate to a solitary retreat into the forest for a couple years, so as to "front only the essential facts of life," in the Walden sojourner's words, and "learn what it had to teach." Regardless of the practical and theoretical disjunctions between the two, the nar-rator nevertheless emphasized the metaphysical qualities of his proposition: "I did not know exactly what I wished to study in Cambridge; indeed, I went there to find out." In so doing, he uncovered another layer of romanticism.[12]

Besides entailing voracious reading, which constituted a perpetual modus operandi, that voyage of discovery resulted, at least in the short run, in theological schooling and ecclesiastical training. Even though that decision dovetailed with his philosophical inclinations, the remembered Higginson's spiritual turn did not pivot on a fierce religiosity. Rather, the "potent" standards set by the Unitarian clergymen James Freeman Clarke and Theodore Parker propelled him to seize the idea-shaping and rhetoric-making opportunities of "the 'liberal' ministry." From Clarke, the chronicler averred, he acquired lessons on "the immense value of simplicity of statement and perfect straightforwardness of appeal." From Parker, the commemorator added, he gained instruction on the clerical mode "of pure thought and advanced independence." Together, they had proven that "one might accomplish something and lead a manly life even in the pulpit." Therein lies the key to understanding Higginson's pastoral calling and romantic predisposition. As *Cheerful Yesterdays* shows, both embraced a gendered element, centering on a refined masculinity. The Unitarian pulpit therefore represented an important destination for an aspiring public intellectual and cultural authority because the book's main protagonist hoped to do what paragon Parker particularly had done: hold parishioners "in the hollow of his hand" via forceful, profound, and captivating sermonizing.[13]

In addition to chasing a life of the mind, Higginson capped the new era of the 1840s by espousing abolitionism. Despite never specifying when he took up the slave's cause, the retrospective writer pronounced that after the commencement of his two-year stint at a Newburyport church in September 1847, "I was growing more, not less radical." To verify how radicalized he had gotten, Higginson once again correlated himself to the same Transcendentalist celebrity. In July 1846, Thoreau spent a night in jail for refusing to pay a local poll tax. The memoirist never discussed that disobedience, which the outbreak of the Mexican-American War and the prospect of extending southern servitude westward had sparked. He utilized a Thoreauvian measuring stick, however, to demonstrate that his antebellum "alienation" from the status quo "was almost as great" as the dissenting original's. Even though Higginson penned no memorable manifesto like Thoreau's 1849 "Resistance to Civil Government," the 1890s man of letters noted that his increasing isolation from the social and political mainstream initially manifested itself in a Free-Soil candidacy for public office. He expounded as well on the 1850 Fugitive Slave Act, which especially fomented his risk-taking activities.[14]

An enactment that had manufactured outrage across the North actually assuaged the radicalizing Higginson of *Cheerful Yesterdays*. The raconteur observed that upon entering the antislavery fight, he felt "only sorrow." Just "as Alexander lamented about his father Philip's conquests," the recollected Higginson feared that "nothing had been left for me to do." The thought that abolitionism's revolutionary ferment had bypassed him was originally discouraging; a provocative fugitive slave law altered everything immediately. It confirmed, in the remembered Higginson's estimation, that "there was plenty left to be done, and that Philip had not fought all the battles." For an autobiographer concerned about uniqueness, that legislative development mattered. Scarcely a latecomer, the movement newcomer arrived right on schedule—at least in the storyteller's schema of things.[15]

The next wave of abolitionist radicalism that a controversial statute necessitated also demanded, the author asserted, deeds-driven men: those who "meant business." In "The Fugitive Slave Epoch" chapter, he accordingly featured his heroic response to a loud-ringing tocsin, conversely omitting any resounding sense of commitment while recalling it. Rather than motivated by a mostly "moral conviction," the urge to deliver a dramatic strike against the slaveholding South stemmed, instead, from a powerful biological imperative. Whereas the democratic Higginson had mystically absorbed the egalitarianism of old Cambridge, as an antislavery partisan he reputedly inherited a penchant for gallantry from Revolutionary-era forebears. "Probably I got from my two soldier and sailor grandfathers," the personal historian surmised, "an intrinsic love of adventure which [has] haunted me" ever since "childhood." That "early emotion," he admitted, "was not created by the wish for praise alone, but was mainly a boyish desire for a stirring experience." By foregrounding such quixotic cravings, the littérateur's dashing rendition of his 1850s self came at the expense of an ethical and just protest tradition.[16]

To substantiate the seriousness of his pugnacious past, the retrospective writer separated himself from other white activists, as exhibited by his reminiscences of the runaway Thomas Sims's 1851 arrest. About an emergency session of Boston's Vigilance Committee, which had taken place at the publishing headquarters of William Lloyd Garrison's *Liberator*, Higginson painted the attendees in an unflattering light. Despite "personally admirable" attributes, the narrator could not fathom another gathering of dissidents "less fitted . . . to undertake any positive action in the direction of forcible resistance to authorities." Two alleged defects incapacitated such allies of Sims. On the one side, stood the ideological Garrisonian "non-resistants," who evinced more enthusiasm for "purifying . . . a nation," rather than the seemingly mundane issue of freeing someone from confinement.

On the other, the more pragmatic "political Abolitionists," who, regardless of their professed "indignation," evidenced greater anxiety about the prospect of seeming "outside the pale of good citizenship." As an ostensible agency of one, the book's main protagonist viewed things entirely differently.[17]

In comparison to well-intentioned but utterly inept comrades, the recollected Higginson comprehended that effective abolitionism required vigorous, physical opposition. He was not totally alone, though. A fellow committee member merited encomiums—the Greek War of Independence veteran and future Secret Six co-conspirator Samuel Gridley Howe. Yet, the authorial plaudits accorded to him appear not in *Cheerful Yesterdays* but an 1876 eulogy that reappears, in slightly revised form, in *Contemporaries*. In both accounts, Higginson revealingly esteemed the subject's antislavery life as "that of a man of chivalrous nature, with a constitutional love for freedom and daring enterprises, taking more interest in action than in mere agitation, and having, moreover, other fields of usefulness which divided his zeal." The beyond-words activism advocated by the memoirist and the memorialized Howe never flared up in 1851, because hundreds of police guarded the courthouse that held the recaptured Sims, chained doors restricted access to and from the building, and iron rods on windows barred any alternative entry or exit. However disappointed, Higginson reportedly learned to ultimately rely on himself should a similar happening transpire.[18]

The 1854 arrest of the runaway Anthony Burns the chronicler essentially presented as a godsend, one that had thankfully terminated an interregnum of "minor anti-slavery work." Apparently, assuming the pastoral office of a Worcester church that anchored a vibrant community of reformers, submitting articles to Free-Soil and "liberal Democratic" newspapers, frequenting abolitionist conventions, and occasionally escorting freedom seekers to Underground Railroad safe spots constituted insufficiently exhilarating service. The very event from which Higginson would build a public reputation as a bold freedom fighter produced, at first, another purportedly useless Vigilance Committee meeting. It sank to a pitifully farcical level, in this retelling, after participants abruptly adjourned their discussion so that the moralizers could gaze upon Burns's captors passing by outside and wag "'the finger of scorn.'" Such behavior warranted nothing but commemorative contempt: "as if Southern slave catchers," the author mordantly quipped, "were to be combated by such weapons." The remembered Higginson thus knew not only that "something must be done" but that he personally had to do it. Better to fail, according to his logic, "than acquiesce tamely as before, and see Massachusetts henceforward made a hunting-ground for fugitive slaves."[19]

Thanks to that vow, forcible-resister Higginson emerged as a starring player
in a spectacular free-for-all, which climaxed not with the glorious release of a detained runaway but the stunning death of a deputy US marshal. Decades after the
fact, the autobiographer invested the incidents surrounding James Batchelder's
"killing" with tremendous worth. They did not just precede the Kansas territorial imbroglio or John Brown's Harpers Ferry expedition. Rather, the storming
of the Boston courthouse doors, the push to seize the apprehended fugitive, and
the bloodshed that ensued marked the start of an advancing sectional crisis and
impending military conflict. "Like the firing on Fort Sumter," he maintained, the
foiled Anthony Burns rescue signified "that war had really begun." Regardless
of the actual or imagined outcomes, it enabled a propagandist of the antislavery
deed to showcase subversive mettle.[20]

The storyteller irradiated how he, along with a "stout negro," occupied the forefront of a fracas in which the assailants strove to smash open a locked entrance
with a wooden beam. As soon as they did so, the recollected Higginson and his
"black ally" then rushed inside the building, only to come across "six or eight
policemen" awaiting them. Whereas the two rescuers relied on their fists, the op-
posing guardsmen "hammer[ed] away" at their "heads" with clubs. Even though
the raconteur referred to some earlier "boxing lessons" that allowed for a modest
counterattack, the charge collapsed, but not for want of pluck or stamina. Unfortunately, nonresistant Garrisonians and political abolitionists helped undermine
the push, at least in this reckoning. Instead of joining the melee, they safely remained among the onlookers, inaction that the personal historian characterized
as spineless and effete. Moralistic and reputable abolitionism, quite simply, fell
woefully short of the militant antislavery banner that Higginson championed at
the time. If nothing else, the valor of an anonymous African American made a
strong impression. It "was of inestimable value to me," the memoirist attested,
removing "once and for all every doubt of the intrinsic courage of the blacks."
Such an arbitrary admission, however, only complicates the narrative. Evidently,
a Civil War decision to command the First South Carolina Volunteer Infantry
and its freedom-seeking enlistees depended on the 1854 behavior of a single person of color (namely, Lewis Hayden), whom the narrator neglected or declined
to identify.[21]

Besides counting himself as among the select few who had acquitted themselves valiantly, the retrospective writer waxed literarily about his postskirmish
fate. A potential arrest, as well as trial and conviction, reminded him of the
French Catholic priest and philosopher Félicité Robert de Lamennais. Incarceration subsequently raised no terrors, for that nineteenth-century essayist, whom

the man of letters quoted without translation, had taught him "to regard any life as rather incomplete which did not, as in his own case, include some experience of imprisonment in a good cause." If a spell behind bars was the requisite risk and fitting reward for a well-lived existence, the absence of any jailing meant that the autobiographer must rest his revolutionary laurels elsewhere. He therefore viewed the receipt of a cut on the chin not merely as an appropriate battlefield scar but a genuinely romantic achievement. The author further insisted that since "the sincere law-breakers of the world are the children of temperament as well as of moral conviction," he would comport himself in the same manner if 1850s circumstances suddenly repeated themselves. The remembered Higginson assuredly displayed the former trait; the latter, however, had no demonstrable impact on his quarrelsome variety of abolitionism. If the 1890s littérateur meant what he wrote, then he might have equally articulated the humanitarian principles presumably undergirding a previously confrontational career.[22]

Adhering to an authorial pattern fashioned by the Fugitive Slave Law, the recollected Higginson gallantly challenged an additionally divisive governmental directive. By lifting a preexisting prohibition on enslavement throughout Louisiana Purchase lands north of latitude 36°30', the 1854 Kansas-Nebraska Act opened the possibility of slavery's expansion into the Kansas or Nebraska provinces, should the settlers themselves choose to recognize and establish it. Of the two, Kansas's status triggered heated debate and violent contests, largely because of its close proximity to slaveholding Missouri. Even though the memoirist did not delve into the legislative minutiae, he charted an 1856 swashbuckling escapade in which he headed a contingent of men to colonize the territorial battlefront for free soil, free labor, and free men. Purely denouncing the "Border Ruffian" Missourians, who had sought to secure the area for proslavery interests by crossing into neighboring locales and taking part in their elections, could never have slaked his thirst for derring-do.[23]

The personal historian derived much pride from the fact that the migrants under his command carried weapons. Only the Massachusetts Kansas Aid Committee and its branches, with which Higginson affiliated, unhesitatingly did what the more commercially minded New England Emigrant Aid Society either refused to do or reluctantly had done: "arm any party of colonists more openly and thoroughly" against real and potential perils. Akin to the foreshadowing courthouse scuffle to liberate Anthony Burns, the autobiographer viewed the recruitment and mobilization of New England men for the free-state Kansas scrimmage as a "rehearsal . . . of the great enlistments of the Civil War." Since the travelers under the auspices of the Worcester County Kansas Committee also promised to dwell there upon arrival, they exemplified far better settlement stock than the Border Ruffian transients. Whereas the latter vacated the region after casting votes for proslavery candidates, the former tilled the very soil that they fought to preserve for free men like themselves and protect from slavery's invasion. In the storyteller's evaluation, that colonizing component "finally gave Kansas to freedom."[24]

Since the retrospective writer romantically portrayed his frontier stopover, he arguably de-escalated a Great Plains standoff. Regarding a solitary trek from Nebraska to Iowa, he described an unspecified errand as a sort of knight-errant. He recalled the intense thoughts and emotions that overcame him while traversing "about twenty miles of debatable ground," which hostiles from both camps had recently swept. To encapsulate the harsh terrain, the raconteur summoned the setting or mood of a Sir Walter Scott novel. "Every swell of the rolling prairie," he rhapsodized, furnished "a possible surprise, and I had some of the stirring sensations of a [mid-seventeenth-century] moss-trooper." That expanse, even though it did not comprise a veritable no-man's land, constituted an alluringly uncivilized zone in his imagination—the Scottish Highlands of North America. "Never before in my life," the narrator proclaimed, "had I been, distinctively and unequivocally, outside . . . the world of human law." Whatever the lawlessness of the western situation, the remembered Higginson could not help but recite apropos poetic verse. The respective works of the Victorian-era bards Robert Browning and George Walter Thornbury had especially seized his wilderness fancy. Besides buttressing the main protagonist's romantic aura, such allusions underpinned the memoirist's pretentions as a public intellectual and cultural authority.[25]

The man of letters did not solely depend on literary references in order to convey how borderlands uncertainty had inspired him. He also rendered his excursion as an instance in which life and art crisscrossed. Transit through the "Border Ruffian town" of Leavenworth, Kansas, served as the storybook backdrop. The recollected Higginson temporarily halted there, wanting to unofficially monitor the operation of democratic processes in enemy country. The "fifty liquor shops for two thousand inhabitants" appalled him promptly. That "strangers were begged to take a hand in the voting, as if it were something to drink," heightened the community's shady qualities. Despite declining to partake of the suffrage dram himself, the autobiographer indicated that the proslavery locals saw no reason why lack of residency should result in his ballot-box abstinence. The real drama and suspense, though, pertained to a discussion among some antiabolitionists.[26]

While stealthily inspecting Leavenworth, the remembered Higginson over-heard a group of men conversing about an infiltrating antislavery clergyman who preached politics, "'the sufferin' niggers,'" and what should befall the inter-loper if anyone identified him. Permanently etched onto the author's memory, he quoted the exchange verbatim. Amid the talk of his own mobbing, Higginson professed that "I listened with dubious enjoyment." As a consumer of histori-cal romances since childhood—each evening, his mother had read aloud from "one of [Scott's] Waverley novels"—he now found himself at the center of such a tale. Interestingly, in a series of Kansas-themed letters that the *New-York Tribune* printed in 1856, Higginson, under the pseudonym "Worcester," relayed the same eavesdropped conversation without any romantic inflections. Throughout all the dispatches, the correspondent straightforwardly reported on what he saw and heard on the Great Plains field of combat. The artistic flourishes materialized much later only.[27]

Exposure to a disorderly West positively enchanted the recollected Higgin-son. Despite the absence of experiential violence during his stay, "danger," the memoirist italicized, "had always to be guarded against." Returning to regular civilization reputedly debilitated and unnerved the short-lived frontiersman. Once he made it to St. Louis, for example, the remembered Higginson volun-tarily disarmed himself. No longer deeming his revolver as mandatory or useful, he stowed it in a luggage case, a seemingly simple act that the retrospective writer singled out as a transformative moment. With the resumption of the ordinary, he realized that if any threats to his safety arose, he would have "to look meekly about for a policeman." That depressing revelation (which occurs nowhere in the *Tribune* missives) sapped "all the vigor" from him, causing "a despicable effemi-nacy . . . [to] set in." Nothing but a Walter Scott scenario expressed the depths of those feelings, further illuminating his gender-infused romanticism. "I could [now] perfectly understand," he remarked, "how Rob Roy, wishing to repay a debt he owed to the Edinburgh professor, offered to take his benefactor's son back into the Highlands 'and make a man out of him.'" No other autobiographi-cal episodes broadcast a replenishment of lost virility. The narrated Higginson's period of storm and stress reached a high point on the Great Plains.[28]

In the same memorial section in which the personal historian revisited a Kan-sas holiday, he reminisced about Harpers Ferry. As the topic shifted, so too did the authorial tenor. After enumerating antislavery vigilantism with palpable zest, Higginson suddenly scrapped both his sui generis standing among white activ-ists and unique role in aggressive abolitionism's antebellum zenith. In contrast to "Bleeding Kansas" reflections, which reinforced notions of youthful bravado, Higginson's meditations on John Brown severely minimized former radicalism. Ditto for other ones on the South Carolina Volunteers. *Cheerful Yesterdays* thus contains a noticeably imbalanced narrative. Electrifying fugitive slave rescue efforts and galvanizing disputes over slavery's geographical extension represented the stuff of splendid action-and-adventure storytelling. A zealous Brown and his biracial syndicate of insurrectionists, in conjunction with deadly North-South warfare and the arming of freedom-seeking African Americans, elicited comparatively prosaic and restrained ruminations. Truly, the romantic rebelliousness of the book's main protagonist did not survive the roaring 1850s.

Early on, Higginson rebuffed any responsibility for what happened in western Virginia in October 1859. As an abolitionist infiltration of slaveholding country, he insisted that John Brown's commission originally hewed to narrow parameters. That attacking a US Armory and Arsenal never factored into the blueprint the retrospective writer made abundantly clear by summarizing how the mastermind himself had promoted it. Among current and prospective sponsors, the latter would broach an endeavor to permanently station escapees from slavery in the holds of the Alleghany Mountains, "like the Maroons of Jamaica and Surinam," and occasionally shepherd them to Canadian freedom from that topographical sanctuary. Such a sortie, as presented by Higginson, complemented the already existing Underground Railroad. Since nothing was "objectionable or impracticable," as the memoirist matter-of-factly stated, its Massachusetts backers—Howe, Parker, Franklin Sanborn, George Luther Stearns, and himself—readily cooperated.[29]

Quite tellingly, neither the dramatis personae of the Secret Six nor their clandestine exertions on behalf of a slave-abduction conspiracy ignited the raconteur's literary romanticism. Rather than weave a gripping tale of intrigue, he opted to scrutinize the operational leader. To extract John Brown's essence, the public intellectual categorized him as "a high-minded, unselfish, belated Covenanter." He noted that his face bore no marks of "pettiness or baseness," but its "thin, worn, [and] resolute" features betrayed "the signs of a fire which might wear him out, and practically did so." He also mentioned that his mode of speech was "calm, persuasive, and coherent." To crown the portrayal, the cultural authority reverted to a tried-and-true practice. Just as the historical novel permitted the autobiographer to colorfully picture his western borderlands romp, it enabled him to evocatively profile Brown's person, which he likened to something that "Sir Walter Scott might have drawn." In his habitually bookish vein, Higginson deduced that the Harpers Ferry raider, despite a humorless nature, possessed "no more of coarseness than was to be found in [Scott's] Habakkuk Mucklewrath or in [novelist] George Eliot's Adam Bede." Expressed in less learned terms, such a real-life character evinced an elevated religiosity that approximated "a kind of refinement."[30]

Even though Higginson's Brown epitomized the uncompromising, one-idea man—a "pure enthusiast . . . fanatic, if you please"—he reportedly applied that fervor to a harmless belief that an omniscient deity had predestined the Alleghenies as a refuge for runaways. Regardless of the impressive power of Brown's religious probity, the personal historian affirmed that it wielded zero influence over himself. Only basic logistics evidently persuaded him to lend assistance. To his satisfaction, Brown, as a former surveyor, "knew points which could be held by a hundred men against a thousand." That the latter had arranged "charts of some of those localities and . . . connected mountain fortresses" also carried extra weight. Such an explanation proved to late-nineteenth-century readers that nothing could swindle a shrewd Higginson, who could easily detect a sound venture from a farfetched one. In that way, the romantic revolutionary mellowed into a remarkably levelheaded investor.[31]

However newfound, that sensible genius comprises something more than a fleeting storyline. Pragmatic considerations not only steered the recollected Higginson's undercover partnership with Brown. They accounted for why he never accompanied him southward as well. Before learning of the Harpers Ferry assault, via the popular press, the retrospective writer avowed that he had had little contact with the ringleader for over a year. He alluded to a spring of 1858 development to substantiate the claim. When a Brown collaborator—namely, Hugh Forbes—threatened to expose everything unless the Secret Six purchased his silence, a membership majority agreed to postpone the pending mission. After that, the remembered Higginson assumed that the "project had been abandoned." Despite acknowledging that a group insider notified him, in June 1859, that "'Brown has set out on his expedition,'" the author denied having prior knowledge of what eventually took place. As if to counteract skepticism, he tersely proclaimed: "Nobody mentioned Harper's Ferry [to me]." Brown's attempted takeover of a US arms depot, then, not only shocked other Americans. It allegedly took Higginson by surprise, too.[32]

Upon reading about Brown's blitz, the memoirist confessed to instant remorsefulness. The recollected Higginson felt sorrow not for the unfortunate souls who, in fact, journeyed to western Virginia but for the financiers who never literally followed Brown to the Southland. To further justify his own absence from the convoy, the autobiographer declared that given the frequent delays, he came to see the whole undertaking as "rather vague and dubious." Whereas he had grown less and less absorbed with each passing month, repeated deferments supposedly wrought a contrary effect on Brown. They irreparably upset the "delicate balance of the zealot's mind," in the storyteller's estimation, causing his Covenanter enthusiasm to attain alarmingly monomaniacal proportions. Prudence had, indeed, rewarded the remembered Higginson, who ostensibly backed Brown contingently: based on the relative reasonability of the planner and overall feasibility of his plan.[33]

Despite that commemorative act of divestment, the chronicler did not totally sever himself from the Harpers Ferry raider. Concerning why he never absconded from the United States in order to evade possible legal ramifications for affiliating with Brown, the raconteur's 1859 self seemingly mustered the courageousness that had defined his participation in the unsuccessful Anthony Burns rescue. Since Secret Six members "befriended" Brown's enterprise as "we understood" it, he contended that each had an obligation to stand firmly behind the captured crusader. Yet given a purportedly loose association with Brown and fixed awareness of his intentions, the 1890s narrator apprised audiences that he never worried about his destiny. Hardly trying, a trial would have provided an official venue to both absolve himself and acquit Brown of a major criminal charge. Even though he never faced a jury of his peers, the man of letters testified before readers that inciting a slave uprising, "in the ordinary sense of the word, was remote from [Brown's] thoughts." Such a depiction symbolizes how the littérateur specifically retreated from forcible-resistance abolitionism on the very pages of *Cheerful Yesterdays*. Since later scholarship has demonstrated that Higginson fully comprehended the insurrectionary lineaments of Brown's design, the memorialist also withheld information and manipulated facts while revising antislavery history.[34]

Several years before Higginson neutralized his life story, he more graciously analyzed John Brown's curriculum vitae for the 1888 *Appletons' Cyclopædia of American Biography*. In an entry that spans four double-columned pages, he predominantly covered the subject's exploits in Kansas Territory and western Virginia. Whereas the memoirist barely commented on the Pottawatomie massacre, the encyclopedist forthrightly addressed the infamous nighttime occurrence of May 24–25, 1856, in which Brown, his sons, and others whom he commanded executed five proslavery settlers. Even though Higginson endorsed the slaughter not at all, he harnessed a tit-for-tat rationalization in order to soften a brutal affair that "friends and foes" alike had deemed as Brown's "most questionable" deed. The midnight murders came about, he pointed out, "in avowed retribution for the assassination of five free-state men, and was intended to echo far beyond Kansas, as it did, and to announce to the slave-holding community that blood for blood would henceforth be exacted in case of any further invasion of rights." Unlike that defense, the autobiographer doubted the very necessity of Brown's frontier bloodletting. In a 1906 article for *Alexander's Magazine*, Higginson basically sidestepped the issue.[35]

Regarding Brown's slave-abduction scheme and the Secret Six schemers, the encyclopedist sketched both mainly in the same style as the 1898 memoirist. In contrast to the personal historian's judgmental conclusions about the firebrand's mental state, the 1888 essayist employed greater judiciousness, innocently observing that the evolution of Brown's machinations "no doubt bore marks of the over-excited condition of his mind." Of the three publications, the author asserted only in the first that Brown's Massachusetts backers supplied much-needed money and munitions from their "personal faith in him" and "a common zeal for his objects." They did so, he additionally specified, "without asking to know details." The sole certainty reportedly pertained to the Allegheny mountain range, which continually formed the project's literal and figurative bastion in Higginson's various delineations.[36]

The encyclopedist next turned to the sundry events around the Harpers Ferry dustup. He discussed where Brown and his men stationed themselves in the weeks leading up to the invasion; the initiation of the assault itself; and the capture, trial, and hanging of the principal architect. Concerning what motivated Brown to effectively wage warfare on the US government by targeting one of its arsenals, Higginson hypothesized that he had "desire[d] . . . to alarm the country at large, and not merely to secure arms, but attract recruits to his side after he should have withdrawn." Even though Brown had always hoped to obtain weapons, the essayist quickly tempered that aspiration's radical magnitude. Any confiscated hardware would end up in the hands of freedom seekers so that they could defend themselves, if necessary, while either ensconced in the regional mountains or before embarking northward for Canada. A violent slave revolt never entered the equation—at least according to Higginson's 1888, 1898, and 1906 treatments.[37]

As for Brown's inability to evacuate the armory complex and adjoining village before US forces had arrived, the encyclopedist offered no interpretation. He, instead, paraphrased a remark that the jailed ringleader putatively uttered about losing control of himself for the "first time" and swiftly getting "punished" for it. The essayist also pointed out that of the few followers who fled from the attack site, none could answer for the captain's remaining there. In the *Alexander's*

Magazine piece, Higginson classified Brown's Harpers Ferry decision-making as an impenetrable enigma. No analyst, he argued, "has ever precisely solved or will solve the strange impulse which led him to substitute a hopeless bit of self-sacrifice—of himself and others—for the more deliberate and wholly practicable plans of his earlier days." The Brown conundrum, he tendered, was as "perplexing to many students as the Negro question itself." The memoirist, however, discarded his 1888 tentativeness and definitively cracked the riddle that he would pose in 1906.[38]

For the autobiographer, an astonishing raid and a forsaken retreat boiled down to an agitated psyche. Based on an 1860 interview with an incident survivor, Charles Plummer Tidd, he underscored that "a final loss of mental balance," caused by "overbrooding on one idea," had induced Brown's strike against a US arms depot. The encyclopedist, by comparison, cited the contemporaneous opinions of Governor Henry Wise of Virginia, which had rejected the notion of a madman Brown, as a "final and trustworthy estimate." During a ten-year interval, then, appraiser Higginson significantly reconsidered a controversial figure. In 1888, he highly rated Brown's career, in consideration of "the important part he played in events preliminary to the great civil war, and for the strong and heroic traits shown in his life and death." By 1898, he patently dismissed Brown as an unhinged extremist. Despite a 1906 recognition of the nobility with which Brown deported himself both on the Osawatomie battlefield and Charleston scaffold, Higginson criticized the reputed hero. He therefore pinpointed Brown's "needlessly artificial and elaborate mode of organization for a band of men whose methods and aims appear indeterminate," in tandem with "the growing unsteadiness of mind," as the sources of his demise. In contrast to such surety about Brown's insanity, Higginson's Secret Six never constituted a revolutionary cadre. If recollecting Harpers Ferry represented a memorial Rubicon, after crossing it the personal historian virtually renounced antislavery radicalism.[39]

Not even the Civil War refreshed the raconteur's gusto. Since Higginson had already set down his martial experiences in an 1869 book, a single chapter on the First South Carolina Volunteers raises no red flags. That he described army life in a Black regiment with little romantic flair sticks out nonetheless. Despite declaring that his military assignment "took my breath away, and fulfilled a dream of a lifetime," his remembrances downplay the uniqueness of fighting against slavery alongside the formerly enslaved. Closer to the conflict, Colonel Higginson powerfully articulated the post's meaningfulness. "I had been an abolitionist too long," he pronounced, "and had known and loved John Brown too well, not to feel a thrill of joy at last finding myself in the position where he only wished to be." Whereas an 1860s Higginson proudly viewed himself as a new Brown, the 1890s man of letters once more buffered himself from old Brown's fanaticism.[40]

Over multiple paragraphs the memoirist gauged the general characteristics of his "warlike material," particularly vouching for the inherent manliness and soldierly fitness of freed-slave fighters. Yet since the autobiographical agenda never surpassed an acknowledgment that Black troops had neither humiliated themselves nor disappointed their white commander, such an account scarcely functioned as a rousing call for racial equity and inclusion amid unfolding Jim Crow discrimination and segregation. Even though the storyteller summed up an actually historic situation as regretfully humdrum, consisting mostly of un-eventful "outpost and guerilla duty," he nevertheless compared himself with an exalted Union Army officer. Just as references to Thoreau allowed Higginson to accentuate his Transcendentalism, he now referred to Robert Gould Shaw with the apparent intention of amplifying his Civil War reputation.[41]

Owing to a nameless African American coadjutor during the failed Anthony Burns rescue, the main protagonist of Cheerful Yesterdays knew "in advance of the essential courage of the blacks." Higginson's Shaw was initially skeptical about their bravery. The leader of the Fifty-fourth Massachusetts Volunteers, the retrospective writer divulged, had once admitted that African American enlistees might require a line of whites directly at their rear, thereby ensuring that they would not refuse to fire and flee from the front. Such a confession ut-terly "amazed" the recollected Higginson, for he "never should have dreamed of . . . such a step." Even though the author observed that Shaw's unit amply proved its audacity and fearlessness, he added nothing else of substance about the "young hero" or Black men who had lost their lives in the 1863 Battle of Fort Wagner. The only thing that evidently mattered: how he personally stacked up against another Bay State legend.[42]

Besides outdoing Shaw on a race-related detail, the autobiographer presum-ably merited a pedestal for other reasons. The experiment of enlisting people of color in order to perpetuate the Union not only officially began with himself but allegedly expanded thanks to his pathbreaking colonelcy. That approximately two hundred thousand African Americans "march[ed] in that column where the bayonets of the First South Carolina had once gleamed alone" brought him im-mense happiness. Regardless of that contentment, readying the formerly enslaved for combat amounted to no apogee of aggressive abolitionism—certainly not in the 1890s. The Black soldiers whom he recalled possessed a definite purpose—they had donned blue uniforms on behalf of African American liberty—but an unmistakably emancipatory message never emerges from the narrative. How the narrator finished the chapter sheds insight onto the forces affecting his postbellum priorities. Whereas active duty "checked" the remembered Higginson's "literary pursuits," demobilization relit his "love of letters." As a civilian, though, he did not simply recommence aesthetic interests. After the cessation of hostilities, the littérateur practically discharged himself from militant activism as well.[43]

In an 1867 *Atlantic Monthly* essay, Higginson postulated that "we seem nearly at the end of those great public wrongs . . . requir[ing] a special moral earthquake" to topple them. The perceived absence of compelling social issues—excepting women's suffrage, which apparently proceeded along "very peaceably"—meant that the man of letters could earnestly fight for culture. Since the United States had lacked a Europeanesque "literary class," he accordingly trumpeted the guidelines that would elevate American writing to a fine art. Higginson still engaged in reform over the next forty years, but his allegiance to "poetry, *belles-lettres*, or pure literature" continuously triumphed. Other post–Civil War writings further spotlight the belletristic mindset that informed and impaired his memorial and historical pen. Some even expose a distinctive mutation, whereby a radical activist degenerated into a sectional reconciliationist.[44]

Shortly after the publication of *Cheerful Yesterdays*, Higginson released another collection of previously printed pieces. Of *Contemporaries'* nineteen chapters, most revolve about an eminent Transcendentalist, an accomplished verse and prose stylist, a well-known statesman, or a famous abolitionist. Despite sections on the writer-reformers Lydia Maria Child and John Greenleaf Whittier, those dealing with William Lloyd Garrison and Wendell Phillips particularly document how Higginson divorced himself from a movement that he professedly "loved." Even though the commentator primarily assessed the artistic output of Child and Whittier, to the neglect of their respective antislavery contributions, he notably scanned the abolitionism of Garrison and Phillips from a public intellectual's standpoint. As a knowing observer, Higginson progressively retreated from an ongoing African American freedom struggle. His personal push for cultural authority coalesced with a stance on southern race relations that, however conflicted occasionally, was conciliatory far more regularly.[45]

Higginson opened the audit of Garrison, portions of which had appeared in the *International Review* (in 1880) and *Atlantic Monthly* (in 1886), with accolades. Recognizing that a "single hand" did not slay enslavement, he nonetheless attributed the "ultimate result" to the leader of the "Garrisonian or Disunion Abolitionists." The *Liberator's* editor alone, the author averred, operated as "an original and creative force," while everyone else "reflect[ed] the current of popular progress." Despite the 1840 splintering of the AASS into competing factions, which had rendered the Garrisonians as "the narrowest of the streams . . . mak[ing] up the mighty river" of organized abolitionism, Higginson decided that they comprised the "loftiest height" and "greatest head of water." Regardless of numerical insignificance, the clique over which Garrison presided was enormously influential.[46]

Unlike the memoirist's mocking finger-wagging Garrisonians in *Cheerful Yesterdays*, they no longer obstruct a new phase of revolutionary abolitionism in this authorial text. The proponents of "physical[ly] rescu[ing]" fugitive slaves, the essayist maintained, were the Garrisonians' "pupils." The partisans who cast ballots for antislavery political candidates "drew strength from them" as well. The veteran officer of the First South Carolina Volunteers even argued that despite the limited role of the Garrisonians in raising Civil War troops, "the tradition of their influence did much to impel the army." Yet simply extolling Garrison and his disciples did not motivate Higginson in 1880, 1886, or 1899. The group's easygoing ally, after all, never developed into a full-fledged acolyte. Once the man of letters deployed his critical gaze, anyone and anything was assailable.[47]

The inveterate critic parsed Garrison's corpus selectively in *Contemporaries*, concentrating not on the editorialist but the speechmaker. Besides possessing a "firm and well-built person," the expert analyst found especially impressive the "moral strength" that the orator's countenance exuded. A reverend solemnity also characterized his utterances, which Higginson described as "grave, powerful, with little variety or play." Even though the appraiser mentioned a "sonorous" voice, an otherwise pleasing quality quickly became a rhetorical shortcoming. Rather than conceal, the deep and resonating vocal sounds evidently accented Garrison's "usually monotonous" and "sometimes fatiguing" speechifying. Despite his reputation as a "leading figure on the platform," the vaunted abolitionist showcased no silver tongue. That drawback practically displaced any other oratorical virtue that the auditor introduced.[48]

Garrison's "reason," according to an aesthetically attuned Higginson, "marched like an army *without* banners." The elocutionary problem surrounded the scathing invectives that the antislavery crusader commonly vented from the rostrum. As a judicious reviewer, and not some hero worshipper, he stressed that the denunciations bore no signs of "personal anger." Rooted in Holy Scripture, they, instead, "seemed like a newly discovered chapter of Ezekiel." Such Old Testament seriousness never registered with a cosmopolitan Higginson. Since the orator in question "constantly reiterated . . . his argument with ample details, and had a journalist's love for newspaper cuttings, which he inflicted without stint upon his audience," the evaluator adjudged him as stylistically deficient overall.

"I cannot honestly say," the littérateur decreed, "that I ever positively enjoyed one of his speeches." Nor did he always "fai[l] to listen with a sense of deference and of moral leadership," a disclosure that apparently upheld Garrison's controlling presence at old-time gatherings.[49]

Wendell Phillips, by comparison, occupied premier space in Higginson's pantheon of rhetoricians. For the perceptive investigator, who first delivered his verdict in an 1884 copy of the *Nation*, Phillips enjoyed "the perfect moulding of the orator." A "conversational" manner reputedly constituted the indispensable ingredient of his public-speaking flawlessness. No one else, the essayist supposed, spoke so effortlessly, beginning each event "as if he simply repeated" more loudly what he had just said to "some familiar friend at his elbow." Despite an early tendency to formulate addresses beforehand, the commemorated Phillips largely depended on his wits and thrived on improvisation. The results, according to the chronicler, were completely "disarming." The unaffected informality and colloquialisms of the master speechmaker, in conjunction with the "poise of his manly figure, the easy grace of his attitude, the thrilling modulation of his [superbly] trained voice, the dignity of his gesture, [and] the keen penetration of his eye," mesmerized audiences. The man of letters inferred that Phillips's performances had personally transported him, too.[50]

Concomitant with the oratorical prestige conferred on Phillips, Higginson underlined the downside of a platform-speaking vocation. Such a path, he pontificated, presented hazards and produced pitfalls. While persistently traveling it, one "acquires . . . the mood of the gladiator, and, the better his fencing, the more he becomes the slave of his own talent." To the detriment of an entrancing antebellum lecturer, in the examiner's judgment, he never surrendered combative Garrisonianism. Higginson thus determined that the unrelenting verbal jousting of Phillips's abolitionist training and profession not only marred his postbellum effectiveness but also made him into a misguided and outmoded reformer.[51]

After slavery's destruction, the recollected Phillips manifested "a certain restlessness," perpetually longing for "some new tournament." As proof of the pitiable depths to which an august personage had fallen, Higginson alluded to a Greenback Party collaboration between Phillips and Benjamin F. Butler, supposedly "the most unscrupulous soldier of fortune who ever posed as a Friend of the People on this side of the Atlantic." He additionally noted that an anachronistic Phillips contested the rising power of industrial capitalism while still dressed in the garb of crusading abolitionism. "Preaching" holy wars on "complex" Gilded Age problems, in the author's evaluation, was terribly unfashionable and inappropriate. Rather than alleviate the plight of downtrodden laborers, Higginson's

Phillips only depreciated himself. The critic consequently discarded the ossified agitator's thoughts on workers' rights and money matters, alleging that he never "profoundly studied" the topics anyway. In the days of chattel servitude, "appealing to sympathy and passion" might have sufficed. For the clear-eyed commentator, though, modern questions demanded up-to-date solutions.[52]

Mature self-reflection evidently revealed to Higginson the time-specific nature of "a great moral movement." That a late-in-life Phillips adhered to a "'Let my people go'" mindset and equated everything as absolutely right or wrong served as the requisite evidence of his inability to evolve. While concocting such a sad story and cautionary tale, Higginson briefly pondered Edmund Quincy's antithetical—and subsequently apposite—pathway. As freedom for the enslaved accelerated during the Civil War, the remembered Quincy resolved that "there was no other battle worth fighting." Rather than tilt at windmills, à la Phillips, he gladly "reverted . . . to that career of cultivated leisure" from which decades of championing the slave's cause had "wrenched him." That "*désœuvré*," or aimless, abolitionist therefore devoted his twilight years to music appreciation and theatergoing. The cultural authority enlarged on that synopsis in an 1898 article for the *Outlook*, invoking other French concepts and deriving the same lessons about the appropriately refined existence of "reformer *emeritus*" Quincy.[53]

Even though Higginson celebrated Phillips as undoubtedly "heroic," his sometimes stinging assessment commands attention, all the more so since it originally circulated but a few days after the renowned orator's death. A recent decease did not necessarily elicit a similarly probing analysis of the *Liberator's* editor, for newly published biographies had mobilized the public intellectual into action during the 1880s. In an 1886 book review, for example, he welcomed the filiopietistic account prepared by Garrison's sons, applauding the multivolume work's "intellectual thoroughness" and "admirable tone." Rather than provide an overview, Higginson fixated on whether the offspring refuted the accusations that opponents within and without abolitionism had leveled at the Garrison family patriarch. Despite omitting entire paragraphs of the *Atlantic* essay in the *Contemporaries* composition, the auditor labeled the iconic agitator as imperious in both.[54]

Higginson mused that because of a putatively arrogant and domineering streak, the *Liberator's* editor had probably accrued more broken alliances than any other "great reforme[r]." As confirmation, the author referred to fallouts with such antislavery loyalists as James Birney, William Goodell, Benjamin Lundy, Amos Phelps, and the Tappan brothers. He seemingly qualified the claim by interjecting his own experiences, announcing that a "thoroughly established" Garrison, once the philanthropic tribulations of the 1830s had subsided, was "wholly patient and considerate with younger recruits." Notwithstanding that personal history, Higginson ruled that given the "weight of testimony," Garrison proffered far less leniency and understanding toward longstanding immediatists. He further corroborated the damnatory charge of egoism by citing other abolitionist insiders. Partaking in hagiography interested him not at all; delivering magisterial pronouncements surely did.[55]

Higginson's frank appraisal of Garrison's foibles and flaws focused on the matter of moral absolutism. Whether from the assembly-hall dais or the editor's desk, the customary vituperation of the *Liberator*'s editor had troubled many Americans. His "whole vocabulary," the essayist expounded, logically stemmed from the "stern school of old-fashioned Calvinism" that had reared him, which detractors "overlooked and still overlook." Given that religious background, Higginson's Garrison conducted himself as an exceedingly unyielding and forbidding protestor. So, too, did his entourage. The entire lot, Higginson avouched, held "the least of sins worthy of death, and ha[d] no higher penalty for the greatest" of infractions. Even though the commentator conceded that that notion of sinfulness comprised some of the group's foundational "power," he simultaneously detected it as a structural "weakness."[56]

On several publishing occasions, the man of letters disapproved of the Garrisonians' "Draconian inflexibility." In the biographical essay, he took umbrage with their reputedly imprudent and unfair fusillade against the Old South's ruling race. Higginson highlighted that the slaveholders whom Garrison and his followers indiscriminately pilloried faced legal barriers deterring individual antislavery enactments. Those self-righteous crusaders, according to Higginson's admonition, were ill-suited to constructively solve "the tremendous practical difficulties studiously accumulated by skillful lawgivers in the way of sundering the relation between master and the slave." In a surprising authorial move, the former forcible-resistance abolitionist did what extremist Garrisonians had allegedly refused to do: confront slave owning with sensitivity and charitableness.[57]

In South Carolina, Georgia, Alabama, and Mississippi, the compassionate critic expatiated, inheritors of human property could only emancipate chattels personal with the local legislature's permission. Such a dispensation, Higginson avowed, was "usually impossible to get." Even though Virginia statute allowed masters to manumit bondservants, it also mandated that "converted slaveholders" remove them from the state's borders. Failing to comply, he added, would result in the reenslavement of the newly freed, "at auction to the highest bidder." The Old Dominion's expatriation stipulation only inflated Higginson's ex post facto kindness, for he professed that it had encumbered already burdened Chesapeake planters. Because of their general "impoverish[ment]," he avowed, they lacked the financial means to relocate the formerly enslaved. In the book review, the author emphasized that the estates of would-be emancipators were "mortgaged and deeply indebted." Beset by those predicaments, the conscientious Virginian evidently had no choice but to keep Black people in bondage.[58]

The decent Deep South slave owner, according to Higginson, could not do much either. He provocatively propounded that such a southerner, "had he been Garrison himself, was as powerless to free his slaves without the formal consent of the state authorities as he would have been to swim the Atlantic with those slaves on his back." Garrisonian ideologues never contemplated such niceties; their purported rigidity and reductionism made no room for the slaveholder's dilemma. Even though the critique ends positively—the *Liberator*'s editor "kept far higher laws than he broke" and represented a hardworking "man of iron in an iron age"— the pundit arguably dealt too much damage by that narrative point. Higginson, however, did more harm to his own reputation than Garrison's. Acquiring empathy for the antebellum master class came at the expense of his radical past; it also advanced a present-day quest for sectional reconciliation.[59]

As a degenerating abolitionist, the retrospective writer never metamorphosed into a latter-day apologist of the Old South. His solicitude for the enslavers "who had begun to open their eyes to [slavery's] evils, yet found themselves bound hand and foot by its laws," connotes a startling development nonetheless. The idea that a burdensome social arrangement victimized slave owners could function as a convenient myth on behalf of intersectional comity after 1876. Years before the littérateur brought his influence to bear on amicable North-South relations, Colonel Higginson showered no pity on the world that slaveholders had made. In an April 1865 newspaper report, he contrasted the "fanaticism of magnanimity," which had taken hold of white northerners in the aftermath of Confederate General Robert E. Lee's surrender, with the vengeful popular reaction that swept across northern locales following Abraham Lincoln's assassination. For Higginson and other "radical Republicans," nothing about Honest Abe's shocking death "astonished" them. "Slavery," he unconditionally stated, "is perpetual violence, and its career had been a catalogue of murders." Reenter his graciousness of 1886 and 1899, which obfuscated a history of virulent antiabolitionism among masterclass members. Once the Republican Party's postwar rebuilding program unraveled, the belletrist seemingly sided more and more with those whom he had challenged as a militant activist and military commander.[60]

In an April 1877 letter to the *New-York Tribune*, Higginson publicized his disillusionment with outside intervention in the South's politics and race relations.

While instructing old abolitionists and stalwart Republicans to accept the southern strategy of President Rutherford B. Hayes as a fait accompli, he himself "heartily, cordially, and unreservedly" endorsed the removal of US Army protection from the remaining Republican-occupied statehouses in the former Confederacy. The erstwhile radical argued that since congressional readmission of the secessionist states had heralded Reconstruction's completion, any subsequent policies or actions treating those entities as conquered provinces represented an alarming innovation. The assumption of "arbitrary authority" by the Hayes administration, he deduced, would "endanger the liberties of every State," setting the stage for a "consolidated despotism" in the future. Upholding a governmental system of limited power and responsibility at the national level now counted more than the "immediate welfare" of African Americans.[61]

Regardless of previous and prospective anti-Black terrorism, the epistler defended a hands-off protocol based on the perceived tranquility that had typified the South "for months." "So long as the peace is kept and the Constitution is obeyed," he reasoned, each "State in the Union" possessed an unqualified "right . . . to manage its own local affairs in its own way, well or badly." Higginson thus advertised an embrace of new golden rules—states' rights and laissez-faire—prescriptive positions that effectively overlapped with the reactionary mission of southern Democrats. Letting people do as they pleased, however admirable in theory, actually enabled racially conservative whites to rid the Southland of interracial Republican governments, ones that had supposedly plagued the region with ignorant freed-slave voters, corrupt African American officeholders, and their exploitative northern "carpetbagger" allies.[62]

Even though the Hamburg Massacre of July 1876 had prompted Higginson to condemn the outburst of old-line recalcitrance, the murders of six African Americans and plundering of Black homes and businesses did not reawaken his radicalism. After deploring the "utterly unprovoked" South Carolina atrocity in a *New York Times* missive, the correspondent revealingly indicated that the viciousness would rouse Republicans to unfurl the vote-getting bloody shirt during the upcoming presidential contest. "I have been trying to convince myself," Higginson confessed, "that the Southern whites had accepted the results of the war, and that other questions might now come uppermost." "Of what use are all our efforts to lay aside" sectional issues, he rhetorically asked, if such southerners kept them alive? Months later, Higginson expanded on the political grief brought about by the Hamburg incident. Since it proved that a "barbarous spirit prevailed," he declared that "the whole course of the [Hayes] campaign" must change. He therefore blamed Palmetto State rebelliousness for "instantly postpon[ing] . . . all those fine questions of civil service reform," the very stuff on which good-government Republicans like himself wanted to concentrate.[63]

Despite comparing the Hamburg Massacre to territorial border ruffianism in an August 1876 article, Higginson's self-imposed blinders remained intact. While looking for historical lessons or parallels, the veteran abolitionist never demanded that white northerners resume the battle against an unvanquished Slave Power. For him, flare-ups of racial violence in the South, however heinous, warranted a resolute response among state-level officials solely. Citizens of the readmitted states, he insisted in an 1878 issue of the *Atlantic Monthly*, must "work out their own salvation." Should any abuses arise, he counseled Black southerners to exert their strength at the ballot box or utilize their "power of locomotion." Following Reconstruction's collapse, Higginson espied nothing major that would compel African Americans to vote with their feet. Ironically, in December 1876 he derided all notions about "peace and order" distinguishing the ex-Confederate places wherein white Democrats had regained control, sarcastically equating them to the "old assertions of Northern travelers that the slaves were happy and well off in slavery." Tragically, the man of letters helped fabricate a New South mythos thereafter.[64]

After pronouncing a firm states'-rights stance, the belletrist did very little for the rest of his public life to defy the evolution of another regime of white supremacy, Black subordination. He readily capitalized on civic engagements in order to pledge his conciliatory attachments. In early 1881, the former officer of the First South Carolina Volunteers returned to the cockpit of secession. An invitation to speak at a centennial commemoration of the Battle of Cowpens had taken him to the Palmetto State. The setting of a Revolutionary War celebration did not merely permit the New Englander to honor the martial exploits achieved by the "men of the Southern Colonies" against the British Redcoats. The past and present converged for Higginson at the memorial moment, as he appropriated the earlier history of a nation in the making so as to re-cement national unity following decades of internal strife.[65]

Since white northerners and southerners no longer constituted enemies, the orator beckoned both to rise above "the terrible wounds of the lat[e] contest." The "new social problems of the new age," he avouched, necessitated that they do so. Even though Higginson never specified what those troubles were, he did not leave his words open to interpretation. "No State," he opined, "can dare to be permanently clouded by the ignorance of any class of its people, or to allow any class to oppress any other." Despite that declaration's apparent universality, the sectional reconciliationist targeted landless and uneducated African Americans.

To remove any doubts as to where he stood and with whom he identified, Colonel Higginson generously decreed: "We of the North [apprehend] the difficulties, the temptations, the mutual provocations" between the races of the South. "Nor can we forget," he continued, "that the greater responsibility must rest upon the more educated and enlightened race." To overcome a cross-generational racial quandary, the Yankee lecturer peddled nothing resembling a radical abolitionist or stalwart Republican panacea.[66]

After advocating the "great healer" of time, Higginson promulgated "*Noblesse oblige!*" as the region's next great watchword. In so doing, he probably sought to rally benevolent and paternalistic white southerners on behalf of gradually improving the status and condition of African Americans. Whatever his hopes, the speaker's contrite tone in no way controverted the dreams of unreconstructed ex-Confederates in and outside South Carolina. "There are sins enough for all to repent [and] errors enough for all to correct," he acknowledged, ostensibly apologizing for the Republican Party's Reconstruction-era blunders. Nor did the concessions stop there. Even though every state in the Union had "its own ordeals," a mollifying Higginson contended that the South faced tougher ones than any other section of the country. Its white and Black populations, he affirmed, "are yet learning . . . to adapt themselves" to the transformations wrought by the Civil War. Regardless of whether the orator had pleased listeners, his sentiments radically deviated from prior activism.[67]

Higginson's ardor for rapprochement burned even more intensely at a 1904 Decoration Day gathering. On Harvard's campus, the Harvard alumnus delivered a speech eulogizing the Harvard graduates who had sacrificed their lives on behalf of the Union war effort. Much of what he said he had already stated in an 1870 oration at nearby Mount Auburn Cemetery. Unlike that address, the later one includes a noticeable addendum, whereby the speaker praised the noble cause of each Civil War sectional combatant. As one century concluded and another commenced, Higginson arguably smothered any lingering racial justice impulses while continually rewriting history.[68]

The public intellectual prefaced his paean to appeasement by mentioning that the "contesting parties" of the warring 1860s finally recognized the opponent's "qualities," "fatigues," and "daring." The passage of time worked its magic far more profoundly, however, allowing men like Higginson to personally ascertain the real source of turmoil between the Union and Confederacy. No "mere quarrel," the Civil War veteran professed, temporarily severed the United States; nor did any "institution, even that of slavery," do so. "Two principles of government," he decreed, bred the honest differences that had divided white Americans into hostile camps, namely, "state rights and the sovereignty of the nation." In that way, the former forcible-resistance abolitionist reduced the slaveholders' revolt to a constitutional quarrel, normalizing and legitimating it in the process.[69]

Higginson's revisionism encompassed placatory nomenclature as well, further demonstrating the tremendous mental and emotional distances that he traversed, over forty years, in order to arrive at intersectional insight and bliss. In his estimation, the originally named "war of the rebellion" was a politically charged designation whose very partisan meaning had made it passé. The current and more suitable term "civil war" appropriately captured the North-South concord and healing that had taken place. Despite that expressed preference, Higginson's causation observations aligned with a different appellation altogether. By the early 1900s, he essentially viewed the past via the same lens as unreconstructed ex-Confederates, as both (mis)understood it as the "War between the States." For the sectional reconciliationist, in particular, memories of fighting for Black liberty and equality had receded into virtual nothingness.[70]

An abolitionist homily that Higginson gave at an 1857 AASS meeting displays the disconnection between the authorial past and present. A few years before Lincoln's election to the presidency sparked the departure of seven Deep South states from the United States, he predicted the Union's imminent dissolution. An omnipotent southern system of slavery, according to his thinking, would shatter the republic to pieces. In stark contrast to the after-Reconstruction man of letters, a fiery antebellum activist inveighed against an overbearing slaveocracy, because it

> has governed this nation since its formation . . . has for half a century elected every President, dictated every Cabinet, controlled every Congress, [is] the power that has demoralized the religion of the nation, and emasculated its literature[,] . . . the power that has ruled as easily its Northern creditors as its Northern debtors, the power that at this moment stands with all the patronage of the greatest nation of this world in its clutches, and with the firmest financial basis in the world . . . beneath its feet.

Individuals may, of course, modify their opinions and beliefs as they get older. As Higginson adjusted his own throughout the postbellum period, he routinely downgraded or disowned principled abolitionism.[71]

That retreat from antislavery radicalism and corresponding obsession with sectional reconciliation surfaces in *Cheerful Yesterdays*, too. The author's miniature portrait of an uncle's Virginia plantation, for instance, mirrored his steadily regressive take on slavery as it was and the reasons for fratricidal warfare. During a sojourn at the estate in question, a college-aged Higginson had discovered "nothing to suggest anything undesirable" about chattel servitude. The "head servant," according to the autobiographer, was a "grave and dignified man, with the most unexceptionable manner," a description that could apply to the household help of any respectable New Englander. Besides recalling the commonplace occurrence of children of both races "play[ing] together," he remembered a more extraordinary sight, whereby an enslaved girl learned her letters while white youths received their schooling. That it happened, contrary to state law that had forbidden such literacy, reinforced the benignant representation of enslavement. As an ostensible microcosm, those and other unfree African Americans "seemed merely to share in the kindly and rather slipshod methods of a Southern establishment." The only thing amiss about human bondage in this scenario pertained to an overheard conversation, in which an overseer had spoken of "the domestic relations of the negroes . . . precisely as if they had been animals." Given the absence of additional commentary, the reader will never know if generations of captivity imbruted Black people or their exploiters.[72]

Higginson mulled over an everyday Old South in his chapter "The Rearing of a Reformer," wherein he announced that the immediate emancipation campaign had deeply pierced his "conscience." Reminiscences of a not-so-dreadful institution of slavery hardly serve as fodder for a budding activist. They instead illumine the limitations of an autobiography that simply contains no neoabolitionist objectives. On the occasions that the chronicler discussed other proponents of abolitionism—beyond the belittling of moralistic Garrisonians and scrutinizing of an unstable John Brown—he often did so in a lighthearted way. The commemorator specifically lavished attention on the movement's idiosyncratic qualities, its "picturesque ingredients," to use his evocative phrase.[73]

The retrospective writer pointed out that many women serenely knitted amid the excitement and din of antislavery assemblages. Yet their exceptional piety had nothing to do with the special assignment at hand (the proceedings themselves) but the kind literally in their hands (the stitching). Since they bore "the look of prolonged and self-controlled patience," those diligent and devout needleworkers reminded the memoirist of the present-day Catholic Sisters of Charity. He remarked that abolitionist events attracted uncommonly bearded agitators like Charles C. Burleigh. The hirsute reformers of yesteryear brought to his mind the sort of revolutionists now "noticed in European Socialist meetings." The Hutchinson Family Singers constituted another hallmark of antislavery get-togethers, prompting the personal historian to outline the songsters as "natural . . . actors, indeed unconscious *poseurs,* easily arousing torpid conventions with . . . stirring melodies." Regardless of whom Higginson recollected, he never commented on the humanitarianism behind physical appearances.[74]

He more fully canvassed abolitionism's theatrical dimensions in an 1899 essay fittingly entitled "The Eccentricities of Reformers." First published in the *Outlook* and republished in *Contemporaries,* it illustrates Higginson's disregard for a useable antislavery past amid a developing Jim Crow present. Ever the raconteur, he disbursed whimsical anecdotes of the colorful characters collectively comprising an early-nineteenth-century counterculture. Foregrounding the harmless peccadilloes and endearing oddities of such crusaders intersected with a hugely popular fictional rendition of bohemian life by the English illustrator and writer George du Maurier. Americans initially encountered the story of an enclave of British art students in 1850s Paris on the pages of *Harper's Monthly Magazine,* which serialized du Maurier's novel in 1894. That same tale, which stars a working-class artist's model who turns into a hypnotized operatic diva, also thrilled audiences as a stand-alone book and stage production. Du Maurier himself made a cameo in *Cheerful Yesterdays.* In the "Literary London Twenty Years Ago" chapter, the transatlantic cultural insider recounted a banquet interaction with the well-known satirical cartoonist several years before he "added literary to artistic successes." Whatever inspiration Higginson derived from *Trilby,* his firsthand account conjures real-world bohemianism that social-reform nonconformists had unknowingly created.[75]

By surveying the quirks of sundry individuals, the essayist verified that every reformatory endeavor enveloped itself with "a fringe of the unreasonable and half-cracked." Higginson enlisted more details about a long-bearded Burleigh who came of age during "a beardless period." He also reported that James Russell Lowell jocularly likened himself to a "young neophyte accompanying his father confessor," because of public reactions to the shorter, less prominently hairy Lowell walking alongside the taller and shaggier Burleigh. The author additionally expanded on the Hutchinsons. Besides referring to the troupe's male members as "raven-haired and keen-eyed . . . Bohemians [who] had a melodramatic look, with their wide collars and long locks," he mentioned that all the siblings sporadically exuded genius. Beyond those familiar personages, the littérateur reviewed a whole new cast of zany agitators.[76]

Higginson invoked Father Lamson and Abby Fulsom in partial confirmation that a variety of unconventional types gravitated to abolitionism. Even though such "professional lunatics" had tried the patience of antislavery proselytizers, for the storyteller they functioned as wonderful backdrops magnifying the drama of any old-fashioned convocation. The "white habiliments" and equally "white beard" of Lamson, he declared, "seemed almost like a stage make-up" for some philanthropic spectacle. Fulsom's shrieking fulminations against capitalists, he similarly stated, "seemed like the rehearsal of a play." The narrator alluded to several more one-of-a-kind abolitionists to justify his thesis, such as Stephen Symonds Foster, Parker Pillsbury, Nathaniel Peabody Rogers, and Henry Clarke Wright. Nor did he restrict his inquiry to fellow travelers in the immediate emancipation campaign.[77]

Other quaint madcaps included a transplanted southern belle of singular independence. The ballad of Miss Ora Noon, whose proper name Higginson withheld, entailed the freeing of inherited slaves upon reaching her twenty-first birthday, enrollment in a Philadelphia medical college, ownership of a set of revolvers, subscriptions to a local theater and "pistol-gallery," as well as advocating feminism. Another curious reformer, Percy Taylor, differentiated himself as an inimitable farmer not because of his excellent agricultural practices but a vegetarian lifestyle of total freedom, as if inhabiting a "lonely island." Unlike the sinister character in du Maurier's fiction, Higginson's saintly Svengalis wielded no mesmerizing capabilities, certainly not on behalf of past and present reformism. The belletrist-reconciliationist chose countercultural weirdness over racial justice.[78]

In another *Outlook* article, Higginson addressed the exceptionality of antislavery evangelists without delving into their peculiarities. By rehashing many already explored ideas and themes, the public intellectual distilled twenty years of writing into a single 1898 composition. From the onset, he underscored abolitionism's mystical orientation, asserting that it embodied "a cult, a moral organization, a tie akin to freemasonry." In the absence of secret handshakes and elaborate passwords, the congregations of the immediatist faithful approximated those of the "early Christians or . . . French Huguenots." That common zeal, the commemorator emphasized, begat no lasting cohesion, as evidenced by the movement's irreparable division. Even though the chronicler noted his previous transactions with both the disunionist Garrisonians and "voting Abolitionists," he expressly favored the former's meetings. Not only did the man of letters find them as "far more attractive and . . . stimulating," he also thought that among all the reformers whom he ever met, no others shined with "the same glamour" as William Lloyd Garrison's crew.[79]

Despite Higginson's proclamation that the abolitionists belonged to the most "disinterested" undertaking of his lifetime, requiring "the largest proportion of sacrifice and the smallest of personal benefit," he never upheld their selflessness as relevant. Whatever his Garrisonian predilections, the knowing observer still intermixed a healthy dosage of criticism into the narrative. Just as he had done in the 1886 book review and would do in an 1899 *Contemporaries* chapter, the essayist complained that otherwise liberal altruists never lent their generosity to "humane" elements of the Old South's ruling race. Such men, the author granted, comprised "a very small minority," but morally inflexible Garrisonians only made the catch-22 of manumission-inclined slaveholders more difficult. As foes of inequity, quite simply, those antislavery crusaders were themselves unjust.[80]

Interestingly, neither *Outlook* piece suggests the radical renaissance that the littérateur seemingly underwent at the time. By the end of 1898, the veteran abolitionist and resolute reconciliationist suddenly vindicated Reconstruction-era Black enfranchisement. He decried a recent spate of anti-Black terrorism throughout the Southland, too. In so doing, he ultimately urged African Americans to politically punish the Party of Lincoln, emancipation, and equal rights by supporting the presidential prospects of Democrat William Jennings Bryan. That development, however, pertained not at all to the free-silver monetary views of the Boy Orator of the Platte. Rather, it stemmed from the imperialistic turn that the Spanish-American War had taken and the subsequent anti-imperialism championed by the Nebraska Populist on the campaign trail.[81]

What began as an anticolonial insurgency in the Spanish-held island of Cuba resulted not only in eventual US military involvement but also the country's acquisition of territories in the Caribbean and Pacific from a defeated Spain. The American occupation of the Philippines and the ensuing push to conquer indigenous resistance under the leadership of Emilio Aguinaldo reanimated Higginson's moribund militancy. That a nation born from a revolutionary war against a distant mother country and founded on republican principles of government should itself procure an overseas empire and violently suppress Filipino independence disturbed him immensely. He therefore joined in the 1898 founding of the Boston-based Anti-Imperialist League. More significantly, amid a racialized foreign policy premised on the alleged savagery and inferiority of Filipinos, Higginson defended brown people abroad and Black ones at home.[82]

His rejuvenated racial justice advocacy manifested itself in several ways. He publicized it in a March 1899 dispatch to the *Nation*, wherein he offered a historical apologia of African American voting rights. The man of letters particularly vented his critical spleen on Thomas Nelson Page's 1898 fictional work *Red Rock: A Chronicle of Reconstruction*. Besides dissecting the malevolent carpetbagger stereotype lurking throughout the book's pages, the public intellectual took the Virginia novelist to task for failing to apprehend the "absolute" necessity of Black suffrage. Enfranchising the freedmen, according to his reprimand, constituted "the only method" by which the formerly enslaved, "almost the sole Southern friends of the Union," could protect themselves against the belligerent whites who sought to keep them in a slave-like condition. He also maintained that had African American males not gained the ballot, the US government "would have disgraced it[self] forever" by perpetrating such a flagrant "act of desertion." With a solitary epistle, Higginson conceivably communicated a recommitment to the ideals that in the spirit of intersectional harmony he had stifled since the 1870s.[83]

Another 1899 public performance apparently confirmed the recovery of his radical abolitionist's mettle. At a Boston gathering protesting racial lynching in the South, speaker Higginson received a celebratory introduction: as "'one who comes to us [now] as he came to the rescue of Anthony Burns some forty years ago and answers the call of his country [today] as he did in '61.'" That living legend, according to press coverage, told attendees that liberty and equality for African Americans did not merely consist of exemption from perpetual servitude. It comprehended the right to such grander things as the vote, personal cultivation, and "a position as free men that is worth having." Anti-Black violence caused him, however belatedly, to bristle with uncontained indignity, so much so that he issued a stern warning to white southerners. "There is a limit," he avowed, "to even the patience which a great Christian civilization can demand" of mistreated and oppressed populations. He implicitly condoned the usage of force or retaliatory measures, so that African Americans could enjoy actual freedom, not the "nominal" kind that they currently endured across the former Confederacy.[84]

If anti-imperialism enlivened Higginson's lethargic sense of racial justice, both concerns dovetailed during the presidential election of 1900. In a leaflet, Higginson, William Lloyd Garrison Jr., and George S. Boutwell encouraged Black voters to forgo their conventional Republican backing. "If ever there was a war of the races in this world," the authors argued, then colonial turbulence in the Philippines "precisely" represented one. Given such combat, as team Higginson cautioned, white troops daily learned racist lessons in the Pacific, "constantly" describing Filipinos as "'niggers'" in letters to friends and family. Since the subjugation of "darker races" abroad, under US imperial rule, did not bode well for Black freedom at home, the undersigned exhorted African Americans to leave "the party you once had reason to love." They should, however, enter into an electoral alliance with a traditional adversary not despite but because of the Democracy's bigoted history.[85]

The very unwillingness of white southern Democrats "to give equal political rights to the American negro," according to this appeal, inadvertently benefited people of color globally. As opponents of colonialism, those prejudicial politicos had no desire to "undertake the government of 10,000,000 more belonging to the colored race." If nothing else, casting ballots for Bryan represented the lesser of two evils for Black voters. To further justify their presidential recommendation, the canvassers referenced their humanitarian credentials and the Civil War itself. "Trained from youth in the strictest school of anti-slavery conviction," they pleaded with African Americans to renounce the Republican William McKinley in order to thwart a malicious doctrine, one that "we fought through a four years' war to get rid of . . . and enlisted nearly 200,000 black soldiers" to help demolish. In other words, persisting racial conquest in the tropics, under a renewed McKinley administration, would ensure that notions of Anglo-Saxon superiority reigned supreme once more.[86]

The return of vintage Higginson was a transitory phenomenon. A few notable actions did not fundamentally invert a trajectory that had rendered and continued to render the tenets of revolutionary abolitionism and achievements of Radical Reconstruction as nearly obsolescent. Another passage from the 1904 Decoration Day address elucidates Higginson's albatross. The Civil War, he proclaimed, "gave peace to the nation; it gave union, freedom, equal rights; and . . . it has given to all survivors the sacred sympathy of th[e] names" inscribed on gravestones. Those panegyrics might have suited the earlier 1870 Decoration Day occasion, when Higginson first uttered them, but their reiteration shows the orator's tone-deafness thirty-five years later. Nothing in the past or present effected adjustments to his declaration that the warring 1860s had yielded beautiful gifts. A postwar career focusing on belles-lettres and sectional reconciliation overwhelmed a revival of midcentury militancy.[87]

Yet as indicated by the 1904 essay "'Intensely Human,'" the littérateur never completely suppressed antislavery-oriented egalitarianism. Among antebellum whites, Higginson apprised the *Atlantic*'s readers, only the abolitionists truly understood "the negro . . . as he was." The master class did not, by comparison, because property-in-man values had perverted its vision. As reputed race experts, the exponents of immediatism thus anticipated that Black people, once emancipated, "would have human temptations—to idleness, folly, wastefulness, even sensuality." Even though such frailties were racially unique to nobody, which denoted a rejection of contrary claims, Higginson saw them as perfectly natural given the generations of captivity that African Americans withstood. The same applied to other antislavery advocates. Since the humanity of Black people resided in their "virtues" as well as their "vices," they fully recognized that the formerly enslaved, like any "abused and neglected" group, would require "education, moral instruction, and, above all, high example." Regardless of the postbellum reverses to his radicalism, the public intellectual never second-guessed African Americans' developmental capacities.[88]

Having affirmed a pedigree as pure as any Anglo-Saxon's, Higginson next trounced on the charge of Black sexual aggressiveness. Once suspected of assaulting a white woman, an African American man, he declaimed, "will [likely] be put to death without trial, and perhaps with fiendish torture." He did not cite any exact incidents but referred to a disturbing scene that increased in frequency during the late nineteenth and early twentieth centuries. The uptick of lynching in the United States, along with the associated communal participation and ritualistic sadism, disproportionately affected African Americans in the South. To explode the falsehood of rape often surrounding it, the Civil War veteran mentioned the good behavior of freed-slave servicemen as proof. He also trusted in logic. On behalf of a larger point, the essayist hypothetically allowed that the Black male constituted a sexual threat to white womanhood. "Does any one suppose for a moment," he rhetorically asked, "that the mob which burns him on suspicion of such a crime is doing it in defense of chastity?" "Not at all," the old abolitionist quickly professed, for "it is in defense of caste." Besides exposing the lies that had framed another phase of anti-Black terrorism, Higginson indicted southern white men. Their actual lechery had not only given birth to mixed-race populations but also made chattel bondage into a "hell" for its female victims.[89]

Despite denouncing the "half-freedom" characterizing the African American experience in the New South, which "chain-gangs, lynching, and the lash" only worsened, Higginson concluded the article optimistically. "As the memories of the slave period fade away," he expected that the "fetich of colorphobia will cease to control our society; and marriage may come to be founded, not on the color of the skin, but upon the common courtesies of life, and upon genuine sympathies of heart and mind." However admirable, such hopefulness evaded the troublesome reality that existed. Rather than hazard a substantive remedy to racial matters, the erstwhile radical took solace from the nebulous feeling that anti-Black prejudices would abate slowly but surely. He proffered a similar cure-all more than twenty years previously as a sectional reconciliationist at the Cowpens commemoration. In that way, he retained fealty to gradualism and became a firm patron of Booker T. Washington.[90]

From his Alabama base of operations, the *Up from Slavery* autobiographer and Tuskegee Institute founder promoted industrial schooling, or manual labor training, so as to elevate African Americans in the present and improve race relations in the future. The economic growth of Black communities and obtainment of middle-class standards, Washington believed, represented a better means of racial uplift than political activism. As a powerful figure in African American education and social reform, the Wizard of Tuskegee sought to accommodate, as opposed to openly contesting, ruling white interests in the South. Such an anti-racism strategy attracted Higginson—as well as many other northern white philanthropists—who served as a trustee of the Black Belt–located and Washington-backed Calhoun Colored School. The author's "'Intensely Human'" composition coincided with an educational trip to the New South, in which he visited both the Tuskegee and Calhoun institutions. Whatever the connection between the two, the essayist prefaced his trust in a colorblind tomorrow with a puzzling statement. The "enfranchisement of the negroes," he avowed, "once established, will of course never be undone." The poll taxes, literary tests, and other discriminatory maneuvers that southern state legislatures had taken in order to virtually eliminate African American voting rights apparently upset him none whatsoever. Intersectional cooperation and Washingtonian cautiousness essentially immobilized Higginson.[91]

Whereas the Great Accommodator operated as a Daniel in the New South lion's den, the formerly militant abolitionist espoused appeasement from a comfortable New England radius. Two years before his death, an eighty-six-year-old Higginson dismissed a 1909 assemblage that contributed to the NAACP's formation. He spurned an invitation to participate, according to a news report, on the grounds that an "unwise" expansion of the suffrage had instigated "great friction between the races" and "injur[ed] . . . the negro himself." Remarkably, Higginson alleged that those judgments comprised an article of faith since 1868. In his assessment, not only had "existing law" made an equal civil and political status for African American men unattainable, but only "a conflict of terrible consequence" could effectuate it. The prosperity and progress of Black southerners, then, should squarely rest on a Washingtonian model: "industrial and educational development."[92]

Higginson also deemed the National Negro Conference as unwarranted given the ascent of the Republican William Howard Taft to the presidency. A brand-new Black rights organization would therefore "embarrass" and frustrate a fledgling Taft administration, whose "purpose seems to be to conciliate the more progressive class of Southern white citizens." So that no one misconstrued his opinions, Higginson marketed his bona fides, noting that he was "almost the sole survivor of the early abolitionists"; a commander of the First South Carolina Volunteers; and an "organizer and supporter of the Calhoun, Ala., school." Notwithstanding that personal exoneration, when a venerable activist directly disputed a rising neoabolitionist movement, the meaning and significance of his antebellum militancy met its postbellum nadir.[93]

Well before that happened, an unalloyed revolutionary delivered a moving address on the relationship between religion and abolitionism at the 1855 New England Anti-Slavery Convention. Based on audience cheers and applause, which newspaper accounts recorded, the speaker scored a resounding success. While making the case that the drive for immediate emancipation did more for American Christianity than any divinity school, the Unitarian minister and aspiring man of letters "thanked God" that it had transformed the slavery subject into an "absorbing" and pressing problem. Responding to the complaints of unidentified churchmen, literati, and other professionals that antislavery agitation disturbed "science and literature and theology," a younger Higginson memorably intoned: "We have something more important to do in this age than to be mere scholars."[94]

Some thirteen years later, Higginson announced that women's suffrage formed "The Next Great Question" in a piece for the *Independent*. While conceding that some "tired Abolitionist" might need a respite after decades of strenuous labor, he tolerated no such relaxation among reformers like himself. For those "who had the luck to be born ultraists and men of the future," Higginson motioned them onward in the service of unrelenting activism. At about the same time, the littérateur effectively forecasted that art and aesthetics would consume his hardiness and fervor. "American literature," he notified the *Atlantic*'s readership, "is not yet copious, American scholarship not profound, [and] American society not highly intellectual." The real worth of any nation, he averred, depended not on wealth accumulation or diffusion of "elementary knowledge, but the high-water mark of its highest mind." As a prolific belletrist, the postemancipation Higginson consecrated himself to converting a cultural backwater into a mighty artistic empire. In that respect, he made no compromises and never rested.[95]

7

What Was Antislavery For?

From the Disbandment of the AASS to the Determination of Abolitionist Women

Organized abolitionism, as led by the adherents of the American Anti-Slavery Society, officially ended on April 9, 1870. At the final meeting of the AASS, participants celebrated the Fifteenth Amendment's recent ratification as the consummation of a nearly forty-year fight. At the gathering's commencement, President Wendell Phillips remarked that, since the nation-state now legally actualized their founding organizational promises on behalf of African American liberty and equality, "we have nothing to do but to thank God and to throw our exertions henceforth into channels more fitting the hour which dawns upon us." Even though the latest constitutional victory evidently allowed working abolitionists to discontinue their partnership, several contributors disallowed a simple retirement. During an otherwise joyous occasion, a tone of duty resounded throughout as speakers articulated their personal sentiments or read aloud those of others who could not attend.[1]

An epistle from John Greenleaf Whittier acknowledged that the elderly ages of many antislavery agitators likely precluded them from rigorous reformism in the future. Regardless of how "frosted" their heads had gotten or how "worn and weary" their bodies had grown, the esteemed poet of abolitionism instructed movement loyalists to "give our word of cheer and sympathy to those who are to take our places and make" the Reconstruction-era gains "so dearly purchased a blessing to all." A communication from the husband and wife humanitarians David Lee and Lydia Maria Child registered an even stronger reminder about the enduring responsibilities of true-blue crusaders. After expressing gratitude to the Almighty for making the abolitionists "His instruments to right a monstrous wrong," they decreed that "we must not consider ourselves dismissed from service." Despite chattel slavery's extinction and the adoption of equalitarian legislation and constitutional amendments, the necessity of "constant activity" and "incessant vigilance," in their opinion, had diminished not one jot. "The world is far enough from being able to dispense with bold reformers, who proclaim the truth without fear or favor," the Childs added, "and nowhere are they more needed than in this country at the present time." Even though the Underground Railroad conductor Thomas Garrett concluded his letter by encouraging the longtime "friends of the slave" to help solve the "Woman Suffrage question" by pushing for another addendum to the US Constitution, he, too, reminded them that "there is much yet for philanthropists to do" before the formerly enslaved "can fully enjoy the great boon" that the Fifteenth Amendment had bestowed. For Whittier, the Childs, and Garrett, the followers of the AASS must not stop toiling individually.[2]

Besides encomiums, Phillips vocalized the same themes in a prayerful address that ultimately silenced the proceedings. Halting the AASS's institutional existence, according to his comments, spelled the concomitant death of antislavery agitation not in the slightest. "There is no mustering out in this warfare," he averred, because "that day will never come." "Do not imagine," he notified younger constituents, "that the age of heroism and of martyrdom is over; that there are to be no more mobs." To each and every listener, the orator declared that nobody possessed "a right to take off the harness." Grand contests, then, would not merely await abolitionist veterans and their successors on some nearby or distant juncture. They had already summoned them to the front lines.[3]

In justification, Phillips referenced the immense "self-conceit of the Saxon race" in the United States, as well as a tenacious "spirit of caste" across the nation. The orator therefore imparted a personally inspirational vision as the next crusading agenda for all the celebrants. "What I want," he professed, "is a more broad and tolerant civilization." "What we have to do," he enjoined, "is to lift American Statesmanship and American Christianity to the level of ignoring race." Given such an errand, Phillips hardly indulged in empty rhetoric when, in a *National Anti-Slavery Standard* editorial that wrapped up the convocation coverage, he stated that the AASS "may dissolve, or adjourn indefinitely, only to be called together in case of some unexpected emergency." Despite their dispersal, the abolitionists could not lessen their consideration for the recently emancipated, who still required, in the chieftain's judgment, "counsel, aid, education, [and] land." Despite Phillips's sincerity, no actual or perceived calamities induced anyone to reassemble the immediatist clan.[4]

After 1876 the pursuits of veteran white abolitionists, as displayed in their memorial and historical writings, ceased to revolve substantively about racial justice. To be sure, the exponents of immediate and unconditional emancipation never represented one-idea reformers. Most, if not all, embraced myriad causes at once, both before and after the Civil War. Whereas undoing racially based servitude had mainly taken precedence over other altruistic endeavors, the interconnected problem of racism did not constitute a central concern during the nineteenth century's closing decades. The uncertain or worsening status and condition of the freedpeople and their descendants failed to elicit the attentiveness that the plight of the enslaved had previously aroused. As the imperatives of an ongoing African American freedom struggle steadily receded in significance and value, the veteran white abolitionists of this examination rerouted reformist time and energy. As the twentieth century neared, none seriously aimed at reinvigorating defunct antislavery networks.[5]

Even though Oliver Johnson did not approach the subject of abolitionism as a detached or disinterested scholar, his partisan discourses partly concentrated on the objective and impartial histories of the future. In his book-length biography of the *Liberator*'s editor, as well as other essays on antislavery issues, the seasoned newspaperman dedicated his golden years not to history for history's sake. Nor did the author, despite his awareness of a persisting past—one that never dies—contemplate bygone times for activist reasons. Rather, by battling postbellum detractors and pulverizing antiabolitionist fallacies, he sought to secure the Garrisonians' important historical place. The misinformation assailing bona fide abolitionism also mobilized Parker Pillsbury into action. While Johnson's vindicatory undertaking prompted him to unmask Protestant ministers and churches as ethically and religiously odious, Pillsbury's twilight-years quest resulted in more extensive muckraking. He conscripted saintly abolitionists' prior conflicts with a thoroughly corrupted and proslavery Christian establishment on behalf of a current campaign in which the Free Religious Association targeted persistent spiritual bondage and clerical tyranny.

Aaron Macy Powell also deployed the humanitarian past in order to exalt present-day altruism. Whereas Pillsbury invoked the pure Christianity of antebellum antislavery apostles for his particular postbellum purposes, Powell likened morally sublime, pre–Civil War abolitionists as harbingers of post–Civil War purity crusaders who launched a new transatlantic offensive against slavery—the state-regulated variety wherein white girls and women approximated sex slaves. Thomas Wentworth Higginson, in stark contrast, reflected on antislavery days of yore with no intentions of reproducing radical abolitionism's life force or reusing its ethos for the next cycle of militant activism. Through sundry pieces that debuted in premier periodicals, he narrated antislavery history from a romantic inclination or handled the careers of high-ranking abolitionists from a public intellectual's vantage point.

Taken together, those motivations and preoccupations marked the dislocation of racial justice from the mindsets of antislavery chroniclers and commemorators at precisely those moments that commanded alertness: after the restoration of white Democratic rule across the former Confederacy and amid the rebirth of white mastery in the New South. The collapse of the Republication Party's reconstruction project disrupted and compromised the willingness of veteran white abolitionists to apply original movement principles to regressive developments in American race relations. The public works of such retrospective writers consequently represent highly suggestive, if not totally symbolic, signposts documenting instances of apathy, negligence, and/or desertion. When viewed within a wider timeframe, they broadcast a story of declension as well.

Regardless of the middle-class notions of respectability that informed Samuel Joseph May's 1869 depiction of immediate emancipation movers and shakers, he in no way disengaged from an ongoing African American freedom struggle. He disseminated recollections of responsible and dutiful reformers partly in favor of just congressional policies for the formerly enslaved as well as a more racially inclusive United States. Given the code bourgeois and uplift evangel that William Wells Brown spotlighted in his gallery of outstanding people of color, he continually cultivated transcendent abolitionism in an 1874 survey of the Black Atlantic. He further exhibited a deeply internalized antislavery way of life in an 1880 autobiography addressing race relations in the pre–Civil War and post-Reconstruction South. Antiracism was always inseparable from the Black activist Brown's memorial and historical writings. Beyond enhancing his own literary prospects or prestige, he knew that everything he authored had racial implications, proving or disproving the past, present, and future abilities of Africans in America. If, indeed, a process of decline transpired during the waning decades of the nineteenth century, Johnson, Pillsbury, Powell, and Higginson were either individually unaware of it, at best, or personally contributed to it, at worst. Whatever the case, the deterioration of equal Black rights did not compel them to launch sustained rhetorical attacks or lengthy jeremiads. Notwithstanding the passing lamentations in the publications of Johnson, Pillsbury, and Powell, racial justice in the postbellum present figured secondarily in their reflections on the antebellum past. A belletristic or sectional-reconciliationist Higginson never vented any harangues while recounting abolitionism.

Yet, the real demise of antislavery-oriented egalitarianism arguably predated, by several years, the attenuation of racial justice in the post-1876 publications of the veteran white abolitionists of this investigation. On the same day that AASS members shut down their operation, more than a few installed a successor without delay. The initial boosterism surrounding the Reform League illustrates that its backers wanted to simultaneously preserve and extend the immediate emancipation campaign in some form. In copies of the *National Anti-Slavery Standard* during the month of March, a recurring announcement had apprised readers that the upcoming AASS get-together supplied the perfect opportunity to both complete the old business of abolitionism and inaugurate a neoabolitionist enterprise.

Appearing under the names of thirty female reformers, the notification emphasized that antislavery crusaders could not solely revel in current events and forever rest on their laurels, because "the proscriptive prejudice, born of slavery, which still closes schools, workshops, and hotels, to colored applicants, and denies to them equal social advantages, may be removed." Antislavery crusaders, it further stressed, should soldier on with their efforts, for "human rights, in the broadest sense, may yet be more fully recognized and guaranteed, and the ideal Republic be attained." Since the AASS membership needed to persevere with philanthropic fighting, the memorandum's sponsors—which included the likes of Louisa May Alcott, Lydia Maria Child, Ellen Craft, Abigail Kelley Foster, Mary Grew, Sallie Holley, Julia Ward Howe, Laura Giddings Julian, Amy Post, and Caroline F. Putnam—wanted "to use in the new era the machinery which has wrought so well in the past." They specifically pledged themselves to acquiring much-needed patronage for the *Standard*, which would function as the Reform League's analogue to, and replacement of, the abolitionist original.[6]

As the mouthpiece of the Reform League, the *Standard* embodied a modernized immediate emancipation initiative against a host of societal ills. In a publishing prospectus for 1870–1871, Powell, the paper's editor, promulgated that it would press for "the abolition of caste" as well as the equal rights of native peoples, Asian immigrants, and women. It would push the cause of labor as "closely allied . . . to that of Slavery," as well as plead for the "speedy" prohibition of capital punishment. It would also highlight "intemperance as one of the worst enemies of all classes" and "hasten . . . true and abiding" international peace. That far-reaching venture, unfortunately, had an extremely short lifespan. In comparison to the three-decade print run of the first *Standard*, the second one lasted for a measly two years. By the start of 1873, veteran abolitionists essentially inhabited a lonely world. The absence of a formal alliance or national clearinghouse meant that anyone committed to racial justice would proceed as an army of one. The white retrospective writers of this examination indicate that such solitary forces basically withdrew from the Black-rights battlefield during the 1880s, 1890s, and 1900s.[7]

Regardless of a publishing prospectus advertising that the *National Anti-Slavery Standard* would circulate under a slightly different visage, and despite a

newspaper announcement in which female reformers advocated for a neoabolitionist adaptation of time-honored AASS devices, not everyone rested easily. The
Black pastor, activist, and educator Henry Highland Garnet shared personally
bittersweet feelings of "gratification" and "regret" during the 1870 celebration.
Whereas southern slavery's demise produced the first emotion; organized abolitionism's dissolution, the second. If AASS partisans executed his wishes, then
they would stay together "until not a slave should tread on the soil" anywhere
in the Western Hemisphere as well as the wider world. Even though an absent
William Wells Brown generally lauded the accomplishments of antislavery allies
and "rejoice[d] that the Society has finished its labors and comes to an honorable
close," his missive to the congregation hinted at a profounder sense of sorrow
and trepidation. The departure of the AASS, in his estimation, was a potentially
devastating loss for African Americans, as they "are no longer to have the vigilant eye and watchful care of their old and tried friends." He only hoped that the
latter "will, individually, insist on having the new laws" concerning Black civil
and political equality "crystallized into fact, until not an atom of distinction shall
grace the American character." Rather than a profession of absolute confidence,
Brown's observation suggests uncertainty about the reformatory power of un-
aligned white abolitionist veterans.[8]

The famed Spiritualist medium Cora L. V. Tappan more openly challenged
fellow crusaders during the business session of the AASS confab. From her angle,
most of the shareholders had prematurely buried a living community. Even with
the "earnest words of farewell" that had defined the public portion of the assembly, Tappan tried to reorient the conference mood and thereby rearrange its outcome. "Law is good," she pronounced on the one hand, while pointing out that
"bad men will have their day," on the other. So long as the wrong sort lingered,
the speaker expounded, the abolitionists could not merely rely on directives that
would "have no effect in the Southern States but by military force." Based on
her perceptions of unceasing defiance throughout the former Confederacy, conscience dictated her disapproval of any institutional breakup.[9]

In lieu of disbanding, she submitted a resolution providing for a literal retention and revitalization of the AASS. Despite, and because of, the ratification of
the Fifteenth Amendment, the motion recommended three actions: keeping intact the agency's structure, enlarging its corporate "capacities" so as "to meet the
increasing demands" of African Americans, and rechristening it the "American
Human Rights Association." Such a proposal revealingly made no headway. In
consecutive order, the prominent immediatists Charles C. Burleigh and Henry
Clarke Wright squarely disagreed with Tappan, claiming that AASS members

lacked the necessary constitutional authority to fulfill her prescriptions. Nothing could apparently sway a determined majority against desisting abolitionism.[10]

That did not deter another agitator from making a last-ditch attempt to save a vital syndicate. Since "the liberty of the negro" was still unwritten "in the hearts" of whites, Stephen Symonds Foster could find no solace. The very prospect of a humanitarian landscape without the AASS caused him to inject a stern dosage of reality into the assemblage, just as he had done in 1865. Regardless of the abolitionists' valorous deeds, he expected "looming up," somewhere in the United States on some day, "a great work to be done." Whereas Tappan referred to recalcitrant white southerners in order to make her case for the AASS's continuation and renovation, Foster cited untrustworthy northern Republicans in defense of his position. The emancipation of the enslaved, he fulminated, came about from an opprobrious "military necessity"; the enfranchisement of African American men, unprincipled "party necessity." To protect the freedpeople from the whims of political expediency in the short and long terms, Foster stood against the organization's cessation. "We should resolve never to lay aside our armor," he argued, "until the negro as well as the white man has the land upon which he can exercise an independent vote." Since the former was "the victim of years of plunder," the relentless activist stipulated that "[he] must have the means of providing for himself, before he is left to himself."[11]

Unlike Wright, who motioned that the attendees should simply wind up their meeting without scheduling a later one, Foster introduced a firmly worded countermotion that, had it passed, would have mandated that veteran abolitionists, as AASS minutemen, should prepare to reconvene at a moment's notice:

> *Resolved*, That in view of the great danger which still attends the future of our colored fellow citizens, we deem it unsafe to dissolve this Society, but will adjourn *sine die*, with instructions to the Executive Committee to call its members together whenever in their judgment a crisis shall have arisen which calls for farther united and organized action.

According to Foster's reckoning, a sleeping organizational giant "might possibly be a terror to evil doers"; a dead one would, of course, frighten nobody. An antislavery crusader could occasionally relax but must never quit—at least, not anytime soon.[12]

Even though that vigorous brand of abolitionism did not prevent the AASS from closing its doors, something like it factored in the formation of the Reform League. Frederick Douglass, for instance, flatly disagreed with Foster's resolution, not to mention his overall outlook. Earlier in the day, he expressed sheer amazement and appreciation for what had transpired over the past few years. Thanks to the "great triumph of justice and liberty that this association has been so largely instrumental in achieving," a renowned abolitionist lecturer now admittedly lacked the language to articulate those sensations appropriately. Sadness surfaced nowhere in his later remarks. "The work of the Society," in his appraisal, "had already been so well done, even better than was anticipated in the beginning, that it would be superfluous" to maintain the consortium any longer. The influential race leader accordingly captured the attitudes of many when he placed his trust in the forthcoming *Standard*. "One blast from that bugle," he confidently predicted, "will bring together again all that remain to us, ready again to do battle for the right." After that new altruistic trumpet fell silent, however, steadfast activism on behalf of the freedpeople and their descendants steadily faded away among those remaining white racial progressives during and after the 1880s.[13]

Ironically, in the absence of the neoabolitionist Reform League, the only body of potentially sympathetic whites on which Douglass could rely belonged to the Party of Lincoln. His 1892 autobiography records the closer ties that he had formed with Republican politicos. "Since 1872," he declared, "I have been regularly what my old friend Parker Pillsbury would call a 'field hand' in every important political campaign, and at each national convention have sided with what has been called the stalwart element of the Republican party." The final installment of his memoirs also documents not merely the governmental appointments that Republican presidents had awarded him for his campaigning services (namely, US marshal of the District of Columbia, recorder of deeds for the same area, and minister resident and consul general to Haiti) but also his disappointment with a partisan band that often betrayed its alleged heart and soul: "liberty" and "justice," "freedom" and "progress." In the years during and after the Rutherford B. Hayes administration, the autobiographer discerned a terrible renaissance of the Old South master class and proslavery Democracy in the United States. "When the Republican party," he moralized, "ceased to care for and protect its Southern allies, and sought the smiles of the Southern negro murderers, it shocked, disgusted, and drove away its best friends." At no narrative point did Douglass criticize veteran white abolitionists as apostates.[14]

In the penultimate chapter of his life story's updated 1881 edition, he commended, instead, the sturdy antislavery friends who had facilitated the rise of a famous "'self-made man.'" He thus honored more than fifty white male companions, all of whom were "helpful and confiding" and unhesitatingly treated him as "a man and a brother," such as John Brown, Arnold Buffum, Charles C. Burleigh, Samuel Buffington Chace, Stephen Symonds Foster, Samuel J. May, Wendell Phillips, Nathaniel P. Rogers, Edmund Quincy, and Joseph Southwick. Douglass also singled out numerous white women—from well-known Lucretia Mott and Lydia Maria Child to little-known Lucinda Wilmarth and Amorancy Paine—whose inspirational devotion to the slave's cause and "recognition of the equal manhood of the colored race" factored into his proudly becoming "a woman's-rights man." The author readjusted none of that praise for the book's 1892 printing.[15]

Not even a passing barb at the expense of John A. Collins disrupts those positive reminiscences. In a recounted conversation that had occurred during a steamboat excursion, a Kentucky-born US congressman from California essentially exposed a retrogressive Collins after Douglass inquired about an antislavery colleague who had mentored him at the start of his career. Replying that he certainly knew the man in question, the interlocutor explained that, as an opposing-party candidate, Collins had competed for the same House of Representatives position that he currently held. "'I charged him with being an abolitionist,'" the narrator recalled the Democrat's boast, "'but he denied it; so I sent off and got the evidence of his having been general agent of the Massachusetts Anti-Slavery Society, and that settled him.'" Even though the remembered exchange also debuted in the 1881 volume—in an unrelated chapter—it sheds no light on the Reconstruction-era loyalties of a white activist. Since Collins had migrated from New England to the Pacific Coast during the Gold Rush, his purported betrayal of the immediate emancipation campaign took place years before the Civil War.[16]

Elsewhere in the text, however, Douglass lamented the abolitionists' organizational disbandment and concurrent abandonment of "systematic" agitation, which he misattributed to Garrison's 1863–1865 actions. The autobiographer committed another factual error by claiming that, immediately after slavery's abolition, "the cause of the freedmen was left mainly to individual effort and to hastily-extemporized [benevolent] societies of an ephemeral character." Regardless of such mischaracterizations, which first appear in the 1881 version and remain in the 1892 finale, Douglass notably professed that the new philanthropic combinations "were not as effective for good as the old society would have been had it followed up its work and kept its old instrumentalities in operation." Approximately ten years removed from the actual dissolution of the AASS, the personal historian apparently recognized the problem that Brown had alluded to in his 1870 missive and Foster strove to avert during the conference proceedings: a world without organized abolitionism.[17]

Yet, the post-1876 instances of apathy, negligence, and/or desertion among Johnson, Pillsbury, Powell, and Higginson were scarcely anomalous. The appearance of two compact publications at the start of the 1890s indicates that white women had also moved on with their humanitarian lives after Reconstruction's termination. In 1891, Elizabeth Buffum Chace released *Anti-Slavery Reminiscences*, the narrative of which numbers about forty pages. That same year, Lucy N. Colman issued a somewhat longer memorial offering, *Reminiscences*, whose main text encompasses seventy-seven pages. Each author previously combined with the AASS and/or a subsidiary. In the process of recording past abolitionist exertions—in Massachusetts and Rhode Island, for Chace; western New York, Pennsylvania, and the Old Northwest, for Colman—both reproached the racial antipathies of antebellum Americans. The personal historians additionally communicated different postbellum passions: feminism, in Chace's case; freethought, in Colman's.[18]

Chace opened her memoir by outlining the evolution of antislavery among the Society of Friends in Rhode Island, as well as mapping the emancipationist march of Quaker relatives during the late eighteenth and early nineteenth centuries. After noting that a grandfather had associated with a local manumission organization, the daughter of the New England Anti-Slavery Society's first president especially prized her father's pathway. Arnold Buffum, a reverent Chace underscored, had detested enslavement since his childhood. That juvenescent abolitionism reportedly blossomed thereafter. He initially backed the American Colonization Society, on the presupposition that it genuinely intended to solve an iniquitous social arrangement. He then took up the sincere gradual emancipation program of Quaker coreligionist Benjamin Lundy. He ultimately befriended "the Garrisonian Anti-Slavery movement." Whereas the *Liberator*'s editor converted the Buffum head of household to the doctrine of immediatism, Chace's dad scattered the good news among his kindred, bringing about new births and baptisms.[19]

From the moment of that domestic revival onward, the memoirist informed readers that she labored as a diehard disciple of William Lloyd Garrison. She and her husband, Samuel, reared their youngsters as loyal Garrisonians. Their Valley Falls residence lodged high-profile Garrisonians as they proselytized throughout Rhode Island, such as William Wells Brown, Charles C. Burleigh, Stephen and Abigail Kelley Foster, Wendell Phillips, Parker Pillsbury, Charles Lenox Remond, Lucy Stone, Henry Clarke Wright, and Garrison himself. They always accommodated Frederick Douglass, too, despite the latter's distancing himself from group orthodoxy on such matters as the US Constitution's proslavery essence (an estrangement that comes up nowhere in the narrative). Lastly, they stayed "firm in the Garrisonian idea," even though the retrospective writer never explicitly addressed the 1840 AASS schism that would have required such a faithful showing.[20]

That the Buffum paterfamilias had sided with the Liberty Party political abolitionists, as well as the later antislavery politicos of the Republican Party, constitutes a tacit authorial acknowledgment of abolitionism's fragmentation. Regardless of father's turn toward partisan politics, the deferential descendant never doubted his philanthropic commitments, asserting that he perpetually advocated "some enterprise that promised immediate results." As for the autobiographer, both she and Samuel refused to countenance the Libertyites or partake in a US government that "sanctioned slavery." After the congressional adoption of the 1850 Fugitive Slave Law, their homestead further functioned as a busy station on the Underground Railroad. About a dozen pages of Chace's story certify both the righteousness of that disobedience to an ungodly statute and the "intelligence and sharp-sightedness" of the freedom seekers who had fled from the Old South prison-house.[21]

Beyond the family circle, the narrator explained that Garrisonian abolitionism met with little acceptance among others. Despite an eagerness to share the immediatist gospel, she quickly discovered that intersectional political, commercial, and spiritual ties had "blinded the eyes" and "hardened the hearts" of most white northerners. Even her Quaker coterie disapproved of the *Liberator*'s editor, partly because of the supposed religious infidelity of the abolitionist leader and the severe denunciations that regularly discharged from his press. Endemic racism also played a role. "At the time," Chace remarked, caste prejudices were "stronger than the pro-slavery spirit." Of the two, the latter prompted the decision to personally vacate the Society of Friends. But a few years after she, her spouse, and their children relocated from the Bay State to neighboring Rhode Island, the author intimated that "many occurrences" proved that the ancestral church had forgotten its earlier antislavery history and "submitted to the domination of the slave-holding power." Conscience therefore dictated that she must relinquish her membership.[22]

Besides the backsliding of fellow Quakers, Chace illumined the anti-Black biases that contaminated New England before and even during the Civil War. She recalled that a Taunton, Massachusetts, railroad had denied "a highly respected, well-dressed colored man and his wife" with passage to Boston until the remonstrations of white antislavery allies forced a temporary policy change. She pointed out that colorphobia had once polluted her Fall River, Massachusetts, domicile during a dinner party for visiting abolitionists. When invited to join in the meal, a recollected white domestic servant declined to sit at any table that also welcomed "'niggers.'" Decades afterward, Chace suggested that an ostensibly Christian woman, of a Baptist persuasion, likely "went hungry that day." The memoirist disclosed that such bigotry blighted the views of several abolitionists, too. Without naming any names, she attested that some patrons of the Fall River Female Anti-Slavery Society had "strongly objected" to formally admitting African Americans, as they did not want to put such persons "on an equality" with themselves. That small-mindedness, however, represented an exception to the rule, for "none except the long-tried Abolitionists," the autobiographer affirmed, sought the "removal of all racial prejudice" and the "establishment of the principle of a common humanity." Well before the reality of the Thirteenth, Fourteenth, and Fifteenth Amendments, she declared that observation and conviction had taught her that everyone's betterment would ensue as soon as whites ensured that Black people, as "members of our body politic," possessed the same rights and privileges as well as received treatment on merit-based qualifications exclusively.[23]

Notwithstanding remembered protests of public services, private agencies, and charitable institutions that had discriminated against free Black northerners and resisted racial integration, the half-finished reformism that the octogenarian Chace detected did not involve the formerly enslaved. Since the "diadem of citizenship" crowning African Americans had supplanted the shackles of perpetual servitude, "it is too late," according to the retrospective writer's memorable phrase, "to become an Abolitionist now." While working for the liberty of southern slaves, as well as assisting slavery escapees who sojourned at her home, she recounted how "experience revealed the great injustice . . . of the subordinate, disfranchised condition of woman." Even though the sexist lashes and chains that degraded and restrained were figurative, the memoirist believed that women's liberation should not only galvanize veteran abolitionists but also their progeny and all post-Reconstruction others whom they still inspired.[24]

On behalf of that "broader more world-wide reformation," Elizabeth Buffum Chace accordingly bequeathed the lessons of the immediate emancipation campaign. Contemporary feminists, in her evaluation, could learn much from the antebellum abolitionists' uncommon sense of self-sacrifice and "consecration to duty." They also owed them tremendous gratitude, for when chattel bondage ended in the United States, antislavery agitators headed "the Woman Suffrage cause." Based on how the personal historian concluded her brief account, the new workers evidently needed models and encouragement. The "next generation of reformers," Chace observed, must carry out a task whose "significance to the progress of all mankind" exceeded that of abolitionism itself, insights that she reiterated in a publicly read letter at an 1893 Danvers commemorative event.[25]

The "liberal education" afforded by the prewar movement thus prepared Chace to enlist in the greater "warfare for the emancipation . . . and elevation" of another class of subaltern people. The veteran abolitionist unquestionably practiced what she preached, committing her life's last thirty years to feminism. For example, shortly after helping organize the New England Woman Suffrage Association, Chace cofounded a Rhode Island counterpart in 1868, functioning as its chief executive from 1870 to 1899. She likely would have participated in the 1869 formation of the American Woman Suffrage Association had not illness intervened, but she attended its annual convocations and served as its president in 1882–1883, and her state-level alliance affiliated with it. Just as freeing humanity's female half preoccupied an inexhaustible crusader, it also underwrote her reminiscences. An ongoing African American freedom struggle did not.[26]

Lucy Colman broached the topic of race in the early-nineteenth-century United States as well. She pointed out that white northerners habitually practiced a "bitter prejudice against color," treating anyone with the slightest trace of "dark blood," regardless of refinement or attainments, as an outcast. To quash that aversion to blackness, the autobiographer sarcastically stated that otherwise observant racists manifested no qualms toward "black dog[s]." Many "ladies," she exclaimed, will "caress with the greatest affection" a dusky-coated canine, "bringing the mouth of that four-footed pet into the closest contact with their own!" Colman did not merely expose the absurdity of colorphobia or ridicule the slipshod logic behind it. As a scrappy and cantankerous memoirist, she rivaled the caustic and cranky Pillsbury. She also belonged to a like-minded freethinkers' guild, as her autobiography demonstrates. The retrospective writer therefore eviscerated irrationality and conservatism, castigating religious hypocrisy and intolerance, as well as condemning racism and sexism.[27]

Even though the author asserted that she had gained "the reputation of an earnest Abolitionist" and recounted how she toiled assiduously as a lecturing agent of the Western Anti-Slavery Society, the first pages of her narrative fixate on orthodox Protestantism and its oppressiveness. After recollecting how, as a child, she wrestled with weighty theological questions concerning God's justness or goodness but received no satisfactory answers either from pious relatives or the Christian Bible itself, Colman shared the program that propelled her adult career. "Until the majority of the people are emancipated from authority over their minds," she maintained, "we are not safe." Nor should sympathetic readers take solace in the apparent liberalization of Protestant sects over time. Such a softening, in her assessment, only "nicely covered" their elemental "hideousness," exactly why real "Liberals [must] be on the alert." "Christianity demands entire subordination to its edicts," she avouched. Since its emissaries allegedly enthralled persons from their earliest days, at Sunday schools as well as public classrooms, Colman wanted infidels and skeptics everywhere to unite. Alluding to Giordano Bruno, whose unorthodox beliefs and cosmological views ran afoul of the Catholic Church and resulted in his death in 1600 by burning, she advised American freethinkers to "use the utmost diligence" in order to topple all laws that criminalized "*free speaking.*" The memoir's additional pages suggest, in pronounced and subtle ways, that the cause of "mental liberty" and the intertwined matters of spiritual tyranny and patriarchal misrule governed her late-in-life ruminations.[28]

To be sure, not every story that the retrospective writer told redounded to the benefit of freethought. She nevertheless revisited the antislavery past as an actively engaged, critical commentator. Her remembrances of abolitionist fieldwork often had nothing to do with the proslavery or racist obstacles that blocked the immediate emancipation campaign's headway in a specific region or locality. She, instead, labeled mostly all Hoosiers as "too stupid" to obtain any stimulation from antislavery agitation. She also publicized the "appalling . . . ignorance" of the people whom she had met in Pennsylvania. More notably, Colman contended that, beyond antiabolitionist churchmen, Spiritualism obstructed abolitionism as well. At a WASS annual meeting, in Detroit, she recalled that the Spiritualists in attendance had nearly usurped the proceedings. An ardent Garrisonian like Henry Clarke Wright "lost all zeal" for abolitionist activism, according to her accusation, "saying that now the *spirits* would . . . bring about" the slaves' freedom. Despite favoring that alternative faith during the 1850s, the memoirist could never personally stomach a designated antislavery get-together devolving into a séance. Besides characterizing the omnipresence of Spiritualism in Michigan as "like some outbreak of disease," that menace had reputedly overtaken the northern parts of Illinois, too. At the sites usually available to traveling abolitionist speakers, the Spiritualists monopolized them: "Heaven in another world," she opined, "was a greater temptation than a free country here and now."[29]

While retelling her antislavery excursions in Ohio, Colman further dwelled on the "dreadful" illiteracy that she had seen among clerics and parishioners alike. Regarding the unintelligence of Buckeye State Methodists, she announced: "If a man could speak loud enough, and pray long enough, and shout with sufficient fervor, he had the principal requisite for the ministerial office." The narrator divulged an especially dismal tale about a Presbyterian woman. Reportedly driven to madness by a revival of religion, she killed two of her offspring and attempted to slice the throat of another. After her confinement in an asylum had ended, she birthed three more children, each of whom suffered from a developmental disability (idiocy, to use the author's terminology). The seemingly loyal husband, known only as "Mr. L—," received the brunt of the retrospective writer's criticism, though. When Colman asked how he could permit a deranged person to get repeatedly pregnant, the quoted man said that "'she was *harmless, and she was my WIFE!*'" Such an allegory allowed the autobiographer to shine a light on the "cruelty" of long-established religious credos that not only condemned untold portions of humankind to hell but also commanded womenfolk to obediently submit to male heads of household. In this scenario, wifehood was nothing but sanctioned prostitution.[30]

Iconoclasm thus pervades this personal history, as does a pugnacious, common-sense rationalism. Both specifically materialize on the occasions in which Colman explicitly formulated feminist viewpoints. Regarding the dimwitted Pennsylvanians of her recollections, she explicated how, in response to an election query by a male colleague, the men at one meet and greet uttered that "*Ginral Jackson*" would get their votes. When notified that the war hero had long since passed away, Colman's dumbfounded dialogists still stood by their decision, expressing undying electoral allegiance not to the Jacksonian Democrats per se but Old Hickory himself. Voters such as those, the memoirist interjected, served as "a good text whereon to base an argument" for the enfranchisement of women. Colman related another Keystone State tour stop at which she was the sole female participant. Hardly a scandalous antislavery affair, the retrospective writer underlined how she herself kept an entire audience of "coarse men on their good behavior." Since she had done it there, according to the rationalist sermonizing, other ladies could perform just as admirably at the traditionally masculine polling places and legislative chambers. Her feminism, however, did not just encompass a fully impartial suffrage and equal political opportunities for both sexes.[31]

Colman elucidated that as an itinerant lecturer, "I always" addressed "the *legal slavery* in which every *white* woman is held," stressing that governments had subjected them to statutes to which they never gave their consent. Before she joined the ranks of abolitionism, the autobiographer revealed that entering the age-old profession of motherhood was eye-opening. Maternity evidently enabled her to identify closely with enslaved African American women. Noting the incomparable joy that she had felt when she first saw her newborn baby, the ecstasy instantly evaporated while thinking about "the slave-mother's agony, as she looked upon her child and knew its fate." Such an affinity catalyzed her "work for the slave's deliverance." Maternity additionally compelled her to more intently cogitate manmade marriage laws, as well as reflect on the godlike power that men customarily wielded. A twenty-eight-year-old Colman painfully discovered that the father completely "owned" and "controlled" the babe to which she herself had "gone down to death's door to give life." Throughout the account she appropriately interlaced nonfictional parables in order to illustrate "something about wrongs that do not belong exclusively to the 'Anglo-African.'" She similarly remarked elsewhere in the text that "I find so much of *wrongs* that I have no space for [women's] *rights*."[32]

Whether reminiscing about herself as a circuit-riding abolitionist or pioneering feminist, Colman exhibited an indomitable freethought mentality that did not slacken with age. An acute sense of reason apparently saved her from a premature quietus as well. "Intimately acquainted" with John Brown and deeply interested in his plans to erect a fugitive slave stronghold in the mountains of western Virginia, Colman nonetheless refrained from enrolling in his expedition. Even though they possessed a mutual "hatred" of enslavement, their sacred compasses profoundly deviated from each other. The author portrayed Brown as the "most thorough Calvinist" that she had ever known, one who "positively believed" that an omnipotent deity had chosen him to effectuate his designs. Since Colman no longer put her "faith in special providences" and "ceased to regard the Hebrew laws as binding," she could not entrust herself to such an old-school leader.[33]

The recollected Harpers Ferry occurrence encapsulates the septuagenarian memoirist's outlook. Conventional religion never satisfied her, philosophically repulsing her ultimately. In contrast to the Holy Scriptures that ordered the existences of countless Christians, Colman disclosed that the *Truth Seeker* constituted her "bible," as it did for thousands of other postbellum freethinkers. Her autobiography contains more references to that periodical, which D. M. Bennett originally edited, than Garrison's *Liberator* or another antislavery newspaper. Having lost two husbands and a daughter earlier in life, the personal historian treasured the journal's managers, contributors, and supporters, all of whom she had adopted as "family." Besides noting the *Truth Seeker's* invaluable functions, the narrator occasionally cited other freethought publications.[34]

Colman indicated, in the memoir's last paragraphs, that her unyielding secularism found a partial outlet in the National Liberal League, too. Founded in 1876, the group championed the total separation of church and state, as well as freedom of conscience for all Americans. Its patrons particularly sought to counteract intrusive evangelical Protestants who conspired to implement or had successfully implemented the US government on behalf of Christianizing initiatives (such as the National Reform Association's constitutional-amendment drive and Anthony Comstock's crusade against obscenity). The narrative also makes clear that rather than sit idly by amid ubiquitous bigotry, she "preferred" to do her own work in her own manner, the effectiveness of which depended on her own wits, not the guidance or "dictat[ion]" of otherworldly spirits.[35]

A strong-willed individual unequivocally takes center stage in Colman's chronicle, as further evinced by descriptions of Civil War activities. The commemorator remembered that during the slaveholders' rebellion, she served several months as matron of the National Colored Orphan Asylum in Washington, DC; was the district's superintendent of eleven African American schools for a longer spell; and twice accompanied the Black activist Sojourner Truth to the White House. In the first role, the author discussed how her reformism had focused on removing an abusive female teacher who enjoyed the patronage of important Massachusetts politicos and well-connected religious liberals. In an endeavor to cure the food-deprived, parasite-ridden Black children under her care, Colman's campaign against a "wicked woman" nearly failed until the threat of media exposure resulted in the desired outcome. In the second role, the author had to contend not only against the generations of captivity that rendered the lessons of cleanliness, sobriety, and prudence as difficult ones to impart among the newly liberated. She also confronted the American Tract Society, "the most proslavery organization in this country," whose petty, evangelical Protestant proponents tried to deny her access to young and old African Americans inhabiting the Freedmen's Village, which was located on the estate of the Confederate general Robert E. Lee. In the third role, the author debunked the posthumous grandeur of Abraham Lincoln. According to her rendition, a renowned storyteller shared no amusing anecdotes or folksy wisdom during his meeting with Truth. President Lincoln, instead, regarded the visitor as an "ordinary washer woman," condescendingly greeting her as "aunty." Nor did the critique halt there.[36]

For the retrospective writer, the Great Emancipator was a reluctant liberator, at best, a white supremacist, at worst. She matter-of-factly stated that the inexorable course of military events had forced Lincoln into abolitionist glory. "Perhaps he came to rejoice over" the Emancipation Proclamation's release, Colman mused, "when he realized" that the command would immortalize his name, "but at that time he did not see it." She more derisively propounded that Honest Abe "believed in the white race, not in the colored," and wished none whatsoever to place the latter on an equality with the former. The memoirist more favorably sketched the assassinated president's substitute, however. During a second excursion to the Executive Mansion with Truth, Colman perceived that Andrew Johnson "was quite at home with his colored guest, asking her . . . to be seated, and refusing to be seated himself while she should stand." Except for that alleged gentility, the autobiographer listed nothing else about the Tennessean. She ostensibly wanted to use him as a foil to diminish Lincoln's legacy solely. Despite asserting about herself that "if anything was to be done for any special colored person, everybody, far and near, knew I was the one to be called upon to do it," Colman's racial justice services apparently expired circa 1865. Thanks to chattel slavery's demolition, she confessed, "I had fairly earned rest." Nor did the narrator harbor any regrets about the physical toll that roving abolitionism had taken, for "a race redeemed . . . is a memory like a benediction." The memoir shows that the eventual restoral of her energies aided not the formerly enslaved but the freethinkers' fight.[37]

Regardless of a text's male or female creator, the antislavery memorial and historical literature of the 1890s uniquely conveys the protracted fallout from Reconstruction's downfall. No all-consuming abolitionist fires reignited the movement's white veterans. Even Sarah H. Southwick's succinct 1893 production *Reminiscences of Early Anti-Slavery Days* conforms to that commemorative template. In a narrative of some thirty-five pages, the chronicler italicized an immediate emancipation upbringing and maturity. She started her review by publicizing familial assistance for Garrison and his *Liberator*. Her father had subscribed to the legendary reformer's newspaper from its inception, when the author herself was "ten years old." Her mother's sisters had married husbands who read Garrison's weekly from the beginning, too, "heartily" investing their "money and interest" on the journalist's behalf. Her humanitarian tutelage further consisted of dad's cofounding the AASS; loyally frequenting with mom the gatherings of the Boston Female Anti-Slavery Society as well as the annual fairs that Maria Weston Chapman and other abolitionist women had put together; and a parental abode that once hosted the eminent English agitator, George Thompson, and often housed Henry Clarke Wright.[38]

As a profile of a rank-and-file activist, Southwick's concise account illustrates that she had been a spectator at several remarkable incidents in abolitionist history: the 1835 mobbing of Garrison; the mixed-sex, or "promiscuous," assembly lectures of Sarah and Angelina Grimké; the 1837 Faneuil Hall speech of Phillips; the 1838 incineration of Pennsylvania Hall; the 1840 schism of the AASS; and the inaugural public address of Frederick Douglass at a Nantucket antislavery convention. Besides covering each in individual sections, the author briefly catalogued regnant anti-Black prejudices of white northerners in another. The first example concerns the bigotry that the racially mixed son of an English governor of Sierra Leone had experienced. Despite a "gentlemanly" pedigree and an Oxford education, the nameless person of color returned homeward when he found that his complexion, which Southwick classified as "jet black," deterred his prospects as a businessman in the northeastern United States. The second pertains to the racial segregation that a daughter of a leading Black Baptist preacher in Boston had encountered. Regardless of how "educated and intelligent" Susan Paul was, as well as the fact that she was not "very dark," her African ancestry barred her admission to a steamboat ladies' cabin. Forced to travel on the lower deck and exposed to inclement weather during a nighttime passage, racism's repercussions were literally deadly in this scenario, for Paul had contracted "a severe cold" that eventuated in life-taking tuberculosis. The "Prejudice against Color" inventory, however, never surpasses the early 1840s; the colorphobia "prevailing" then presumably lasted no longer from Southwick's 1890s standpoint. Not even a sparsely discussed 1887 dinner with Douglass stirred the memoirist to ruminate on what he had done or continued to do since his first speaking foray.[39]

Mostly featuring teenaged experiences and adhering to an "I was there, too" framework, her pithy remembrances of philanthropic yesteryears comprise a registry of an ordinary but reliable follower of antebellum abolitionism. The narrator nevertheless surmised that since "her parents, relatives, and best friends were all abolitionists," any dissent from their reformism would have taken "much moral heroism." Such an aside suggests that the pressure of kinfolk and peers was powerful and potentially restrictive. When pondering the present day, she did so only to share her amazement and gratefulness that a formerly reviled and "shunned" *Liberator*'s editor, and the crusaders linked to him, now garnered popular adoration and "reverence." So astounding were those reversals that the anti-Garrisonian past seemed like a foreign country to a septuagenarian Southwick. Nor did an 1893 assemblage of antislavery veterans prompt her to reflect more materially, as the speaker largely reminisced about a family history in Danvers and Salem that stretched back to the earliest English settlers.[40]

The autobiography of a generally independent agitator provides a possible exception to the authorial trajectory herein delineated. Originally published in 1881, Laura Smith Haviland's *A Woman's Life-Work: Labors and Experiences* went through four subsequent editions. The fifth and final updated version of 1897 came with a revised subtitle: *Including Thirty Years' Service on the Underground Railroad and in the War*. Despite affiliating with the Logan Female Anti-Slavery

Society (Lenawee County, Michigan) that the Quaker poet and reformer Elizabeth Margaret Chandler had established in 1832, as well as sometimes attending the meetings of the Garrisonian Michigan Anti-Slavery Society (founded in
Adrian, in 1853), Haviland mainly toiled outside such collaborative channels. The
memoirist herself lightly touched on the former coalition and never mentioned
the latter. Even though she made passing references to preeminent white abolitionists, such as James G. Birney, William Lloyd Garrison, and Gerrit Smith, her
fellow Underground Railroad operative Levi Coffin represents the only figure
who regularly shows up in her narrative. Regardless of whom she recalled and
how, the personal historian surveyed an immediate emancipation vocation in
which she often plodded as an association of one.[41]

In the opening chapter, the author recounted a spiritual struggle that commenced early in life. "I well remember," she remarked, "the perplexities and
doubts that troubled my young mind in trying to find the whys and wherefores
of existing facts." As a five-year-old seeker, Haviland learned that all things biblical were not literally true, especially the idea that a man and woman, once united
together in holy matrimony, ceased as dual entities. When the youngster inter-
rogated her mother one day about the whereabouts of father, the incorrect answers had proven to her that husband and wife shared neither a single person
nor the same mind. Years later, a teenaged seeker personally discovered Methodist praying, singing, and exhortations at a relative's home in upstate New York.
For Quaker-raised Haviland—whose dad was a Society of Friends minister, and
mom, a denominational elder—that first contact affected her immensely. From
there on, according to the retrospective writer, she sought out a new birth. Haviland reminisced about such a life-changing decision with precision, quoting
word for word her self-resolution: "'I *never* will give up trying, if it takes as long
as I live, until I receive an evidence that I am the Lord's child [and] realize that
peace and joy those men and women expressed in that [prayer] meeting.'" The
numerous chapter pages that follow predominantly concern a years-long quest
for Methodist justification and sanctification. The recollected Haviland initially
pursued it secretly, for fear of troubling her parents. She then suppressed or tried
to redirect it, with much mental and emotional anguish, given their opposition
to enthusiastic, or what they had called "'overheated,'" religion.[42]

Beyond the spiritual, an inquisitive Haviland thirsted for knowledge of all
kinds in her youth. That other yearning brought about an antislavery awakening, which the memoirist also addressed in the leadoff chapter, albeit in less detail. While imbibing books seemingly wherever she found them, the avid reader
made yet another important personal discovery: the eighteenth-century writ-

ings of John Woolman. The autobiographer did not cite the specific title, but she presumably happened upon the Quaker abolitionist's *Some Considerations on the Keeping of Negroes: Recommended to the Professors of Christianity of Every Denomination* (which was published in two parts, in 1754 and 1762, respectively). The essay's descriptions of transatlantic slave trading and its African victims during and after the Middle Passage immersed and terrified her, driving her to tears while reading and rereading the text during an evening's sitting. "My sympathies," the author shared, "became too deeply enlisted for the poor negroes who were thus enslaved for time to efface."[43]

Toward the close of the same chapter, Haviland additionally referred to the Logan Female Anti-Slavery Society. Even though she pointed out that it constituted Michigan's first abolitionist organization and admitted interested persons regardless of sect, she offered nothing revealing about the partnership's founding values. Nor did she reflect at length on the institution's leading light, merely noting that Elizabeth Chandler identified as a progressive, Hicksite Quaker. At that narrative moment, then, Haviland made no revelations about whether she had seen or heard Chandler's activist verse; whether she had taken inspiration from the "Ladies' Repository" section that Chandler managed for Lundy's *Genius of Universal Emancipation*; or whether the twenty-six-year-old Chandler's death, in 1834, had impaired organized abolitionism locally or across the county. (Much later in the text, however, the remembered Haviland defended a "noble" Chandler during a conversation in which a white southerner had dismissed the Quaker's antislavery poems as a northern "'pack of lies.'") The memoirist did not fail to explain that, as a result of the Logan group's interdenominational spirit, she and her family separated from Orthodox Quakerism. A soul's journey that had earnestly commenced in the early 1820s culminated not just in Laura Smith Haviland's joining the Wesleyan Methodist Church but also a mother and father who had originally discouraged her attraction to Methodism.[44]

Throughout many of the other twenty-five chapters Haviland presented herself as an undaunted foe of iniquitous slaveholders, duplicitous slave catchers, and unrepentant ex-Confederates. She simultaneously emerges from the text as a fierce ally of freedom seekers before the Civil War, as well as a staunch friend of the freedpeople during and after that sectional conflagration. While recalling the ways in which she thwarted the slave-hunting machinations of nefarious white southerners in Michigan, Ohio, and Indiana, the autobiographer transmitted tales of courageous and cunning African Americans who went to great lengths in order to secure their own autonomy and that of loved ones. Never a sweet land of liberty during the antebellum decades, Haviland continually stressed that the fugitives from southern servitude whom she assisted had to abscond from the United States entirely. Only through Canadian relocations did their recollected search for safety reach fruition. While narrating missionary and relief efforts among the formerly enslaved across a war-torn Southland during the 1860s and 1870s, she similarly related the accounts of Black men and women who broke away from white brutality. In a postbellum America wherein enslavement no longer legally existed, Haviland ultimately emphasized that tens of thousands of new runaways, as Kansas Exodusters, sought sanctuary on the Great Plains.[45]

If any readers of the 1880s and 1890s doubted the Civil War's rightfulness or necessity, then the author's recitation of southern horrors reminded them that the Lincoln administration had justifiably suppressed the slaveholders' rebellion. To edify audiences, she repeated what fleeing African Americans had personally told her during a wartime nursing stint in Mississippi and Louisiana. As slavery's survivors, Haviland's informants disclosed that they suffered not merely harsh working regimes but also cruel and unusual punishments that had killed some and scarred or crippled many more. Besides lashings that had shredded flesh, the ruling race contrived terrifying devices so as to discipline supposedly disobedient bondservants. References to neck-irons, knee-stiffeners, and other tortuous contraptions demonstrated how sadistic whites had wreaked havoc on Black bodies. In the pathetic case of "Uncle Tim," finger-sized metal joints rubbed the skin completely away, causing worm-infested sores to develop around the collar. Even though death prevented additional agony, the barbarity did not cease. Because of the victim's swelled head and neck, "Massa George Ralston" reportedly resorted to decapitation in order to remove the apparatus and potentially reuse it in the future. Despite the intel that she had acquired over years of Underground Railroad service, what Haviland first encountered as a self-constituted charitable worker, then as an officially appointed agent of a Michigan Freedmen's Aid Society, exceeded her preexisting understanding of southern depravity and backwardness. The memoirist explained that she confiscated sundry slave-irons because she wanted to show fellow northerners "'what sort of jewelry the colored people had to wear down here.'" As visual reinforcement, she inserted a full-length portrait of herself propagandistically exhibiting those sinister wares.[46]

Since white southerners had created a Hell on Earth, Haviland communicated a story in which very few could ever end up in paradise. Nor did she limit her Dantean anathemas to the Old South and CSA monstrosities. In the "Present Condition of the Freedmen" chapter, the autobiographer berated the neoslavery that had taken form after 1865. By citing an array of depredations that unreconstructed and seemingly irredeemable whites inflicted on the formerly enslaved,

Haviland put forward a damning record that approximated, if not overwhelmed, the racial atrocities that had defined the antebellum period. Since "re-enlivened treason" amounted to the "true sentiment" and prevalent power across the "ex-slave States," an apparently tireless adversary of systemic exploitation, racism, and ungodliness reported on what she had found out while working in Kansas among African American escapees from the not-so-new South then materializing.[47]

In defense of the Exoduster Movement, the author declared that "after fifteen years of patient hoping, waiting, and watching for the shaping of government," the freedpeople faced a future encompassing either "submissive vassalage, a war of races, or emigration." The resurgence of "tyrannous" ex-slaveholders, according to Haviland, compelled multitudes of African Americans to bolt from the Southland once again. Based on interviews conducted, as well as private letters and printed articles, the memoirist disseminated testimonial after testimonial documenting the violence that not only made the Southland solidly Democratic by 1877 but also persisted after Reconstruction's collapse. In many regional parts, Haviland proclaimed, "the greatest crime . . . is being a Republican." The very skin color of such Black partisans, she further elucidated, made the criminal offense especially heinous for countless white southerners, as evidenced by the verbal, physical, sexual, and aggravated assaults that the latter had perpetrated. As a result of that reign of terror, the autobiographer felt duty-bound to "ventilate these facts." Whatever the sensationalist accusations that might accompany her exposé, a Black migrant's recited words encapsulated one of the section's overarching themes: "'I do not believe there are Democrats in heaven.'" That terrorism induced Haviland to appeal forthrightly to her readership as well. "Let every man, woman, and child," she summoned, "arise and work for the refugees, who are suffering for food, fuel, and clothing." To forcefully punctuate that supplication to Good Samaritans, she admonished northerners about the "debt our nation owes to the ex-slaves," which "should be paid."[48]

Had the memoirist made no textual emendations, the narrative would arguably rate as the most potent racial justice statement penned by a veteran white abolitionist. No comparable annalist of abolitionism so extensively or compellingly wrote, as Haviland did during the early 1880s, about the resilience of enslaved people, the incredible wickedness of southern slaveholders, the unvanquished rebelliousness of ex-Confederates, and the strivings of freedmen and women amid hardship and persecution. In the book's original arrangement, the nineteen chapters, totaling 520 pages, the author wholly concentrated on "a long and sorely oppressed race." Yet, the fifth edition, which contains over a hundred pages of additions, reveals that she had moved away from an ongoing African

American freedom struggle. The commemorative tone therefore veers dramatically beginning with the twentieth chapter, one that Haviland composed for the fourth manuscript installment of 1887. After detailing a personal history about a noninstitutional antislavery activist, never once referring to the AASS, the chronicler expanded the tale by pledging allegiance to the nationally influential Woman's Christian Temperance Union (WCTU). By the late 1880s and for the remainder of her life, Laura Smith Haviland contested an altogether different moral and social monster.[49]

Despite the persistent abuse that Black southerners endured, a pestilential liquor traffic now outstripped that humanitarian concern. Such a commerce, the autobiographer opined, consumed the "body, soul and spirit of 100,000 annually." As the next "'Irrepressible Conflict,'" Haviland contended that antialcohol demanded "persevering, energetic, self-sacrificing" crusaders. Among the fresh soldiers enlisting in the fighting, the narrator specifically extolled the advocates of the WCTU, whose watchwords were "Agitation—agitation, keep the ball rolling!" Repeatedly deploying martial language and imagery, she asserted that the "Grand Army of Temperance," under the nationwide direction of Frances E. Willard, would topple all alcoholic strongholds. With a firm conviction that the campaign against the saloon represented a Christ-like cause, the memoirist avouched that God's "battalion of forces" could not fail. Equipped with the Bible and principle, as well as "voice," "pen," *and* the "ballot," Haviland announced that lasting success against drunkenness depended on the "onward march [of] women." In her estimation, societal progress and female advancement went hand in hand. As emblematic of the former, the latter evidently ensured both the regeneration of America and salvation of besotted Americans. Just as remorseless slaveholders and ex-Confederates never entered the Promised Land, so, too, were the tippler and dram seller blocked from a heavenly afterlife, thereby making feminine intervention absolutely crucial.[50]

The peal of a new alarm bell also carried over to chapter add-ons for the book's 1897 printing. An aggrieved and sickened autobiographer highlighted the daily reports of the "mighty giant, Alcohol," and the deadly scourge that it had spawned. Since that murderous fiend purportedly claimed more money and lives each year by the late 1890s than the financial and human costs of the four-year Civil War, Haviland redoubled her backing of earnest and uncompromising temperance activism. "Is it not well," she rhetorically asked, "that more than 300,000" WCTU members "are banded together, shoulder to shoulder, heart to heart, to battle against this monst[rous] evil?" Since the liquor traffic's corruptive tentacles had pierced legislative chambers and partisan politics, the former abolitionist evolved into a full-fledged Christian feminist during her last years. Indeed, in the memoir's fifth edition she more strongly called for the enfranchisement of women. Once armed with voting rights throughout the United Sates, female Protestants like herself could decisively protect the fireside and family, as well as purify municipal, state, and national environments.[51]

For a nearly ninety-year-old commemorator, rampant drunkenness generated a grave sense of danger, not resurrected white supremacy. Even before significantly enlarging the autobiographical contents, she underscored "appalling fact[s]" in the preface of the 1884 third edition: the existence of some "7,000,000" drinkers in the United States and the allotment of "$100 for drink for every dollar" that Americans spent on clergymen. The seventy-five-year-old chronicler thus unleashed her life story once more, beseeching the conscientious and devout to "look to the Lord Jesus for ability and wisdom to cry aloud and spare not until our day's work is done for the Master." By the late 1890s, furthermore, only diabolical alcohol inspired biblical notions of déjà vu. "Surely history is repeating itself," the author prophesied, imploring readers to consult pertinent scriptural passages in Isaiah 28 so as "to see the sad picture" of the present. By equating the darkness of olden times to inebriated nowadays, Haviland displayed that prohibition had overshadowed antiracism. A previously vocal critic of neoslavery was essentially speechless amid the outburst of racial lynching throughout the South and the dismantling of the African American suffrage across the region. Even though the first imprint of Haviland's autobiography diverges from the tenor of other memorial and historical literature that veteran white abolitionists had written after 1876, the final one does not.[52]

However much her humanitarianism revolved about transnational antislavery work across the Great Lakes; educational work on behalf of Black people in Adrian, Michigan, Toledo, Ohio, and Windsor, Canada; as well as Civil War–era missionary and relief work among African Americans in Kentucky, Tennessee, Mississippi, Louisiana, Washington, DC, Virginia, and Kansas, the central message of *A Woman's Life-Work* pertains to religious devotedness. Whether as a birthright Quaker, an adult follower of Wesleyan Methodism, or an eventual returnee to the Society of Friends, the opus demonstrates that Haviland pursued reform in order to honor her Savior and testify to her faith. With good reasons did the composer deploy a works/working motif, as epitomized in two declarations in chapter 7. Writing on behalf of all true believers, the memoirist moralized that whatever the responsibility, "how careful we should be to attend to every little errand as we are passing through our life-work." Despite the "neglected duties" dotting her existence with occasional regret, each one had taught, as she attested, that "greater faithfulness in the Master's work" was fundamental. Haviland could have easily dubbed her assignment "A Christian's Course," "Holy Witness," or the "Lord's Instrument," because no ambiguity surrounds for whom she toiled and why.[53]

That the autobiographer made it known, toward the volume's end, that a branch of the Young Woman's Christian Temperance Union had designated itself the "L. S. Haviland Union" constituted an appropriate this-worldly reward for such a well-lived life. The same applied to a Kansas town and the Quaker academy located there bearing her last name. The epistles that she incorporated into the text from the school's officials aptly express the perceived usefulness of her memoir as the twentieth century approached. "We are accustomed to think of slavery as a thing of the past," the missive writers observed. Naturally, they knew better, stating that bondage still thrived in the United States. The "demon of intemperance and other social vices," Haviland's correspondents added, "stalk boldly through our fair land," subjecting postbellum inhabitants to a thralldom that was "much more immoral and degrading" than the antebellum predecessor. As a major authorial development, the serpent of alcoholism suddenly portended a bigger threat than racial injustice in Haviland's narrative.[54]

Interestingly, when not privileging antialcohol the author earmarked other sections in the fifth edition in cementing her position as an organizational pioneer and innovator. In two chapters, Haviland utilized an 1875 essay that she had published, newspaper clippings, annual society reports, and personal correspondence in order to authenticate her catalytic role behind an 1871 enactment setting up the State Public School for Dependent and Neglected Children at Coldwater, Michigan. Her genealogy charted that institution's origins to three establishments to which she herself had intimate ties: the Raisin Institute, which began in 1837 as a manual labor school before its academic focus shifted to the model of Ohio's interracial and coeducational Oberlin College; the Haviland Home for Homeless Freed Children, which had replaced the Raisin Institute after its 1864 closure; and the Michigan Orphan Asylum for all destitute or discarded youths, which had succeeded the Haviland Home in 1868. As the direct precursor of the State Public School, the retrospective writer likened the formation of the Michigan Orphan Asylum to an "untried experiment." Rather than benefit a particular locale, the refuge that she envisaged targeted waifs statewide. Not solely a new charitable cause, it comprised an additional "specialty" on her Christian stewardship vita.[55]

Even though recollections of training indigent and abandoned youngsters for good character and citizenship surface in other parts of the text, only in 1897 did a remembered Haviland spring up as the moving spirit in the drive to save juvenile souls from careers as "convicts within prison walls." By comparison, the autobiographer initially avowed that "it matters not by whom this great work was accomplished [or] by what agencies our prayer of more than four years . . . was answered." Her earlier self-professed care, moreover, revolved about the Michigan Legislature's adopting a bill that converted a Lenawee County shelter into the State Public School. The memoirist now desired due recognition, as the book's final rendering indicates. Since she had labored for so long without an associational nexus, the independence and self-reliance that Haviland attained meant that, if no one else respected her benevolent contributions, she would validate them herself.[56]

In yet another chapter added to the fifth edition, the retrospective writer advertised that after the State Public School, involvement in the 1879 founding of the Industrial School for Girls at Adrian ranked as "next in importance." She especially underlined her resistance to a reform-school appellation in conversations with Michigan general assemblymen. "I insisted," Haviland explicated, "that the memory of having been in an Industrial School would be a far better one" for female or male beneficiaries, as "industry was honorable," and an institution structured upon it would lack the negative connotations that so often encircled reformatories. Since building right-mindedness was the priority, the narrator pinpointed a scholastic charge that would prepare individuals for appropriate decision-making "under all circumstances and in all places," as well as "inspire them with high and noble aims both for this life and the life to come." Years after its creation, the facility hosted WCTU gatherings that resulted in the personally cherished young ladies' L. S. Haviland affiliate. The author apprised readers that, as soon as the 1897 version of her autobiography issued from the presses, she planned on gifting a dozen to the group's two-hundred-plus constituents. Concerning those "dear girls who are endeavoring to make of themselves good women," she employed the words of Christ, as set down in John 8:11, to conclude her sermon: "'Neither do I condemn thee; go and sin no more.'" The memoir's later copies modify the composition's meaning and import, showcasing an altruist who finally consecrated herself to reclaiming the parentless, wayward, and intoxicated.[57]

To the Grand Army of Temperance, in particular, an unretiring Haviland paid unlimited fealty. Capping a provocative, uncensored survey of an unreconstructed South, the personal historian spotted a silver lining. Despite the gruesome circumstances impelling Exoduster migrations, she thankfully reported that the "heaven-born cause" of antialcohol "is gaining a foothold in our

Southern States." To publicize her total engagement in that divinely ordained undertaking, in the hopes of accelerating its "conquering" across the continent and around the globe, the autobiographer appropriated the stirring sentiments of the *Liberator*'s editor elsewhere in the narrative. Similar to an "old-time friend," the activist-author chimed: "'I will not retreat a single inch. I will not prevaricate, and I will be heard.'" Among the rare instances in which Garrison's abolitionist testimony makes a textual appearance, Laura Smith Haviland invoked it twice, on back-to-back pages, in order to strengthen another life-and-death contest against slavery, the one in which the WCTU fought to liberate drinkers and drunkards. The stakes were huge, for the inveterate worker, because the ramifications were everlasting.[58]

Coda

Complicated Legacies

D espite individual acts of apathy, negligence, or desertion, Oliver Johnson, Parker Pillsbury, Aaron Macy Powell, and Thomas Wentworth Higginson did not amount to philanthropic failures. Their memorial and historical publications evince that they wanted to correct and improve the United States and its inhabitants—morally, socially, or culturally. The same basically applies to the retrospective writers Elizabeth Buffum Chace, Lucy N. Colman, Sarah H. Southwick, and Laura Smith Haviland. Even though all members of the research cohort sought to enhance understandings of the past in some manner, only two indisputably marshaled it in order to advance African Americans in the present and future. Nothing deflected the attention or redirected the gaze of the Black activist William Wells Brown from abolitionism's equalitarian values and aspirations; ditto for the white memoirist Samuel Joseph May. The tales that the eight others told accentuated divergent callings and avocations.

The thoughts that such storytellers emitted on and omitted from the printed page confirm that an ongoing African American freedom struggle no longer engrossed the minds of veteran white abolitionists. None powerfully sounded a tocsin for the immediate emancipation campaign's renewal in support of at-risk Black populations. Nor did any strenuously appeal to younger Americans to resume the antislavery crusade against racism. The emergence and spread of draconian Jim Crow regimes throughout the former Confederacy simply did not provoke the outrage that the Southland's system of slavery had done. Haviland's authorship constitutes a dynamic case in point. At the outset of the 1880s, she undoubtedly belonged to the veteran abolitionist side combating southern inhumanity and racial injustice. She moved about the alternative-preoccupation crowd before the completion of that decade and during the following one. Whereas the Civil War and Reconstruction revolutionized American race relations, the Gilded Age and Progressive era ushered in reactionary transformations as well as humanitarian eclipses. Well before the latter actually happened, Charles Lenox Remond worried about the very prospect.

At the same 1865 AASS gathering during which Remond reproved Garrison, he dissected the dependability of virtually all white allies as well. One can only imagine how startled or dismayed many attendees were as he doubted, if not disputed outright, their empathetic capabilities. To be sure, Remond recognized that white friends had "so often put their souls in his [the Black man's] stead." "However much they may have tried," he frankly informed listeners that their voluntary guises did not subsequently render them as authorities on African Americans. Well-intentioned whites, according to his analysis, had wrongfully assumed that they totally understood the needs of Black people or genuinely comprehended the difficulties that they confronted. Even though he acknowledged that a couple or possibly twelve qualified as racially enlightened, a preponderance did not. At the height of abolitionism as an antislavery movement, the fate of its corresponding antiracism mission therefore weighed heavily on Remond's shoulders. Numerous white comrades—more than a dozen, assuredly—felt similarly for several more years, but their attachments to racial equity and inclusion, as measured in this study, became increasingly slighter after 1876. Since Remond passed away in 1873, he neither saw Radical Reconstruction's destruction nor white abolitionism's declension. Given the interconnections between the two and the allyship limitations that they convey, historians should carefully consider the source of his apprehensions.[1]

Regardless of the ways in which later civil rights agitators expanded on abolitionist foundations, the careers of immediate emancipation partisans neither plainly spoke for themselves nor simply ceased after the Civil War. That dozens of movement adherents prepared antislavery narratives in the years and decades following enslavement's eradication readily attests to the first claim. How those authors commemorated antebellum persons and events and why they chronicled them at various postbellum junctures more problematically testifies to the second. Toward the end of the nineteenth century (and their own lives), the veteran white crusaders herein surveyed still showcased an unbreakable reformatory spirit. The twilight truths that they published, however, scarcely illumined a passageway to such twentieth-century groups as the National Association for the Advancement of Colored People or Congress of Racial Equality. Truly, abolitionism's legacy is complex.[2]

Acknowledgments

ΑΛΣ ΙΧΗ ΧΑΝ

In the spirit of an illustrious Netherlandish visual artist of the fifteenth century, I imprint quasi-Greek letters at the top of the page in order to announce a meaningful motto. Transcribed in Dutch, Jan Van Eyck's aphorism "Als Ich Can" refers to a Greco-Roman saying highlighting, according to my understanding, a proud personal accomplishment and the inevitable human limitations surrounding it. Initially conceived while I was a graduate student; slowly revised while I was a full-time lecturer typically teaching four classes every semester and at least one each summer; and finally perfected, to some degree, as an assistant professor of history, this book constitutes "the best I can do." Were it not for numerous individuals and institutions, however, my work never would have attained levels of finish.

At Purdue University, where I conducted my doctoral studies, Robert E. May was a consummate advisor. Besides dispensing prompt feedback and swiftly fulfilling requests for letters of recommendation, Bob established a wonderful academic model through his scrupulous attention to detail not only as an historical researcher and writer but also as a curriculum designer and lecture builder. I am also grateful to Cornelius L. Bynum, John L. Larson, and the late Michael A. Morrison, whose individual critiques collectively formed a much-needed program for fashioning a book manuscript. At Youngstown State University, where I commenced postbaccalaureate studies, undecided about a scholarly course of action, the late Frederick J. Blue inspired me to explore the nineteenth-century United States and commit myself to the intellectually rich field of antislavery and abolition. I vividly remember Fred, about a year before his retirement, hunched over a classroom desk and actively taking notes during a conference presentation on the campus of the Ohio State University. At John Carroll University, where a first-generation college-goer discovered entirely new worlds, the art historians Leslie Curtis, the late Robert H. Getscher, Linda Koch, and Charles Scillia taught me how to see, discern, and decipher. I am tremendously indebted to Dr. Getscher, my first mentor. Not only did he spark my passion for prints via the seminars he taught and the impressive personal collection he displayed; by taking an interest in my development, he additionally made me more confident about my academic capabilities.

I could not have completed this project without indispensable libraries and archives. I would therefore like to thank the interlibrary loan teams at Purdue University and Boise State University, as well as the librarians, archivists, and support staffs at the American Antiquarian Society, Houghton Library at Harvard University, Huntington Library, Library Company of Philadelphia, and Newberry Library. As a Boise State faculty member, I have received invaluable assistance from departmental chairs—Joanne Klein, Jill Gill, Nick Miller, and Lisa Brady—and continually benefit from the goodwill and conviviality of all my history department colleagues. I would like to recognize countless undergraduates and graduate students as well. Whether taking my courses or workshops; discussing ideas, career pathways, and less serious matters with me in and outside of class; serving as my teaching assistants; attending Phi Alpha Theta conferences with me; or extending postgraduation friendship, they have greatly shaped my Boise State career.

For several years I mainly toiled quietly, formally sharing my findings with few other scholars. Hugh Davis commented on an early version of a chapter so long ago that he has probably forgotten about it. Ditto for Thomas Mackey and Richard Newman. More recently, John David Smith has provided project encouragement and helpful advice that I will always appreciate. More broadly, I hope that my reference notes and historiographical remarks convey a deep admiration for the generations of scholarship without which this book would read very differently.

Concise words cannot adequately express my gratitude to Fordham University Press. Director Fredric Nachbaur made the publishing process for an anxious author much less stressful. Beyond imparting necessary information, Fred graciously responded to all my concerns. As the manuscript entered the production phase, both Project Editor Kem Crimmins and Managing Editor Eric Newman clearly laid out the publication steps and quickly answered my questions. The design team crafted an attractive and thought-provoking cover, members of the Board of Directors offered important manuscript suggestions, and Rob Fellman delivered expert copyediting. To Andrew L. Slap, the editor of the "Reconstructing America" series, I am eternally thankful. Andy's extensive and no less incisive criticism pushed me to transform my work in subtle and profound ways. So too did John A. Casey's similarly insightful observations. I could not have done what I did without their counsel; only I, of course, am responsible for the book's remaining shortcomings.

Many loved ones also enabled me to do my best. My mother, Mary Lou Krohn, epitomizes the self-sacrificing parent; her support I can never repay. The diligent labor required to execute this authorial undertaking I owe to her devout, hardworking example. I appreciate the generosity of my brothers, Robert, Marc, Michael, and Steven; the kindness of my uncle and aunt Robert and Kathy Testa; and the parental solicitude of Stephen and Cathy Rodabaugh. A fellow historian and good friend, Cathy additionally introduced me to my spouse. As my favorite poet, Hannah Rodabaugh has affected my work in manifold respects. Her creative reflections on the natural spaces and native species that we humans cherish and destroy often refocused my historical ruminations on presence and absence over the last few years. Besides exposing me to unique Western landscapes as well as a wider artistic universe, she helped sustain my writing amid the inescapable high and low points that frame long-term intellectual endeavors. I dedicate this book to her.

Notes

Introduction. What Is Abolitionism Now? From the Disposition of the AASS to the Determinants of Abolitionist History

1. On the abolitionist centrality of African Americans, see, for example, Ira Berlin, *The Long Emancipation: The Demise of Slavery in the United States* (Cambridge, MA: Harvard University Press, 2015); Kelli Carter Jackson, *Force and Freedom: Black Abolitionists and the Politics of Violence* (Philadelphia: University of Pennsylvania Press, 2019); Jesse Olsavsky, *The Most Absolute Abolition: Runaways, Vigilance Committees, and the Rise of Revolutionary Abolitionism, 1835–1861* (Baton Rouge: Louisiana State University Press, 2022); Timothy Patrick McCarthy and John Stauffer, eds., *Prophets of Protest: Reconsidering the History of Abolitionism* (New York: New Press, 2006); Manisha Sinha, *The Slave's Cause: A History of Abolition* (New Haven, CT: Yale University Press, 2016).

2. Frederick Douglass, *Life and Times of Frederick Douglass*, rev. and enl. ed. (Boston: De Wolfe, Fiske & Co., 1892), 620–23, 633–35, 647–73. No recent historian has given more sustained attention to Douglass than David W. Blight; see his *Frederick Douglass' Civil War: Keeping Faith in Jubilee* (Baton Rouge: Louisiana State University Press, 1989); and *Frederick Douglass: Prophet of Freedom* (New York: Simon & Schuster, 2018). On Douglass the autobiographer, see William L. Andrews, *To Tell a Free Story: The First Century of Afro-American Autobiography, 1760–1865* (Urbana: University of Illinois Press, 1986), chap. 6; Robert S. Levine, *The Lives of Frederick Douglass* (Cambridge, MA: Harvard University Press, 2016); Waldo E. Martin Jr., *The Mind of Frederick Douglass* (Chapel Hill: University of North Carolina Press, 1984), chap. 4; and the collection of essays dealing with iterations of *Life and Times* in a special issue of the *Journal of African American History* 99, no. 1–2 (Winter/Spring 2014): 4–88. The well-known Black activist William Still published two editions of his antislavery experiences. For the second, see *Still's Underground Rail Road Records: With a Life of the Author*, rev. ed. (Philadelphia: William Still, 1886).

3. *Platform of the American Anti-Slavery Society and Its Auxiliaries* (1853; New York: American Anti-Slavery Society, 1860), 4, 12; *Constitution of the New-England Anti-Slavery Society: With an Address to the Public* (Boston: Garrison and Knapp, 1832); "Constitution of the Female Anti-Slavery Society of Philadelphia," *The Liberator*, April 19, 1834. Paul J. Polgar's *Standard-Bearers of Equality: America's First Abolition Movement* (Williamsburg, VA, and Chapel Hill: Omohundro Institute of Early American History and Cultures and the University of North Carolina Press, 2019) argues that pre-1830 abolitionism constituted an antiracism movement, too.

4. Herbert Aptheker, *Anti-Racism in U.S. History: The First Two Hundred Years* (Westport, CT: Greenwood, 1992), 129–30; Kate Masur, *Until Justice Be Done: America's First Civil Rights Movement, from the Revolution to Reconstruction* (New York: Norton,

2021); Sinha, *The Slave's Cause*, 1–3. For other positive assessments of antebellum abolitionism's equalitarian features, see Herbert Aptheker, *Abolitionism: A Revolutionary Movement* (Boston: Twayne, 1989); David Brion Davis, *The Problem of Slavery in the Age of Emancipation* (New York: Knopf, 2014); Merton L. Dillon, *The Abolitionists: The Growth of a Dissenting Minority* (DeKalb: Northern Illinois Press, 1974); Paul Goodman, *Of One Blood: Abolitionists and the Origins of Racial Equality* (Berkeley: University of California Press, 1998); Stanley Harrold, *Subversives: Antislavery Community in Washington, D.C., 1828–1865* (Baton Rouge: Louisiana State University Press, 2003); Nancy A. Hewitt, *Radical Friend: Amy Kirby Post and Her Radical Worlds* (Chapel Hill: University of North Carolina Press, 2018); Gary J. Kornblith and Carol Lasser, *Elusive Utopia: The Struggle for Racial Equality in Oberlin, Ohio* (Baton Rouge: Louisiana State University Press, 2018); Carlton Mabee, *Black Freedom: The Nonviolent Abolitionists from 1830 through the Civil War* (New York: Macmillan, 1970); J. Brent Morris, *Oberlin, Hotbed of Abolitionism: College, Community, and the Fight for Freedom and Equality in Antebellum America* (Chapel Hill: University of North Carolina Press, 2014); Richard S. Newman, *The Transformation of American Abolitionism: Fighting Slavery in the Early Republic* (Chapel Hill: University of North Carolina Press, 2002); Olsavsky, *The Most Absolute Abolition*; Stacey M. Robertson, *Hearts Beating for Liberty: Women Abolitionists and the Old Northwest* (Chapel Hill: University of North Carolina Press, 2010); Milton C. Sernett, *Abolition's Axe: Beriah Green, Oneida Institute, and the Black Freedom Struggle* (Syracuse, NY: Syracuse University Press, 1986); Milton C. Sernett, *North Star Country: Upstate New York and the Crusade for African American Freedom* (Syracuse, NY: Syracuse University Press, 2002); John Stauffer, *The Black Hearts of Men: Radical Abolitionism and the Transformation of Race* (Cambridge, MA: Harvard University Press, 2002); James Brewer Stewart, "Comfortable in His Own Skin: Wendell Phillips and Racial Egalitarianism," in *Wendell Phillips, Social Justice, and the Power of the Past*, ed. A. J. Aiséirithe and Donald Yacovone (Baton Rouge: Louisiana State University Press, 2016), 111–32; Kyle G. Volk, *Moral Minorities and the Making of American Democracy* (New York: Oxford University Press, 2014); Dana Elizabeth Weiner, *Race and Rights: Fighting Slavery and Prejudice in the Old Northwest, 1830–1870* (DeKalb: Northern Illinois University Press, 2013).

5. On the egalitarian limitations of white abolitionists, see Lawrence J. Friedman, *Gregarious Saints: Self and Community in American Abolitionism, 1830–1870* (New York: Cambridge University Press, 1982), chap. 6; Kerri K. Greenidge, *The Grimkes: The Legacy of Slavery in an American Family* (New York: Liveright, 2022); Leon F. Litwack, "The Abolitionist Dilemma: The Antislavery Movement and the Northern Negro," *New England Quarterly* 34 (March 1961): 50–73; Leon F. Litwack, *North of Slavery: The Negro in the Free States, 1790–1860* (Chicago: University of Chicago Press, 1961); Jane H. Pease and William H. Pease, "Ends, Means, and Attitudes: Black-White Conflict in the Antislavery Movement," *Civil War History* 18 (June 1972): 117–28; Jane H. Pease and William H. Pease, *They Who Would Be Free: Blacks' Search for Freedom, 1830–1861* (New York: Atheneum, 1974); William H. Pease and Jane H. Pease, "Antislavery Ambivalence: Immediatism, Expediency, Race," *American Quarterly* 17 (Winter 1965): 682–95; C. Vann Woodward, "The Northern Crusade Against Slavery," in *American Counterpart: Slavery and Racism in the North-South Dialogue* (Boston: Little, Brown, 1971), 140–62.

6. Erica Ball, *To Live an Antislavery Life: Personal Politics and the Antebellum Black Middle Class* (Athens: University of Georgia Press, 2012). On the wider uplifting efforts of white philanthropists, see Robert H. Abzug, *Cosmos Crumbling: American Reform and the Religious Imagination* (New York: Oxford University Press, 1994); Steven Mintz, *Moralists and Modernizers: America's Pre-Civil War Reformers* (Baltimore, MD: Johns Hopkins University Press, 1995); Ronald G. Walters, *American Reformers, 1815–1860*, rev. ed. (New York: Hill and Wang, 1997). For more critical assessments of white reformers' motivations, see, for example, Nicholas Guyatt, *Bind Us Apart: How Enlightened Americans Invented Racial Segregation* (New York: Basic Books, 2016); Ibram X. Kendi, *Stamped from the Beginning: The Definitive History of Racist Ideas in America* (New York: Nation Book, 2016), chaps. 13–15; Susan M. Ryan, *The Grammar of Good Intentions: Race and the Antebellum Culture of Benevolence* (Ithaca, NY: Cornell University Press, 2003).

7. Martin Robison Delany, *The Condition, Elevation, Emigration, and Destiny of the Colored People of the United States Politically Considered* (Philadelphia: Martin Robison Delany, 1852), 24–29. For a fuller treatment, see Robert S. Levine, *Martin Delany, Frederick Douglass, and the Politics of Representative Identity* (Chapel Hill: University of North Carolina Press, 1997), chaps. 1–2.

8. For other memorial literature authored by white men partly or wholly concerning antislavery history, see Adin Ballou, *Autobiography of Adin Ballou, 1803–1890* (Lowell, MA: Vox Populi, 1896); James Freeman Clarke, *Anti-Slavery Days. A Sketch of the Struggle Which Ended in the Abolition of Slavery in the United States* (New York: R. Worthington, 1884); Cassius Marcellus Clay, *The Life of Cassius Marcellus Clay. Memoirs, Writings, and Speeches* (Cincinnati, OH: J. Fletcher Brennan & Co., 1886); Levi Coffin, *Reminiscences of Levi Coffin, the Reputed President of the Underground Railroad* (Cincinnati, OH: Western Tract Society, 1876); Moncure Daniel Conway, *Autobiography, Memories and Experiences of Moncure Daniel Conway* (London: Cassell and Co., 1904); Calvin Fairbank, *Rev. Calvin Fairbank During Slavery Times. How He "Fought the Good Fight" to Prepare "The Way"* (Chicago: R. R. McCabe & Co., 1890); John G. Fee, *Autobiography of John G. Fee* (Chicago: National Christian Association, 1891); Octavius Brooks Frothingham, *Theodore Parker: A Biography* (Boston: James R. Osgood and Co., 1874); Octavius Brooks Frothingham, *Gerrit Smith: A Biography* (New York: G. P. Putnam's Sons, 1879); Octavius Brooks Frothingham, *Recollections and Impressions, 1822–1890* (New York: G. P. Putnam's Sons, 1891); George Julian, *Political Recollections, 1840 to 1872* (Chicago: Jansen, McClurg & Co., 1884); George Julian, *The Life of Joshua R. Giddings* (Chicago: Jansen, McClurg & Co., 1892); Samuel May Jr., "Anti-Slavery," in *James Freeman Clarke: Autobiography, Diary and Correspondence*, ed. Edward Everett Hale (Boston: Houghton, Mifflin and Co., 1891), 213–60; Alexander Milton Ross, *Recollections and Experiences of an Abolitionist: from 1855 to 1865*, 2nd ed. (Toronto: Roswell & Hutchinson, 1876); Alexander Milton Ross, *Memoirs of a Reformer, 1832–1897* (Toronto: Hunter, Rose & Company, 1893); Franklin B. Sanborn, *The Life and Letters of John Brown; Liberator of Kansas, and Martyr of Virginia*, 3rd ed. (1885; Concord, MA: F. B. Sanborn, 1910); Franklin B. Sanborn, *Recollections of Seventy Years*, 2 vols. (Boston: Richard G. Badger, 1909); Henry B. Stanton, *Random Recollections*, 3rd ed. (New York: Harper & Brothers, 1887); Giles B. Stebbins, *Upward Steps of Seventy Years. Autobiographic, Biographic, Historic* (New York:

United States Book Company, 1890); Lewis Tappan, *The Life of Arthur Tappan* (New York: Hurd and Houghton, 1870); Austin Willey, *The History of the Antislavery Cause in State and Nation* (Portland, ME: Brown Thurston and Hoyt, Fogg & Donham, 1886); Elizur Wright, *Myron Holley; and What He Did for Liberty and True Religion* (Boston: Elizur Wright, 1882).

9. Elizabeth Cady Stanton, *Eighty Years and More (1815–1897): Reminiscences of Elizabeth Cady Stanton* (New York: European Publishing Company, 1898); Elizabeth Cady Stanton, Susan B. Anthony, and Matilda Joslyn Gage, ed., *History of Woman Suffrage*, 3 vols. (1881–1886; Rochester, NY: Charles Mann, 1889). For a scholarly account, see Lori Ginzburg, *Elizabeth Cady Stanton: An American Life* (New York: Hill and Wang, 2009).

10. For other memorial literature by white women that partly concerns antislavery history, see Ednah Dow Cheney, *Reminiscences of Ednah Dow Cheney* (Boston: Lee & Shepard, 1902); Julia Ward Howe, *Reminiscences, 1819–1899* (Boston: Houghton, Mifflin and Co., 1899); Jane Grey Swisshelm, *Half a Century* (Chicago: Jansen, McClurg and Co., 1880). Also see *James Mott: A Biographical Sketch* (New York: William P. Tomlinson, 1868), wherein Mary Grew composed a seventeen-page biography of a deceased comrade and compiled more than twenty pages of veteran-abolitionist tributes to him.

11. James M. McPherson, *The Struggle for Equality: Abolitionists and the Negro in the Civil War and Reconstruction* (1964; Princeton, NJ: Princeton University Press, 1992). On Reconstruction's course and collapse, Eric Foner's *Reconstruction: America's Unfinished Revolution, 1863–1877* (New York: Harper & Row, 1988) remains the starting point. Also see Douglas R. Egerton, *The Wars of Reconstruction: The Brief, Violent History of America's Most Progressive Era* (New York: Bloomsbury, 2014); Michael Fitzgerald, *Splendid Failure: Postwar Reconstruction in the American South* (Chicago: Ivan R. Dee, 2007); William Gillette, *The Retreat from Reconstruction, 1869–1879* (Baton Rouge: Louisiana State University Press, 1979). On the notion that white mastery in a postemancipation world required a reconstruction of its own, especially see Stephen Kantrowitz, *Ben Tillman and the Reconstruction of White Supremacy* (Chapel Hill: University of North Carolina Press, 2000).

12. Dominick LaCapra, "Rethinking Intellectual History and Reading Texts," *History and Theory* 19 (October 1980): 274–75; John Patrick Diggins, "The Oyster and the Pearl: The Problem of Contextualism in Intellectual History," *History and Theory* 23 (May 1984): 151–69.

13. James M. McPherson, *The Abolitionist Legacy: From Reconstruction to the NAACP* (1975; Princeton, NJ: Princeton University Press, 1995). Also see Mark R. Schneider, *Boston Confronts Jim Crow, 1890–1920* (Boston: Northeastern University Press, 1997). John T. Cumbler's *From Abolition to Rights for All: The Making of a Reform Community in the Nineteenth Century* (Philadelphia: University of Pennsylvania Press, 2008) stresses that untiring New England radicals expanded on antebellum abolitionism throughout the postbellum period, subsequently preparing the way for Progressive-era reformers. For notable exceptions to a historiographical tradition that McPherson helped establish, see Kornblith and Lasser, *Elusive Utopia*, chaps. 8–9, which surveys how Oberlin's white reformers, by the start of the twentieth century, ditched an "experiment in radical racial egalitarianism" that town founders had inaugurated in the 1830s; David N. Gellman, *Lib-*

erty's Chain: Slavery, Abolition, and the Jay Family of New York (Ithaca, NY: Three Hills, 2022), chap. 15, which shows that John Jay II basically jettisoned his earlier antislavery radicalism after 1876 while increasingly combating the perceived problems of governmental corruption and Catholic immigration; and Stauffer, *The Black Hearts of Men*, chap. 8, which suggests that Gerrit Smith particularly sundered personal bonds with Black antislavery allies after 1860, thereby abandoning an uncommon racial egalitarianism that had typified his radical abolitionism.

14. Julie Roy Jeffrey, *Abolitionists Remember: Antislavery Autobiographies and the Unfinished Work of Emancipation* (Chapel Hill: University of North Carolina Press, 2008); Manisha Sinha, "Memory as History, Memory as Activism: The Forgotten Abolitionist Struggle after the Civil War," *Common-Place* 14 (Winter 2014), http://www.common -place-archives.org/vol-14/no-02/sinha/#.WdRdK1tSxdg. By comparison, Larry Gara, in "A Glorious Time: The 1874 Abolitionist Reunion in Chicago," *Journal of the Illinois State Historical Society* 65 (Autumn 1972): 280–92, alluded to the tensions that combating still-entrenched racial prejudices had generated among former antislavery advocates. Scot Gac, in *Singing for Freedom: The Hutchinson Family Singers and the Nineteenth-Century Culture of Antebellum Reform* (New Haven, CT: Yale University Press, 2007), 24–48, noted the avoidance of present-day racial justice among the old abolitionists at an 1893 commemorative gathering.

15. John David Smith, *An Old Creed for the New South: Proslavery Ideology and Historiography, 1865–1918* (1985; Carbondale: Southern Illinois Press, 2008); John David Smith, *Slavery, Race, and American History: Historical Conflict, Trends, and Method, 1866–1953* (Armonk, NY: M. E. Sharpe, 1999). W. Caleb McDaniel, in his recent historiographical essay "The Bonds and Boundaries of Antislavery," *Journal of the Civil War Era* 4 (March 2014): 84–105, appropriately referred to the late nineteenth century as a neglected era in abolitionist scholarship. Corey Brooks repeated that sentiment in his literature review "Reconsidering Politics in the Study of American Abolitionists," *Journal of the Civil War Era* 8 (June 2018): 291–317. Manisha Sinha, in "The Future of Abolition Studies," *Journal of the Civil War* Era 8 (June 2018): 187–89, also identified that very same period as "the next frontier in abolition studies."

16. David W. Blight, *Race and Reunion: The Civil War in American Memory* (Cambridge, MA: Harvard University Press, 2001); David W. Blight, *Beyond the Battlefield: Race, Memory, and the American Civil War* (Amherst: University of Massachusetts Press, 2002); Edward J. Blum, *Reforging the White Republic: Race, Religion, and American Nationalism, 1865–1898* (Baton Rouge: Louisiana State University Press, 2005); Alice Fahs and Joan Waugh, eds., *The Memory of the Civil War in American Culture* (Chapel Hill: University of North Carolina Press, 2004); K. Stephen Prince, *Stories of the South: Race and the Reconstruction of Southern Identity, 1865–1915* (Chapel Hill: University of North Carolina Press, 2014); Kirk Savage, *Standing Soldiers, Kneeling Slaves: Race, War, and Monument in Nineteenth-Century America*, new ed. (1997; Princeton, NJ: Princeton University Press, 2018); Nina Silber, *The Romance of Reunion: Northerners and the South, 1865–1900* (Chapel Hill: University of North Carolina Press, 1993). Also see Donald Yacovone, *Teaching White Supremacy: America's Democratic Ordeal and the Forging of Our National Identity* (New York: Pantheon, 2022), whose examination of US history

textbooks and how they ultimately reinforced and nationalized Lost Cause narratives appeared in print while I made finishing touches to this manuscript. For scholarly works redressing the extent of reconciliation among white northerners, see M. Keith Harris, *Across the Bloody Chasm: The Culture of Commemoration among Civil War Veterans* (Baton Rouge: Louisiana State University Press, 2014); Caroline E. Janney, *Remembering the Civil War: Reunion and the Limits of Reconciliation* (Chapel Hill: University of North Carolina Press, 2013); John R. Neff, *Honoring the Civil War Dead: Commemoration and the Problem of Reconciliation* (Lawrence: University Press of Kansas, 2005). Also see Nina Silber, "Reunion and Reconciliation, Reviewed and Reconsidered," *Journal of American History* 103 (June 2016): 59–89. On the sizable scholarship of Civil War–era historical memory, see Barbara A. Gannon, *Americans Remember Their Civil War* (Santa Barbara, CA: Praeger, 2017); K. Stephen Prince, "Reconstruction: Intellectual Life and Historical Memory," in *Interpreting American History: Reconstruction*, ed. John David Smith (Kent, OH: Kent State University Press, 2016), chap. 7.

17. On the declining unity among the AASS membership, see McPherson, *The Struggle for Equality*, chaps. 12–13. Also see Francesca Gamber, "The Public Sphere and the End of American Abolitionism, 1833–1870," *Slavery and Abolition* 28 (December 2007): 351–68; Stanley Harrold, *Lincoln and the Abolitionists* (Carbondale: Southern Illinois University Press, 2018), chap. 7; W. Caleb McDaniel, *The Problem of Democracy in the Age of Slavery: Garrisonian Abolitionists and Transatlantic Reform* (Baton Rouge: Louisiana State University Press, 2013), chap. 10.

18. *Proceedings of the American Anti-Slavery Society, at Its Third Decade, Held in the City of Philadelphia, Dec. 3d and 4th, 1863* (New York: American Anti-Slavery Society, 1864), 27, 111–12.

19. Kirk H. Porter and Donald Bruce Johnson, comp., *National Party Platforms: 1840–1960* (Urbana: University of Illinois Press, 1961), 35. On slavery's many deaths, see, for example, Bruce Levine, *The Fall of the House of Dixie: The Civil War and the Social Revolution That Transformed the South* (New York: Random House, 2013); James Oakes, *Freedom National: The Destruction of Slavery in the United States, 1861–1865* (New York: Norton, 2013); Michael Vorenberg, *Final Freedom: The Civil War, the Abolition of Slavery, and the Thirteenth Amendment* (New York: Cambridge University Press, 2001).

20. "Thirty-Second Anniversary of the American Anti-Slavery Society," *The Liberator*, May 26, 1865. For complete coverage of the 1865 gathering, see the May 19, 26, and June 2 editions of the *Liberator*. Also see "Thirty-Second Anniversary of the American Anti-Slavery Society," *National Antislavery Standard*, May 20 and May 27, 1865. For scholarly accounts, see Friedman, *Gregarious Saints*, 264–70; McPherson, *The Struggle for Equality*, 302–7.

21. "Thirty-Second Anniversary," May 26.

22. "Thirty-Second Anniversary," May 26. Remond issued a similar remonstration at an 1863 abolitionist gathering. For the newspaper coverage, see "Annual Meeting of the Massachusetts Anti-Slavery Society," *National Anti-Slavery Standard*, February 6, 1863.

23. "Thirty-Second Anniversary of the American Anti-Slavery Society," *The Liberator*, June 2, 1865. In *Proceedings of the American Anti-Slavery Society, at Its Third Decade*, 56–59, Foster's convention speech also sounded a somber note.

24. "Thirty-Second Anniversary," May 26; "Thirty-Second Anniversary," June 2. In *Proceedings of the American Anti-Slavery Society, at Its Third Decade*, 27, Garrison also asserted that retired abolitionists must still work on behalf of the freedpeople's betterment.

25. "Thirty-Second Anniversary," June 2. On the AASS exodus of Garrison and other abolitionists, see Friedman, *Gregarious Saints*, 264–65; McPherson, *The Struggle for Equality*, 305.

26. "Thirty-Second Anniversary," June 2. For scholarly accounts of Remond's activities, see James Oliver Horton and Lois E. Horton, *Black Bostonians: Family Life and Community Struggle in the Antebellum North*, rev. ed. (1979; New York: Holmes and Meier, 2000); Stephen Kantrowitz, *More Than Freedom: Fighting for Black Citizenship in a White Republic, 1829–1889* (New York: Penguin, 2012); Patrick G. Wheaton and Celeste M. Condit, "Charles Lenox Remond (1810–1882), Abolitionist, Reform Activist," in *African-American Orators: A Bio-critical Sourcebook*, ed. Richard W. Leeman (Westport, CT: Greenwood, 1996), 302–10.

27. "Thirty-Second Anniversary," June 2. For a different approach to the language of abolitionism, see Brycchan Carey, *From Peace to Freedom: Quaker Rhetoric and the Birth of American Antislavery, 1657–1761* (New Haven, CT: Yale University Press, 2012). Even though my investigation does not adhere to the variety of linguistic contextualism emphasizing that prevailing language paradigms determine the meanings of historical texts, I have found the methodological writings of J. G. A. Pocock thought-provoking. See his essays "The State of the Art," in *Virtue, Commerce, and History: Essays on Political Thought and History, Chiefly in the Eighteenth Century* (New York: Cambridge University Press, 1985); and "Languages and Their Implications: The Transformation of the Study of Political Thought," in *Politics, Language, and Time: Essays on Political Thought and History* (1971; Chicago: University of Chicago Press, 1989). The same applies to Quentin Skinner's brand of contextualist intellectual history, which places a premium on the location of a text and its author within an original discursive context in order to unlock textual meaning and authorial intentions. See his classic essays "Meaning and Understanding in the History of Ideas," *History and Theory* 8 (1969): 3–5; and "Motives, Intentions, and the Interpretation of Texts," in *On Literary Intention*, ed. D. Newton de Molina (Edinburgh: Edinburgh University Press, 1976), 210–21.

28. On the abolitionists as sophisticated political thinkers and activists, see McDaniel, *The Problem of Democracy in the Age of Slavery*; Peter Wirzbicki, *Fighting for the Higher Law: Black and White Transcendentalists against Slavery* (Philadelphia: University of Pennsylvania Press, 2021). On the political consequences of generations of antislavery activism, see Stanley Harrold, *American Abolitionism: Its Direct Political Impact from Colonial Times into Reconstruction* (Charlottesville: University of Virginia Press, 2019). On the instrumental and political dimensions of autobiography, see Susanna Egan "'Self'-Conscious History: American Autobiography after the Civil War," in *American Autobiography: Retrospect and Prospect*, ed. Paul John Eakin (Madison: University of Wisconsin Press, 1991), 70–94; Jacqueline Dowd Hall, "'You Must Remember This': Autobiography as Social Critique," *Journal of American History* 85 (September 1998): 439–65. Also instructive are the critical essays in Julia Swindells, ed., *The Uses of Autobiography* (London: Taylor & Francis, 1995).

1. Antislavery Moderated:
Samuel Joseph May and the Lessons of Respectable Reform

1. Samuel J. May, *Some Recollections of Our Antislavery Conflict* (Boston: Fields, Osgood, & Co., 1869), 172–75. For biographical information, see Donald Yacovone's fine study, *Samuel Joseph May and the Dilemmas of the Liberal Persuasion, 1797–1871* (Philadelphia: Temple University Press, 1991). Also see Jane H. Pease and William H. Pease, "The Gentle Humanitarian: Samuel Joseph May," in *Bound with Them in Chains: A Biographical History of the Antislavery Movement* (Westport, CT: Greenwood, 1972), 277–307. George B. Emerson, Samuel May, and Thomas J Mumford, comp., *Memoir of Samuel Joseph May* (Boston: Roberts Brothers, 1873), contains useful diary excerpts and personal letters.

2. May, *Some Recollections*, 170, 175–77, 184. In a *Letter Addressed to the Editor of the Christian Examiner* (Boston: Garrison & Knapp, 1835), 3–6, May elaborated on points that he had privately debated with Channing. For scholarly accounts, see Andrew Delbanco, *William Ellery Channing: An Essay on the Liberal Spirit in America* (Cambridge, MA: Harvard University Press, 1981); Molly Oshatz, *Slavery and Sin: The Fight against Slavery and the Rise of Liberal Protestantism* (New York: Oxford University Press, 2012), chap. 2.

3. My interpretation partly concurs with Jeffrey's *Abolitionists Remember*, 27–49, 57–59, which depicts May's recollections as promoting equal Black rights. Unlike my respectability emphasis, Jeffrey situated the publication within the additional contexts of sentimental culture and history of the book.

4. "Prospectus of *The Liberator*, Volume VIII," *The Liberator*, December 15, 1837. For scholarly accounts of Garrisonian abolitionism, see Aileen Kraditor, *Means and Ends in American Abolitionism: Garrison and His Critics on Strategy and Tactics, 1834–1850* (1967; Chicago: Ivan R. Dee, 1989); McDaniel, *The Problem of Democracy in the Age of Slavery*; Lewis Perry, *Radical Abolitionism: Anarchy and the Government of God in Antislavery Thought* (1973; Knoxville: University of Tennessee Press, 1995); James Brewer Stewart, *William Lloyd Garrison and the Challenge of Emancipation* (Arlington Heights, IL: Harlan Davidson, 1992); William Wiecek, *Sources of Antislavery Constitutionalism in America, 1760-1848* (Ithaca, NY: Cornell University Press, 1977).

5. "Declaration of Sentiments Adopted by the Peace Convention," *The Liberator*, September 28, 1838; "Prospectus of *The Liberator*."

6. "No Compromise with Slavery," *The Liberator*, January 19, 1844; "The American Union," *The Liberator*, January 10, 1845; "The Constitution—Political Action," *The Liberator*, April 24, 1846; "Prospectus of *The Liberator*." For early announcements of Garrison's disunionist stance, see the following *Liberator* articles: "The Annual Meeting at New York," April 22, 1842; "Repeal of the Union," May 6, 1842. Also see concurrent issues of the *National Anti-Slavery Standard*, the New York–based publication that functioned as the mouthpiece of the Garrisonian-directed AASS. For a comprehensive Garrisonian statement on human bondage and constitutional framers, see Wendell Phillips, *The Constitution, a Pro-Slavery Compact: or, Selections from the Madison Papers, etc.* (New York: American Anti-Slavery Society, 1844). For a scholarly treatment, see Paul Finkelman, *Slavery and the Founders: Race and Liberty in the Age of Jefferson*, 3rd ed. (New York: Routledge, 2015), chap. 1.

7. "Prospectus of *The Liberator*, Volume VIII"; *Proceedings of the National Women's Rights Convention, Held at Cleveland, Ohio, on Wednesday, Thursday, and Friday, October 5th, 6th, and 7th, 1853* (Cleveland: Gray, Beardsley, Spear & Co., 1854), 54–56. On abolitionism and feminism, see, for example, Kathryn Kish Sklar and James Brewer Stewart, eds., *Women's Rights and Transatlantic Antislavery in the Age of Emancipation* (New Haven, CT: Yale University Press, 2007); Kathryn Kish Sklar, ed., *Women's Rights Emerges within the Antislavery Movement, 1830–1870: A Short History with Documents*, 2nd ed. (Boston: Bedford/St Martin's, 2019).

8. "Prospectus of *The Liberator*, Volume VIII." On the 1840 AASS schism, see Kraditor, *Means and Ends in American Abolitionism*, chaps. 3–5; John R. McKivigan, *The War against Proslavery Religion: Abolitionism and the Northern Churches, 1830–1865* (Ithaca, NY: Cornell University Press, 1984); Richard H. Sewell, *Ballots for Freedom: Antislavery Politics in the United States, 1837–1860* (New York: Oxford University Press, 1976), chaps. 2–3; Stewart, *William Lloyd Garrison*, chap. 7; James Brewer Stewart, *Holy Warriors: The Abolitionists and American Slavery*, rev. ed. (New York: Hill and Wang, 1996), chap. 4; Bertram Wyatt-Brown, *Lewis Tappan and the Evangelical War against Slavery* (1969; Baton Rouge: Louisiana State University Press, 1997), chap. 10.

9. "The 'Infidelity' of Abolitionism," *The Liberator*, December 21, 1855.

10. May, *Some Recollections*, iii, 404.

11. May, *Some Recollections*, 181, 396.

12. On the politics of Reconstruction, see the sources listed in the Introduction, n11.

13. On May's ancestry, see Emerson et al., *Memoir of Samuel Joseph May*, 1–3. For a scholarly account of his upbringing and schooling, see Yacovone, *Samuel Joseph May*. On Unitarian culture and gentility, see, for example, Daniel Walker Howe, *The Unitarian Conscience: Harvard Moral Philosophy, 1805–1861* (Cambridge, MA: Harvard University Press, 1970). On the apparent elitism of past and present Unitarianism, see, for example, the Unitarian-Universalist minister Mark W. Harris's account *Elite: Uncovering Classism in Unitarian Universalist History* (Boston: Skinner House, 2011).

14. Yacovone, *Samuel Joseph May*, 3, 60, 80. In "The Fourth and the First: Abolitionist Holidays, Respectability, and Radical Interracial Reform," *American Quarterly* 57 (March 2005): 129–51, W. Caleb McDaniel examined the relationship between respectability and abolitionism, particularly the respectable manner in which the Garrisonian celebrated holidays.

15. *Proceedings of the American Anti-Slavery Society, at Its Third Decade*, 87. May, *Some Recollections*, 266. On May's Civil War–era activities, see Yacovone, *Samuel Joseph May*, 169–81. For scholarly treatments of Lincoln's handling of the slavery issue, see Eric Foner, *The Fiery Trial: Abraham Lincoln and American Slavery* (New York: Norton, 2010); Allen C. Guelzo, *Lincoln's Emancipation Proclamation: The End of Slavery in America* (New York: Simon & Schuster, 2004); James Oakes, *The Radical and the Republican: Frederick Douglass, Abraham Lincoln, and the Triumph of Antislavery Politics* (New York: Norton, 2007).

16. May, *Some Recollections*, 4–5, 32–33. On abolitionists and the American Revolutionary heritage, see Daniel J. McInerney, *The Fortunate Heirs of Freedom: Abolition and Republican Thought* (Lincoln: University of Nebraska Press, 1994); Margot Minardi,

Making Slavery History: Abolitionism and the Politics of Memory in Massachusetts (New York: Oxford University Press, 2010).

17. May, *Some Recollections*, 15–20. In *A Brief Account of His Ministry, Given in a Discourse, Preached to the Church of the Messiah, in Syracuse, N.Y., September 15th, 1867* (Syracuse: Masters & Lee, 1867), 19, May similarly expressed the life-changing impact that Garrison had upon him. For scholarly treatments, see Henry Mayer, *All on Fire: William Lloyd Garrison and the Abolition of Slavery* (New York: St. Martin's, 1998); Stewart, *William Lloyd Garrison*; John L. Thomas, *The Liberator: William Lloyd Garrison* (Boston: Little, Brown, 1963).

18. Emerson et al., *Memoir of Samuel Joseph May*, 261.

19. Joseph May, *Samuel Joseph May: A Memorial Study* (Boston: George H. Ellis, 1898), 9–10, 13, 32–33. On middle-class notions of respectability, especially as reflected in etiquette manuals, see Richard H. Bushman, *The Refinement of America: Persons, Houses, Cities* (New York: Knopf, 1992); C. Dallett Hemphill, *Bowing to Necessities: A History of Manners in America, 1620–1860* (New York: Oxford University Press, 1999); John F. Kasson, *Rudeness and Civility: Manners in Nineteenth-Century Urban America* (New York: Farrar, Straus and Giroux, 1990). On the cultural makeup of the emerging middle class, see Jennifer L. Goloboy, "The Early American Middle Class," *Journal of the Early Republic* 25 (Winter 2005): 537–45. Also see Stuart Blumin, *The Emergence of the Middle Class: Social Experience in the American City, 1760–1900* (New York: Cambridge University Press, 1989), which stresses the material conditions surrounding middle-class formation.

20. May, *Some Recollections*, 18, 22, 33-34; see 37–39 for how May, in another symposium with Channing, used the distinguished divine's own words to bolster his apologia of Garrison in both the 1830s and 1860s.

21. May, *Some Recollections*, 27–30, 35–37.

22. May, *Some Recollections*, 33; May, *Samuel Joseph May*, 34.

23. May, *Samuel Joseph May*, 14–15.

24. May, *Some Recollections*, 323. On abolitionism in upstate New York, see Sernett, *North Star Country*.

25. May, *Some Recollections*, 323–25, 327.

26. May, *Some Recollections*, 325–26, 328. For a scholarly account, see Norman K. Dann, *Practical Dreamer: Gerrit Smith and the Crusade for Social Reform* (Hamilton, NY: Log Cabin, 2009).

27. May, *Some Recollections*, 329. For scholarly accounts, see Robert E. McGlone, *John Brown's War against Slavery* (New York: Cambridge University Press, 2009); David S. Reynolds, *John Brown, Abolitionist: The Man Who Killed Slavery, Sparked the Civil War, and Seeded Civil Rights* (New York: Knopf, 2005). On Brown's covert allies, see Edward J. Renehan, *The Secret Six: The True Tale of the Men Who Conspired with John Brown* (New York: Crown, 1995). Also see Stauffer, *The Black Hearts of Men*, which partly focuses on the Smith-Brown relationship.

28. May, *Some Recollections*, 326–27, 329.

29. May, *Some Recollections*, 385–88.

30. Samuel J. May, *An Address Delivered Before the American Peace Society, in Park Street Church, Boston, May 26th, 1860* (Boston: American Peace Society, 1860), 4–5, 18.

31. May, *An Address Delivered Before the American Peace Society*, 18–20. For a fuller discussion of May's ambivalence toward the Harpers Ferry ringleader, see Yacovone, *Samuel Joseph May*, 166–68. On the memory of Brown in American culture, see R. Blakeslee Gilpin, *John Brown Still Lives! America's Long Reckoning with Violence, Equality, and Change* (Chapel Hill: University of North Carolina Press, 2011); Merrill D. Peterson, *John Brown: The Legend Revisited* (Charlottesville: University of Virginia Press, 2002).

32. May, *Some Recollections*, 224–25.

33. May, *Some Recollections*, 222–25; May, *An Address Delivered Before the American Peace Society*, 19. On Lovejoy and the Alton riot, see Merton L. Dillon, *Elijah P. Lovejoy, Abolitionist Editor* (Urbana: University of Illinois Press, 1961); Ken Ellingwood, *First to Fall: Elijah Lovejoy and the Fight for a Free Press in the Age of Slavery* (New York: Pegasus, 2021).

34. *The Emancipator*, December 28, 1837. For additional information on May's reception of the Alton tragedy, see Yacovone, *Samuel Joseph May*, 108–10.

35. May, *Some Recollections*, 94–96.

36. *Emancipator*; May, "Anti-Slavery Reminiscences," nos. 1–5, *National Anti-Slavery Standard*, December 16, 1841; December 23, 1841; January 6, 1842; January 27, 1842; and February 3, 1842, which the memoirist later incorporated into his narrative; May, *Some Recollections*, 225.

37. May, *Some Recollections*, 7–8, 345–49, 373–75. For recent treatments of the Fugitive Slave Law and its fallout, see R. J. M. Blackett, *The Captive's Quest for Freedom: Fugitive Slaves, the 1850 Fugitive Slave Law, and the Politics of Slavery* (New York: Cambridge University Press, 2018); John L. Brooke, *"There Is a North": Fugitive Slaves, Political Crisis, and Cultural Transformation in the Coming of the Civil War* (Amherst: University of Massachusetts Press, 2019).

38. May, *Some Recollections*, 356–62. May similarly rationalized violence in his 1867 publication *A Brief Account of His Ministry*, 50–51. Also see Emerson et al., *Memoir of Samuel Joseph May*, 221. On May's complex relationship with violent means after the 1850 Fugitive Slave Law's passage, see Yacovone, *Samuel Joseph May*, 151–54. For additional reading on white abolitionists' general accommodation to violent means, see Friedman, *Gregarious Saints*, chap. 7; Stanley Harrold, *The Rise of Aggressive Abolitionism: Addresses to the Slaves* (Lexington: University Press of Kentucky, 2004); Mabee, *Black Freedom*, chaps. 17–19; Perry, *Radical Abolitionism*, chap. 8. For important reconsiderations of abolitionism and violent means, see Jackson, *Force and Freedom*; Olsavsky, *The Most Absolute Abolition*.

39. May, *Some Recollections*, 362–63, 375–79.

40. May, *Some Recollections*, 377. In *Human Government Subordinate to the Divine. Speech of Samuel J. May, in the County Convention at Syracuse, October 14, 1851* (Syracuse: Agan & Summers, 1851), May publicized his rescue role, thereby daring authorities to arrest and prosecute him. For scholarly treatments, see Angela F. Murphy, *The Jerry Rescue: The Fugitive Slave Law, Northern Rights, and the American Sectional Crisis* (New York: Oxford University Press, 2016); Sernett, *North Star Country*, 136–45.

41. May, *Some Recollections*, 251. On behalf of a new history of abolition, Sinha's *The Slave's Cause*, 1–2, 13–14, 253–54, discounts, if not dismisses, abolitionism's liberal-bourgeois dimensions.

42. May, *Some Recollections*, 28–30, 81–82. On the ways in which many other antebellum whites utilized liberal individualism very differently, see Joshua A. Lynn, *Preserving the White Republic: Jacksonian Democracy, Race, and the Transformation of American Conservatism* (Charlottesville: University of Virginia Press, 2019).

43. Samuel J. May, *These Bad Times the Product of Bad Morals: A Sermon Preached to the Second Church in Scituate, Mass., May 21, 1837* (Boston: Isaac Knapp, 1837). On the historiographical problem concerning the relationship between transatlantic abolitionism and industrial capitalist economies and work relationships, consult the stimulating essays, respectively by John Ashworth, David Brion Davis, and Thomas L. Haskell, in Thomas Bender, ed., *The Antislavery Debate: Capitalism and Abolitionism as a Problem in Historical Interpretation* (Berkeley: University of California Press, 1992). Also see John Ashworth, *Slavery, Capitalism, and Politics in the Antebellum Republic*, vol. 1: *Commerce and Compromise, 1820–1850* (Cambridge: Cambridge University Press, 1995); Robin Blackburn, *The American Crucible: Slavery, Emancipation, and Human Rights* (London: Verso, 2013), 304–28, 386–90; Seymour Drescher, *Capitalism and Antislavery: British Mobilization in Comparative Perspective* (New York: Oxford University Press, 1986); Louis S. Gerteis, *Morality and Utility in American Antislavery Reform* (Chapel Hill: University of North Carolina Press, 1987); Goodman, *Of One Blood*, chaps. 7–8, 13; James L. Huston, "Abolitionists, Political Economists, and Capitalism," *Journal of the Early Republic* 20 (Autumn 2000), 487–521; Sinha, *The Slave's Cause*, 347–58; Ronald G. Walters, *The Antislavery Appeal: American Abolitionism after 1830* (Baltimore, MD: Johns Hopkins University Press, 1978), chap. 7.

44. May, *Some Recollections*, 238–39. For scholarly considerations of working-class involvement in antislavery activism, see Goodman, *Of One Blood*, chaps. 11–12; Bruce Laurie, *Beyond Garrison: Antislavery and Social Reform* (New York: Cambridge University Press, 2005); Edward Magdol, *The Antislavery Rank and File: A Social Profile of the Abolitionist Constituency* (Westport, CT: Greenwood, 1986).

45. May, *Some Recollections*, 64–66.

46. May, *Some Recollections*, 97–100.

47. May, *Some Recollections*, 249–55.

48. May, *Some Recollections*, 91–97, 230–39, 244–45, 285–96.

49. May, *Some Recollections*, 39–72, quotations at 49, 50, 51, 66, 71.

50. May, *Some Recollections*, 266–78, 285. On racial thought in the nineteenth century, see Mia Bay, *The White Image in the Black Mind: African-American Ideas about White People, 1830–1925* (New York: Oxford University Press, 2000); Bruce Dain, *A Hideous Monster of the Mind: American Race Theory in the Early Republic* (Cambridge, MA: Harvard University Press, 2002); George M. Fredrickson, *The Black Image in the White Mind: The Debate on Afro-American Character and Destiny, 1817–1914*, new ed. (1971; Hanover, NH: Wesleyan University Press, 1987). On how free Black northerners skillfully pursued the politics of respectability, see, for example, Ball, *To Live an Antislavery Life*.

51. May, *Some Recollections*, 286–88.

52. May, *Some Recollections*, 290–92.

53. May, *Some Recollections*, 292–96.

54. May, *Some Recollections*, 30, 136.

55. May, *Some Recollections*, 136–37, 234, 395. On antiabolitionist reactions to an emerging immediate emancipation campaign, see Leonard L. Richards, *"Gentlemen of Property and Standing": Anti-Abolition Mobs in Jacksonian America* (New York: Oxford University Press, 1970); Nikki Taylor, *Frontiers of Freedom: Cincinnati's Black Community, 1802–1868* (Athens: Ohio University Press, 2005); Elizabeth R. Varon, *Disunion! The Coming of the American Civil War, 1789–1859* (Chapel Hill: University of North Carolina Press, 2008).

56. May, *Some Recollections*, 119–44, 150–70.

57. May, *Some Recollections*, iv, 147–50, 237–48, 329–45, 365, 366–73. On the relationship between abolitionism and organized religion, see, for example, McKivigan, *The War against Proslavery Religion*.

58. May, *Some Recollections*, 396.

59. Samuel J. May, "A Sermon on Our Civil War," *The Liberator*, May 24, 1861.

60. May, *Some Recollections*, 395–96. On the 1865–1866 Black Codes, see Dan T. Carter, *When the War Was Over: The Failure of Self-Reconstruction in the South, 1865–1867* (Baton Rouge: Louisiana State University Press, 1985), chap. 6; Foner, *Reconstruction*, 199–201, 208–9. On the Ku Klux Klan, see, for example, William A. Blair, *The Record of Murders and Outrages: Racial Violence and the Fight over Truth at the Dawn of Reconstruction* (Chapel Hill: University of North Carolina Press, 2021); Foner, *Reconstruction*, 425–44; Elaine Frantz Parsons, *Ku-Klux: The Birth of the Klan during Reconstruction* (Chapel Hill: The University of North Carolina Press, 2015).

61. May, *Some Recollections*, 395–96.

2. Antislavery Elevated:
William Wells Brown and the Purpose of Black Activism

1. William Wells Brown, *The Rising Son; or, The Antecedents and Advancement of the Colored Race* (Boston: A. G. Brown & Co., 1874), 330, 393–94, 401; William Wells Brown, *My Southern Home: or, The South and Its People* (Boston: A. G. Brown & Co., 1880). Since *The Rising Son* has a copyright of 1873, I will defer to that over the 1874 publication year when referring to the text. The author issued a slightly revised version of the original text in 1882; a few additional pages (552–55) at the end constitute the only substantive difference between the two. For biographical information, Ezra Greenspan's *William Wells Brown: An African American Life* (New York: Norton, 2014) is a fine, up-to-date account. Also useful is William Edward Farrison, *William Wells Brown: Author and Reformer* (Chicago: University of Chicago Press, 1969).

2. Ball, *To Live an Antislavery Life*, has significantly influenced my thinking about the antebellum strategy of Black uplift. Also see Frederick Cooper, "Elevating the Race: The Social Thought of Black Leaders, 1827–50," *American Quarterly* 24, no. 3 (December 1972): 604–25; Eddie S. Glaude Jr., *Exodus!: Religion, Race, and Nation in Early Nineteenth-Century Black America* (Chicago: University of Chicago Press, 2000); James O. Horton and Lois E. Horton, *In Hope of Liberty: Culture, Community, and Protest among Northern Free Blacks, 1700–1860* (New York: Oxford University Press, 1997);

Joanne Pope Melish, "The 'Condition' Debate and Racial Discourse in the Antebellum North," in *Race and the Early Republic: Racial Consciousness and Nation-Building in the Early Republic*, ed. Michael A. Morrison and James Brewer Stewart (Lanham, MD: Rowman & Littlefield, 2002), 75–94; Patrick Rael, *Black Identity and Black Protest in the Antebellum North* (Chapel Hill: University of North Carolina Press, 2002); Donald Wright, *African Americans in the Early Republic, 1789–1831* (Wheeling, IL: Harlan Davidson, 1993).

3. William Wells Brown, *Narrative of William W. Brown, a Fugitive Slave, Written by Himself* (Boston: The Anti-Slavery Office, 1847). On the long African American improvement campaign, see, for example, Kevin Gaines, *Uplifting the Race: Black Leadership, Politics, and Culture in the Twentieth Century* (Chapel Hill: University of North Carolina Press, 1996); Evelyn Brooks Higginbotham, *Righteous Discontent: The Woman's Movement in the Black Baptist Church, 1880–1920* (Cambridge, MA: Harvard University Press, 1993).

4. William Wells Brown, *The Anti-Slavery Harp; A Collection of Songs for Anti-Slavery Meetings* (Boston: Bela Marsh, 1848); William Wells Brown, *Three Years in Europe; or, Places I Have Seen and People I Have Met* (London: Charles Gilpin, 1852); William Wells Brown, *The American Fugitive in Europe. Sketches of Places and People Abroad* (Boston: John P. Jewett and Company, 1855); William Wells Brown, *Clotel: or, The President's Daughter: A Narrative of Slave Life in the United States. With a Sketch of the Author's Life* (London: Partridge & Oakey, 1853); William Wells Brown, *Clotelle: A Tale of the Southern States* (Boston: James Redpath, 1865); William Wells Brown, *Clotelle; or, The Colored Heroine. A Tale of the Southern States* (Boston: Lee & Shepard, 1867); William Wells Brown, *The Escape; or, A Leap for Freedom. A Drama in Five Acts* (Boston: R. F. Wallcut, 1858); William Wells Brown, *The Black Man, His Antecedents, His Genius, and His Achievements* (New York: Thomas Hamilton, 1863); William Wells Brown, *The Negro in the American Rebellion: His Heroism and His Fidelity* (Boston: Lee & Shepard, 1867). Besides the biographical studies already cited, on Brown the song compiler, see Aaron D. McClendon, "Sounds of Sympathy: William Wells Brown's *Anti-Slavery Harp*, Abolition, and the Culture of Early and Antebellum American Song," *African American Review* 47, no. 1 (Spring 2014): 83–100; on Brown the travel writer, see Charles Baraw, "William Wells Brown, *Three Years in Europe*, and Fugitive Tourism," *African American Review* 44, no. 3 (Fall 2011), 453–70; Martha Schoolman, *Abolitionist Geographies* (Minneapolis: University of Minnesota Press, 2014), chap. 3; on Brown the novelist, see John Ernest, *Resistance and Reformation in Nineteenth-Century African-American Literature: Brown, Wilson, Jacobs, Delany, Douglass, and Harper* (Jackson: University Press of Mississippi, 1995), chap. 1; Judith Madera, *Black Atlas: Geography and Flow in Nineteenth-Century African American Literature* (Durham, NC: Duke University Press, 2015), chap. 1; Christopher Stampone, "'[H]eroic bravery in more than one battle': The Creation of Heroes in William Wells Brown's Multi-Edition *Clotel*," *African American Review* 49, no. 2 (Summer 2016): 75–91; on Brown the playwright, see John Ernest, "The Reconstruction of Whiteness: William Wells Brown's *The Escape; or, A Leap for Freedom*," *PMLA* 113, no. 5 (October 1998): 1108–21; on Brown the historian, see Stephen G. Hall, *A Faithful Account of the Race: African American Historical Writing in Nineteenth-Century America* (Chapel

Hill: University of North Carolina Press, 2009), chaps. 3–4; Marnie Hughes-Warrington, "Coloring Universal History: Robert Benjamin Lewis's *Light and Truth* (1843) and William Wells Brown's *The Black Man* (1863)," *Journal of World History* 20, no. 1 (March 2009): 99–130.

5. Brown, *My Southern Home*, 237, 253; William Wells Brown, *St. Domingo: Its Revolutions and Its Patriots. A Lecture, Delivered before the Metropolitan Athenaeum, London, May 16, and at St. Thomas' Church, Philadelphia, December 20, 1854* (Boston: Bela Marsh, 1855). On the development of Black historical discourse, see John Ernest, *Liberation Historiography: African American Writers and the Challenge of History, 1794–1861* (Chapel Hill: University of North Carolina Press, 2004); Hall, *A Faithful Account of the Race*; Laurie F. Maffly-Kipp, *Setting Down the Sacred Past: African-American Race Histories* (Cambridge, MA: Belknap, 2010); Benjamin Quarles, "Black History's Antebellum Origins," *Proceedings of the American Antiquarian Society* 89 (April 1979): 89–122.

6. William Goodell, *Slavery and Anti-Slavery; A History of the Great Struggle in Both Hemispheres; with a View of the Slavery Question in the United States* (New York: William Harned, 1852); R. B. Lewis, *Light and Truth; Collected from the Bible and Ancient and Modern History, Containing the Universal History of the Colored and Indian Race, from the Creation of the World to the Present Time* (1836; Boston: A Committee of Colored Men, 1844).

7. Brown, *The Rising Son*, v–x, 418; Lewis, *Light and Truth*, 304–8, 326–34. On Lewis and his book, see Bay, *The White Image in the Black Mind*, 44–46; Ernest, *Liberation Historiography*, 101–13; Hall, *A Faithful Account of the Race*, 62, 65, 71–73, 79–81; Hughes-Warrington, "Coloring University History."

8. Brown, *The Rising Son*, 37–44. In *The Black Man*, 32–33, Brown similarly ruminated on the significance of Ethiopia as well as Egypt. Hall, *Faithful Account of the Race*, 130, contends that Brown downplayed ancient Africa's contemporary relevance. On the transatlantic identity of African-descended people, see Paul Gilroy's classic account, *Black Atlantic: Modernity and Double-Consciousness* (Cambridge, MA: Harvard University Press, 1993); as well as Rael, *Black Identity and Black Protest*, chaps. 1–2.

9. Brown, *The Rising Son*, 51–64. On the significance of ancient history in early African American historical discourse, see Hall, *A Faithful Account of the Race*, 63–73; Maffly-Kipp, *Setting Down the Sacred Past*, chap. 1; Wilson Jeremiah Moses, *Afrotopia: The Roots of African American Popular History* (New York: Cambridge University Press, 1998), chaps. 2–3. Also see Scott Trafton, *Egypt Land: Race and Nineteenth-Century American Egyptomania* (Durham, NC: Duke University Press, 2004).

10. Brown, *The Rising Son*, 44–47, 58. For an earlier African American inquiry into the African origins of ancient civilization as well as the environmental causes of skin-color differences, see James W. C. Pennington, *A Text Book of the Origin and History of the Colored People* (Hartford, CT: L. Skinner, 1841), which Brown cited. For a scholarly treatment of such themes, see Bay, *The White Image in the Black Mind*, chaps. 1–2.

11. Brown, *The Rising Son*, 46. On Brown's nondenominational religious identity, see Greenspan, *William Wells Brown*, 174–75.

12. Brown, *The Rising Son*, 78–82.

13. Brown, *The Rising Son*, 84–85, 88.

14. Brown, *The Rising Son*, 85–86.

15. Brown, *The Black Man*, 33–35. On the British past in early African American thought, see Rael, *Black Identity and Black Protest*, 227–34.

16. Brown, *The Rising Son*, 85–86. On cyclical theories in Western historical thought, see, for example, Ernst Breisach, *Historiography: Ancient, Medieval, and Modern*, 3rd ed. (Chicago: University of Chicago Press, 2007). On progress and decline in Black historiography, see Moses, *Afrotopia*, chaps. 3–4. On racial thought in the nineteenth century, see the sources listed in Chapter 1, n50. Also see Terrence D. Keel, "Religion, Polygenism, and the Early Science of Human Origins," *History of the Human Sciences* 26, no. 2 (April 2013): 3–32; Colin Kidd, *The Forging of Races: Race and Scripture in the Protestant World, 1600–2000* (Cambridge: Cambridge University Press, 2006), chap. 5.

17. Brown, *The Rising Son*, chaps. 3, 8; quotation at 69.

18. Brown, *The Rising Son*, 68, 70.

19. Brown, *The Rising Son*, 70–71.

20. Brown, *The Rising Son*, 101–2, 106–8.

21. Brown, *The Rising Son*, 97–100, 102, 127, 129–34.

22. Brown, *The Rising Son*, 87, 118–24, 135–37. See Hall, *A Faithful Account of the Race*, 1–2, for a cogent reading of *The Rising Son*'s main title.

23. In *The Black Man*'s updated 1863 edition, Brown added four more entries—African Americans all. For scholarly analyses of the earlier works, see Farrison, *William Wells Brown*, 255–58, 366–77; Greenspan, *William Wells Brown*, 328–29, 367, 383–90, 402–3. On Brown's penchant for grafting old work onto new writing, including his own and others, see Ernest, *Resistance and Reformation*, 24–34; Geoffrey Sanborn, *Plagiarama! William Wells Brown and the Aesthetics of Attraction* (New York: Columbia University Press, 2016).

24. On Brown's European sojourn, see Farrison, *William Wells Brown*, chaps. 10–15; Greenspan, *William Wells Brown*, chaps. 6–7.

25. Brown, *St. Domingo*, 24–25, 32–33, 37–38. On Haiti's impact on antebellum African American thought, see Bruce Dain, "Haiti and Egypt in Early Black Racial Discourse in the United States," *Slavery and Abolition* 14, no. 3 (December 1993): 139–61; Hall, *A Faithful Account*, chap. 3; Rael, *Black Identity and Black Protest*, 220–26. On Haiti's postbellum significance among leading African Americans, see Brandon R. Byrd, *The Black Republic: African Americans and the Fate of Haiti* (Philadelphia: University of Pennsylvania Press, 2019). For a comprehensive account of the Haitian Revolution's presence in American popular culture, see Matthew J. Clavin, *Toussaint Louverture and the American Civil War: The Promise and Peril of a Second Haitian Revolution* (Philadelphia: University of Pennsylvania Press, 2010). For a broader analysis of African American activists and violent means, see Jackson, *Force and Freedom*.

26. For Brown's pioneering book about Black Civil War experiences, see *The Negro in the American Rebellion*. On the Fugitive Slave Law and popular opposition to it, see the sources listed in Chapter 1, n37.

27. Brown, *The Rising Son*, 145–46, 156, 160, 162, 170–72.

28. Brown, *The Rising Son*, 150–51, 171, 174–75, 179–83, 197.

29. Brown, *The Rising Son*, 206, 208–12, 214, 216, 220–22, 226–27.

30. Brown, *The Black Man*, 116, 138.

31. Brown, *The Rising Son*, 263–64. For Brown's positive assessments of other Haitian rulers, see 216–19, 232–33, 236–37, 239. On the attempted 1869 annexation of the present-day Dominican Republic, see, for example, Millery Polyné, "Expansion Now!: Haiti, 'Santo Domingo,' and Frederick Douglass at the Intersection of U.S. and Caribbean Pan-Americanism," *Caribbean Studies* 34, no. 2 (July–December 2006): 3–45. Also see Byrd, *The Black Republic*, chap. 1.

32. Brown, *The Rising Son*, 296. For Brown's coverage of those topics, see chaps. 30–40, 42–48.

33. Brown, *The Rising Son*, 291–95, 319, 331, 336–39, 387–88.

34. Brown, *The Rising Son*, 413–15.

35. Brown, *The Black Man*, 47–48; Brown, *The Rising Son*, 417. On Franklin's impact on African American literature, see Robert S. Levine, "The Slave Narrative and the Revolutionary Tradition of American Autobiography," in *The Cambridge Companion to the African American Slave Narrative*, ed. Audrey Fisch (New York: Cambridge University Press, 2007), 99–114. For a broader analysis, see Carla Mulford, "Figuring Benjamin Franklin in American Cultural Memory," *New England Quarterly* 72, no. 3 (September 1999): 415–43.

36. Brown, *The Rising Son*, 418–552.

37. Brown, *The Rising Son*, 418–25, 463–68, 489–93, 495–508, 510–12, 514, 517–20, 536–42, 544–45, 547–48.

38. Brown, *The Rising Son*, 434–40, 458–63, 468–69, 481–83, 486–89, 493–95, 520–22, 531–32, 534–35, 548–49.

39. For Brown's utilization of the first three words, see Brown, *The Rising Son*, 433, 435, 440, 454, 464, 471, 473, 474, 483, 497, 505, 536, 522, 524, 543, 544, 546, 552, 553; for his deployment of the two other descriptors, see 435, 438, 442, 445, 447, 448, 449, 450, 452, 455, 456, 459, 469, 470, 471, 472, 474, 481, 483, 493, 494, 496, 498, 500, 504, 511, 513, 514, 517, 519, 520, 522, 523, 524, 526, 530, 532, 536, 545, 548, 549, 550, 551, 552.

40. Brown, *The Black Man*, 7–9, 42, 48–49.

41. Brown, *The Rising Son*, 425–26, 430–32; Brown, *The Black Man*, 51–58. On the sources that Brown personally expropriated in the former, see Sanborn, *Plagiarama!*, 152–60.

42. Brown, *The Rising Son*, 413; Brown, *The Black Man*, 35. On Reconstruction's demise, see the sources listed in the Introduction, n11.

43. Brown, *My Southern Home*, v–viii. For scholarly treatments, see William L. Andrews, introduction to *From Fugitive Slave to Free Man: The Autobiographies of William Wells Brown* (New York: New American Library, 1993); John Ernest, "William Wells Brown Maps the South in *My Southern Home: Or, The South and Its People*," *Southern Quarterly* 45, no. 3 (Spring 2008): 88–107; John Ernest, introduction to *My Southern Home: Or, The South and Its People* (Chapel Hill: University of North Carolina Press, 2011); M. Clay Hooper, "'It Is Good to Be Shifty': William Wells Brown's Trickster Critique of Black Autobiography," *Modern Language Studies* 38, no. 2 (Winter 2009): 28–45; Bryan Sinche, "William Wells Brown's Economy of Entertainment," *African American Review* 25, no. 1–2 (Spring/Summer 2012): 83–98. Also see Sanborn, *Plagiarama!*, 14–16, 55–56, 160–61.

44. On Brown's temperance mission and overseas contacts, see Farrison, *William Wells Brown*, 423–36; Greenspan, *William Wells Brown*, 477–86.

45. Brown, *My Southern Home*, iii, 107. For Brown's discussion of the antebellum South as an ignorant, superstitious, and barbaric place, see chaps. 6–8, 12, 16; for the cruelties surrounding slave trading, see chaps, 4, 10, 11.

46. Brown, *My Southern Home*, 91; Sinche, "William Wells Brown's Economy of Entertainment," 83. Also see the other sources cited in n43.

47. Brown, *My Southern Home*, chaps. 1–2, 5, for the discussion of the subversive wit and guile of the enslaved.

48. Brown, *My Southern Home*, 163–66.

49. Brown, *My Southern Home*, 165, 182, 219–21, 224–29, 245–48. On the Exoduster Movement, see Nell Irvin Painter, *Exodusters: Black Migration to Kansas after Reconstruction* (1976; New York: Norton, 1992); Quintard Taylor, *In Search of the Racial Frontier: African Americans in the American West, 1528–1990* (New York: Norton, 1998), chap. 5.

50. Brown, *My Southern Home*, 166, 239.

51. Brown, *My Southern Home*, 234, 237–38, 243–44, 251; Brown, *The Rising Son*, 316, 358, 381; Brown, *The Black Man*, 71.

52. Brown, *My Southern Home*, 166, 179, 182, 225, 250. On the shifting significance of Black martial manhood in later African American literary works, see John A. Casey Jr., *New Men: Reconstructing the Image of the Veteran in Late-Nineteenth-Century American Literature and Culture* (New York: Fordham University Press, 2015), chap. 5.

53. Brown, *My Southern Home*, iii, 179, 181–83, 188–89, 212–13, 229–30.

54. Brown, *My Southern Home*, 188–90.

55. Brown, *My Southern Home*, 191–98, 232–33.

56. Brown, *My Southern Home*, 198–99, 229–30, 239.

57. Brown, *My Southern Home*, 233–35, 239–41.

58. Brown, *My Southern Home*, 241–43.

59. Brown, *The Black Man*, 35–36; Brown, *My Southern Home*, 234, 248.

60. Brown, *My Southern Home*, 243.

3. Antislavery Vindicated:
Oliver Johnson and the Value of Abolitionism's Grand Old Party

1. Oliver Johnson, *William Lloyd Garrison and His Times; or, Sketches of the Anti-Slavery Movement in America, and of the Man Who Was Its Founder and Moral Leader* (Boston: Houghton, Mifflin and Co., 1881), 449–50. A different Boston-based publishing firm, B. B. Russell & Company, issued the book's 1880 edition under the same title. The revised and enlarged text is herein cited unless otherwise noted. For biographical information, see Steven M. Raffo, *A Biography of Oliver Johnson, Abolitionist and Reformer, 1809–1889* (Lewiston, NY: Edwin Mellon, 2002). Johnson's Civil War–era activities are discussed within a broader abolitionist context in McPherson, *The Struggle for Equality*; McPherson, *The Abolitionist Legacy*.

2. "Sketch of William Lloyd Garrison by Oliver Johnson," *Chicago Daily Tribune*, June 12, 1874; Oliver Johnson, "William Lloyd Garrison. Death of the Philanthropist,"

New-York Tribune, May 26, 1879; Oliver Johnson, *Garrison: An Outline of His Life* (New York: Charles Scribner's Sons, 1879); Oliver Johnson, "The Fall of Slavery. Recollections of an Abolitionist," *New-York Tribune*, June 14, 1879, to January 10, 1880; Oliver Johnson, *William Lloyd Garrison and His Times*, xiii–xiv.

3. Johnson, *William Lloyd Garrison and His Times*, xiv–xv. On Garrisonian abolitionism, see the sources listed in Chapter 1, n4; on the 1840 AASS schism, Chapter 1, n8.

4. Johnson, *William Lloyd Garrison and His Times*, xvi, xv, v. On Johnson's role as an antislavery organizer, see 82–89; John Myers, "The Beginning of Antislavery Agencies in Vermont, 1832–1836," *Vermont History* 36 (Summer 1968): 126–41; Raffo, *Oliver Johnson*, 25–30.

5. Johnson, *William Lloyd Garrison and His Times*, 65–66.

6. Johnson, *William Lloyd Garrison and His Times*, 65–66. On the notion of northern political subservience to slaveholding interests, see Corey M. Brooks, *Liberty Power: Antislavery Third Parties and the Transformation of American Politics* (Chicago: University of Chicago Press, 2016); Leonard L. Richards, *The Slave Power: The Free North and Southern Domination, 1780–1860* (Baton Rouge: Louisiana State University Press, 2000).

7. On Reconstruction's demise, see the sources listed in the Introduction, n11. Also see Charles W. Calhoun, *Conceiving a New Republic: The Republic Party and the Southern Questions, 1869–1900* (Lawrence: University Press of Kansas, 2006), which emphasizes not a Republican retreat from Reconstruction but party efforts to preserve the era's accomplishments by retaining control of national politics. On the backroom bargaining allegedly surrounding the disputed 1876 election, see C. Vann Woodward's classic study *Reunion and Reaction: The Compromise of 1877 and the End of Reconstruction* (Boston: Little, Brown, 1951).

8. Johnson, *William Lloyd Garrison and His Times*, 66, 102.

9. Johnson, *William Lloyd Garrison and His Times*, 66. On the bloody shirt's electoral significance, see Charles W. Calhoun, *From Bloody Shirt to Full Dinner Pail: The Transformation of Politics and Governance in the Gilded Age* (New York: Hill and Wang, 2010); Stanley P. Hirshson, *Farewell to the Bloody Shirt: Northern Republicans and the Southern Negro, 1877–1893* (Bloomington: Indiana University Press, 1962).

10. Mr. Greeley's Reply," in *Proceedings of the Liberal Republican Convention, in Cincinnati, May 1st, 2d and 3d, 1872*; Horace Greeley's Letter of Acceptance; *Address of the New York State Committee to Their Fellow-Citizens* (New York: Baker & Godwin, 1872), 38–40; "The Platform," in *Proceedings of the Liberal Republican Convention*, 19–21.

11. Oliver Johnson, *What I Know of Horace Greeley* (New York, 1872), 3, 4, 8, which originally appeared as the article "Horace Greeley for President," *The Golden Age* (New York), August 24, 1872. On the liberal republican movement, see Andrew L. Slap, *The Doom of Reconstruction: The Liberal Republicans in the Civil War Era* (New York: Fordham University Press, 2006); John G. Sproat, *"The Best Men": Liberal Reformers in the Gilded Age*, new ed. (1968; Chicago: University of Chicago Press, 1982). On Johnson and the 1872 presidential contest, see James M. McPherson, "Grant or Greeley? The Abolitionist Dilemma in the Election of 1872," *American Historical Review* 71 (October 1965): 43–61; Raffo, *Oliver Johnson*, 312–16.

12. *Orange Journal* (New Jersey), March 17, 1877, quoted in McPherson, *The Abolitionist Legacy*, 91.

13. Oliver Johnson, "Bitter Dregs of Slavery. A Letter from Oliver Johnson," *New-York Tribune*, October 11, 1879. On Johnson's positions toward Hayes's appeasement policy, see James M. McPherson, "Coercion or Conciliation? Abolitionists Debate President Hayes's Southern Policy," *New England Quarterly* 39 (December 1966): 474–97; James M. McPherson, *The Abolitionist Legacy*, 87, 91, 98, 101.

14. Johnson, *William Lloyd Garrison and His Times*, 19, 65, 318, 320, 345.

15. Johnson, *William Lloyd Garrison and His Times*, 29–34, 37–44, 46, 51–53, 112–19, 147–55, 194–200, 454.

16. Johnson, *William Lloyd Garrison and His Times*, 23–24, 52–58, 110, 336.

17. Johnson, *William Lloyd Garrison and His Times*, 46, 67, 366.

18. Johnson, *William Lloyd Garrison and His Times*, 24, 67–70, 273–74, 363. For Johnson's full discussion of Garrison's religious orthodoxy and supposed infidelity, see chaps. 4, 22.

19. Johnson, *William Lloyd Garrison and His Times*, 44–45, 82, 111, 174–78. For an insightful examination of Beecher's influence on Garrison, see Abzug, *Cosmos Crumbling*. For other scholarly considerations of the relationship between evangelical revitalization and antebellum reformism, see Gilbert Hobbes Barnes, *The Anti-Slavery Impulse, 1830–1844*, intro. William G. McLoughlin (1933; New York: Harcourt, Brace & World, 1964); Mintz, *Moralists and Modernizers*; Walters, *American Reformers*; Michael P. Young, *Bearing Witness against Sin: The Evangelical Birth of the American Social Movement* (Chicago: University of Chicago Press, 2006).

20. Johnson, *William Lloyd Garrison and His Times*, 111.

21. Johnson, *William Lloyd Garrison and His Times*, 44–45, 89.

22. Johnson, *William Lloyd Garrison and His Times*, 67, 278–79, 363–65, 370–71, 444.

23. Johnson, *William Lloyd Garrison and His Times*, 55, 336, 370.

24. Johnson, *William Lloyd Garrison and His Times*, 123, 368–69.

25. Johnson, *William Lloyd Garrison and His Times*, 43–44, 321.

26. Johnson, *William Lloyd Garrison and His Times*, 44, 48–49, 70, 74–75, 98, 105, 109, 224–53.

27. Johnson, *William Lloyd Garrison and His Times*, 44, 70, 91, 159–61, 224–53.

28. Johnson, *William Lloyd Garrison and His Times*, 74–75, 91–93, 98, 157–59.

29. Johnson, *William Lloyd Garrison and His Times*, 52, 82–83, 110, 337, 344.

30. Johnson, *William Lloyd Garrison and His Times*, 37, 102–3, 112–15, 119–24, 129–31.

31. Johnson, *William Lloyd Garrison and His Times*, 101, 113–15, 124–27, 419. On Reconstruction-era violence, see John Patrick Daly, *The War after the War: A New History of Reconstruction* (Athens: University of Georgia Press, 2022); Carole Emberton, *Beyond Redemption: Race, Violence, and the American South after the Civil War* (Chicago: University of Chicago Press, 2013); George C. Rable, *But There Was No Peace: The Role of Violence in the Politics of Reconstruction* (Athens: University of Georgia Press, 1984); and the sources listed in Chapter 2, n60.

32. Johnson, *William Lloyd Garrison and His Times*, 99–105.

33. Johnson, *William Lloyd Garrison and His Times*, 101–2, 339–42, 348. For newspaper coverage of the famous Framingham gathering, including a representative speech of Garrison's denouncing the Constitution, see the *Liberator*, July, 7, 14, 21, 1854.

34. Oliver Johnson, "The Future of the Negro," *North American Review* 89 (July 1884): 93–95.

35. Johnson, *William Lloyd Garrison and His Times*, 94–95; Johnson, "Bitter Dregs of Slavery." James McPherson similarly highlighted Johnson's gradualist program as a race-relations solution but ultimately italicized his rejecting that position once Hayes's appeasement policy had failed. See "Coercion or Conciliation," 488, for his suggestion that Johnson's recommendations for improved race relations foreshadowed Booker T. Washington's; *The Abolitionist Legacy*, 101, for his statement that Johnson's repudiation of sectional reconciliation signified radical revivalism on his part.

36. Stewart, *Holy Warriors*, chap. 6; James Brewer Stewart, "Emergence of Racial Modernity and the Rise of the White North, 1790–1840," *Journal of the Early American Republic* 18 (Spring 1998): 181–217; James Brewer Stewart, "Modernizing 'Difference': The Political Meaning of Color in the Free States, 1776–1840," in *Race and the Early Republic: Racial Consciousness and Nation-Building in the Early Republic*, ed. Michael A. Morrison and James Brewer Stewart (Lanham, MD: Rowman & Littlefield, 2002), 113–33. On the antebellum strategy of Black uplift, see the sources listed in Chapter 2, n2.

37. Johnson, "The Future of the Negro," 94. On the ways in which veteran abolitionists of the 1870s and 1880s viewed time, education, and economic growth as important ingredients of racial progress, see McPherson, *The Abolitionist Legacy*, chaps. 4, 7.

38. *Proceedings of the American Anti-Slavery Society, at its Third Decade*, 78–79.

39. *Proceedings of the American Anti-Slavery Society, at its Third Decade*, 79.

40. Oliver Johnson, "To the Readers of the Anti-Slavery Standard," *National Anti-Slavery Standard*, May 20, 1865; Raffo, *Oliver Johnson*, 148–49, 284–85.

41. Johnson, *William Lloyd Garrison and His Times*, 237.

42. Johnson, *William Lloyd Garrison and His Times*, 72–73, 140–44, 155–58, 163, 165, 184–85, 190–91, 209–10, 220–22, 271–301.

43. Johnson, *William Lloyd Garrison and His Times*, 299, 306–8.

44. Johnson, *William Lloyd Garrison and His Times*, 308–15. For scholarly treatments, see Frederick J. Blue, *No Taint of Compromise: Crusaders in Antislavery Politics* (Baton Rouge: Louisiana State University Press, 2005); Brooks, *Liberty Power*; Sewell, *Ballots for Freedom*.

45. Johnson, *William Lloyd Garrison and His Times*, 276–77, 286–91.

46. Johnson, *William Lloyd Garrison and His Times*, 283–84, 293, 429–30.

47. Johnson, *William Lloyd Garrison and His Times*, 277–78, 291–92.

48. Johnson, *William Lloyd Garrison and His Times*, 296–99, 320, 322, 325–26.

49. Johnson, *William Lloyd Garrison and His Times*, 293–99, 448.

50. Johnson, *William Lloyd Garrison and His Times*, 200–2, 315, 317, 428.

51. Johnson, *William Lloyd Garrison and His Times*, 315, 320, 325–27, 345–46, 379, 427–28, 440–41, 448–50.

52. "Garrison and the Churches . . . A Letter from the Rev. Dr. Whedon," *New-York Tribune*, September 25, 1879.

53. "Anti-Slavery History. Oliver Johnson Answers Dr. Whedon," *New-York Tribune*, October 2, 1879.

54. "Slavery and Methodism. A Rejoinder by the Rev. Dr. Whedon," *New-York Tribune*, November 8, 1879; "Slavery and Methodism. Surrejoinder to the Rev. Dr. Whedon," *New-York Tribune*, November 15, 1879; Johnson, *William Lloyd Garrison and His Times*, 404–54. In the first edition of *William Lloyd Garrison and His Times*, 75–81, Johnson directly contested Whedon's newspaper arguments; in the revised and expanded version, xi, the author excised the entire discussion.

55. George W. Julian, "The Genesis of Modern Abolitionism," *International Review*, June 1882, 538–42, 543–48; Oliver Johnson, "Charles Osborn's Place in Anti-Slavery History," *International Review*, September 1882, 191–206.

56. Johnson, "Charles Osborn's Place," 191, 193–95, 198–205. For Julian's response, see "The Truth of Anti-Slavery History," *International Review*, November 1882, 437–54. He later reissued his articles as a pamphlet, *The Rank of Charles Osborn as an Anti-Slavery Pioneer* (Indianapolis: Bowen-Merrill Company, 1891), 1–37.

57. Theodore Bourne, "Rev. George Bourne, The Pioneer of American Antislavery," *Methodist Quarterly Review* 64 (January 1882): 68–70, 73–75; Oliver Johnson, "Unwritten History. An Anti-Slavery Boanerges," *Boston Commonwealth*, June 6, 1885. William Oland Bourne, in "Anti-Slavery Leaders. The Pioneer Abolitionist," *Boston Commonwealth*, July 25, 1885, responded to Johnson's qualified praise and reinforced his brother's celebratory representation of dad's abolitionism.

58. Wright, *Myron Holley*, 230–36; Lawrence B. Goodheart, *Abolitionist, Actuary, Atheist: Elizur Wright and the Reform Impulse* (Kent, OH: Kent State University Press, 1990), 63, 74, 112–13.

59. Leonard Woolsey Bacon, "A Good Fight Finished," *Century Magazine* 25 (March 1883): 656–59. For scholarly accounts, see Hugh Davis, *Leonard Bacon: New England Reformer and Antislavery Moderate* (Baton Rouge: Louisiana State University Press, 1998); Oshatz, *Slavery and Sin*, chap. 4.

60. Oliver Johnson, "On the Late Dr. Bacon and the Abolitionists," *Century Magazine* 26 (May 1883): 153–55; Oliver Johnson, *William Lloyd Garrison and His Times*, 104. Johnson's reply elicited Woolsey Bacon's "Did 'Abolition' Abolish?," *Century Magazine* 26 (August 1883): 636–37; in *Anti-Slavery before Garrison* (New Haven, CT: The Tuttle, Morehouse & Taylor Company, 1903), 9–11, 36–37, the latter issued some final anti-Garrisonian jabs to which a deceased Johnson could not counter. Before that feuding, Johnson quarreled with the older Bacon. From February 11, 1874, to December 30, 1874, the *Christian Union* printed twenty-four installments of his abolitionist remembrances. After reading Johnson's "Early-Anti-Slavery Days" pieces, Leonard Bacon penned four of his own for the same journal, under the heading "The Earlier Anti-Slavery Days," December 9, 1874, to January 20, 1875. On January 27, 1875, Johnson responded to his disputant in "Dr. Bacon's 'Earlier Anti-Slavery Days.'"

61. Eli Thayer, *The New England Emigrant Aid Company and Its Influence, through the Kansas Contest, upon National History* (Worcester, MA: Franklin R. Price, 1887), 13–19, 26–27, 46–47. Two years later, Thayer issued a book-length account: *A History of the Kansas Crusade: Its Friends and Foes*, intro. Rev. Edward Everett Hale (New York: Harper & Brothers, 1889).

62. Thayer, *The New England Emigrant Aid Company and Its Influence*, 6, 9–13, 19, 33.

63. Oliver Johnson, *The Abolitionists Vindicated in a Review of Eli Thayer's Paper on the New England Emigrant Aid Company* (Worcester, MA: Franklin R. Price, 1887), 7–11, 15, 26.

64. Oliver Johnson, "Anti-Slavery. Congregational Club Addressed by an Old Abolitionist," *Brooklyn Daily Eagle*, February 26, 1889.

65. *New-York Tribune*, January 25, 1880.

66. Johnson, *William Lloyd Garrison and His Times*, 52; Oliver Johnson, *Garrison's Piety* (n.p.: 1890[?]).

4. Antislavery Sanctified:
Parker Pillsbury and the Spirit of Abolitionism in the Fields

1. Parker Pillsbury, *Acts of the Anti-Slavery Apostles* (Concord, NH: Clague, Wegman, Schlicht, & Co., 1883), iv, 47–48, 80, 292. For biographical information, see Stacey M. Robertson's fine study *Parker Pillsbury: Radical Abolitionist, Male Feminist* (Ithaca, NY: Cornell University Press, 2000) and her earlier article "'A Hard, Cold, Stern Life': Parker Pillsbury and Grassroots Abolitionism, 1840–1865," *New England Quarterly* 70 (June 1997): 179–210. Also see Louis Filler, "Parker Pillsbury: An Anti-Slavery Apostle," *New England Quarterly* 19 (September 1946): 315–37.

2. Pillsbury, *Anti-Slavery Apostles*, iii–iv, 250–51, 364, 479.

3. In "Political Abolitionists, Fanatics, and Philanthropists," *The Revolution*, April 8, 1869, Pillsbury contested other anti-Garrisonian viewpoints years before preparing a book-length account.

4. Pillsbury, *Anti-Slavery Apostles*, iii–iv, 503. On Pillsbury's itinerant abolitionism, see Robertson, *Parker Pillsbury*, chaps. 2, 5.

5. Pillsbury, *Anti-Slavery Apostles*, 307, 324, 366, 369. On Pillsbury's Congregationalist training and denominational breakaway, see Robertson, *Parker Pillsbury*, chap. 1. On comeouterism, see John R. McKivigan, "The Antislavery 'Comeouter' Sects: A Neglected Dimension of the Abolitionist Movement," *Civil War History*, June 1980, 142–60; John R. McKivigan, *The War against Proslavery Religion*; Perry, *Radical Abolitionism*.

6. Pillsbury, *Anti-Slavery Apostles*, 48. On the 1875 Civil Rights Act, see Hugh Davis, *"We Will Be Satisfied With Nothing Less": The African American Struggle for Equal Rights in the North during Reconstruction* (Ithaca, NY: Cornell University Press, 2011), chap. 4; David Herbert Donald, *Charles Sumner and the Rights of Man* (New York: Knopf, 1970); Foner, *Reconstruction*, chap. 11; James M. McPherson, "Abolitionists and the Civil Rights Acts of 1875," *Journal of American History* 52 (December 1965): 495–510; James M. McPherson, *The Abolitionist Legacy*, chap. 1. On the *Civil Rights Cases* of 1883, see Linda Przybyszewski, *The Republic according to John Marshall Harlan* (Chapel Hill: University of North Carolina Press, 1999), 90–96.

7. In contrast to my interpretation, Jeffrey's *Abolitionists Remember*, 192–201, views Pillsbury's efforts to publish antislavery remembrances as a testament to his continued engagement in racial justice activism. On Pillsbury's Spiritualist sympathies and FRA membership, see Robertson, *Parker Pillsbury*, 164–71. For broader accounts, see Molly

McGarry, *Ghosts of Futures Past: Spiritualism and the Cultural Politics of Nineteenth-Century America* (Berkeley: University of California Press, 2008); R. Laurence Moore, *In Search of White Crows: Spiritualism, Parapsychology, and American Culture* (New York: Oxford University Press, 1977); Stow Persons, *Free Religion: An American Faith* (New Haven, CT: Yale University Press, 1947); Eric Leigh Schmidt, *Restless Souls: The Making of American Spirituality* (San Francisco: Harper & Row, 2005). On the idea that uncertainty surrounded southern race relations before they hardened into legalized segregation, see C. Vann Woodward's classic account, *The Strange Career of Jim Crow*, 3rd ed. (New York: Oxford University Press, 1974).

8. Despite virtually vacating the AASS, Pillsbury participated in the association's final gathering, as documented by "American Anti-Slavery Society—Commemorative Meeting," *National Anti-Slavery Standard*, April 16, 1870. On abolitionist divisions over impartial suffrage for Black men and all women, as well as Pillsbury's siding with Stanton and Anthony, see Robertson, *Parker Pillsbury*, chap. 8. Also see Faye E. Dudden, *Fighting Chance: The Struggle over Woman Suffrage and Black Suffrage in Reconstruction America* (New York: Oxford University Press, 2011); Eleanor Flexner and Ellen Fitzpatrick, *Century of Struggle: The Woman's Rights Movement in the United States*, enlarged ed. (Cambridge, MA: Belknap, 1996), 137–43; James M. McPherson, "Abolitionists, Woman Suffrage, and the Negro, 1865–1869," *Mid-America* 47 (January 1965): 40–47; James Brewer Stewart, *Wendell Phillips: Liberty's Hero* (Baton Rouge: Louisiana State University Press, 1986), 281–86.

9. Stanton, *Eighty Years and More*, v. For Pillsbury's *Revolution* contributions championing impartial suffrage and broader women's rights, see "'Universal Suffrage,'" February 5, 1868; "Educated Suffrage," April 16, 1868; "Is Woman Capable of the Ballot?," April 23, 1868; "Educated Suffrage," June 18, 1868; "The Work of the Hour," October 22, 1868; "Constitutional Patchwork," February 18, 1869; "Voting a Natural Right," March 11, 1869; "The Fifteenth Amendment," July 1, 1869; "Woman in History," July 8, 1869; "Fifteenth Amendment—Its Ludicrous Side," July 22, 1869; "Call to All Hands," August 26, 1869; "The Sixteenth Amendment," March 24, 1879; "Mr. Julian and the XVI Amendment," April 14, 1870. Also see his women's rights pamphlet *The Mortality of Nations: An Address Delivered before the American Equal Rights Association, in New York, Thursday Evening, May 9, 1867* (New York: R. I. Johnston, 1867), as well as his later tract partly addressing the topic, *Ecclesiastical vs. Civil Authority: God in the Federal Constitution; Man and Woman Out* (Concord, NH: Republican Press Association, 1891). In *Old Anti-Slavery Days: Proceedings of the Commemorative Meeting, Held by the Danvers Historical Society, at the Town Hall, Danvers, April 26, 1893* (Danvers, MA: Danvers Mirror Print, 1893), 32, speaker Pillsbury briefly privileged women's rights over persistent racial justice activism. On the founding of *The Revolution* and the National Woman Suffrage Association, see Ellen Carol DuBois, *Feminism and Suffrage: The Emergence of an Independent Women's Movement in America, 1848–1869* (Ithaca, NY: Cornell University Press, 1978), 104; Flexner and Fitzpatrick, *Century of Struggle*, 143–48.

10. William J. Potter, *The Free Religious Association: Its Twenty-Five Years and Their Meaning* (Boston: The Free Religious Association of America, 1892), 9; *Report of Addresses at a Meeting Held in Boston, May 30, 1867, to Consider the Condition, Wants,*

and Prospects of Free Religion in America (Boston: Adams & Co., 1867), 3, 54–55; Parker Pillsbury, *The "Party of Progress." Letter to a Radical Member of Congress* (n.p., 1867); Parker Pillsbury, *Second Letter to a Radical Member of Congress* (Concord, NH: n.p., 1867). For Pillsbury's *Revolution* contributions scolding northern political conservatism, see "Who Are the Friends of the Negro?," April 30, 1868; "Democracy Restored," July 16, 1868; "The Constitutional Amendment," August 13, 1868; "Grant and Negro Suffrage," September 10, 1868; "Wendell Phillips and the National Prospect," October 8, 1868; "The Present Danger," December 3, 1868; "South Carolina—Letter from Parker Pillsbury," October 14, 1869; "The South as It Is," November 4, 1869; "The South as It Is," November 11, 1869; "Wendell Phillips on Freedmen's Suffrage," November 18, 1869; "Colorphobia," December 2, 1869; "What the South Needs," January 6, 1870; "Condition of the Freemen," April 7, 1870.

11. For Pillsbury's replicating antislavery circuit-riding networks as an FRA activist, consult his "Notes from the Field" communications that appeared in *The Index* on May 6, 1871; May 20, 1871; July 1, 1871; July 6, 1871; August 10, 1872; and October 12, 1872. For a fuller discussion of Pillsbury's FRA activism, see Robertson, *Parker Pillsbury*, 158–83.

12. Parker Pillsbury, "Slave-Holding Christianity," *The Index*, July 2, 1874. For other Pillsbury exposés concerning the relationship between southern slavery and American Christianity, see the following *Index* contributions: "Chattel Slavery and the Church," July 23, 1874; "Did Churches Own Slaves?," August 13, 1874; "'What Was American Slavery?,'" August 20, 1874; "What Was Slavery?," August 27, 1874; "What Was Slavery?," September 17, 1874; "What Was Slavery?," October, 8 1874; "What Was Slavery?," November 5, 1874; "What Was Slavery?," December 3, 1874, all of which formed a foundation for the book-length memoir.

13. Pillsbury, *Anti-Slavery Apostles*, 15–16, 18.

14. Pillsbury, *Anti-Slavery Apostles*, 490, 495–97.

15. Pillsbury, *Anti-Slavery Apostles*, 328–29. In a *Letter from Mr. Pillsbury to the Editor of the Anti-Slavery Standard* (n.p., 1862), the author challenged the seemingly growing abolitionist support for a formal dissolution of the AASS. On Garrisonian infighting over the AASS's course of action during and after the Civil War, see the sources listed in the Introduction, n17. On the Pillsbury-Garrison reconciliation, see Robertson, *Parker Pillsbury*, 184–85. Also see Robertson, *Parker Pillsbury*, chaps. 7–8, for Pillsbury's abolitionist positions during the 1860s.

16. Pillsbury, *Anti-Slavery Apostles*, 12–14, 16–22.

17. Pillsbury, *Anti-Slavery Apostles*, 16, 21–23.

18. Pillsbury, *Anti-Slavery Apostles*, 23, 25–26; Parker Pillsbury, "Notes from the Field," *The Index*, July 1, 1871.

19. Pillsbury, "Notes."

20. Pillsbury, *Anti-Slavery Apostles*, 24–27.

21. Parker Pillsbury, *Address of Parker Pillsbury at the Unveiling of the Garrison Statue in Newburyport, Mass., July 4, 1893* (n.p.). In "Address of Hon. Parker Pillsbury," in *The Man with the Branded Hand, or a Short Sketch of the Life and Services of Jonathan Walker* (Muskegon, MI: Chronicle Steam Publishing House, 1879), 17, 19, Pillsbury

also announced that Garrison had finished the Revolutionary generation's incomplete work.

22. Pillsbury, *Anti-Slavery Apostles*, 102–22, 159–81, 184–203, 241–49, 308–12.

23. Pillsbury, *Anti-Slavery Apostles*, 30–31, 44, 251; Parker Pillsbury, "Nathaniel Peabody Rogers," *The Revolution*, March 18, 1869.

24. Pillsbury, *Anti-Slavery Apostles*, 30–31, 44–45.

25. Pillsbury, *Anti-Slavery Apostles*, 31–41.

26. Pillsbury, *Anti-Slavery Apostles*, 34, 45.

27. Pillsbury, *Anti-Slavery Apostles*, 31, 43, 369. For the bound-with-them biblical language, see Heb. 13:3.

28. Pillsbury, *Anti-Slavery Apostles*, 43–44. See 93–95, 132–33, 173–79, 221–33, 251–63, for examples of how Pillsbury deployed *Herald of Freedom* editorials in order to enhance Rogers's posthumous reputation and document the stiff clerical antagonism that antislavery field laborers had encountered.

29. Pillsbury, *Anti-Slavery Apostles*, 35, 44; Pillsbury, "Nathaniel Peabody Rogers"; *A Collection from the Miscellaneous Writings of Nathaniel Peabody Rogers*, intro. John Pierpont, 2nd ed. (Manchester, NH: William H. Fisk, 1849).

30. Pillsbury, *Anti-Slavery Apostles*, 328–30. On the Pillsbury-Rogers friendship, see Robertson, *Parker Pillsbury*, 21–22, 64–65.

31. Pillsbury, *Anti-Slavery Apostles*, 44, 248–49, 263, 265. On Garrisonian abolitionism, see the sources listed in Chapter 1, n4. On the extreme antiauthoritarianism of Rogers, as well as the Garrisonian infighting that stemmed from his no-organizational views, see Perry, *Radical Abolitionism*, 117–28; Robertson, *Parker Pillsbury*, chap. 4; Stewart, *Wendell Phillips*, 131–32.

32. On the 1840 AASS schism, see the sources listed in Chapter 1, n8. On the Rogers affair as a Garrisonian family feud, see Friedman, *Gregarious Saints*, 59–61.

33. Robertson, *Parker Pillsbury*, 70–75.

34. Pillsbury, *Anti-Slavery Apostles*, 28–29, 495–96.

35. Pillsbury, *Anti-Slavery Apostles*, 85, 123–55; Parker Pillsbury, "Stephen Symonds Foster," *Granite Monthly*, August 1882, 1–7.

36. Pillsbury, *Anti-Slavery Apostles*, 124, 145–46, 148–49, 276–77.

37. Pillsbury, *Anti-Slavery Apostles*, 124–26.

38. Pillsbury, *Anti-Slavery Apostles*, 128–29, 145–47, 297–98. For scholarly accounts of Foster's provocative tactic, see Troy Duncan and Chris Dixon, "Denouncing the Brotherhood of Thieves: Stephen Symonds Foster's Critique of the Anti-Abolitionist Clergy," *Civil War History* 47 (June 2001): 97–117; McKivigan, *The War against Proslavery Religion*, 56–73; Jane H. Pease and William H. Pease, "The Perfectionist Radical: Stephen Symonds Foster," in *Bound with Them in Chains: A Biographical History of the Antislavery Movement* (Westport, CT: Greenwood, 1972), 191–217.

39. Pillsbury, *Anti-Slavery Apostles*, 145, 272–74.

40. Pillsbury, *Anti-Slavery Apostles*, 130–32, 146–48, 265–72, 276, 281–82, 308–17.

41. Pillsbury, *Anti-Slavery Apostles*, 146, 204–5, 276, 288. See Acts. 6–7 for the New Testament account of Stephen's stoning.

42. Pillsbury, *Anti-Slavery Apostles*, 143, 145, 272–73, 276–78, 280, 299.

43. Pillsbury, *Anti-Slavery Apostles*, 145, 156, 279, 292, 322.

44. Pillsbury, *Anti-Slavery Apostles*, 52–60, 71. For a scholarly analysis of abolitionist perceptions of southern slavery and sexual immorality, see Walters, *The Antislavery Appeal*, chap. 5.

45. Pillsbury, *Anti-Slavery Apostles*, 18, 237–40, 331; Henry Wilson, *History of the Rise and Fall of the Slave Power in America*, 3 vols. (Boston: J. R. Osgood and Company, 1872–1877), 1:492–94.

46. Pillsbury, *Anti-Slavery Apostles*, 331–32.

47. Pillsbury, *Anti-Slavery Apostles*, 237, 240.

48. Pillsbury, *Anti-Slavery Apostles*, 237, 481–82.

49. Pillsbury, *Anti-Slavery Apostles*, 237, 325–26, 366–67, 482, 484.

50. Pillsbury, *Anti-Slavery Apostles*, 72, 77, 80–81, 156, 252, 288–91, 361, 366.

51. Pillsbury, *Anti-Slavery Apostles*, 296–97, chaps. 14–15.

52. Pillsbury, *Anti-Slavery Apostles*, 70–71, 82, 104, 207–8, 366, 374, 378–81, 479.

53. Pillsbury, *Anti-Slavery Apostles*, 113, 296, 364, 380, 393.

54. Pillsbury, *Anti-Slavery Apostles*, 77, 283–323, 462, 479–90.

55. Pillsbury, *Ecclesiastical vs. Civil Authority*, 14, the third edition of which appeared in 1894. On the National Reform Association, see Gaines M. Foster, *Moral Reconstruction: Christian Lobbyists and the Federal Legislation of Morality, 1865–1920* (Chapel Hill: University of North Carolina Press, 2002).

56. Parker Pillsbury, *Things New and Old: A Discourse Delivered in Sundry Places* (Concord, NH: The Republican Press Association, 1893), 16, 10, 14. For Pillsbury's criticisms of postbellum economic developments, see his *Plague and Peril of Monopoly: A Lecture on Labor, Laborers, and Employers, Delivered in Lynn, Salem, Haverhill, and Georgetown, Mass., in the Autumn of 1882* (Concord, NH: Republican Press Association, 1887).

57. Parker Pillsbury, *The Church as It Is; or, The Forlorn Hope of Slavery*, rev. ed. (Concord, NH: The Republican Press Association, 1885), 3–4; Parker Pillsbury, *Anti-Slavery Apostles*, 364; James G. Birney, *The American Churches: The Bulwarks of American Slavery*, rev. ed. (Concord, NH: Parker Pillsbury, 1885); Stephen S. Foster, *The Brotherhood of Thieves; or, A True Picture of the American Church and Clergy* (Concord, NH: Parker Pillsbury, 1884). For Pillsbury's references to Birney's and Foster's respective pamphlets, see *Anti-Slavery Apostles*, 120, 127–28, 148, 171, 218, 278–80, 377–78.

58. S. S. Jones, ed., *The Sunday Question, and Self-Contradictions, of the Bible* (Chicago: Religio-Philosophical Publishing House, 1873), iii–iv.

59. Parker Pillsbury, "The Sabbath," in *The Sunday Question*, ed. Jones, 30, 31, 47.

60. H. L. Green, "Parker Pillsbury—A Modern Apostle and His Book," *Free Thought Magazine* 16 (March 1898): 158–59.

61. Parker Pillsbury, *Letter from Mr. Pillsbury to the Editor of the Anti-Slavery Standard* (n.p., 1862).

5. A Tale of Two Slaveries:
Aaron Macy Powell and the Transfiguration of Abolitionism

1. Aaron M. Powell, *Personal Reminiscences of the Anti-Slavery and Other Reforms and Reformers* (Plainfield, NJ: Anna Rice Powell, 1899), 11–12, 16–17; Martha Washing-

ton, *Sojourner Truth's America* (Urbana: University of Illinois Press, 2009), 9, 52–56, 210. For biographical information, Elizabeth Powell Bond's memorial portrait of her brother, in *Personal Reminiscences*, 209–60, still represents the most complete account. Also see *The Philanthropist* 14, no. 3 (July 1899), which dedicated an entire issue to eulogizing the deceased reformer. A brief entry on Powell appears in Rossiter Johnson and John Howard Brown, eds., *The Twentieth Century Biographical Dictionary of Notable Americans*, vol. 8 (Boston: The Biographical Society, 1904); an even briefer one in James Grant Wilson and John Fiske, eds., *Appletons' Cyclopedia of American Biography*, vol. 5 (New York: D. Appleton and Company, 1900). References to Powell's Civil War–era activities occasionally appear in McPherson, *The Struggle for Equality*.

    2. Isaac H. Clothier, "Introduction," in *Personal Reminiscences*, xiv.

    3. In contrast to my interpretation, Jeffrey's *Abolitionists Remember*, 242–45, stresses how a "sense of regret" regarding unfulfilled racial justice in the present characterize Powell's reflections on the antislavery past. On Powell the antivice/antiprostitution reformer, especially see David J. Pivar, *Purity Crusade: Sexual Morality and Social Control, 1868–1900* (Westport, CT: Greenwood, 1973). For other accounts of the social purity movement, see John D'Emilio and Estelle B. Freedman, *Intimate Matters: A History of Sexuality in America*, 3rd ed. (Chicago: University of Chicago Press, 2012), chaps. 7, 9; Alan Hunt, *Governing Morals: A Social History of Moral Regulation* (Cambridge: Cambridge University Press, 1999), chaps. 3–5; Judith R. Walkowitz, *Prostitution and Victorian Society: Woman, Class, and the State* (Cambridge: Cambridge University Press, 1980), part 2.

    4. On Reconstruction-era Black Codes and racial violence, see the sources listed in Chapter 1, n60; and Chapter 3, n31. On the emergence of Jim Crow segregation and discrimination, see Michael Perman, *The Struggle for Mastery: Disfranchisement in the South, 1888–1908* (Chapel Hill: University of North Carolina Press, 2001); John David Smith, "Segregation and the Age of Jim Crow," in *When Did Southern Segregation Begin*, ed. John David Smith (Boston: Bedford/St Martin's, 2002), 1–42; Joel Williamson, *The Crucible of Race: Black-White Relations in the American South since Emancipation* (New York: Oxford University Press, 1984). On racial lynching and the white supremacist myth of the Black rapist, see Paula J. Giddings, *Ida: A Sword among Lions. Ida B. Wells and the Campaign against Lynching* (New York: HarperCollins, 2008); Sandra Gunning, *Race, Rape, and Lynching: The Red Record of American Literature, 1890–1912* (New York: Oxford University Press, 1996); Prince, *Stories of the South*, chap. 6.

    5. "Transcript of Plessy v. Ferguson (1896)," Our Documents: 100 Milestone Documents from the National Archives, https://www.ourdocuments.gov/doc.php?flash=false&doc=52&page=transcript.

    6. "Williams v. State of Mississippi," Legal Information Institute, Cornell University Law School, https://www.law.cornell.edu/supremecourt/text/170/213. On judicial review and the rise of Jim Crow, see, for example, William James Hull Hoffer, *Plessy v. Ferguson: Race and Inequality in Jim Crow America* (Lawrence: University Press of Kansas, 2014); Michael J. Klarman, *From Jim Crow to Civil Rights: The Supreme Court and the Struggle for Racial Equality* (New York: Oxford University Press, 2004).

    7. On the CD Acts and the antiregulation movement, see Hunt, *Governing Morals*; Walkowitz, *Prostitution and Victorian Society*. Also see Josephine E. Butler, *Recollections of George Butler* (Bristol: J. W. Arrowsmith, 1892); Josephine E. Butler, *Personal*

Reminiscences of a Great Crusade (London: Horace Marshall & Son, 1896). In *Laws of the Association for Promoting the Extension of the Contagious Diseases Act of 1866 to the Civil Populations of the United Kingdom* (London: E. Elfick, 1868), proponents of the CD Acts publicized the 1867 founding of a society whose name readily advertised its purpose.

8. Butler, *Personal Reminiscences*, 17–20, which reprints the manifesto; Butler, *Recollections*, 224. My characterizations of an expanding social purity movement additionally draw on sources listed in note 3.

9. Aaron M. Powell, *State Regulation of Vice. Regulation Efforts in America. The Geneva Congress* (New York: Wood & Holbrook, 1878), 42–43; Butler, *Personal Reminiscences*, 108–15, 168–87. On Powell's exposure to and initial involvement with the antiregulationist cause, see Bond, "In Memoriam," in *Personal Reminiscences*, 235–38; Pivar, *Purity Crusade*, 67–72. Gledstone's recollections of the 1876 mission appear in Butler, *Personal Reminiscences*, 214–28, as well as in *The Philanthropist* 12, no. 1 (January 1897). In "The International Federation for the Abolition of State Regulation of Vice," *The Philanthropist* 3, no. 6 (June 1888), Anna Rice Powell examined Butler's role in spearheading a far-reaching movement. For a scholarly account of the multinational scope of Butler's efforts, see Anne Summers, "Which Women? What Europe? Josephine Butler and the International Abolitionist Federation," *History Workshop Journal* 62 (Autumn 2006): 214–31.

10. Butler, *Personal Reminiscences*, 15, for the author's reference to Ephesians 6:13; Powell, *State Regulation of Vice*, 9. For a fuller articulation of Powell's purity philosophy and agenda, see Butler, *Personal Reminiscences*, 11–47, as well as "Fundamental Principles," *The Philanthropist* 7, no. 8 (August 1892).

11. Powell, *Personal Reminiscences*, 3, 10–11, 15, 25–31. Clothier, "Introduction," in *Personal Reminiscences*, vii, xiv, alluded to Powell's original scholastic aspirations; so, too, did the eulogist Hiram Malcolm Jenkins in "Aaron Macy Powell," *Friends Intelligencer* 95 (Fifth Month [May] 20, 1899): 389.

12. Powell, *Personal Reminiscences*, 200–3.

13. Powell, *Personal Reminiscences*, 53–54, 201.

14. Aaron M. Powell, *The Annual Report of the Reform League. Read at Its First Anniversary, Held in Steinway Hall, New York, on Tuesday, May 9, 1871* (New York: Wm. P. Tomlinson, 1871), 5–6, 9, 11, 14, 17–18, 20. The proposed Reform League's mission was announced in the *National Anti-Slavery Standard*, March 5, 1870. As the group mouthpiece, the *National Standard* provides the fullest exposition of its goals and activities. The *New York Times* occasionally covered Reform League events; see, for example, "Caste. The Social Status of the Colored Race—The Subject Considered by the Reform League—Views of Wendell Phillips, Frederick Douglass, and Others," October 11, 1870; "Indian Civilization—Meeting of the Reform League," December 14, 1870; "The Reform League. Proposed Southern Commission—National Education," February 10, 1871; "The Reform League. Views of Wendell Phillips on the Issues of the Day," May 10, 1871; "The Reform League," May 8, 1872.

15. Powell, *The Annual Report of the Reform League*, 6–9.

16. Powell, *The Annual Report of the Reform League*, 4–6, 23; *National Standard*, December 23, 1871. For a succinct scholarly assessment of the Reform League, see McPherson, *The Struggle for Equality*, 430.

17. On the formation of state- and nationwide antiprostitution and antivice associations, see the following *Philanthropist* articles: "The First Decade Meeting," 1, no. 3 (March 1886); "The Social Purity Movement in America," 1, no. 9 (September 1886); "The American Purity Alliance," 10, no. 1 (January 1895). Also see Aaron M. Powell, ed., *The National Purity Congress: Its Papers, Addresses, Portraits* (New York: The American Purity Alliance, 1896).

18. For Powell's antialcohol pamphlets, see *The Relation of the National Government to the Drink-Traffic* (n.p., 1876); *The Beer Question* (New York: National Temperance Society and Publications House, 1881); *The National Government and the Liquor Traffic* (New York: National Temperance Society and publications House, 1882); for antiprostitution ones, see *State Regulation of Vice. Regulation Efforts in America. The Geneva Congress*, which collects three separate paper presentations; *Regulation of Prostitution: An Open Letter to the President of the New York Academy of Medicine* (n.p., 1883); *The State and Prostitution. A Paper Read before the Section of Public Health of the New York Academy of Medicine* (New York: The Philanthropist, 1894). On Powell's involvement in the Chicago-based purity congress, see the following *Philanthropist* articles: "World's Congress on Social Purity," 6, no. 4 (April 1891); "The World's Congress on Social Purity," 8, no. 7 (July 1893); "The World's Congress on Social Purity," 8, no. 8 (August 1893). On his involvement in the Baltimore-based purity congress, see "National Purity Congress," *The Philanthropist* 10, no. 7 (July 1895); Powell, ed., *The National Purity Congress*. Also see the press coverage that the *New York Times* provided: "Purity Congress Meets," October 15, 1895"; "Purity Alliance Work," October 16, 1895; "Friends of Purity Awake," December 10, 1895.

19. *Centennial Anniversary of the Pennsylvania Society, for Promoting the Abolition of Slavery, the Relief of Free Negroes Unlawfully Held in Bondage, and for Improving the Condition of the African Race* (Philadelphia: Grant, Faires & Rodgers, 1875), 69. On the perceived need for moral purity among the freedpeople, see the following *Philanthropist* articles: "The Legacy of Slavery," 3, no. 2 (February 1888); "A Legacy of Immorality," 3, no. 10 (October 1888); "Thirteenth Annual Meeting of the New York Committee. Remarks of Aaron M. Powell," 4, no. 3 (March 1889); "The Immoral Legacy of Slavery," 6, no. 4 (April 1891). On the early activities of the Pennsylvania Abolition Society, see Newman, *The Transformation of American Abolitionism*; Polgar, *Standard-Bearers of Equality*.

20. *Commemoration of the Fiftieth Anniversary of the Organization of the American Anti-Slavery Society in Philadelphia* (Philadelphia: Thos. S. Dando & Co., 1884), 47–48.

21. *Commemoration of the Fiftieth Anniversary*, 48.

22. Powell, *Personal Reminiscences*, 40, 42–45, 47–52.

23. Powell, *Personal Reminiscences*, 31–37; Francis Jackson Garrison and Wendell Phillips Garrison, *William Lloyd Garrison, 1805–1879, The Story of His Life Told by His Children*, 4 vols. (New York: Century Company, 1885–1889).

24. Powell, *Personal Reminiscences*, 21, 31, 37, 47–50.

25. Powell, *Personal Reminiscences*, 41–42, 54.

26. Powell, *Personal Reminiscences*, 42–46, 59–61.

27. Powell, *Personal Reminiscences*, 58–59.

28. Powell, *Personal Reminiscences*, 58–60. In *Recollections*, 265–67, Butler discussed Garrison's Liverpudlian visit. In "William Lloyd Garrison on State Regulation of Vice,"

The Philanthropist 12, no. 3 (July 1898), Powell also reported on Garrison's 1878 homecoming speech.

29. Powell, *Personal Reminiscences*, 60–61.

30. Powell, *Personal Reminiscences*, 62–63.

31. "Fundamental Principles," *Philanthropist* 4; "Nineteenth Annual Meeting," *The Philanthropist* 10, no. 1 (January 1895): 4; Clothier, "Introduction," in *Personal Reminiscences*, xvi–xvii.

32. Powell, *Personal Reminiscences*, 90–94, 96–98. For scholarly accounts, see Aiséirithe and Yacovone, eds., *Wendell Phillips, Social Justice, and the Power of the Past*; Irving Bartlett, *Wendell Phillips: Boston Radical* (Boston: Beacon, 1961); and Stewart, *Wendell Phillips*.

33. Powell, *Personal Reminiscences*, 77–81, 83. A special fundraising edition of the famous speech appeared as the pamphlet *The Freedom Speech of Wendell Phillips. Faneuil Hall, December 8, 1837, with Descriptive Letters from Eye Witnesses* (Boston: Wendell Phillips Hall Association, 1891). On Lovejoy and the Alton riot, see the sources listed in Chapter 1, n33.

34. Powell, *Personal Reminiscences*, 58, 98–102. On the Geneva gathering, see Powell, *State Regulation of Vice*, chap. 3; Butler, *Personal Reminiscences*, chap. 8.

35. Powell, *Personal Reminiscences*, 131–34, 143. For scholarly accounts, see Margaret Hope Bacon, *Valiant Friend: The Life of Lucretia Mott*, new ed. (Philadelphia: Quaker Press of Friends General Conference, 1999); Carol Faulkner, *Lucretia Mott's Heresy: Abolition and Women's Rights in Nineteenth-Century America* (Philadelphia: University of Pennsylvania Press, 2011).

36. Powell, *Personal Reminiscences*, 132–133. On the World Anti-Slavery Convention, see Betty Fladeland, *Men and Brothers: Anglo-American Antislavery Cooperation* (Urbana: University of Illinois Press, 1972), 261–70; Kathyrn Kish Sklar, "'Women Who Speak for an Entire Nation': American and British Women Compared at the World Anti-Slavery Convention, London, 1840," *Pacific Historical Review* 59 (November 1990): 453–99.

37. Powell, *Personal Reminiscences*, 129–30.

38. Powell, *Personal Reminiscences*, 83–84, 134.

39. Powell, *Personal Reminiscences*, 120.

40. Powell, *Personal Reminiscences*, 120–21; Moore, *In Search of White Crows*, chap. 5; Janet Oppenheim, *The Other World: Spiritualism and Psychical Research in England, 1850–1914* (Cambridge: Cambridge University Press, 1985), chaps. 4–6.

41. Powell, *Personal Reminiscences*, 122–23.

42. Powell, *Personal Reminiscences*, 122, 124. See 114–24 for Powell's complete discussion of his antislavery experiences in the Old Northwest.

43. Powell, *Personal Reminiscences*, 140–42.

44. Powell, *Personal Reminiscences*, 155, 158–59.

45. Powell, *Personal Reminiscences*, 142–44, 150–51, 167.

46. "The Responsibilities of Men," *The Philanthropist* 1, no. 5 (May 1886): 4; "Men and Morality," *The Philanthropist* 4, no. 5 (May 1889): 4.

47. Powell, *Personal Reminiscences*, 137, 139–40. On Garrett's Underground Railroad activities, see James A. McGowan, *Station Master on the Underground Railroad: Life and*

Letters of Thomas Garrett, rev. ed. (Jefferson, NC: McFarland, 2005); Priscilla Thompson, "Harriet Tubman, Thomas Garrett, and the Underground Railroad," *Delaware History* 22 (September 1986): 1–21.

48. Powell, *Personal Reminiscences*, 160–63, 165.

49. Powell, *Personal Reminiscences*, 170–71.

50. Powell, *Personal Reminiscences*, 147–48. For a scholarly account, see Margaret Hope Bacon, *But One Race: The Life of Robert Purvis* (Albany: SUNY Press, 2007).

51. Powell, *Personal Reminiscences*, 148.

52. Bond, "In Memoriam," in *Personal Reminiscences*, 218. For Bond's discussion of old abolitionist Aaron, see 218; for temperance Aaron, 228, 230–35, 245–47; and for social purity Aaron, 228–29, 236–45, 247–50, 252–53, 256–58.

53. Powell, *Personal Reminiscences*, 228–30, 258.

54. Powell, *Personal Reminiscences*, 243–44.

55. *The Philanthropist* 15, no. 2 (April 1900): 7.

56. "An Act to further regulate interstate and foreign commerce by prohibiting the transportation therein for immoral purposes of women and girls, and for other purposes," Library of Congress, http://www.loc.gov/law/help/statutes-at-large/61st-congress/session-2/c61s2ch395.pdf. On the white slavery panic among reformers, see Mark Thomas Connelly, *The Response to Prostitution in the Progressive Era* (Chapel Hill: University of North Carolina Press, 1980); Brian Donovan, *White Slave Crusades: Race, Gender, and Anti-Vice Activism, 1887–1917* (Urbana: University of Illinois Press, 2006); D'Emilio and Freedman, *Intimate Matters*, chap. 9; David J. Langum, *Crossing over the Line: Legislating Morality and the Mann Act* (Chicago: University of Chicago Press, 1994). On the neglect of racial justice among reformers, see, for example, David W. Southern, *The Progressive Era and Race: Reaction and Reform, 1900–1917* (Wheeling, IL: Harlan Davidson, 2005).

57. *Old Anti-Slavery Days*, 76.

58. "Thirty-Second Anniversary of the American Anti-Slavery Society," *The Liberator*, June 2, 1865. On the election of 1876, see the sources listed in Chapter 3, n7.

6. Songs of Innocence and Experience:
Thomas Wentworth Higginson and the Abdication of Abolitionism

1. Thomas Wentworth Higginson, *Cheerful Yesterdays* (Boston: Houghton, Mifflin and Co., 1898), 2; Thomas Wentworth Higginson, *Contemporaries* (Boston: Houghton, Mifflin and Co., 1899). For biographical information, Tilden G. Edelstein's *Strange Enthusiasm: A Life of Thomas Wentworth Higginson* (1968; New York: Atheneum, 1970) remains the most thorough and revealing account. Also see Howard N. Meyer, *Colonel of a Black Regiment: The Life of Thomas Wentworth Higginson* (New York: Norton, 1967); Anna Mary Wells, *Dear Preceptor: The Life and Times of Thomas Wentworth Higginson* (Boston: Houghton Mifflin, 1963). For more specialized investigations, see James W. Tuttleton, *Thomas Wentworth Higginson* (Boston: Twayne, 1978), which analyzes Higginson's literary career; Leslie Butler, *Critical Americans: Victorian Intellectuals and Trans-atlantic Liberal Reform* (Chapel Hill: University of North Carolina Press, 2007), which

examines a postbellum Higginson's cultural reformism in conjunction with like-minded men of letters. Still useful is Mary Thacher Higginson, *Thomas Wentworth Higginson: The Story of His Life* (Boston: Houghton Mifflin, 1914), a biography by Higginson's second wife.

2. In contrast to my interpretation, Jeffrey's *Abolitionists Remember*, 248–54, views Higginson's autobiography as an anomaly among the antislavery authors who deployed movement memories on behalf of a more racially just society. Also see W. Scott Poole, "Memory and the Abolitionist Heritage: Thomas Wentworth Higginson and the Uncertain Meaning of the Civil War," *Civil War History*, June 2005, 202–17, which contends that Higginson grew increasingly radical amid mounting Gilded Age conservatism.

3. Regardless of the literary merits of Higginson's autobiographical writings, Lawrence Buell has argued that autobiography generally functioned as an unfulfilled artistic endeavor throughout much of the nineteenth century. Lawrence Buell, "Autobiography in the American Renaissance," in *American Autobiography: Retrospect and Prospect*, ed. Paul John Eakin (Madison: University of Wisconsin Press, 1991), 47–69.

4. Higginson, *Cheerful Yesterdays*, 101–02; Thomas Wentworth Higginson, *The Afternoon Landscape: Poems and Translations* (New York: Longmans, Green, and Co., 1889); Thomas Wentworth Higginson, *Such as They Are: Poems* (Boston: Roberts Brothers, 1893). T. W. Higginson and Mabel Loomis Todd, eds., *Poems by Emily Dickinson*, 2 vols. (Boston: Little, Brown, and Company, 1890–1891). Winifred Mather's *A Bibliography of Thomas Wentworth Higginson* (Cambridge, MA: J. A. Cummins, 1906) represents a convenient starting place to track Higginson's voluminous authorial output. On the Higginson-Dickinson relationship, see Edelstein, *Strange Enthusiasm*, 342–52; Tuttleton, *Thomas Wentworth Higginson*, 143–47; Brenda Wineapple, *White Heat: The Friendship of Emily Dickinson and Thomas Wentworth Higginson* (New York: Knopf, 2008).

5. Higginson, *Cheerful Yesterdays*, 171–72, 183–84, 186; Thomas Wentworth Higginson, "Malbone: An Oldport Romance," *Atlantic Monthly* 23, nos. 1–6 (January–June 1869). On the importance of print culture for the postbellum Higginson, see Butler, *Critical Americans*. On the *Atlantic*'s origins and development, see Ellery Sedgwick, *A History of the 'Atlantic Monthly,' 1857–1909: Yankee Humanism at High Tide and Ebb* (Amherst: University of Massachusetts Press, 1994).

6. Mather, *Bibliography of Thomas Wentworth Higginson*, 28–29.

7. Higginson, *Cheerful Yesterdays*, 87, 90, 92, 97–98, 100–1.

8. Higginson, *Cheerful Yesterdays*, 100, 102–4.

9. Higginson, *Cheerful Yesterdays*, 3–4, 12–16, 69–72, 77. Whereas this analysis explores how the autobiographer romanticized aspects of his life and career, Ethan J. Kytle's *Romantic Reformers and the Antislavery Struggle in the Civil War Era* (New York: Cambridge University Press, 2014), chap. 5, examines the impact of indigenous and external sources of romanticism on Higginson's militant abolitionism of the 1850s. For a fine survey of Transcendentalism, see Philip F. Gura, *American Transcendentalism: A History* (New York: Hill and Wang, 2007).

10. Higginson, *Cheerful Yesterdays*, 79–81, 87–90.

11. Higginson, *Cheerful Yesterdays*, 77–78.

12. Higginson, *Cheerful Yesterdays*, 90–92; Henry David Thoreau, *Walden and Resistance to Civil Government*, ed. William Rossi, 2nd ed. (New York: Norton, 1992), 61; Laura Dassow Walls, *Henry David Thoreau: A Life* (Chicago: University of Chicago Press, 2017), chap. 8.

13. Higginson, *Cheerful Yesterdays*, 16, 97–98. On divinity-school Higginson, see Edelstein, *Strange Enthusiasm*, chap. 5.

14. Higginson, *Cheerful Yesterdays*, 112–14, 119, 128; Walls, *Henry David Thoreau*, chap. 6. On Higginson's Newburyport pastorate, see Edelstein, *Strange Enthusiasm*, 69–95.

15. Higginson, *Cheerful Yesterdays*, 126, 131. On the Fugitive Slave Law and popular opposition to it, see the sources listed in Chapter 1, n37; on abolitionism and violent means, see Chapter 1, n38.

16. Higginson, *Cheerful Yesterdays*, 132, 135–38, 141. Among the "New Romantic" activists at the center of Kytle's *Romantic Reformers*, Higginson serves as a prime example of how second-wave abolitionists broke away from the original strategies and tactics of first-wave counterparts who had launched the immediate emancipation campaign.

17. Higginson, *Cheerful Yesterdays*, 139–40.

18. Higginson, *Cheerful Yesterdays*, 140–45; Thomas Wentworth Higginson, "Remarks of Colonel Higginson," in *The Memoir of Dr. Samuel Gridley Howe. By Julia Ward Howe: with Other Memorial Tributes* (Boston: The Howe Memorial Committee, 1876), 122; Thomas Wentworth Higginson, "Dr. Howe's Anti-Slavery Career," in *Contemporaries*, 300.

19. Higginson, *Cheerful Yesterdays*, 146–54. On Higginson's Worcester pastorate, see Edelstein, *Strange Enthusiasm*, 129–205.

20. Higginson, *Cheerful Yesterdays*, 155.

21. Higginson, *Cheerful Yesterdays*, 152–55, 157–58. On Lewis Hayden's activism, see Kantrowitz, *More Than Freedom*.

22. Higginson, *Cheerful Yesterdays*, 160–62, 166. Regarding Higginson's radical, as opposed to romantic, response to Anthony Burns's rendition, see his *Massachusetts in Mourning: A Sermon in Worcester, on Sunday, June 14th* (Boston: James Munroe and Company, 1854). On his anti–Fugitive Slave Law activities, see Edelstein, *Strange Enthusiasm*, 110–19, 154–74; Meyer, *Colonel of the Black Regiment*, chaps. 11, 13. Also see Albert J. Von Frank, *The Trials of Anthony Burns: Freedom and Slavery in Emerson's Boston* (Cambridge, MA: Harvard University Press, 1998).

23. "Kansas-Nebraska Act (1854)," Our Documents: 100 Milestone Documents from the National Archives, https://www.ourdocuments.gov/doc.php?flash=false&doc=28. For scholarly accounts, see Jonathan Earle and Diane Mutti Burke, eds., *Bleeding Kansas, Bleeding Missouri: The Long Civil War on the Border* (Lawrence: University Press of Kansas, 2013); Nicole Etcheson, *Bleeding Kansas: Contested Liberty in the Civil War Era* (Lawrence: University Press of Kansas, 2004); James Rawley, *Race and Politics: "Bleeding Kansas" and the Coming of the Civil War* (Philadelphia: J. B. Lippincott, 1969).

24. Higginson, *Cheerful Yesterdays*, 197–200.

25. Higginson, *Cheerful Yesterdays*, 201–2.

26. Higginson, *Cheerful Yesterdays*, 210–12.

27. Higginson, *Cheerful Yesterdays*, 14, 210–12; Thomas Wentworth Higginson, "A Ride through Kanzas," in *The Magnificent Activist: The Writings of Thomas Wentworth Higginson, 1823–1911*, ed. Howard N. Meyer (New York: Da Capo, 2000), 74–100, which reproduces the *Tribune* letters that additionally appeared as a standalone tract.

28. Higginson, *Cheerful Yesterdays*, 205, 214. On Higginson's Kansas adventures, see Edelstein, *Strange Enthusiasm*, 182–92; Meyer, *The Colonel of the Black Regiment*, chaps. 17–18.

29. Higginson, *Cheerful Yesterdays*, 217–18, 220–21. For scholarly accounts of Brown, see the sources listed in Chapter 1, n27. On Higginson's Secret Six involvement, see Edelstein, *Strange Enthusiasm*, 204–36; Ethan J. Kytle, "'A Transcendentalist above All': Thomas Wentworth Higginson, John Brown, and the Raid at Harpers Ferry," *Journal of the Historical Society* 12, no. 3 (September 2012): 283–308; Ethan J. Kytle, *Romantic Reformers*, 225–35; Meyer, *Colonel of the Black Regiment*, 139–48; Renehan, *The Secret Six*.

30. Higginson, *Cheerful Yesterdays*, 219.

31. Higginson, *Cheerful Yesterdays*, 220–21.

32. Higginson, *Cheerful Yesterdays*, 222–23.

33. Higginson, *Cheerful Yesterdays*, 223. For very different accounts of Higginson's reactions to the Harpers Ferry news, see Edelstein, *Strange Enthusiasm*, 221; Kytle, "'A Transcendentalist above All,'" 300.

34. Higginson, *Cheerful Yesterdays*, 224–25. See, for example, Edelstein, *Strange Enthusiasm*, 213–26; Tilden G. Edelstein, "John Brown and His Friends," in *The Abolitionists: Immediatism and the Question of Means*, ed. Hugh Hawkins (Boston: D.C. Heath and Co., 1964), 71–79.

35. Thomas Wentworth Higginson, "John Brown," in *Appletons' Cyclopædia of American Biography*, ed. James Grant Wilson and John Fiske (New York: D. Appleton and Co., 1888), 1:405–6; Higginson, *Cheerful Yesterdays*, 207–08; Thomas Wentworth Higginson, "John Brown at Osawotamie," *Alexander's Magazine* 2 (August 1906): 23–26.

36. Higginson, "John Brown," 406; Higginson, *Cheerful Yesterdays*, 220–21; Higginson, "John Brown at Osawotamie," 25.

37. Higginson, "John Brown," 406–7.

38. Higginson, "John Brown," 406–7; Higginson, "John Brown at Osawotamie," 25–26.

39. Higginson, *Cheerful Yesterdays*, 229; Higginson, "John Brown," 406–7; Higginson, "John Brown at Osawotamie," 23. Higginson, in *Young Folks' History of the United States* (Boston: Lee and Shephard, 1875), 283–84, 286–89, highlighted Brown's historical significance without negatively addressing his mental state. For a positive assessment of Higginson's common-school textbook, see Yacovone, *Teaching White Supremacy*, 134–38. For scholarly discussions of Brown's memory in American culture, see the sources listed in Chapter 1, n31.

40. Higginson, *Cheerful Yesterdays*, 251–52, 266; Thomas Wentworth Higginson, *Army Life in a Black Regiment*, intro. Howard N. Meyer (1869; New York: Norton, 1984), 29. On Higginson's Civil War activities, see Edelstein, *Strange Enthusiasm*, chaps. 14–16; Kytle, *Romantic Reformers*, 235–50; Meyer, *Colonel of the Black Regiment*, chaps. 25–27.

Also see Kytle, "'A Transcendentalist above All,'" for an insightful discussion of how Higginson executed Harpers Ferry tasks during the Civil War.

41. Higginson, *Cheerful Yesterdays*, 249, 254, 257, 259–63, 266–67. Higginson previously defended the manliness of enslaved men in a series of *Atlantic Monthly* essays: "Maroons of Jamaica," 5 (February 1860): 213–22; "Maroons of Surinam," 5 (May 1860): 549–57; "Denmark Vesey," 8 (June 1861): 728–44; "Nat Turner's Insurrection," 8 (August 1861): 173–87; "Gabriel's Defeat," 10 (September 1862): 337–45, all of which he republished in *Travelers and Outlaws: Episodes in American History* (Boston: Lee and Shepard, 1888).

42. Higginson, *Cheerful Yesterdays*, 256–57.

43. Higginson, *Cheerful Yesterdays*, 254, 269–70.

44. Thomas Wentworth Higginson, "Literature as an Art," *Atlantic Monthly* 20 (December 1867): 745–54, reproduced in *Atlantic Essays* (Boston: Lee and Shepard, 1882), 23–47.

45. Higginson, *Cheerful Yesterdays*, 328; Higginson, *Contemporaries*, 60–71, 108–41. In *John Greenleaf Whittier* (New York: The Macmillan Company, 1902), Higginson more fully addressed Whittier's literary career and reformism, largely through quoted letters and some personal commentary.

46. Higginson, *Contemporaries*, 244, 246; Higginson, "Two Anti-Slavery Leaders," *International Review* 9 (1880): 143–48; Higginson, "William Lloyd Garrison," *Atlantic Monthly* 52 (January 1886): 120–28.

47. Higginson, *Contemporaries*, 246–47; Higginson, "Two Anti-Slavery Leaders," 145.

48. Higginson, *Contemporaries*, 245–46; Higginson, "Two Anti-Slavery Leaders," 144–45.

49. Higginson, *Contemporaries*, 245–46; Higginson, "Two Anti-Slavery Leaders," 145.

50. Higginson, *Contemporaries*, 265–69; Thomas Wentworth Higginson, "Wendell Phillips," *The Nation*, February 7, 1884, 116–18. Besides including the *Nation* piece in *Contemporaries*, Higginson utilized it as the basis for a biographical entry in *The Encyclopædia Britannica: A Dictionary of Arts, Sciences, Literature and General Information*, 11th ed. (1899; New York: The Encyclopædia Britannica Company, 1911), 21:407–8.

51. Higginson, *Contemporaries*, 259–60, 264, 268, 272–74; Higginson, "Wendell Phillips," 116, 118.

52. Higginson, *Contemporaries*, 275–78; Higginson, "Wendell Phillips," 118. On Phillips's postbellum humanitarianism, see Aiséirithe and Yacovone, eds., *Wendell Phillips, Social Justice, and the Power of the Past*, chaps. 7–10; Timothy Messer-Kruse, "Eight Hours, Greenbacks, and 'Chinamen': Wendell Phillips, Ira Steward, and the Fate of Labor Reform in Massachusetts," *Labor History* 42 (May 2001): 133–58; Stewart, *Wendell Phillips*, chap. 13; David A. Zonderman, *Uneasy Allies: Working for Labor Reform in Nineteenth-Century Boston* (Amherst: University of Massachusetts Press, 2011), chaps. 3–4.

53. Higginson, *Contemporaries*, 275; Higginson, "Wendell Phillips," 118; Higginson, "Anti-Slavery Days," *The Outlook* 60 (September 3, 1898): 52.

54. Higginson, *Contemporaries*, 275; Higginson, "Wendell Phillips," 118; Higginson, "William Lloyd Garrison," 120. In "Two-Anti-Slavery Leaders," Higginson sternly critiqued Oliver Johnson's partisan biography of Garrison.

55. Higginson, *Contemporaries*, 248–51; Higginson, "William Lloyd Garrison," 121–22, 126; Higginson, "Two Anti-Slavery Leaders," 144.

56. Higginson, *Contemporaries*, 250–53; Higginson, "William Lloyd Garrison," 122–24.

57. Higginson, *Contemporaries*, 253–54; Higginson, "William Lloyd Garrison," 125.

58. Higginson, *Contemporaries*, 254; Higginson, "William Lloyd Garrison," 125.

59. Higginson, *Contemporaries*, 254–56; Higginson, "William Lloyd Garrison," 125, 128.

60. Higginson, *Contemporaries*, 255; Higginson, "William Lloyd Garrison," 125; Higginson, "The Popular Reaction," *The Commonwealth* (Boston), April 29, 1865.

61. "Abolitionists and Mr. Hayes. Letter from Col. T. W. Higginson," *New-York Tribune*, April 28, 1877. On the abolitionist reception of Hayes's southern strategy, see McPherson, "Coercion or Conciliation," 474–97; McPherson, *The Abolitionist Legacy*, chap. 5.

62. "Abolitionists and Mr. Hayes."

63. Thomas Wentworth Higginson, "The Hamburg (S.C.) Massacre," *New York Times*, July 19, 1876; Thomas Wentworth Higginson, "Miss Forten on the Southern Question," *Woman's Journal*, December 30, 1876. On the Hamburg Massacre, see Foner, *Reconstruction*, 570–71; Kantrowitz, *Reconstruction of White Supremacy*, 64–71. On Higginson as a civil-service reformer and good-government advocate, see Butler, *Critical Americans*, 191–208; Edelstein, *Strange Enthusiasm*, 374–81.

64. Thomas Wentworth Higginson, "'Border Ruffianism' in South Carolina," *The Independent* (New York), August 10, 1876; Thomas Wentworth Higginson, "Some War Scenes Revisited," *Atlantic Monthly* 42 (July 1878): 9; Higginson, "Miss Forten on the Southern Question." In that *Atlantic* piece and "The Southern Outlook," *Woman's Journal*, March 16, 1878, Higginson provided a rosy assessment of African American prosperity in the Age of Redemption. In "An Old Abolitionist on the Negro Vote," *New York Evening Post*, September 30, 1885, he attributed declining Black participation in southern politics to "poverty and ignorance," not racial violence and intimidation.

65. *Address of Thomas Wentworth Higginson at the Celebration of the Battle of the Cowpens at Spartanburg, S.C.: May 11, 1881* (Charleston: n.p., 1881), 1.

66. *Address of Thomas Wentworth Higginson*, 3–4.

67. *Address of Thomas Wentworth Higginson*, 3–4.

68. Thomas Wentworth Higginson, *Address on Decoration Day in Sanders Theatre, Harvard Memorial Hall, May 30, 1904* (n.p., 1904); Thomas Wentworth Higginson, *Decoration Day Address at Mount Auburn Cemetery, May 30th, 1870* (Cambridge, MA: n.p., 1870).

69. Higginson, *Address on Decoration Day in Sanders Theatre*, 1.

70. Higginson, *Address on Decoration Day in Sanders Theatre*, 1. On the significance of Civil War appellations, see John M. Coski, "The War between the Names: What Should the American War of 1861 to 1865 Be Called?," *North & South* 8 (January 2006): 62–71; Gaines M. Foster, "What's Not in a Name: The Naming of the American Civil War," *Journal of the Civil War Era* 8 (September 2018): 416–54.

71. Thomas Wentworth Higginson, *The New Revolution: A Speech before the American Anti-Slavery Society, at their Annual Meeting in New York, May 12, 1857* (Boston: R.F. Wallcut, 1857), 5.

72. Higginson, *Cheerful Yesterdays*, 124.

73. Higginson, *Cheerful Yesterdays*, 117, 122.

74. Higginson, *Cheerful Yesterdays*, 117–19.

75. Higginson, *Cheerful Yesterdays*, 289–91; Thomas Wentworth Higginson, "The Eccentricities of Reformers," *The Outlook* 62 (July 1899): 510–17; George du Maurier, *Trilby*, intro. Elaine Showalter (Oxford: Oxford University Press, 2009). For scholarly assessments, see Simon Cooke and Paul Goldman, eds., *George Du Maurier: Illustrator, Author, Critic* (London: Routledge, 2016).

76. Higginson, *Contemporaries*, 329, 332–36; Higginson, "The Eccentricities of Reformers," 510–12.

77. Higginson, *Contemporaries*, 330–33, 336; Higginson, "The Eccentricities of Reformers," 510–12.

78. Higginson, *Contemporaries*, 339–44; Higginson, "The Eccentricities of Reformers," 513–16.

79. Higginson, "Anti-Slavery Days," 47–50, 55.

80. Higginson, "Anti-Slavery Days," 49–50, 52–55. Whereas the postbellum Higginson acknowledged the existence of small numbers of humane slaveholders, he made no such concession before the Civil War. See, for example, his tract *Does Slavery Christianize the Negro?* (New York: American Anti-Slavery Society, 1855), 1–7.

81. Thomas Wentworth Higginson, *Reasons for Voting for Bryan* (n.p., 1900), which originally appeared in the *Springfield Daily Republican* (Massachusetts) on September 1, 1900.

82. On the Spanish-American War's impact on Higginson, see Butler, *Critical Americans*, chap. 6; Edelstein, *Strange Enthusiasm*, 384–90. On the relationship between anti-imperialism and racial egalitarianism among former abolitionists and their descendants, see McPherson, *The Abolitionist Legacy*, chap. 17. For a general account, see Paul A. Kramer, *The Blood of Government: Race, Empire, the United States and the Philippines* (Chapel Hill: University of North Carolina Press, 2006).

83. Thomas Wentworth Higginson, "The Case of the Carpet-Baggers," *The Nation*, March 2, 1899, 162–63. In "Who Is Responsible for the Carpet-Baggers?," *The Independent* (New York), February 12, 1874, Higginson provided an earlier defense of white northerners who relocated southward during and after the Civil War. In *Stories of the South*, chap. 2, Prince skillfully analyzed the symbolic power of carpetbagger stereotypes. McPherson, in *The Abolitionist Legacy*, 333–37, contended that many former abolitionists (including Higginson) and their neoabolitionist descendants launched a defense of Radical Reconstruction at the turn of the century.

84. *Boston Evening Transcript*, March 10, 1899, parts of which are reproduced as "Southern Barbarity," in Meyer, ed., *Magnificent Activist*, 136–37.

85. Thomas Wentworth Higginson, William Lloyd Garrison Jr., and George S. Boutwell, *How Should a Colored Man Vote in 1900* (n.p., 1900), 2–3, which originally appeared in the *Boston Herald*, October 11, 1900.

86. Higginson, Garrison Jr., and Boutwell, *How Should a Colored Man Vote in 1900*, 3–4.

87. Higginson, *Address on Decoration Day in Sanders Theatre*; Higginson, *Decoration Day Address at Mount Auburn Cemetery*.

88. Thomas Wentworth Higginson, "'Intensely Human,'" *Atlantic Monthly* 93 (May 1904): 589–92, reproduced in *Part of a Man's Life* (Boston: Houghton, Mifflin and Co., 1905), chap. 6. On the place of cultivation in Higginson's thought, see Butler, *Critical Americans*, chap. 4. On racial thought in the nineteenth-century United States, see the sources listed in Chapter 1, n50. Also see McPherson, *The Struggle for Equality*, chap. 6; McPherson, *The Abolitionist Legacy*, chap. 18, which concerns the racial views of old/new abolitionists amid an upsurge of scientific racism.

89. Higginson, "'Intensely Human,'" 590–92. On anti-Black violence in the New South, see the sources listed in Chapter 5, n4.

90. Higginson, "'Intensely Human,'" 590, 596.

91. Higginson, "'Intensely Human,'" 596; Thacher Higginson, *Thomas Wentworth Higginson*, 364–66; Booker T. Washington, *Up from Slavery: An Autobiography* (New York: The Association Press, 1901). On Higginson's Washingtonian support, see Edelstein, *Strange Enthusiasm*, 389–91. On Washington's educational mission and approach to race relations, see, for example, Robert J. Norrell, *Up from History: The Life of Booker T. Washington* (Cambridge: MA: Belknap, 2009). On the erection of voting barriers to curtail Black voting rights, see J. Morgan Kousser, *The Shaping of Southern Politics: Suffrage Restriction and the Establishment of the One-Party South, 1880–1910* (New Haven, CT: Yale University Press, 1974); Perman, *Struggle for Mastery*.

92. "Balk at Negro Conference. Some of Those Invited Disapprove of the Project," *The Sun*, May 30, 1909.

93. "Balk at Negro Conference." My usage of "nadir" is inspired by Rayford Logan's *The Negro in American Life and Thought: The Nadir, 1877–1901* (New York: Dial, 1954), which he later enlarged and retitled. See Mark Elliott's excellent study *Color-Blind Justice: Albion Tourgée and the Quest for Racial Equality from the Civil War to* Plessy v. Ferguson (New York: Oxford University Press, 2006), for an interesting counterpoint to Higginson's postbellum career. On the NAACP as a neoabolitionist organization, see McPherson, *The Abolitionist Legacy*, chap. 20.

94. "Speech of Rev. Mr. Higginson," *The Liberator*, June 8, 1855.

95. Thomas Wentworth Higginson, "The Next Great Question," *The Independent* (New York), November 12, 1868; Thomas Wentworth Higginson, "A Plea for Culture," *Atlantic Monthly* 19 (January 1867): 33, 36, reproduced in *Atlantic Essays*, 1–22.

7. What Was Antislavery For? From the Disbandment of the AASS to the Determination of Abolitionist Women

1. "American Anti-Slavery Society—Commemorative Meeting," *National Anti-Slavery Standard*, April 16, 1870.

2. "American Anti-Slavery Society—Commemorative Meeting."

3. "American Anti-Slavery Society—Commemorative Meeting."

4. "American Anti-Slavery Society—Commemorative Meeting"; Wendell Phillips, "The Fulfillment of Our Pledge," *National Anti-Slavery Standard*, April 16, 1870.

5. In "'Iconoclasm Has Had Its Day': Abolitionists and Freedmen in South Carolina," in *The Antislavery Vanguard: New Essays on the Abolitionists*, ed. Martin Duberman

(Princeton, NJ: Princeton University Press, 1965), 178–205, Willie Lee Rose similarly observed that "the cause of the freedman never equaled the cause of the slave" among veteran abolitionists.

6. "Commemorative Social Reunion," *National Anti-Slavery Standard*, March 5–26, 1870.

7. "The Standard—1870–1871," *National Anti-Slavery Standard*, March 5–26, 1870.

8. "American Anti-Slavery Society—Commemorative Meeting."

9. "American Anti-Slavery Society—Commemorative Meeting."

10. "American Anti-Slavery Society—Commemorative Meeting."

11. "American Anti-Slavery Society—Commemorative Meeting."

12. "American Anti-Slavery Society—Commemorative Meeting." For a scholarly version of Foster's reminders to fellow activists, see Merton Dillon, "The Failure of the American Abolitionists," *Journal of Southern History* 25 (May 1959): 159–77.

13. "American Anti-Slavery Society—Commemorative Meeting."

14. Douglass, *Life and Times of Frederick Douglass*, 506, 649–52, 671, 721.

15. Douglass, *Life and Times of Frederick Douglass*, 566–74.

16. Douglass, *Life and Times of Frederick Douglass*, 554. On the Douglass-Collins relationship, see 267–69, 280–83; for a scholarly treatment, see Blight, *Frederick Douglass*, 106–7, 109–11, 128–29.

17. Douglass, *Life and Times of Frederick Douglass*, 459–60.

18. Elizabeth Buffum Chace, *Anti-Slavery Reminiscences* (Central Falls, RI: E. L. Freeman & Son, 1891); Lucy N. Colman, *Reminiscences* (Buffalo, NY: H. L. Green, Publisher, 1891). For contrary readings of the Chace and Colman texts, see Jeffrey, *Abolitionists Remember*, 233–42.

19. Chace, *Anti-Slavery Reminiscences*, 5–10.

20. Chace, *Anti-Slavery Reminiscences*, 11–12, 23–25, 36, 39, 46.

21. Chace, *Anti-Slavery Reminiscences*, 26–40. For scholarly accounts referencing Chace's activism, see Julie Roy Jeffrey, *The Great Silent Army of Abolitionism: Ordinary Women in the Antislavery Movement* (Chapel Hill: University of North Carolina Press, 1998); Deborah Bingham Van Broekhoven, *The Devotion of these Women: Rhode Island in the Antislavery Network* (Amherst: University of Massachusetts Press, 2002). The fullest account, consisting of personal letters, extracts of speeches and publications, and editorial commentary, is Lillie Buffum Chace Wyman and Arthur Crawford Wyman, *Elizabeth Buffum Chace, 1806–1899: Her Life and Its Environment*, 2 vols. (Boston: W. B. Clarke Co., 1914).

22. Chace, *Anti-Slavery Reminiscences*, 11–15, 18–22.

23. Chace, *Anti-Slavery Reminiscences*, 15–18, 44–45.

24. Chace, *Anti-Slavery Reminiscences*, 44–46.

25. Chace, *Anti-Slavery Reminiscences*, 4, 46–47, *Old Anti-Slavery Days*, 72.

26. Chace, *Anti-Slavery Reminiscences*, 47; Wyman and Wyman, *Elizabeth Buffum Chace*, 1:308–10, 318–21, 324; 2:132, 176, 183, 191. In "Anti-Slavery Education," *The Philanthropist* 6, no. 7 (July 1891), Aaron Macy Powell advertised Chace's remembrances, mentioning that that postemancipation abolitionist had dedicated herself to women's rights *and* social purity.

27. Colman, *Reminiscences*, 51. For scholarly accounts referencing Colman's activism, see Hewitt, *Radical Friend*; Jeffrey, *The Great Silent Army of Abolitionism*.

28. Colman, *Reminiscences*, 5–12, 22–41, 43–48. On Bruno's cosmology and execution, see Alberto A. Martinez, *Burned Alive: Giordano Bruno, Galileo, and the Inquisition* (London: Reaktion, 2018).

29. Colman, *Reminiscences*, 23–25, 30, 45–46.

30. Colman, *Reminiscences*, 32–34, 38–41.

31. Colman, *Reminiscences*, 48–49.

32. Colman, *Reminiscences*, 12, 16, 40–41, 44–45, 53, 70–71.

33. Colman, *Reminiscences*, 56–58.

34. Colman, *Reminiscences*, 11, 25–28, 41, 80. For information about Colman's favorite freethought periodical, see Roderick Bradford, *D. M. Bennett, the Truth Seeker* (New York: Prometheus, 2006).

35. Colman, *Reminiscences*, 25, 80–81. On the Liberal League's founding and principles, see *Equal Rights in Religion. Report of the Centennial Congress of Liberals, and Organization of the National Liberal League, at Philadelphia, on the Fourth of July, 1876* (Boston: National Liberal League, 1876). On the Liberal League's involvement of other veteran abolitionists, see Goodheart, *Abolitionist, Actuary, Atheist*, chap. 12; Robertson, *Parker Pillsbury*, 168–70. On Comstock and the antivice campaign that he headed, see, for example, Amy Werbel, *Lust on Trial: Censorship and the Rise of American Obscenity in the Age of Anthony Comstock* (New York: Columbia University Press, 2018).

36. Colman, *Reminiscences*, 60–67.

37. Colman, *Reminiscences*, 35, 66–68, 79. For a scholarly treatment of Truth's White House visits, see Washington, *Sojourner Truth's America*, 313–14, 323–24. Lerone Bennett Jr., in *Forced into Glory: Abraham Lincoln's White Dream*, 3rd ed. (Chicago: Johnson, 2000), made similar arguments about Lincoln's limitations.

38. Sarah H. Southwick, *Reminiscences of Early Anti-Slavery Days* (Cambridge, MA: Riverside Press, 1893), 5–9, 11–14, 36–37.

39. Southwick, *Reminiscences of Early Anti-Slavery Days*, 10, 17–18, 20–31.

40. Southwick, *Reminiscences of Early Anti-Slavery Days*, 38–39; *Old Anti-Slavery Days*, 56–58. In *Abolitionists Remember*, 226, 233, 234, Jeffrey generally references Southwick's publication.

41. Laura S. Haviland, *A Woman's Life-Work: Labors and Experiences* (Cincinnati: Walden & Stowe, 1881); Laura S. Haviland, *A Woman's Life Work: Including Thirty Years' Service on the Underground Railroad and in the War*, 5th ed. (Grand Rapids, MI: S. B. Shaw, 1897), 32, 155, 160–61, 208, 515, 555. For Haviland's repeated references to Coffin, see 97, 106, 110, 111, 112, 117, 125, 126, 127, 129, 132, 136, 140, 141, 144, 160, 167, 215, 216, 235, 237, 434, 450, 467, 468. In *Reminiscences*, 150, 151, 217, 218, 220, 221, 222, 386, Coffin mentioned Haviland. For scholarly information, see Anthony Patrick Glesner, "Laura Haviland: Neglected Heroine of the Underground Railroad," *Michigan Historical Review* 21, no. 1 (Spring 1995): 19–48; Tiya Miles, "'Shall Woman's Voice Be Hushed?': Laura Smith Haviland in Abolitionist Women's History," *Michigan Historical Review* 39, no. 2 (Fall 2013): 1–20; Robertson, *Hearts Beating for Liberty*, 164, 167, 170, 172, 181–82, 202–3. Charles Lindquist, *The Antislavery Underground Railroad Movement in Lenawee County,*

Michigan, 1830–1860 (Adrian, MI: Lenawee County Historical Society, 1999), also contains useful information. Rob S. Cox, "Finding Aid for Harriet deGarmo Fuller Papers, 1852–1857," William L. Clements Library, University of Michigan, https://quod.lib.umich .edu/c/clementsmss/umich-wcl-M-3210.1ful, establishes basic facts about the Michigan Anti-Slavery Society.

42. Haviland, *A Woman's Life-Work*, 5th ed., 9–10, 15–28.

43. Haviland, *A Woman's Life-Work*, 5th ed., 13–14. For scholarly information, see Thomas P. Slaughter, *The Beautiful Soul of John Woolman, Apostle of Abolition* (New York: Hill and Wang, 2008).

44. Haviland, *A Woman's Life-Work*, 5th ed., 32–34, 144. On Chandler and the Logan Female Anti-Slavery Society, see Benjamin Lundy, *The Poetical Works of Elizabeth Margaret Chandler with a Memoir of Her Life and Character* (Philadelphia: T. E. Chapman, 1845), 40–41; Merton L. Dillon, "Elizabeth Chandler and the Spread of Antislavery Sentiment to Michigan," *Michigan History* 39 (December 1955), 481–94.

45. Haviland, *A Woman's Life-Work*, 5th ed., chaps. 3–15, 18–19.

46. Haviland, *A Woman's Life-Work*, 5th ed., 232, 241, 243, 286–311, 360, 387–88, 392, 400, 442–43.

47. Haviland, *A Woman's Life-Work*, 5th ed., 482, 490.

48. Haviland, *A Woman's Life-Work*, 5th ed., 482–89, 491–94, 496–98, 500–10. On the Exodusters, see the sources listed in Chapter 2, n49.

49. Haviland, *A Woman's Life-Work*, 5th ed., 511, 539, 555. Even though the fifth edition consists of twenty-six chapters, its table of contents does not reflect the post-1887 changes. Jeffrey's contrary reading of the Haviland text, in *Abolitionists Remember*, 131–35, 142–51, neglects the tone-changing emendations. For an even fuller documentary account by a veteran Black abolitionist, see *Still's Underground Rail Road Records*.

50. Haviland, *A Woman's Life-Work*, 5th ed., 540–44, 553–56. On Willard and the WCTU, see Ruth Bordin, *Frances Willard: A Biography* (Chapel Hill: University of North Carolina Press, 1986); Ian Tyrrell, *Woman's World/Woman's Empire: The Woman's Christian Temperance Union in International Perspective, 1880–1930* (Chapel Hill: University of North Carolina Press, 1991).

51. Haviland, *A Woman's Life-Work*, 5th ed., 561–68.

52. Haviland, *A Woman's Life-Work*, 5th ed., 1, 562–63.

53. Haviland, *A Woman's Life-Work*, 5th ed., 9, 34, 142, 166, 481.

54. Haviland, *A Woman's Life-Work*, 5th ed., 611–12, 615, 618–20.

55. Haviland, *A Woman's Life-Work*, 5th ed., chaps. 16–17, 20, 22–23; quotations on 569. On the Raisin Institute, see 34–37, 544–53. On interracial and coeducational Oberlin, see Kornblith and Lasser, *Elusive Utopia*, chaps. 1, 3; Morris, *Oberlin, Hotbed of Abolitionism*, chaps. 1–2.

56. Haviland, *A Woman's Life-Work*, 5th ed., 481, 569.

57. Haviland, *A Woman's Life-Work*, 5th ed., chap. 24; quotations on 610, 611, 612.

58. Haviland, *A Woman's Life-Work*, 5th ed., 510, 541, 546, 553–54. For the Garrison original, see "To the Public," *The Liberator*, January 1, 1831.

Coda: Complicated Legacies

1. "Thirty-Second Anniversary," May 26.

2. For recent considerations of abolitionism's meaning and legacy, see Andrew Delbanco et al., *The Abolitionist Imagination* (Cambridge, MA: Harvard University Press, 2012); Stanley Harrold, "Morality, Violence, and Perceptions of Abolitionist Failure from before the Civil War to the Present," in *Democracy and the Civil War: Race and African Americans in the Nineteenth Century*, ed. Kevin Adams and Leonne Hudson (Kent, OH: Kent State University Press, 2016), 6–26; James Brewer Stewart, ed., *William Lloyd Garrison at Two Hundred* (New Haven, CT: Yale University Press, 2008). On a very different Black abolitionist heritage, see Greenidge, *The Grimke Family*; Keith P. Griffler, *The Freedom Movement's Lost Legacy: Black Abolitionism since Emancipation* (Lexington: University Press of Kentucky, 2023), which appeared in print as my manuscript headed to the presses.

Index

AASS. *See* American Anti-Slavery Society
abolitionism. *See specific topics*
The Abolitionist Legacy (McPherson), 10
Abolitionists Remember (Jeffrey), 10–11
ACS. *See* American Colonization Society
activism: for antiracism, 4, 12; for antislav-
    ery, 79, 140, 215–16, 236n44; by Brown,
    W. W., 54–55, 219; charity and, 216;
    in Civil War, 138; in Europe, 130; for
    feminism, 206; grassroots, 37, 125–26,
    145–46; for human rights, 77–78; by
    Johnson, O., 73–74; in journalism,
    134–35, 153; against oppression, 142;
    politics of, 138–39; for racial justice,
    61–62; reform and, 94–95, 182; sexism
    in, 147–48; against slavery, 94–95;
    social justice, 12; Society of Friends,
    200; for Underground Railroad, 60; in
    US, 114–15; by white abolitionists, 10;
    women and, 92, 127–28, 195, 209–11
Acts of the Anti-Slavery Apostles (Pills-
    bury), 5, 100, 105, 108, 122–24
Adams, John, 142
AFASS. *See* American and Foreign Anti-
    Slavery Society
Africa, 49–50, 52–54
African Americans: Black community
    organizers and, 1–2, 4; to Brown,
    W. W., 64–65, 194, 239n8; in Canada,
    58; Chinese immigrants and, 137; Civil
    War and, 51, 57–58, 66, 155, 162, 171,
    211–12; in Constitution, 24, 60; in cul-
    ture, 48, 66–67; to Democratic Party,
    186–87; depictions of, 161–63; educa-
    tion of, 4–5, 42–43, 54, 60, 79, 179–80;
    Emancipation Proclamation to, 54–55;
    freedom for, 68–69, 76, 102–3, 117–18,

177–78, 193, 236n50; to Higginson,
    261n64; history of, 39, 58; human rights
    for, 121–22, 124, 187–88; incarceration
    of, 162–63; to Johnson, O., 86–87, 93;
    journalism and, 61; NAACP, 152, 155,
    189, 220; National Colored Orphan
    Asylum, 207; National Negro Con-
    ference, 189–90; neoabolitionism
    for, 10; in politics, 60–63, 178–79;
    prejudice against, 14–15, 35–36, 45–46,
    62–63, 83–84, 148–49; public prejudice
    against, 2–3; racial justice for, 29; rac-
    ism against, 61–62, 119, 149–50, 219–20;
    reform for, 103–4; to Republican
    Party, 126; reputation of, 68, 185–86;
    on slavery, 188–89; social justice for,
    12; stereotypes of, 188–89; suffrage for,
    23, 86, 103, 127–29, 164, 215; tyranny
    to, 211–13; in US, 64; violence against,
    8–9, 31–32, 56–57; voting rights for, 129;
    welfare of, 178; white abolitionists for,
    29, 45; women and, 38, 103, 130, *131–34*,
    134, 141, 205–6
Aguinaldo, Emilio, 185
Alcott, Louisa May, 195
alcohol, 214–18
Allen, Nathaniel, 121
American and Foreign Anti-Slavery Soci-
    ety (AFASS), 90–92
American Anti-Slavery Society (AASS):
    antiracism to, 14; Christianity and, 28;
    after Civil War, 153; culture and, 91–92;
    defectors, 73, 89–91, 98; Douglass and,
    208–9; exponents of, 12; factions from,
    172–73; Garrison and, 21–22, 89, 220,
    232n6, 249n15; history of, 1–9; Johnson,
    O., in, 88; in journalism, 103, 112;

American Anti-Slavery Society (*continued*)
leadership in, 32, 129–30, 146; lectur-
ing circuit, 145; Lincoln and, 105–6;
May in, 24, 33; partisanship in, 16–17;
Phillips, W., and, 191–92; philosophy of, 112–13; politics of, 13, 15–16,
78–79, 95–96, 101, 181; to Powell, A.
M., 125–26, 129–30, *131–34*, 134, 136–37;
racial justice and, 194–201
American Colonization Society (ACS), 25,
28, 53–54, 81, 85, 96
American Peace Society, 30, 32
American Purity Alliance, 135–36, 147
American Women Suffrage Association,
203
Amistad revolt, 58
antebellum abolitionism, 10–11, 13
Anthony, Susan B., 7, 38, 103, 121, 149
anti-abolitionists, 42, 110–11, 120
anti-authoritarianism, 250n31
anti-Blackness, 27, 84–85, 87–88, 185–86,
201–2, 209
anti-imperialism, 262n82
Anti-Imperialist League, 185
antiracism, 4, 12, 14, 87–88, 134–35, 194–95
antislavery. *See specific topics*
The Anti-Slavery Harp (songbook), 46
Anti-Slavery Reminiscences (Chace, E. B.),
7–8, 200
*An Appeal in Favor of That Class of Ameri-
cans Called Africans* (Child), 37
appeasement, 245n35
atonement, 106

Bacon, Leonard, 96, 246n60
Bacon, Leonard Woolsey, 96
Ball, Erica L., 4, 237n2
Banneker, Benjamin, 62–63, 71
Baptists, 109–10, 119–20
Batchelder, James, 162
Battle of Fort Wagner, 171
Beach, Thomas Parnell, 121
Beecher, Lyman, 80–81
Bennett, D. M., 206

BFASS. *See* Boston Female Anti-Slavery
Society
Birney, James G., 89, 122, 175–76, 210
Black Codes, 43, 126
Black community organizers, 1–2, 4
*The Black Man, His Antecedents, His
Genius, and His Achievements* (Brown,
W. W.), 46, 51, 55–57, 62–63, 70
Black people. *See* African Americans
Black refugees, 8
Blight, David, 12
Blum, Edward J., 12
Bond, Elizabeth Powell, 150–51, 251n1
Boston Female Anti-Slavery Society
(BFASS), 8, 208
Boston Vigilance Committee, 160–61
Bourne, George, 95
Bourne, Theodore, 95
Boutwell, George S., 186
Boyer, Jean-Pierre, 58
Brooks, Corey, 229n15
Brown, Erastus, 121
Brown, John: Burns, A., and, 162; financ-
ing for, 29; Fugitive Slave Act and, 155;
Harpers Ferry, 29–31, 165–70, 206;
Higginson and, 259n39; legacy of, 7, 58,
165–70, 182; on trial, 30–31
Brown, William Wells: activism by, 54–55,
219; African Americans to, 64–65,
194, 239n8; Banneker and, 62–63, 71;
on Carthaginians, 48–49; for Christianity, 68–69; Douglass and, 10, 61;
ethics of, 56–57, 69–70; Foster, S. S.,
and, 199; on freedom, 47–48; Garnet
and, 196; Garrison to, 45; legacy of, 38,
119; on Liberia, 53–54; Louverture to,
55–56; oppression to, 67; philanthropy
by, 64; philosophy of, 5–7, 9; poverty
to, 67–68; on racial justice, 46–47; on
racism, 52; on Reconstruction, 60–61;
religion to, 50–51; on slavery, 46–47,
58–59; on violence, 52–53, 65–66; white
abolitionists to, 59–60; women and,
60–61

Browning, Robert, 164
Bruno, Giordano, 204
Bryan, William Jennings, 185
Buell, Lawrence, 257n3
Buffum, Arnold, 8, 199–201
Burleigh, Charles C., 36–38, 104, 121,
    182–83, 196–97, 199–200
Burns, Anthony, 7, 161–62
Burns, Robert, 109
Butler, Benjamin F., 174–75
Butler, Josephine, 128–29, 139–40, 143, 151,
    253n9
Byron, Lord, 109

Calhoun, John, 138
Calvin, John, 22
Calvinism, 176, 206
Canada, 34, 40, 58, 166, 212
capitalism, 36, 122
Carpenter, Joseph, 148–50
Carthaginians, 48–49
Cary, Mary Ann Shadd, 60
caste prejudice, 3, 40, 135, 201
Catholicism, 109, 228n13
Chace, Elizabeth Buffum, 7–8, 200–3, 219,
    264n26
Chace, Samuel Buffington, 199-200
Chandler, Elizabeth Margaret, 210–11
Channing, William Ellery, 19–20
Chapman, Maria Weston, 7, 38, 208
charity, 146–47, 182–83, 216
chastity, 128, 141
Cheerful Yesterdays (Higginson), 5, 154–57,
    159–61, 166, 168, 171–73, 181–83
Child, David Lee, 191–92
Child, Lydia Maria, 7, 37–38, 151, 172,
    191–92, 195, 199
Chinese immigrants, 137, 153
Christianity: AASS and, 28; American,
    190; antislavery and, 193; Brown,
    W. W., for, 68–69; Catholicism and,
    109, 228n13; Civil War and, 98, 104–5;
    to Colman, 203–4; corruption in, 101;
    culture before, 49; ethics of, 19–20, 32,

54, 60, 82–84, 116; evangelicalism in,
    109–10; feminism and, 214–15; to FRA,
    123; to Garrison, 106–7; history of, 115;
    human rights and, 85; to Johnson, O.,
    79–81; journalism and, 93–94, 106, 192;
    philosophy of, 47, 79–80, 114, 120–21;
    politics in, 118–20, 173–74; racial justice
    in, 52; racism in, 201–2; reform in,
    121–22; sects of, 110; slavery and, 115–16,
    249n12; Spiritualism to, 119; in US, 27,
    42, 83, 101–2, 121–22, 204–5; violence
    in, 30–31, 34; WCTU, 214–18; women
    in, 128–29
Christophe, Henri, 55–58
The Church as It Is (Pillsbury), 122
Cinqué, Joseph, 58
citizenship, 23, 86, 179
Civil Rights Act (1866), 127
Civil Rights Act (1875), 102
Civil War: AASS after, 153; activism in, 138;
    African Americans and, 51, 57–58, 66,
    155, 162, 171, 211–12; anti-abolitionists
    after, 120; antiracism after, 88; Chris-
    tianity and, 98, 104–5; culture after,
    69, 105, 126, 172, 178–79, 220, 262n80;
    freedom after, 63; gradualism after,
    87; Grant in, 76–77; Great War and,
    1; Higginson in, 170–71; Lincoln and,
    124, 207; May on, 41–42; NEEAC and,
    163–64; philosophy of, 173, 212; politics
    before, 74; Reconstruction and, 59, 63,
    219; religion and, 83, 173–74; Repub-
    lican Party after, 177; as revolution,
    56; scholarship after, 5; Underground
    Railroad and, 2; US after, 11–12, 23;
    white supremacy after, 9; Women's
    Loyal National League after, 7
Clarke, James Freeman, 159
Clay, Henry, 138
Clothier, Isaac H., 125–26, 141
Coffin, Levi, 210
Coleridge, Samuel Taylor, 157
Collins, John A., 199
Colman, Lucy, 7–8, 203–8, 219

colorblindness, 86–87, 189
colorphobia, 3–4, 27, 85, 118, 149, 188, 201, 203, 209
Confessions of an English Opium Eater (De Quincey), 157
Congregationalism, 113–14, 119–20
Congressional Reconstruction, 28, 70, 74, 135
Congress of Racial Equality, 220
Constitution, US, 1, 24, 60, 102–3, 121–22, 127, 152
Contagious Diseases Acts, 127–28
Contemporaries (Higginson), 5, 154, 161, 172–73, 175, 183, 185
Crandall, Prudence, 6, 38–39, 85
Creole mutiny, 58
culture: AASS and, 91–92; in Africa, 53; African Americans in, 48, 66–67; alcohol in, 214–18; anti-Black bias in, 27, 84–85; antiracism in, 194–95; antislavery in, 78–79; of Canada, 40; before Christianity, 49; after Civil War, 69, 105, 126, 172, 178–79, 220, 262n80; class and, 234n19; education and, 129–30; Emancipation Proclamation in, 98; of France, 175; freedom in, 153; Fugitive Slave Act and, 55, 201, 235n38; Garrison in, 26; of Germany, 37–38; history and, 108–9; inward, 69–70; of Jamaica, 61; with Jim Crow laws, 126–27; Johnson, O., on, 87–88, 92–93; journalism and, 151–52; May and, 232n3; of New York, 148–49; patriarchy in, 96; philosophy and, 192–93; politics and, 74–75, 95–96; progressivism in, 144; racism in, 67–68, 117–18, 212–13; during Reconstruction, 180, 191–92; saintliness in, 82–83; secularism in, 206–7; segregation in, 152; of slavery, 176–77, 181–82; social purity, 150–51; Spiritualism in, 103–4; of Switzerland, 143; of US, 100–1, 112–13, 123–24, 145–46, 163–65, 176–77; violence in, 30–32; women in, 143, 146–47

Dante, 156
Davis, Edward M., 146–47
Declaration of Independence, 8, 35
Delany, Martin Robison, 4–5, 61
democracy, 2, 21, 153
Democratic Party, 9, 75, 161, 179, 186–87, 194, 213
Dessalines, Jean-Jacques, 55–58
Dickinson, Anna, 14–15
Dickinson, Emily, 155
Diggins, John Patrick, 9–10
diversity, 49–50
divine justice, 42
Dominican Republic, 58
Douglass, Frederick: AASS and, 12, 197–98; autobiographies of, 2, 198–99; Brown, W. W., and, 10, 61; to Chace, 200–1; to May, 38, 40–41; to Pillsbury, 119; on racism, 12; Reform League to, 198; to Southwick, 208–9
Dudevant, Amantine-Lucile-Aurore, 156

"The Eccentricities of Reformers" (Higginson), 183
Ecclesiastical vs. Civil Authority (Pillsbury), 121–22
education: of African Americans, 4–5, 42–43, 54, 60, 79, 179–80; for Black girls, 6; Colman on, 204–5; to Crandall, 85; culture and, 129–30; history of, 143–44; philosophy from, 98–99; public, 217; religion and, 114, 210–11; to Smith, G., 28–29; women and, 136, 217
egalitarianism, 194–95
Egypt, 48–49, 239n8
Eighty Years and More (Stanton, E. C.), 7, 103
Eliot, George, 167
elitism, 233n13
Elliot, Robert Brown, 60, 102
Emancipation Proclamation, 12, 17, 36–37, 54–55, 59–60, 98
Emerson, Ralph Waldo, 157–58
environmentalism, 49–50

Episcopalians, 119–20
The Escape (Brown, W. W.), 46
The Estray (Longfellow), 155
ethics: American Purity Alliance, 135–36,
147; of Brown, W. W., 56–57, 69–70; of
Calvinism, 176; in charity, 146–47; of
Christianity, 19–20, 32, 54, 60, 82–84,
116; of Higginson, 162–64; Johnson, O., and, 79–80; May on, 33–34,
37–38; moral agitation, 93; National
Purity Congress for, 136; philosophy
of, 138–39; of Powell, A. M., 146–49;
psychology and, 136–37; of religion, 121;
scholarship on, 139; of slavery, 120–21;
in US, 138
Ethiopia, 48–49, 239n8
eulogies, 112–13, 150–51
Europe: activism in, 130; diversity in,
49–50; history of, 48; racism in, 52–53;
sexism in, 140; US and, 127–28, 172;
women in, 143; World's Anti-Slavery
Convention in, 144
evangelicalism, 79–80, 109–10, 115–16,
244n19

Fall River Female Anti-Slavery Society,
8, 202
feminism, 143–44, 202–3, 206, 214–15. *See
also* women
Fichte, Johann Gottlieb, 156
First South Carolina Volunteers, 166, 170,
179, 189–90
Follen, Charles, 37–38
Forbes, Hugh, 167
Forten, James, 38–40
Foster, Abigail Kelley, 7, 16, 38, 91, 121, 125,
195, 200
Foster, Stephen Symonds, 13–15, 108,
113–17, 125, 184, 197–200
Fourier, Charles, 157
Fox, George, 22
FRA. *See* Free Religious Association
France, 175
Franklin, Benjamin, 60, 62

Franklin, John, 146
freedom: for African Americans, 68–69,
76, 102–3, 117–18, 177–78, 193, 236n50;
antiracism and, 134–35; after Civil War,
63; in culture, 153; to Garrison, 231n24;
philosophy of, 47–48; politics of, 136;
psychology of, 186; of religion, 206–7
Free Religious Association (FRA): anti-
slavery to, 249n11; Christianity to, 123;
missionaries in, 107; philosophy of, 103,
117, 124; Reconstruction to, 111; Republican Party and, 104; Spiritualism to,
121, 193, 247n7
Free-Soil Party, 7, 90, 92, 95–96, 159, 161
Fremont, John C., 105–6
French, John R., 112
Frothingham, Octavius Brooks, 104
Fugitive Slave Act: Brown, J., and, 155;
culture and, 55, 201, 235n38; to Free-
Soil Party, 159; to Higginson, 160, 163;
to May, 33–35; politics of, 7, 33, 58;
Reconstruction and, 67
Furness, William H., 144

Gabriel conspiracy (1800), 58
Garnet, Henry Highland, 61, 196
Garrett, Thomas, 148, 150, 192
Garrison, William Lloyd: AASS and,
21–22, 89, 220, 232n6, 249n15; on
abolitionism, 13; ACS to, 85; anti-Black
bias to, 84–85; antislavery to, 20, 120; to
Brown, W. W., 45; Butler, J., and, 139–
40; Chace, E. B., and, 200–1; Christianity to, 106–7; in culture, 26; Follen and,
37–38; freedom to, 231n24; Higginson
and, 160–61, 172–77; on human rights,
102; to Johnson, O., 72–73, 75–76,
90–91, 95–99; legacy of, 15–16, 74, 78,
92–93, 116, 137, 152, 186, 208; Lincoln
and, 138; May and, 24–25, 27–28, 35–36,
234n17; philosophy of, 5–6, 93–94; to
Pillsbury, 105–8, 193, 247n3; politics of,
12, 15, 21, 83–84; to Powell, A. M., 137–
43; religion to, 79–82, 90–91; Remond,

Garrison, William Lloyd (*continued*)
C. L., and, 13–15; reputation of, 19, 22, 26–27, 100–1, 112, 184–85; Rogers and, 111, 117; violence against, 78–79; white abolitionists and, 89–90
Garrison, William Lloyd, Jr., 186
Geffrard, Fabre, 55, 58
Genius of Universal Emancipation (Lundy), 95, 106, 138, 211
Germany, 37–38, 50
Goodell, William, 47, 175
gradualism, 87, 188
Grant, Ulysses S., 58, 76–77
grassroots activism, 37, 125–26, 145–46
Great War (World War I), 1
Greek War of Independence, 161
Greeley, Horace, 76–77
Green, Beriah, 89
Green, Horace L., 123–24
Greenback Party, 174–75
Grew, Mary, 7, 144, 147, 195, 228n10
Grimes, Leonard, 61
Grimké, Angelina, 7, 121, 208
Grimké, Sarah, 7, 121, 208
Guinea, 52

Haiti, 47–48, 55–58, 67, 240n25
Hamburg Massacre, 178–79
Hancock, John, 142
Harper, Frances Ellen Watkins, 7, 61
Harpers Ferry, 29–31, 165–70, 206. *See also* Brown, John
Harriman, Jesse B., 121
Haviland, Laura Smith, 8–9, 209–19
Hayden, Lewis, 38, 60, 162
Hayes, Rutherford B., 74–76, 178, 198, 245n35
Heine, Heinrich, 156
Henry, William "Jerry," 6, 34–35
Higginson, Thomas Wentworth: African Americans to, 261n64; Brown, J., and, 259n39; Buell on, 257n3; ethics of, 162–64; Garrison and, 160–61, 172–77; on Harpers Ferry, 165–70; militant

abolitionism and, 257n9; racial justice to, 185–90, 257n2; reform to, 256n1; reputation of, 5, 7, 29, 104, 219; retrospective writing by, 154–61, 170–73, 177–85; on stereotypes, 262n83; tactics of, 258n16
History of the Rise and Fall of the Slave Power in America (Wilson), 117
History of Woman Suffrage (Anthony), 7
Holley, Sallie, 7, 38, 121, 195
Holmes, Oliver Wendell, Sr., 155–56
Homer, 156
Howe, Julia Ward, 195
Howe, Samuel Gridley, 29, 161, 166
human rights: for African Americans, 121–22, 124, 187–88; Christianity and, 85; Garrison on, 102; philosophy of, 77–78; to Pillsbury, 123–24; politics of, 105–6; reform and, 142–43; in religion, 109
Hume, David, 51

iconoclasm, 205
immigration, 137, 153
incarceration, 162–63
intellectual history, 231n27
"Intensely Human" (Higginson), 187–88
International Order of Good Templars, 64
international politics, 128–29
inward culture, 69–70

Jamaica, 61
Jay, John, II, 228n13
Jay, William, 89
Jeffrey, Julie Roy, 10–11, 232n3, 247n7, 252n3, 257n2, 264n18, 266n49
Jim Crow laws, 9, 11–12, 17, 126–27, 152, 171
Johnson, Andrew, 23, 43, 208
Johnson, Oliver: in AASS, 88; activism by, 73–74; African Americans to, 86–87, 93; antislavery to, 104; Christianity to, 79–81; on culture, 87–88, 92–93; ethics and, 79–80; Garrison to, 72–73, 75–76, 90–91, 95–99; history to, 82–83;

in journalism, 88–89, 193, 246n57;
McPherson on, 245n35; NEASS to, 85;
philosophy of, 89–90; prejudice to,
94–95; racial justice to, 86; reputation
of, 5–6, 9, 219; retrospective writing
by, 91–92; slavery to, 89; US to, 83–84;
violence to, 77–78; Whedon to, 246
Jones, S. S., 123
journalism: AASS in, 103, 112; for abolitionism, 6; activism in, 134–35, 153;
African Americans and, 61; antislavery
in, 33, 129–30; Christianity and, 93–94,
106, 192; culture and, 151–52; evangelicalism in, 110; Johnson, O., in, 88–89,
193, 246n57; purity in, 150–51; after
Reconstruction, 135–36; religion and,
95, 106–7; retrospective writing and,
31; in US, 108–9; white abolitionists in,
76–77; for women, 151
Julian, George W., 94
Julian, Laura Giddings, 195

Kansas, 97, 162–66, 168–69, 212–13, 215–16
Kansas-Nebraska Act, 163–64
Kingdom of Dahomey, 53
Knights of the White Camelia, 126
Ku Klux Klan, 43, 126, 135

LaCapra, Dominick, 9
Ladies' National Association (LNA),
128
Lafayette, Marquis de, 108
Lamennais, Felicité Robert de, 162–63
Lee, Robert E., 207
Lewis, Edmonia, 60
Lewis, Robert Benjamin, 47
Liberia, 53–54
Liberty Party, 90, 95, 201
Light and Truth (Lewis, R. B.), 47
Lincoln, Abraham: AASS and, 105–6; as-
sassination of, 177; Brown, W. W., on,
51; Civil War and, 124, 207; election
of, 30, 181; Emancipation Proclama-
tion and, 12, 59–60; Garrison and, 138;

legacy of, 98; Republican Party and,
198; US and, 13; white supremacy and,
207–8
LNA. See Ladies' National Association
Loguen, Jermain, 38, 40, 61
Longfellow, Henry Wadsworth, 155
Louisiana White League, 126
Louverture, Toussaint, 55–56
Lovejoy, Elijah, 31–33, 142
Lowell, James Russell, 155–56, 183
Lundy, Benjamin, 95, 138, 149, 175, 200, 211
Luther, Martin, 22

Macaulay, Thomas Babington, 51
"La Madonna di San Sisto" (Higginson),
155
Malbone (Higginson), 156
Mann, James R., 152
Mann Act, 152
Martyr Period, 121
Massachusetts, 116–18
Masur, Kate, 3
maternity, 205–6
du Maurier, George, 183–84
May, Joseph, 26-27
May, Samuel Joseph: in AASS, 24, 33;
antislavery to, 38; on Civil War, 41–42;
Crandall and, 38–39; culture and,
232n3; on ethics, 33–34, 37–38; Forten
and, 39–40; Garrison and, 24–25,
27–28, 35–36, 234n17; for grassroots
activism, 37; Harpers Ferry and, 30–31;
Henry to, 34–35; legacy of, 28–29;
Loguen to, 40; Lovejoy and, 31–32;
memoir of, 19–20, 25–26; philanthropy
by, 22; politics of, 43–44; on racial
justice, 22–23; reputation of, 5–6, 11–12,
194; scholarship on, 24; violence to,
235n38
McDaniel, W. Caleb, 229n15, 233n14
McKenna, Joseph, 127
McKinley, William, 187
McPherson, James, 10, 228n13, 245n35
Memoir of Samuel Joseph May, 25–26

"Memoranda of the Unwritten Chapters,"
130, *131–34*
"Memory as History, Memory as Activism" (Sinha), 11
Methodists, 93, 119–20, 204
Middle Passage, 211
militant abolitionism, 162, 257n9
Mill, John Stuart, 157
Mississippi Rifle Clubs, 126
Missouri, 163
moral agitation, 93
Mott, James, 144, 146
Mott, Lucretia, 7, 38, 104, 143–46, 151, 199
My Southern Home (Brown, W. W.), 5, 46, 63, 67–68, 70

NAACP. *See* National Association for the Advancement of Colored People
Narrative of William W. Brown, a Fugitive Slave (Brown, W. W.), 46
National Association for the Advancement of Colored People (NAACP), 152, 155, 189, 220
National Colored Convention, 1–2
National Colored Orphan Asylum, 207
National Convention of Colored Men, 6–7
National Liberal League, 206–7
National Negro Conference, 189–90
National Purity Congress, 136
National Reform Association (NRA), 121–22
National Women Suffrage Association, 103
NEASS. *See* New England Anti-Slavery Society
Nebraska, 163
NEEAC. *See* New England Emigrant Aid Company
The Negro in the American Rebellion (Brown, W. W.), 46
Nell, William Cooper, 38
New England Anti-Slavery Society (NEASS), 3, 6–8, 85, 200
New England Emigrant Aid Company (NEEAC), 97, 163–64

New England Non-Resistance Society, 106, 111–12
New Hampshire, 108–9, 112, 116
New York, 140–41, 144, 148–49
NRA. *See* National Reform Association

An Old Creed for the New South (Smith, J. D.), 11
oppression, 65–67, 142, 153
orphans, 207, 216
Osborn, Charles, 94–95
Otis, James, 142

pacifism, 20–21
Page, Thomas Nelson, 185–86
Paine, Amorancy, 199
Parker, Theodore, 29, 159, 166
partisanship, 16–17
PAS. *See* Pennsylvania Abolition Society
patriarchy, 39–40, 96, 105
Paul, Susan, 209
Peirce, Sarah H., 147
Pennington, James W. C., 61, 239n10
Pennsylvania Abolition Society (PAS), 136
Personal Reminiscences of the Anti-Slavery and Other Reforms and Reformers (Powell, A. M.), 5, 125
Pétion, Alexandre, 58
PFASS. *See* Philadelphia Female Anti-Slavery Society
Phelps, Amos, 89, 175
Philadelphia Convention, 21
Philadelphia Female Anti-Slavery Society (PFASS), 3, 143, 147
philanthropy, 22, 49, 66
Philippines, 185–86
Phillips, Ann Greene, 142
Phillips, Wendell, 15–16, 141–43, 172, 174–75, 191–92, 199–200
philosophy: of AASS, 112–13; of Brown, W. W., 5–7, 9; of Christianity, 47, 79–80, 114, 120–21; of Civil War, 173, 212; of colorblindness, 86–87; culture and, 192–93; of Democratic Party, 179; from

education, 98–99; egalitarianism, 194–95; of ethics, 138–39; of FRA, 103, 117, 124; of freedom, 47–48; of Garrison, 5–6, 93–94; of government, 180–81; of human rights, 77–78; of Johnson, O., 89–90; of philanthropy, 49; of purity, 90, 107, 126, 129–31, 135–43, 146–53; of reform, 122–23, 183–84; of religion, 51; of retrospective writing, 10, 215–16; of slavery, 119–20; in US, 156–58; of white supremacy, 228n11

Pierce, Esther Carpenter, 147

Pillsbury, Parker: antislavery and, 100–5, 117–24, 247n7; Douglass to, 119; Garrison to, 105–8, 193, 247n3; human rights to, 123–24; religion to, 249n12; Remond, C. L., to, 118; reputation of, 5–6, 9, 184, 219; retrospective writing by, 113–17; on Rogers, 108–13, 250n28

Plessy v. Ferguson, 127

Pocock, J. G. A., 231n27

politics: of AASS, 13, 15–16, 78–79, 95–96, 101, 181; of ACS, 25; of activism, 138–39; of AFASS, 90; African Americans in, 60–63, 178–79; of antislavery, 92–93, 160, 164–65; appeasement in, 245n35; in Christianity, 118–20, 173–74; before Civil War, 74; of Colman, 207–8; in Congress, 40–41; of Contagious Diseases Acts, 127–28; culture and, 74–75, 95–96; of democracy, 153; Emancipation Proclamation in, 36–37; of freedom, 136; Free-Soil Party, 7; of Fugitive Slave Act, 7, 33, 58; of Garrison, 12, 15, 21, 83–84; Greeley in, 76–77; of human rights, 105–6; international, 128–29; of May, 43–44; in New Hampshire, 108; in New York, 140–41; of Non-Resistance Society, 111–12; partisanship in, 16–17; political Abolitionism, 161; populism, 185; prejudice in, 65–66; of progressivism, 3; of racial justice, 177–78; of Reconstruction, 8–9, 23, 66, 118, 123, 127; religion and, 26, 93; of Republican

Party, 73–74, 97; scholarship on, 117; "slaveholding Democracy," 2; slavery in, 11; of Spiritualism, 107–8; of temperance, 214–18; tyranny, 114, 204; in US, 22–23, 243n7

populism, 185

Post, Amy, 7, 195

Post, Joseph, 147

Post, Mary, 147

Potter, William J., 104

poverty, 58–59, 67–68, 158

Powell, Aaron Macy: AASS to, 125–26, 129–30, *131–34*, 134, 136–37; antislavery and, 252n3; on Chace, E. B., 264n26; ethics of, 146–49; Garrison to, 137–43; grassroots activism to, 145–46; racial justice to, 150–53; on reform, 135–36, 195; reputation of, 5–6, 219; retrospective writing by, 127–29; women to, 143–45

Powell, Anna Rice, 136, 253n9

prejudice: against African Americans, 14–15, 35–36, 45–46, 62–63, 83–84, 148–49; anti-Black, 209; caste, 135; to Johnson, O., 94–95; in Massachusetts, 117–18; in politics, 65–66; psychology of, 46–47; public, 2–3; racial justice and, 3–4; racism and, 85; skin color and, 49–50, 149–50; in US, 14

Presbyterians, 119–20

"Presence of God" (Rogers), 109

Prince, K. Stephen, 12

progressivism, 3, 21–22, 144, 219, 228n13

prostitution, 127–29, *131–34*, 135, 151–52

public education, 217

public prejudice, 2–3

Puritans, 110

purity: American Purity Alliance, 135–36, 147; in journalism, 150–51; National Purity Congress, 136; philosophy of, 90, 107, 126, 129–31, 135–43, 146–53; racial justice and, 150; reformation, 147–48; social, 150–51, 264n26

Purvis, Robert, 38, 61, 144, 149–50

Quakerism, 38–39, 81, 94–95, 136, 200–1,
    210–11, 215–16
De Quincey, Thomas, 157
Quincy, Edmund, 112, 175, 199
Quincy, Josiah, 142

racial justice: AASS and, 194–201; activism
    for, 61–62; for African Americans, 29;
    in antebellum era, 16–17; antislavery
    and, 193–94, 201–2, 229n14; Brown,
    W. W., on, 46–47; in Christianity, 52;
    with grassroots activism, 125–26; to
    Higginson, 185–90, 257n2; history of,
    43–44, 48–49; to Johnson, O., 86; May
    on, 22–23; politics of, 177–78; to Powell,
    A. M., 150–53; prejudice and, 3–4;
    purity and, 150; racial egalitarianism,
    262n82; racial essentialism and, 66–67;
    racial rebirth and, 61; religion and, 108;
    to Republican Party, 103; retrospective
    writing on, 122–23; sin and, 27–28; in
    US, 10, 111
racism: in Africa, 53–54; against African
    Americans, 61–62, 119, 149–50, 219–20;
    Brown, W. W., on, 52; in Christianity,
    201–2; in culture, 67–68, 117–18, 212–13;
    Douglass on, 12; environmentalism
    and, 50; in Europe, 52–53; in Philip-
    pines, 186; prejudice and, 85; scholar-
    ship on, 48–50; scientific, 263n88;
    sexism and, 138–39, 207–8; in "slave-
    holding Democracy," 2; slavery and, 39,
    126; in US, 26–28, 41, 124; violence and,
    66, 126; to white abolitionists, 13–14.
    See also specific topics
Radical Reconstruction, 60, 63, 67, 187, 220
Rapier, James T., 102
Reconstruction: Brown, W. W., on, 60–61;
    citizenship in, 179; Civil War and,
    59, 63, 219; Congressional, 70, 74;
    Constitution in, 103; culture during,
    180, 191–92; to Democratic Party, 213;
    to FRA, 111; Fugitive Slave Act and, 67;
    Jim Crow laws during, 11–12; journal-

ism after, 135–36; in literature, 185–86;
    politics of, 8–9, 23, 66, 118, 123, 127;
    Radical, 60, 63; to Republican Party,
    154, 243n7; scholarship on, 5–6
Red Rock (Page), 185–86
reform: activism and, 94–95, 182; for
    African Americans, 103–4; antislavery
    and, 14–15, 19–26, 90; in Christianity,
    121–22; to Douglass, 197–98; to Hig-
    ginson, 256n1; history of, 10, 64, 152–53;
    human rights and, 142–43; in Liberator,
    20; NRA, 121–22; philosophy of, 122–23,
    183–84; Powell, A. M., on, 135–36, 195;
    progressivism and, 228n13; purity
    reformation, 147–48; Reform League,
    130, 135–37, 142, 194–95, 197–98, 253n14;
    in US, 6–7, 72–73
Reid, Whitelaw, 72
religion: anti-abolitionists and, 110–11; to
    Brown, W. W., 50–51; Civil War and, 83,
    173–74; Colman on, 206–7; Congrega-
    tionalism, 113–14, 119–20; divine justice
    in, 42; education and, 114, 210–11; elit-
    ism in, 233n13; ethics of, 121; eulogies
    in, 112–13; evangelicalism, 79–80; FRA,
    103; freedom of, 206–7; to Garrison,
    79–82, 90–91; in Germany, 50; Holy
    Wars, 174–75; human rights in, 109;
    journalism and, 95, 106–7; to May, 23;
    misinformation in, 101; philosophy of,
    51; to Pillsbury, 249n12; politics and,
    26, 93; to Puritans, 110; racial justice
    and, 108; to Republican Party, 86; slav-
    ery and, 114, 119–20; temperance and,
    214–18; in US, 32–33, 98; violence and,
    116. See also specific religions
Reminiscences of Early Anti-Slavery Days
    (Southwick, S. H.), 7–8, 208–9
Remond, Charles Lenox, 13–16, 38, 118,
    149, 200, 219–20
Remond, Sarah Parker, 7, 121, 149
Republican Party: African Americans to,
    126; antislavery to, 98; after Civil War,
    177; Democratic Party and, 9, 75, 194;

FRA and, 104; Free-Soil Party and, 92, 95–96; Hayes to, 76; Liberty Party and, 201; Lincoln and, 198; politics of, 73–74, 97; racial justice to, 103; Reconstruction to, 154, 243n7; religion to, 86; reputation of, 75–76

"Resistance to Civil Government" (Thoreau), 159

retrospective writing: on antislavery, 105–13; by Higginson, 154–61, 170–73, 177–85; history and, 117, 150–51; by Johnson, O., 91–92; journalism and, 31; philosophy of, 10, 215–16; by Pillsbury, 113–17; by Powell, A. M., 127–29; on racial justice, 122–23; revisionism in, 180–81; on Smith, G., 28; on violence, 115

revisionism, 180–81

Revolutionary War, 108

Richter, Johann Paul Friedrich (Jean Paul), 156–58

Right Worthy Grand Lodge of the World, 64

The Rising Son (Brown, W. W.), 5, 45, 47–48, 54, 57–58, 62–63, 67–68

Rogers, Nathaniel Peabody, 108–13, 117, 119, 184, 199, 250n28

Ruggles, David, 38, 61

St. Domingo (Brown, W. W.), 47, 55, 67

Sanborn, Franklin, 29, 166

Sand, George, 156

Savage, Kirk, 12

scientific racism, 263n88

Scott, Orange, 89

Scott, Walter, 109, 164–65, 166–67

Secret Six, 29–30, 161, 166–70

secularism, 206–7

segregation, 152, 171

sexism, 127–28, 138–39, 140, 147–48, 207–8, 264n26

Shakespeare, William, 109

Shaw, Robert Gould, 171

Sierra Leone, 53

Silber, Nina, 12

Sims, Thomas, 160–61

sin, 27–28, 80, 83, 92, 94, 217

Sinha, Manisha, 3, 11

Skinner, Quentin, 231n27

slavery. *See specific topics*

Slavery (Channing), 19–20

Slavery and Anti-Slavery (Goodell), 47

Smith, Gerrit, 7, 28–30, 89, 210

Smith, John David, 11

Snodgrass, Joseph Evans, 16

social justice, 12

social purity, 150–51, 264n26

Society for Psychical Research (SPR), 145

Some Considerations on the Keeping of Negroes (Woolman), 211

Some Recollections of Our Antislavery Conflict (May), 5, 19

South Carolina, 126, 166, 170, 179, 189–90

South Carolina Red Shirts, 126

Southwick, Joseph, 8, 199, 208

Southwick, Sarah H., 7–8, 208–9, 219

Southwick, Thankful, 8, 208

Spanish-American War, 185–86

Spiritualism, 103–4, 107–8, 119, 121, 193, 204, 247n7

SPR. *See* Society for Psychical Research

Stanton, Edwin M., 138

Stanton, Elizabeth Cady, 7, 103

Stanton, Henry Brewster, 7

"State Regulation of Vice" (Powell, A. M.), 139

Stearns, George Luther, 29, 166

stereotypes, 188–89, 262n83

Still, William, 61, 225n2

Stone, Lucy, 7, 121, 200

suffrage: for African Americans, 23, 86, 103, 127–29, 164, 215; women's, 7, 172, 190, 202–3, 205

Sumner, Charles, 102

Switzerland, 143

Tappan, Arthur, 89, 175

Tappan, Cora L. V., 196–97

Tappan, Lewis, 89, 92, 175
Taylor, Percy, 184
temperance, 60, 67, 107, 109, 113, 122, 134–35, 138, 141–43, 214–18
Thayer, Eli, 96–97
Theodore II (emperor), 53
Things New and Old (Pillsbury), 122
Thompson, George, 125, 208
Thoreau, Henry David, 158–59, 171
Thornbury, George Walter, 164
Transcendentalism, 157–59
Truth, Sojourner, 125, 207–8
Tubman, Harriet, 60
Turner, Nat, 58, 67
tyranny, 114, 204, 211–13

Underground Railroad, 2, 6–8, 60, 148, 166, 201, 209–10
Unitarianism, 23, 81, 156, 159, 233n13
United States (US): activism in, 114–15; African Americans in, 64; altruism in, 143, 154; American Peace Society, 30, 32; antislavery in, 35–36; Black refugees in, 8; Canada and, 34, 212; Catholicism in, 228n13; Chinese immigrants in, 137; Christianity in, 27, 42, 83, 101–2, 121–22, 204–5; citizenship in, 23, 86; Civil Rights Act in, 102, 127; after Civil War, 11–12, 23; colonialism by, 58; Constitution, 1, 24, 60, 102–3, 121–22, 127, 152; Contagious Diseases Acts in, 127–28; culture of, 100–1, 112–13, 123–24, 145–46, 163–65, 176–77; democracy in, 21; ethics in, 138; Europe and, 127–28, 172; feminism in, 143–44; Free-Soil Party in, 7; Gilded Age in, 219; Haiti and, 240n25; immigration in, 137, 153; Jim Crow laws in, 9; to Johnson, O., 83–84; journalism in, 108–9; Ku Klux Klan in, 126; Lincoln and, 13; Martyr Period in, 121; National Liberal League in, 206–7; National Purity Congress in, 136; oppression in, 65–66; pacifism in, 20–21; patriarchy in, 39–40; philosophy in, 156–58; politics in, 22–23, 243n7; prejudice in, 14; progressivism in, 21–22; racial justice in, 10, 111; racism in, 26–28, 41, 124; reform in, 6–7, 72–73; religion in, 32–33, 98; in Revolutionary War, 108; slavery in, 54, 104–5, 262n80; Spanish-American War, 185–86
Up From Slavery (Washington, B. T.), 188
US. *See* United States

Vesey, Denmark, 58
violence: against African Americans, 8–9, 31–32, 56–57; by anti-abolitionists, 42; anti-Black terrorism, 185–86; assassination, 177; Brown, W. W., on, 52–53, 65–66; in Christianity, 30–31, 34; in culture, 30–32; evangelicalism and, 115–16; against Garrison, 78–79; history of, 50–51; to Johnson, O., 77–78; by Ku Klux Klan, 135; to May, 235n38; racism and, 66, 126; religion and, 116; retrospective writing on, 115; in slavery, 34, 42–43, 149; white supremacy and, 252n4

Washington, Booker T., 188–89
Washington, George, 108
Washington, Madison, 58
WASS. *See* Western Anti-Slavery Society
WCTU. *See* Woman's Christian Temperance Union
Webster, Daniel, 138
Wesley, John, 93
West Africa, 52
Western Anti-Slavery Society (WASS), 8, 203–4
Western New York Anti-Slavery Society (WNYASS), 6–7
Wheatley, Phyllis, 60, 62
Whedon, D. D., 93–95, 246n54
Whipper, William, 61
white abolitionists: activism by, 10; for African Americans, 29, 45; Anthony as, 149; to Brown, W. W., 59–60; Gar-

rison and, 89–90; history of, 219–20; in journalism, 76–77; racism to, 13–14; reputation of, 126; research on, 6; Stanton, E. C., as, 7; in Underground Railroad, 8

White Slave Traffic Act, 152

white supremacy, 9, 207–8, 228n11, 252n4

Whittier, John Greenleaf, 151, 172, 191–92

Wilberforce, William, 81

William Lloyd Garrison and His Times (Johnson, O.), 5, 72, 77, 88, 93, 95–97

Williams v. Mississippi, 127

Wilmarth, Lucinda, 199

Wilson, Henry, 117

WNYASS. *See* Western New York Anti-Slavery Society

Woman's Christian Temperance Union (WCTU), 214–18

A Woman's Life-Work (Haviland), 8, 209–16

women: in AASS, 91; activism and, 92, 127–28, 195, 209–11; African Americans and, 38, 103, 130, *131–34*, 134, 141, 205–6; American Women Suffrage Association, 203; antislavery and, 191–93, 202–9, 212–18; BFASS, 8; Brown, W. W., and, 60–61; chastity of, 141; in Christianity, 128–29; in culture, 143, 146–47; education and, 136, 217; in Europe, 143; Fall River Female Anti-Slavery Society, 8; feminism, 143–44, 202–3, 206, 214–15; journalism for, 151; LNA, 128; National Women Suffrage Association, 103; PFASS, 3, 143, 147; to Powell, A. M., 143–45; in prostitution, 127–29, *131–34*, 135, 151–52; sexism, 127–28, 138–39, 140, 147–48, 207–8, 264n26; in Underground Railroad, 209–10; WCTU, 214–18; Women's Loyal National League, 7–8; Women's Rights Convention, 144; women's suffrage, 7, 172, 190, 192, 202–3, 205

Woolman, John, 211

World's Anti-Slavery Convention, 144

World War I, 1

Wright, Elizur, 89, 95–96

Wright, Henry Clarke, 14, 107–8, 121, 184, 196–97, 200, 204, 208

Raymond James Krohn is an Assistant Professor of History at Boise State University. As an historian of the United States, he specializes in the eighteenth and nineteenth centuries, slavery and abolition, social movements, and political, intellectual, and cultural history.

RECONSTRUCTING AMERICA
Andrew L. Slap, series editor

Hans L. Trefousse, *Impeachment of a President: Andrew Johnson, the Blacks, and Reconstruction.*

Richard Paul Fuke, *Imperfect Equality: African Americans and the Confines of White Ideology in Post-Emancipation Maryland.*

Ruth Currie-McDaniel, *Carpetbagger of Conscience: A Biography of John Emory Bryant.*

Paul A. Cimbala and Randall M. Miller, eds., *The Freedmen's Bureau and Reconstruction: Reconsiderations.*

Herman Belz, *A New Birth of Freedom: The Republican Party and Freedmen's Rights, 1861 to 1866.*

Robert Michael Goldman, *"A Free Ballot and a Fair Count": The Department of Justice and the Enforcement of Voting Rights in the South, 1877–1893.*

Ruth Douglas Currie, ed., *Emma Spaulding Bryant: Civil War Bride, Carpetbagger's Wife, Ardent Feminist—Letters, 1860–1900.*

Robert Francis Engs, *Freedom's First Generation: Black Hampton, Virginia, 1861–1890.*

Robert F. Kaczorowski, *The Politics of Judicial Interpretation: The Federal Courts, Department of Justice, and Civil Rights, 1866–1876.*

John Syrett, *The Civil War Confiscation Acts: Failing to Reconstruct the South.*

Michael Les Benedict, *Preserving the Constitution: Essays on Politics and the Constitution in the Reconstruction Era.*

Andrew L. Slap, *The Doom of Reconstruction: The Liberal Republicans in the Civil War Era.*

Edmund L. Drago, *Confederate Phoenix: Rebel Children and Their Families in South Carolina.*

Mary Farmer-Kaiser, *Freedwomen and the Freedmen's Bureau: Race, Gender, and Public Policy in the Age of Emancipation.*

Paul A. Cimbala and Randall Miller, eds., *The Great Task Remaining Before Us: Reconstruction as America's Continuing Civil War.*

John A. Casey Jr., *New Men: Reconstructing the Image of the Veteran in Late-Nineteenth-Century American Literature and Culture.*

Hilary Green, *Educational Reconstruction: African American Schools in the Urban South, 1865–1890.*

Christopher B. Bean, *Too Great a Burden to Bear: The Struggle and Failure of the Freedmen's Bureau in Texas.*

David E. Goldberg, *The Retreats of Reconstruction: Race, Leisure, and the Politics of Segregation at the New Jersey Shore, 1865–1920.*

David Prior, ed., *Reconstruction in a Globalizing World.*

Jewel L. Spangler and Frank Towers, eds., *Remaking North American Sovereignty: State Transformation in the 1860s.*

Adam H. Domby and Simon Lewis, eds., *Freedoms Gained and Lost: Reconstruction and Its Meanings 150 Years Later.*

David Prior, ed., *Reconstruction and Empire: The Legacies of Abolition and Union Victory for an Imperial Age.*

Sandra M. Gustafson and Robert S. Levine, eds., *Reimagining the Republic: Race, Citizenship, and Nation in the Literary Work of Albion W. Tourgée.* Foreword by Carolyn L. Karcher.

Brian Schoen, Jewel L. Spangler, and Frank Towers, eds., *Continent in Crisis: The U.S. Civil War in North America.*

Raymond James Krohn, *Abolitionist Twilights: History, Meaning, and the Fate of Racial Egalitarianism, 1865–1909.*

Printed in the USA
CPSIA information can be obtained
at www.ICGtesting.com
LVHW091029090524
779700LV00004B/433